European Commission

information management

Library economics in Europe
An update — 1981-90

Phillip Ramsdale

Institute of Public Finance Ltd
for the European Commission

Directorate-General
Telecommunications, Information Market and Exploitation of Research

1995

EUR 15903 EN

Published by the
EUROPEAN COMMISSION

**Directorate-General XIII
Telecommunications, Information Market and Exploitation of Research**

L-2920 Luxembourg

LEGAL NOTICE

Neither the European Commission nor any person acting on behalf of the Commission is responsible for the use which might be made of the following information

Cataloguing data can be found at the end of this publication

Luxembourg: Office for Official Publications of the European Communities, 1995

ISBN 92-826-9197-7

© ECSC-EC-EAEC, Brussels • Luxembourg, 1995

Printed in Spain

TABLE OF CONTENTS

CHAPTER 1: EXECUTIVE SUMMARY

1.1	Introduction	1
1.2	Framework for the study	1
1.3	Comparisons generated	1
1.4	The overall findings in their econometric context	1
1.5	The findings in more detail : Financial Overview	5
1.6	Activity Overview	7
1.7	European Free Trade Agreement States	7
1.8	Statistical Review	9
1.9	Study Recommendations	9

CHAPTER 2: STUDY OBJECTIVES

2.1	Study Remit	13
2.2	Study Objectives	13
2.3	Study Definitions	14
2.4	Data Sources	14
2.5	Reliability of Results	15

CHAPTER 3: CRITIQUE OF THE ORIGINAL REPORT

3.1	Aims and objectives of the previous report	17
3.2	Summary of the original results	17
3.3	Updated results for the years 1981-1985	18
3.4	Methodology used in the original study	20
3.5	Economic and Social Changes which have occurred since the previous study	20
3.6	Developments in the library world which have occurred since 1986	21
3.7	Maturity of library definitions	21
3.8	Mobile and Static Service Points	22
3.9	Library Staff	22
3.10	Trained Librarians	23
3.11	Total Expenditure	24
3.12	Expenditure relating to the Acquisition of Stock	24
3.13	Expenditure relating to Information Technology	25
3.14	Sources of Income	25

CHAPTER 4: FINANCIAL RESULTS

4.1	Overall Library Expenditure	27
4.2	Staffing Expenditure	28
4.3	Expenditure on the acquisition of stock	29
4.4	Income for Library Services	30
4.5	Remaining Expenditure Items	31

CHAPTER 5: ACTIVITY DATA

5.1	The Provision of Library Services	33
5.2	Book Stocks	34
5.3	Current Periodicals	35
5.4	Audio Visual Material	35
5.5	Staff Numbers	36
5.6	Library Users	37

CHAPTER 6: EUROPEAN FREE TRADE AGREEMENT STATES

6.1	The context of EFTA countries within this study	39
6.2	Summary of financial results	39
6.3	Activity Data	41

CHAPTER 7: THE WAY FORWARD

7.1	The need for standardisation	45
7.2	Any other data which would be of assistance	46
7.3	Maintaining the momentum initiated by these studies	46
7.4	Study proposals	47

APPENDICES

1.	Study specification	49
2.	Methodology used in this study	59
2.2	The relationship between book stocks and library expenditure, and population and library expenditure	69
2.3	Inconsistencies in standard definitions	73
3.	Notes of guidance - Survey questionnaires	77
4.	Study data sets	125
5.	Econometric data	181
6.	Country profiles	199
7.	LIB1-ECON Executive summary.	237

FIGURES AND TABLES

Table 1:	Annual average library expenditure 1986-1990	5
Table 2:	Unesco library sectors and the years where data were available:	14
Table 3:	Average annual revenue expenditure on libraries 1981-1985	17
Table 4:	he increase in registered borrowers / users 1983-1985	18
Table 5:	Annual average library expenditure for the periods 1981-1985 and 1986-1990	27
Table 6:	Annual average staffing costs	28
Table 7:	Annual average acquisition expenditure	29
Table 8:	Annual average fees and charges received by libraries	30
Table 9:	Average number of service points for the five year periods 1981-1985 and 1986-1990	33
Table 10:	Annual average number of volumes in collections	34
Table 11:	Annual average collections of current periodicals	35
Table 12:	Annual average number of audio visual materials in library collections	35
Table 13:	Average annual number of staff employed	36
Table 14:	Annual average number of trained librarians	36
Table 15:	Consultations per thousand population	37
Table 16:	Annual average library expenditure 1981-85 and 1986-90	39
Table 17:	Average annual staffing levels and expenditure	40
table 18:	Annual average expenditure incurred in the acquisition of stock	40
Table 19:	Average number of service points for the two quinquennia 1981-1985 and 1986-1990	41
Table 20:	Average number of volumes in collections	42
Table 21:	Consultations per thousand population	43

Figure 1:	Libraries expenditure (all sectors)	3
Figure 2:	European Union: GDP v RPI 1982 - 1990 EFTA: GDP v RPI 1982 - 1990	4
Figure 3:	Revenue expenditure per annum on Libraries per head of population 1986-1990	8
Figure 4:	Number of library books per head of population 1981-1985 average	10
Figure 5:	Number of library books per head of population 1986-1990 average	10
Figure 6:	Public library expenditure	28
Figure 7:	The sources of income and their respective proportions for all libraries 1986-1990	30
Figure 8:	Public libraries - sources of funding, 1981-1985	30
Figure 9:	Public libraries - sources of funding, 1986-1990	30
Figure 10:	The principal items of expenditure and their respective proportions for all library sectors 1986-1990	31
Figure 11:	Population per service point - public libraries 1986-1990	34
Figure 12:	Population per service point - public libraries 1986-1990	41

CHAPTER 1

EXECUTIVE SUMMARY

1.1 Introduction

The purpose of this study has been to provide a statistical profile of library economics amongst the Member States of the European Union (EU) for the years 1986-1990. It was commissioned by DG XIII of the European Commission and, in addition to providing a profile for the years 1986-1990, was designed to update and complement the findings of a previous study entitled *"A Study of Library Economics in the European Community"* which considered the years 1981-1985.

This current study now extends the coverage of the European Union by including a separate statistical profile for those further states which are signatories to the European Free Trade Agreement (EFTA) relating to the years 1981-1990.

1.2 Framework for the study

The study adopts the six library sector definitions developed by the United Nations Educational, Scientific and Cultural Organisation (UNESCO) and reports the level of expenditure and activities incurred by all libraries within this classification.

Survey questionnaires were despatched to all EU and EFTA states in 1993, and a database constructed on the basis of these returns, other published sources and information provided by UNESCO.

1.3 Comparisons generated

The majority of comparisons are reported as the annual average for each of the two five year periods covered by the respective studies (i.e. 1981-1985 and 1986-1990). This approach substantially eliminates inconsistencies arising in year on year comparisons of the detailed data. These inconsistencies occur as a result of variations concerning the estimates made on the limited data supplied for respective years within the decade.

1.4 The overall findings in their econometric context

(i) Maintenance of libraries continues to be a central element in the cultural programmes of member states of the European Union. However, there has been a marked change in the relative focus of libraries' investment during the decade. Although Public Libraries remain the principal source of library services, accounting for just under one half of gross libraries expenditure (49%), the main areas of investment growth have been devoted towards the Higher Education sector. This reflects an implicit policy to employ the resources of the library services in education programmes, and to some extent illustrates the switch in public sector resources from secondary towards tertiary education.

As the number of pupils attending secondary schools has declined during the decade, so has the investment in their libraries. The changing pattern of investment during the decade also highlights the role of Public Libraries which have barely retained a constant level of real terms funding, and have experienced a slight decline in staff employed. In contrast there has been an increase in the activities of Special Libraries, perhaps revealing the interest of commercial and professional bodies in employing their information resources in the service of modern business affairs.

(ii) Overall library expenditure as a percentage of Gross Domestic Product has remained static throughout the decade for the European Union states, at 0.15%. The corresponding average for the EFTA states has fallen from 0.24% to 0.23%. Figure 1 depicts total library expenditure as a percentage of Gross Domestic Product for the EU and EFTA states for the years 1982-1990. Relative to the retail price index total library expenditure increased by some 1.9% per annum. However, as figure 2a shows the growth in salaries exceeded that of retail price index during the second quiquennium. Some 58% of library expenditure is spent on staff and so the apparent increase in library expenditure relative to retail prices was absorbed by the increase in staffing costs (see Appendix 5). Thus in real terms, investment in libraries has been constrained within the economy as a whole.

(iii) The importance of libraries as a state asset has also been shown by the growth in investment made in National Libraries. Nearly 6.5% of total gross libraries expenditure was devoted on these central facilities, demonstrating their crucial role in the cultural policies of the states of the European Union.

(iv) The "Library industry" employed approximately 237,000 persons in the latter half of the 1980's, and consumed 6.6 billions ECU per annum. When repriced to 1993 constant prices this figure equates to some 8,014 million ECUs. Productivity increased markedly, as the number of staff increased marginally by 0.5% per annum while book stocks grew at an annual average rate of 1.9% per annum to a total of some 1.4 billion volumes. Purchases of current periodicals in all library sectors, except schools, increased, adding to the technical information resources of the estimated 96,000 service points spread across the countries comprising the European Union.

(v) Constraints on public sector funding, which on average accounted for 91.76% of all libraries expenditure during the decade, limited the real terms growth in Public Library funding to 2.2% per annum. Figure 2 plots the relationship between Gross Domestic Product, Retail Prices Index and total library expenditure for the EU and EFTA states which further supports the premise that library expenditure within the economy as a whole has been constrained.

By default, the development in public sector funding was directed towards higher education, and Public Libraries responded by expanding current periodical and audio visual collections to provide greater variety in the choice of available information resources to a general population with more specialist interests. Hence, the growth in general Public Library book stocks was modest (1.9% per annum), while the collections of audio-visual materials increased by 3.3% per annum over the same period. The number of consultations per head of population for the Public Library sector remained static at 5.4 throughout the decade.

(vi) The main trends observed within the European Union were mirrored by the libraries within the states comprising the European Free Trade Agreement. These states principally cover more sparsely populated areas, where the pattern of provision reflects smaller scales of enterprise, and therefore, higher fixed costs per catchment area served by each library service point.

Figure 1:

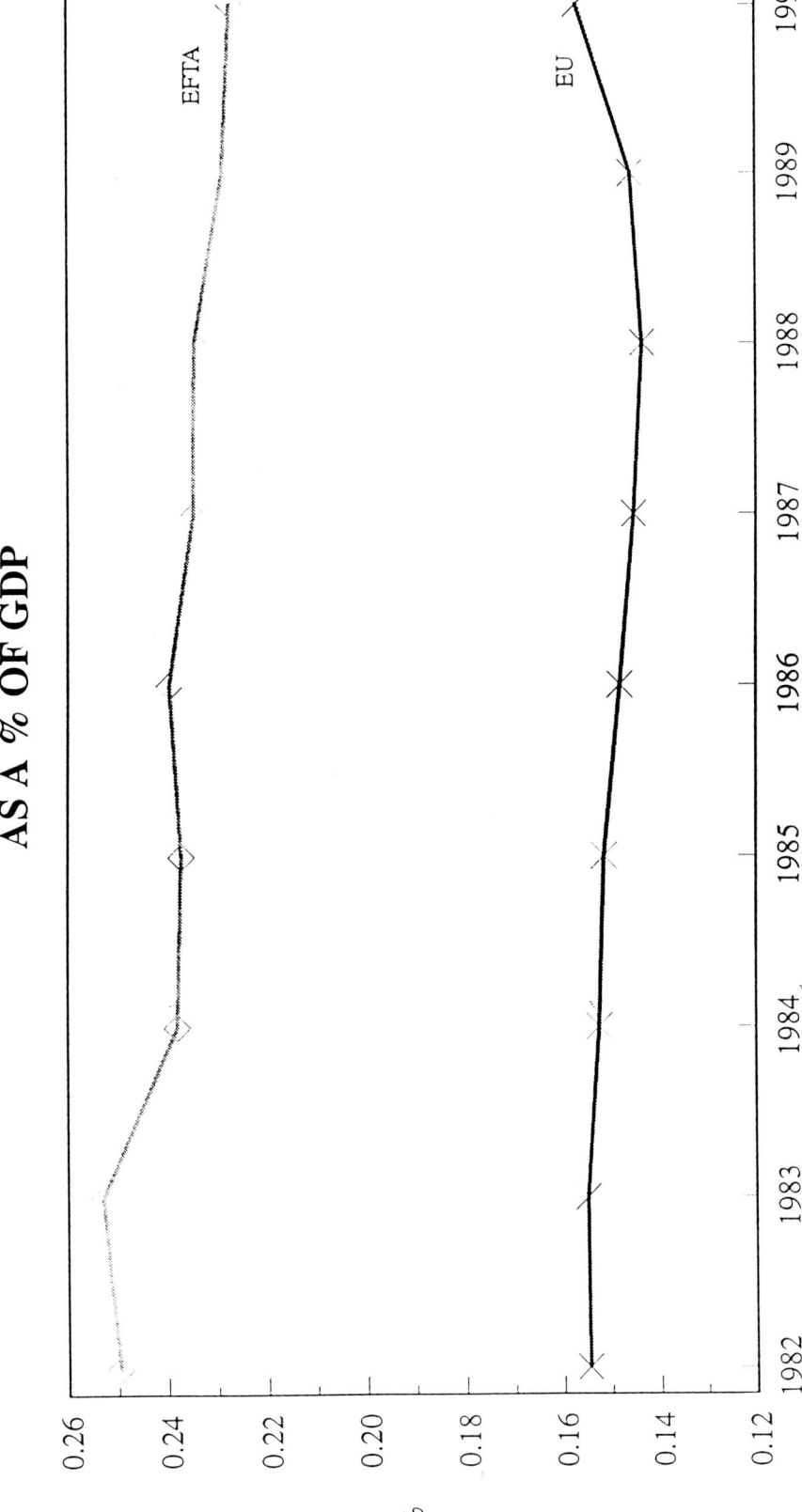

Figure 2:

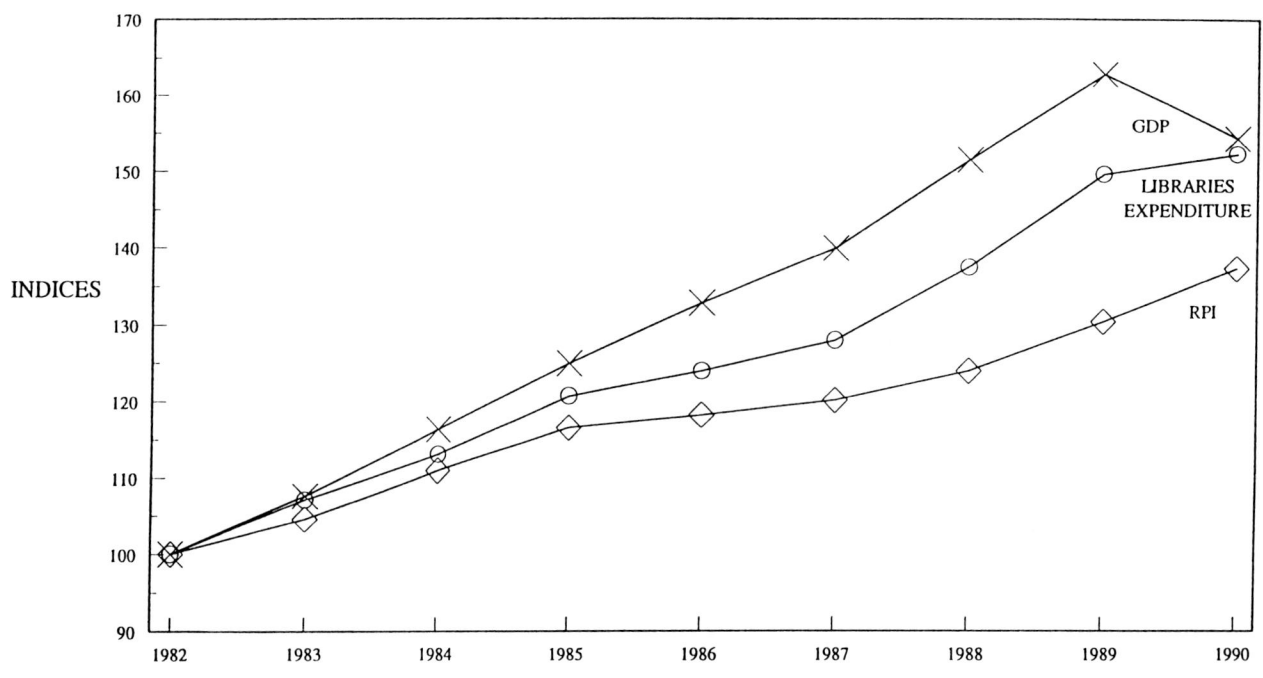

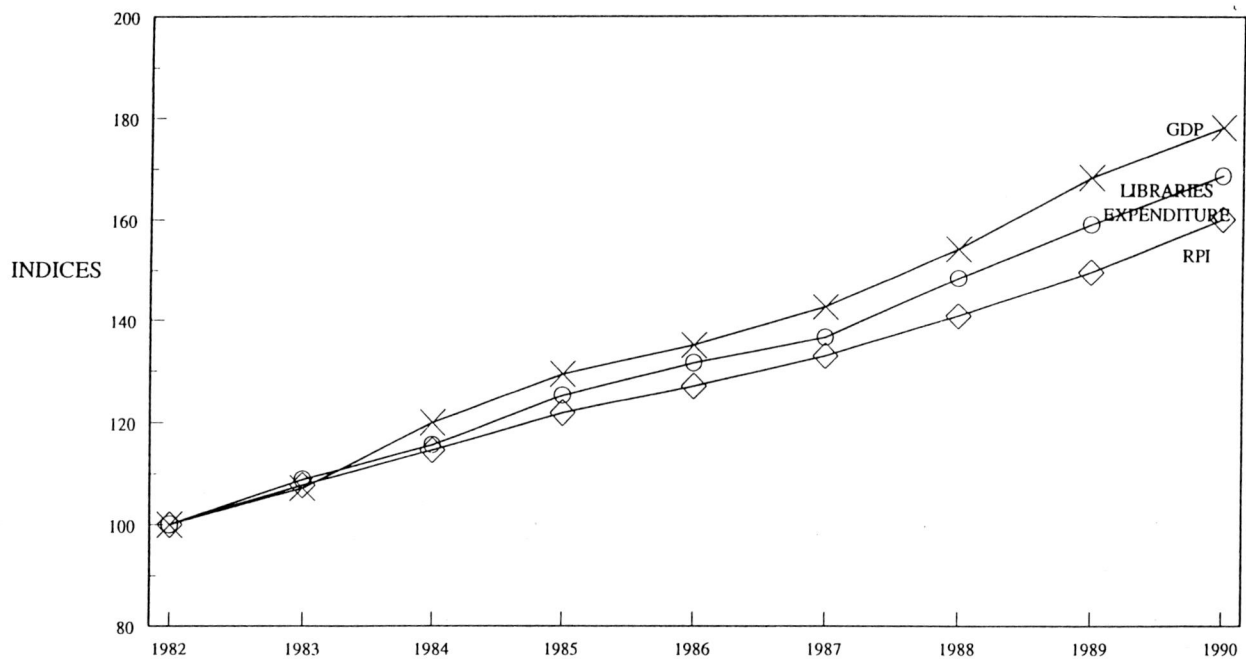

1.5   The findings in more detail : Financial Overview

The average annual total library expenditure for the years 1986-1990 was 6,637 million ECUs expressed at 1990 constant prices. This total equates to 19.52 ECUs per head of population. For the period 1981-1985 the average annual total library expenditure was 6,036 million ECUs expressed at 1990 constant prices, equating to 17.85 ECUs per head of population. Figure 3 shows the average annual expenditure per head of population for the years 1986-1990 for the states participating in this study. This represents an increase in real terms of 1.9% per annum. Increases within the individual sectors varied considerably as Table 1 below shows :

Table 1:

ANNUAL AVERAGE LIBRARY EXPENDITURE 1986-1990

Sector	Expenditure (Million ECUs)	Annual Average % age Increase
National	423.65	1.1%
Higher Education	1,079.75	2.7%
Other Major Non-Specialised	280.97	1.1%
School	981.88	0.3%
Special	607.19	2.7%
Public	3,263.31	2.2%
TOTAL	6,636.75	1.9%

The original study reported an estimated average annual library expenditure for the first quinquennium of 4,448 million ECUs expressed at 1985 constant prices. This has been converted to a total of 5,092 million ECUs expressed at 1990 constant prices. Due to the current availability of more reliable data relating to this period, this estimate has been revised. Furthermore, in order to provide a consistent basis for meaningful comparisons between the two quinquennia, data for the former German Democratic Republic, amounting to some 717 million ECUs per annum, have been included in the estimates for the first quinquennium, leading to a revised estimate of total annual average library expenditure of 6,036 million ECUs. Thus the difference between the two estimates (and after accounting for the incorporation of the former German Democratic Republic) leads to an upward revision of some 227 million ECUs at 1990 constant prices or 0.67 ECUs per head of population.

Reconciliation of the estimates for the period 1981-1985	1985 Prices Million ECUs	1990 Prices Million ECUs
♦ Original Estimate for annual average total library expenditure 1981-1985 (LIB1-ECON)	4,448	5,092
♦ Adjustment in estimates based upon availability of more data		+227
♦ Data relating to the former German Democratic Republic		+717
♦ **Revised Estimate for the years 1981-1985**		= 6,036

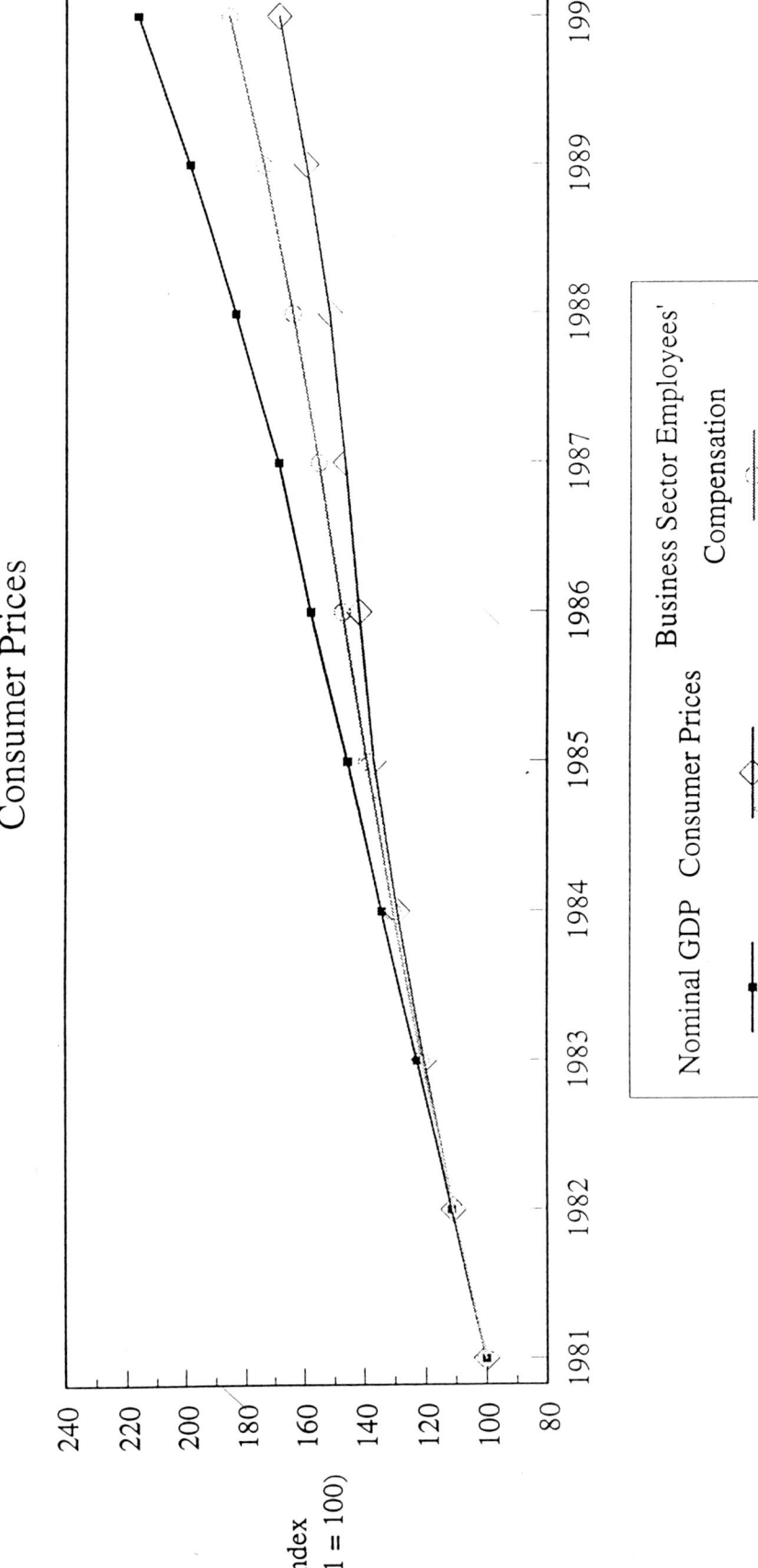

Source: OECD

1.6 Activity Overview

(i) STAFF

The annual average number of staff employed within the library service for the two five year periods has an annual average of 231,600 for the first quinquennium and 237,200 for the second, an average annual increase of 0.5%. Within this figure there appears to have been an increase in the number of "Trained Library Staff" while some sectors have recorded reductions in the number of "Other Library Staff".

Total staffing costs have increased in real terms by an annual average of 1.7%.

(ii) AVAILABILITY OF LIBRARY SERVICES

The annual average number of library service points for the two five year periods has increased from 88,500 to 95,900. This overall increase of 1.6% per annum encompasses a small reduction in the number of service points for the School and Other Major Non-Specialised Library sectors.

(iii) BOOK STOCKS

The number of books within library collections has increased by some 1.7% per annum, rising from some 1,233 million in 1981 to 1,435 million in 1990. The Higher Education sector recorded an above average increase (2.3% per annum, increasing from some 245 million volumes in 1981 to some 300 million in 1990) reflecting the overall growth in student registrations recorded during the study period. While expenditure on acquisition of new materials has increased, the actual purchasing power of the libraries has probably reduced as material prices appear to have risen at a higher rate.

Figures 4 and 5 plot the number of library books per head of population in each state participating in the study, for both quinquennia within the decade. The European Union average figure has increased from 3.76 to 4.11 books per head.

(iv) LIBRARY USERS

Library usage has increased slightly from an average of 8.1 to 8.2 issues or consultations per head of population per annum. However, loans made by the Public Library sector have remained static throughout the decade at 5.4 loans per head of population; while the loans per head of sector population for the Higher Education Libraries have increased from 3.23 to 3.64.

1.7 European Free Trade Agreement States

Annual total library expenditure has increased from an average of 1,419 million to 1,515 million ECUs per annum over the two study periods, representing an annual increase of 1.3%.

The number of service points has reduced from 30,100 to 27,900 with the School Library sector representing the largest reduction of some 2,500 service points (-2.6% per annum).

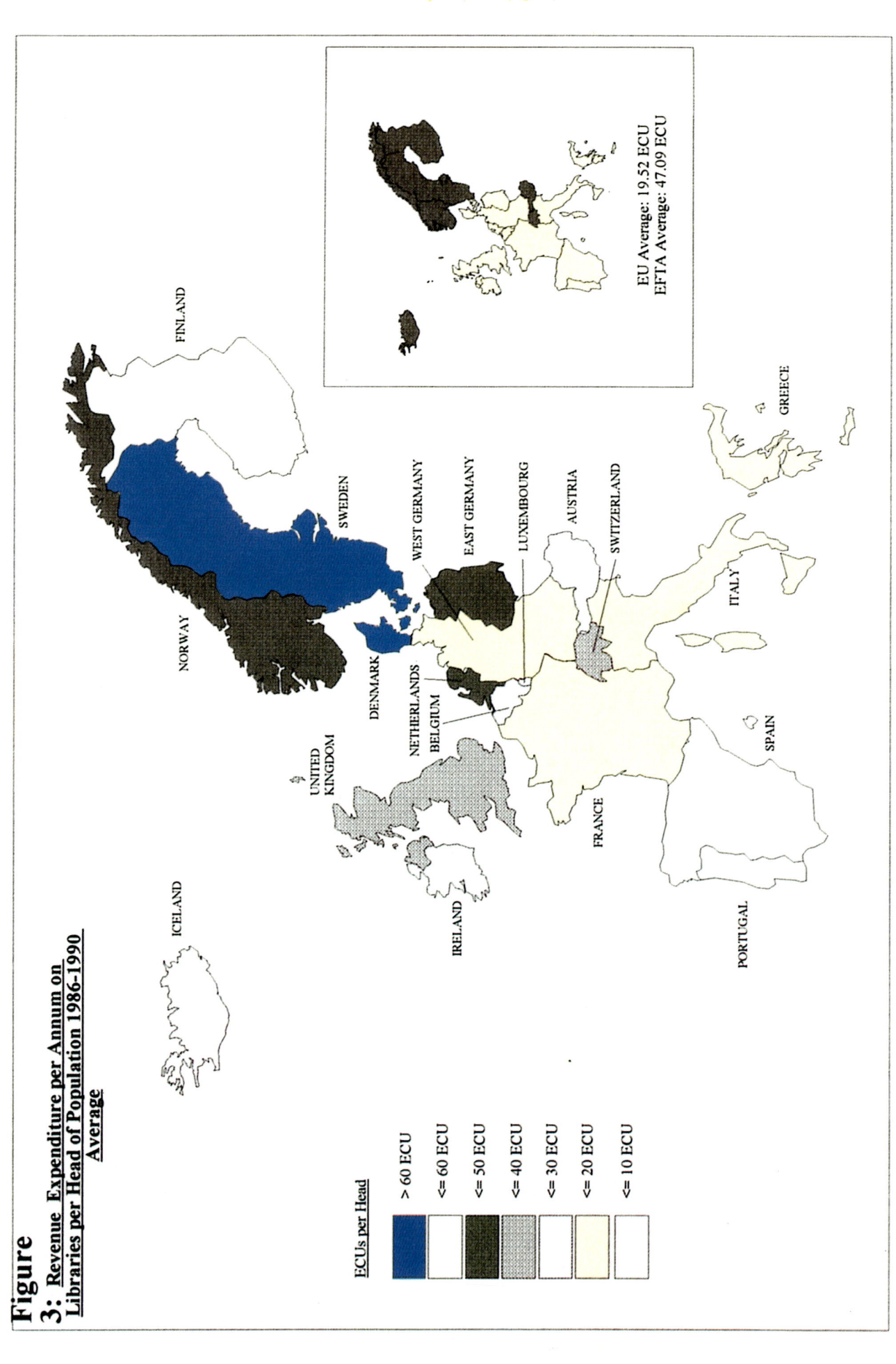

Figure 3: Revenue Expenditure per Annum on Libraries per Head of Population 1986-1990 Average

The estimated number of Library staff employed within the EFTA states has increased slightly, from an annual average of 42,700 to 43,000 for the two quinquennia, representing an annual increase of 0.1%. Within this total staffing figure the School library sector has experienced a reduction in staff employed of some 3% per annum.

The numbers of books in EFTA country libraries have increased by 1.3% per annum from an some 289 million volumes in 1981 to some 324 million in 1990. This equates to a rise in the number of library books per head of population, from 9.2 to 9.8, as the accompanying maps refer (Figures 4 and 5).

1.8   Statistical Review

The study shows that a number of states do not fully comply with the UNESCO and ISO library standards for library statistics (ISO 2789 1989). The number of instances of non-compliance has reduced slightly since the last study which recommended their universal adoption (see Appendix 2.3).

Where responsibility for a library sector is shared by more than one government department or ministry, data can prove to be difficult to collate. In many instances the data are available but are inconsistent and incomplete in any one centre of administrative responsibility.

Data relating to the School Library sector continues to be extremely sparse. Given the importance of the relationship between libraries and education (at all levels) the preparation of data relating to this sector needs to be encouraged.

1.9   Study Recommendations

In summary the following points are recommended for consideration:

1. That the collection of library statistics by the European Commission becomes a regular practice, either annually or biennially, so that information is both timely and consistent. More frequent collection is needed to maintain the development of systems for keeping consistent information which fall into abeyance over longer periods.

2. The benefits of preparing national data to ISO standards and definitions might be recommended by the European Commission to all its member states.

3. A recognised agency or organisation might be jointly appointed by the European Commission and UNESCO to undertake future surveys thus eliminating any duplication of survey effort, and enhancing the information attached to the collection of international statistics.

4. The European Commission may wish to publicise in member states the apparent constraints on the resources available to libraries, as suggested by the study. The closer links between library resources and education programmes might be highlighted as a demonstration of the vital importance of libraries in the cultural development of the European Union.

5. That a review of possible performance measures be undertaken for general use by subscribing states. In this context the European Commission may wish to consider holding a forum on the subject.

Figure 4:

Number of Library Books (All Sectors) per Head of Population 1981-1985 Average

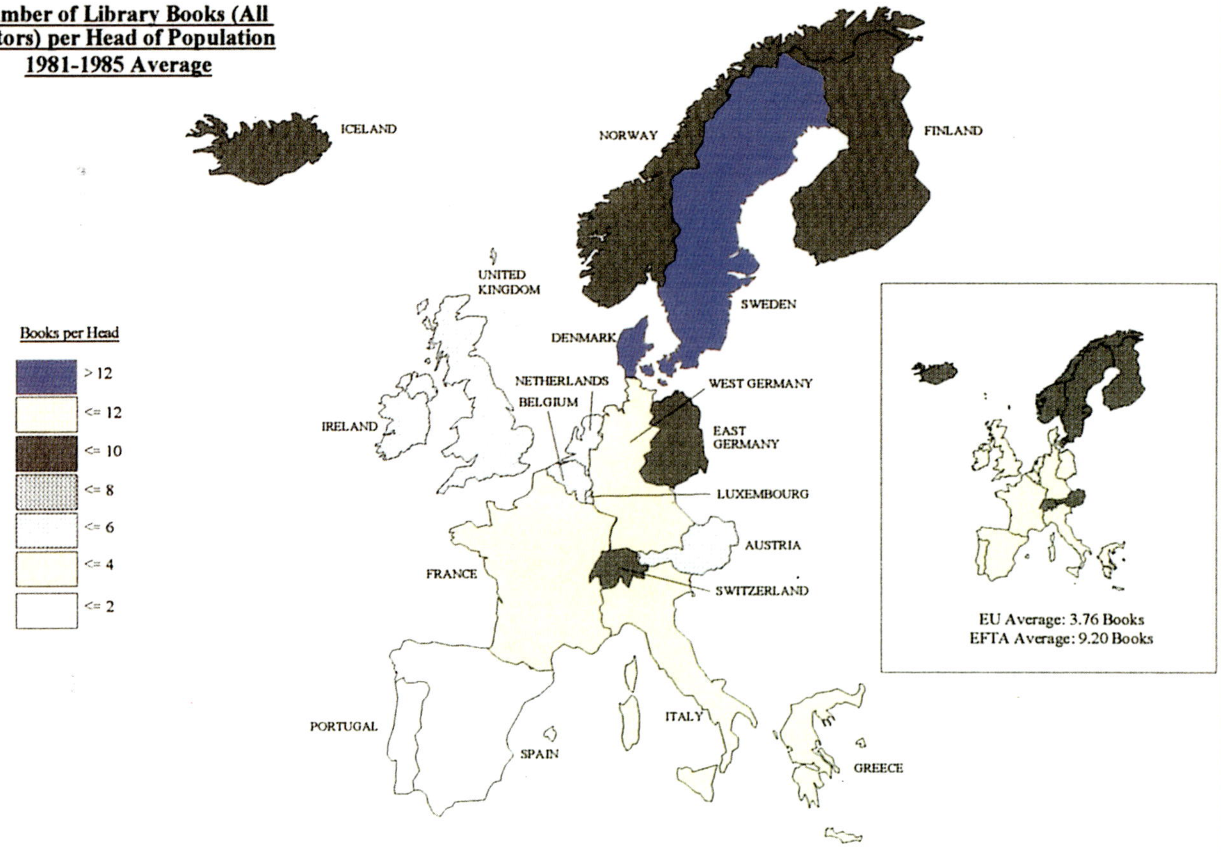

Books per Head:
- > 12
- <= 12
- <= 10
- <= 8
- <= 6
- <= 4
- <= 2

EU Average: 3.76 Books
EFTA Average: 9.20 Books

Figure 5:

Number of Library Books (All Sectors) per Head of Population 1986-1990 Average

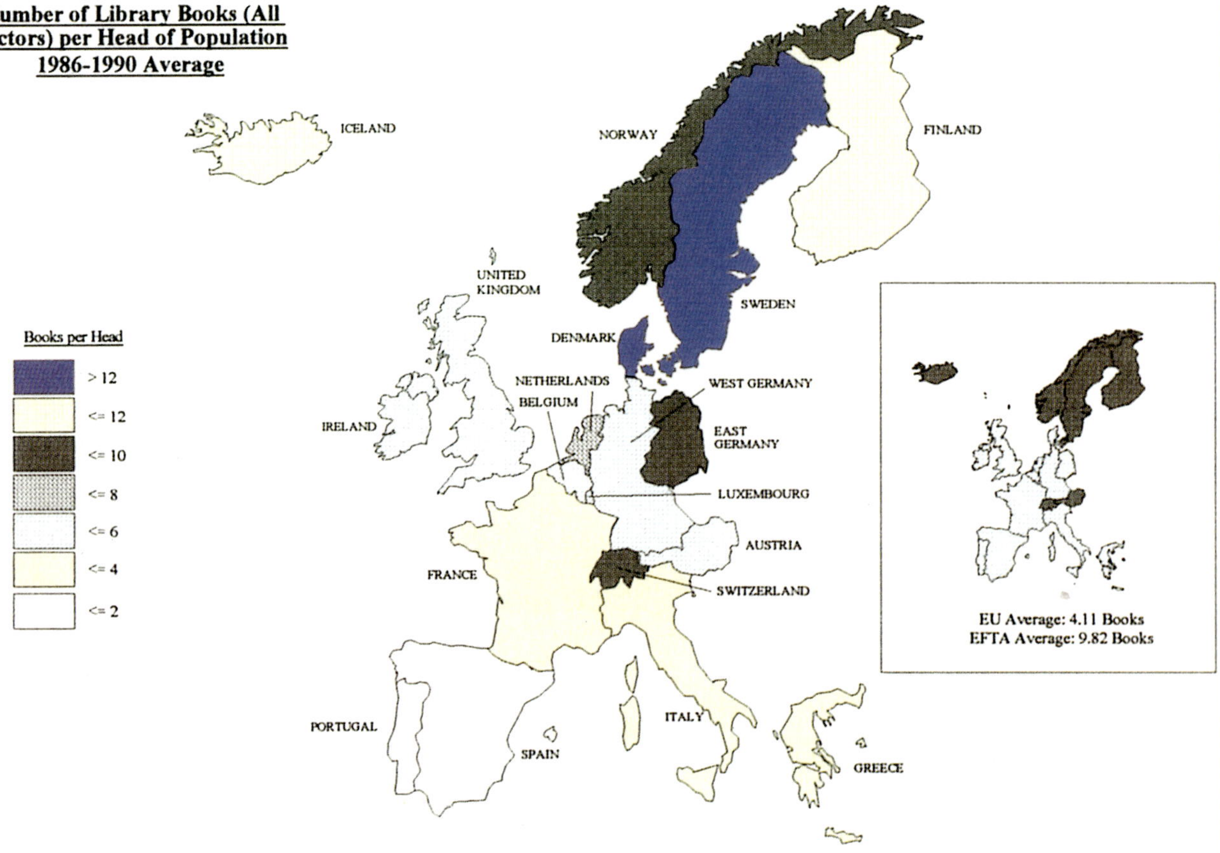

Books per Head:
- > 12
- <= 12
- <= 10
- <= 8
- <= 6
- <= 4
- <= 2

EU Average: 4.11 Books
EFTA Average: 9.82 Books

6. That ISO and IFLA be asked to consider amending the detailed definition and guidance notes relating to the questions asked in this study where apparent inconsistencies in returned data arose (see Appendix 2.3).

CHAPTER 2

STUDY OBJECTIVES

2.1 Study Remit

This report provides a statistical profile of library economics of the Member States of the European Union (EU) for the years 1986-1990. It was commissioned by DG XIII and, in addition to providing a profile for the years 1986-1990, is designed to update and complement the findings of a previous study entitled *"A Study of Library Economics in the European Community"* which considered the years 1981-1985. This former study was published in 1987 under the European Commission study reference LIB1-ECON.

To facilitate the analysis of trends throughout the decade, the current study team have further refined the data set relating to 1981-1985 and repriced all the financial data to 1990 constant prices. Additional activity and financial data, which were not available at the time of the previous study, have also been added to the original data set.

The majority of the comparisons generated within the study are calculated as the annual averages for each of the two five year periods. This approach substantially eliminates inconsistencies arising in year on year comparisons of the detailed data. Such inconsistencies occur as a result of the variations about the estimates made on the fluctuating quantity of data supplied for each year within the ten year study period.

A similar, but separate, statistical profile for those further states which are signatories to the European Free Trade Area (EFTA) relating to the years 1981-1990 is included in this study. This adds further context to the study, although the principal aim has been to trace the trends within the economic block of the European Union over the decade.

Although data have been collated from some states for more recent years it has not proven possible to extend the overall estimates of trends for either the European Union or EFTA states beyond 1990.

2.2 Study Objectives

The aims of this study were:

a) To collate data relating to the volume of Library activities and their associated costs between 1986 and 1990 within the member states of the European Union (including the former Democratic Republic of Germany) and those further states which are signatories to the European Free Trade Agreement, namely:

   Austria, Finland, Iceland, Liechtenstein, Norway, Sweden and Switzerland.

b) To appraise the existing statistical framework and review the action taken by member states since the last study was undertaken. At the time of the original study, difficulties concerning the consistency and completeness of the data were encountered. Consequently a number of recommendations were made in order that the quality of available data relating to library activities and finances might be improved.

c) To update the findings of the previous study, detailing the period 1981-1985, in order that trends over the whole decade (1981-1990) for the member states might be considered. Those states belonging to EFTA were asked primarily for data relating to 1986-1990. Some however, provided data relating to the first five years of the decade thus allowing some comparisons for the complete decade to be made.

A copy of the study specifications is shown at Appendix 1.

2.3 Study Definitions

The United Nations Educational, Scientific and Cultural Organisation (UNESCO) definitions of the six library sectors were employed for both the original and the subsequent study. The use of these definitions ensures consistency, and reinforces their adoption for maintaining national reports.

UNESCO provided the study team with an extract from their statistics relating to various time periods, as shown in Table 2:

Table 2:
UNESCO LIBRARY SECTORS AND THE YEARS WHERE DATA WERE AVAILABLE:

1. National	1986 and 1989
2. Institutions of Higher Education	1987 and 1990
3. Other Major Non-Specialised	1986 and 1990
4. School	1987 and 1990
5. Special	1985
6. Public (or Popular)	1986 and 1989

Specifications for the six library sectors and the more detailed terminology are shown at Appendix 3. The definitions employed in the current survey questionnaires accord with the ISO 2789 (1991) standard. Some of the variations in the year on year data (referred to in 2.1) may be allied to the point at which that particular state adjusted the collation of their national statistics in order to comply with this standard. From the survey returns and subsequent validation work undertaken with individual national sources, it has been found that a number of deviations from the UNESCO and ISO standards still occur.

Activity data relating to Information Technology within Libraries were not collated for this study since they have been the subject of a separate and recent European Commission Study, *"The state of the art of the application of new information technologies in libraries and their impact on library functions"*, study reference EUR 14660 EN January 1992 (which comprises 12 separate reports for each Member State). However, the costs of Information Technology activities were included in this study's survey questionnaires.

2.4 Data Sources

The principal source of data for this study was a survey questionnaire which was similar to that used for the 1981-85 study, but with a simplification of the content on the basis of difficulties previously encountered. Questionnaires for each sector were despatched to at least one contact or institution in each country. Eight countries recorded nil returns for Other Major Non-Specialised Libraries and ten were unable to provide data relating to School Libraries.

Where responsibilities for a particular sector were divided, such as the public libraries in Belgium, questionnaires were sent to both of the responsible ministries.

Further data were collated from the extract of UNESCO statistics. However, the degree of detail required by the study was greater than that contained within the UNESCO statistical framework. For instance, UNESCO statistics do not include any information regarding the level and sources of income received by libraries, nor do they consider specific expenditure items other than staffing and acquisition costs.

Various national publications and articles also proved extremely useful in the preparation of the national profiles. Appendix 6 contains the activity profile for each country, the sources of the data employed in their compilation and the individuals and institutions contacted by the study team.

Where data were available from a number of sources they were sifted in the following manner:

1. Data from the original study were transferred to the new data base;

2. Estimates made in the original study were overwritten by UNESCO data if these were more plausible;

3. Data from national publications were added to the data base;

4. Data provided by survey respondents were then added to the data base, over-riding the previous study estimates and UNESCO data where appropriate.

Plausibility checks of 20% were applied to the data.

2.5 Reliability of Results

The findings of this study depict a reasonable measure of the scale and extent of library activities and their associated costs at a national level. The significance of these findings relates to the overall EU and EFTA perspectives rather than a detailed and explicit examination of each sector within each country. A number of the states included in this study have already undertaken more detailed studies at a local level, and their efforts are of particular interest to local policy-makers. This study is designed to provide a Europe-wide perspective.

Thus the trends identified in this study are indicators of the direction of change as opposed to precise rates of change. This is because the quality and quantity of year on year data collected are not sufficiently refined to enable the study to quantify specific annual movements with confidence in their reliability.

Data relating to activity, and particularly costs, associated with school libraries were extremely scarce. Four of the European Union states and six of the EFTA states were unable to provide any data relating to School libraries. Some states were able to report the number of service points and the book stocks, but few were able to quantify the number of librarians serving these, or any financial data. Hence, data relating to these states have been grossed using fewer "returned" base data than for any of the other library sectors. Therefore, findings relating to the financing of school libraries should be treated with extreme caution.

The majority of special libraries belong to institutions in the private sector and hence rely less on public funding. As a result, the data relating to this sector are not as comprehensive as those relating to the National, Institutions of Higher Education, Public and Other Major Non-Specialised library sectors. As a consequence of the above points concerning the overall perspective and quality of data relating to school and special libraries, caution should be exercised when quoting any individual figures from the study outside their original context.

CHAPTER 3

CRITIQUE OF THE ORIGINAL REPORT
(and lessons learned relating to definitions)

3.1 Aims and objectives of the previous report

The purpose of the original report was to attempt to gauge the level of library activities and their associated costs within the European Community, as it was then known. This represented the first attempt to collate library data at the macro level for the European Community / European Union, and it further identified the differences in recording practices adopted by the constituent Member States.

3.2 Summary of the original results

The original study found that revenue expenditure on library activities, in real terms, remained relatively constant throughout the period 1981-1985; between 13.80 ECUs and 13.97 ECUs per head of population using a 1985 constant price base.

Table 3:
AVERAGE ANNUAL REVENUE EXPENDITURE ON LIBRARIES 1981-1985

Library Sector	Revenue Expenditure at 1985 Prices (Million ECUs)	% of Total
National	207.7	4.6%
Higher Education	523.0	11.8%
Other Major Non-Specialised	105.5	2.4%
School	936.5	21.1%
Special	165.4	3.7%
Public (or Popular)	2,509.8	56.4%
ALL SECTORS	4,447.9	100%

The salient points relating to activity data were:

- There were approximately 75,000 "static service points" in the European Union. One half of these were public libraries and more than a fifth were school libraries.

- The total library book stock was calculated to be some 1.2 billion items. The average School Library was thought to possess 9,200 books compared to 76,000 for institutions of Higher Education and 13,100 for a Public Library.

- Some 243,400 full-time equivalent staff were employed in the library service.

In terms of library usage, approximately 23% of the population were thought to be regular library users or registered borrowers, with 95% of all loan transactions made from public libraries, after discounting School libraries. Table 4 overleaf shows the increase in the number of users of library facilities between 1983 and 1985 in all sectors except school libraries which had experienced a decline in pupil numbers, and hence the number of registered borrowers.

Table 4:
THE INCREASE IN REGISTERED BORROWERS / USERS 1983-1985

Sector	Increase in Users expressed as a percentage per annum
National	3.0%
Higher Education	11.5%
Other Major Non-Specialised	5.0%
Public	1.0%

The collation of data

The original study met with a number of difficulties concerning the collation of financial data, which the current study team has also encountered. These were:

1. It was not common practice to include financial breakdowns in the same surveys used nationally to collect activity based data about libraries. Consequently the figures drawn from different sources were inconsistent, leading to implausible unit costs.

2. There were no common standards for the forms of account.

3. Responsibility for libraries often crossed several government Departments/Ministries, each with their own priorities for identifying the costs of such activities.

Both studies found that activity data appeared to be more readily available than financial data. However, a number of interpretations of the definitions within the returned data emerged. The original study team commented that:

> "The problem which surrounds activity statistics is that of practicability: The definitions are accepted, but when they are difficult to apply on existing national statistical frameworks, then it must be accepted that the wider EC database can only be as good as the level of statistical maturity of its constituent states."

The Executive Summary of the original report which includes the recommendations of the study team is shown at Appendix 7.

3.3 Updated results for the years 1981-1985

The questionnaires for the current study, shown at Appendix 3, set out the data from the original study relating to 1981-1985. Recipients of the questionnaires were asked to validate these data and requested to raise any queries regarding the data for the previous returns. Several respondents supplied additional data which had not been available at the time of the previous study. As a result, it proved possible to create revised grossed estimates relating to 1981-1985, based upon a more extensive set of available data than those which were published in the original report.

The 1981-1985 data contained within this subsequent study include those relating to the former German Democratic Republic. These have been included retrospectively for the whole of the decade rather than from the time of unification only, in order to provide a consistent basis for the figures.

The original study estimated that the annual average library expenditure for the first quinquennium was 4,448 million ECUs, expressed at 1985 constant prices. This figure equates to 5,092 million ECUs at 1990 constant prices. The revised estimate, which includes some 717 million ECUs relating to the Former German Democratic Republic, amounts to the some 6,036 million ECUs. Thus, reducing the difference between the two estimates to 227 million ECUs or 0.67 ECUs per head of population. This difference is the result of more comprehensive data being made available to this current study.

The financial data relating to 1981-1985 have been repriced to 1990 constant prices in order that comparisons with 1986-1990, and for the decade as a whole, might be made.

The significant differences between the original report's findings and those of the updated figures for the 1981-1985 period were:

♦ Service Points

♦ The number of Staff employed by Libraries

Service Points

The original report estimated that there were some 76,547 service points in the European Union. The updated figures show 88,461 service points. This difference may be accounted for by the following factors :

1. The updated figure includes 4,002 service points relating to the former German Democratic Republic.

2. During the decade a reclassification of the number of Institutions of Higher Education in the United Kingdom occurred, increasing the number of libraries in this sector from an annual average of 182 in the original study to 860. In order to ensure consistency, and to be able to make comparisons throughout the decade the latter figure of 860 was used for both quinquennia.

3. The original study estimated that the annual average number of service points in the School Library sector in Italy were 5,866. During this subsequent study data from an national study were made available which reported the number of service points in this sector as 8,920.

4. Further minor adjustments were made as the result of using more robust data which derive from greater clarification of what constitutes a service point in the notes of guidance (see section 3.7).

Staff employed within the Library Service

The original study estimated that the annual average number of staff for the period 1981-1985 was 243,400. However the study team acknowledged that "it is difficult for us to estimate the number of employees with confidence". The revised estimates for the first quinquennium shows the annual average staffing level to be 231,600 (4.8% less than the original figure) with a unit cost per employee of 15,229 ECUs at 1990 constant prices. The unit cost estimated in the original report was 14,130 ECUs at 1990 constant prices.

The annual average staffing costs from the original study were estimated to be 2,965 million ECUs at 1990 constant prices; the updated annual average staffing costs for the period 1981-1985 were 3,527 million ECUs.

3.4 Methodology used in the original study

Other than the UNESCO data there were no sources of information with a European perspective of library activities. The original study designed a set of survey questionnaires based upon the six UNESCO sectors. These foundations were used by the subsequent study and are discussed in paragraph 2.3. The response rate to the original survey was substantially lower, both in terms of quantity and quality. Where data were available for some years but not for others, the missing data had to be inferred by interpolation. Data for non-respondents were estimated by attributing average unit measures to the relevant sector population. Therefore, the relative paucity of returned data available to the previous study team made their conclusions less reliable (see Appendix 2, paragraph 1.2 for the application of population age bands to the six library sectors).

The original study team restricted the application of any assumed relationship between "Activity" and "Financial" data to that of staffing. The subsequent study team extended this relationship to include book stocks when creating estimated data because a clear relationship appeared to exist between book stocks and expenditure levels (Appendix 2, paragraph 1.4 and Appendix 2.2).

The overriding objective when creating the estimated data for non-respondents was confined to establishing credible aggregates which would reasonably depict both the scale and trends of activity within the Community as a whole, as opposed to describing each sector in each individual state. The enhanced methods of estimation employed in the current study are discussed in Appendix 2, paragraph 1.4).

3.5 Economic and Social Changes which have occurred since the previous study

Appendix 5 shows the scale and pattern of population changes of the European Union and the EFTA areas between 1981 and 1990. For the EU the increase in population was very small, (0.22%), over the ten year period.

Paragraph 3.3 discusses the approach taken with regard to data relating to the unification of the former German Democratic Republic and the Federal German Republic, which occurred during the study phase. The earlier data relating to the former German Democratic Republic have been obtained from UNESCO and from Deutsche Bibliotekinstut.

There was throughout Europe a renewed emphasis of continuing education and a general move was made towards the expansion of the Higher (or Tertiary) Education sector in the late 1980's, which appears to be continuing in the early part of the 1990's. This was complemented by an improved economic outlook during the second quinquennia of the 1980's, which would have fed through into investment confidence.

At the end of the decade, the so called "Peace Dividend" and the corresponding reductions in defence expenditure, did not result in any of the funds previously committed to defence being transferred to libraries. Instead, there was a widespread constraint (by the end of the decade) on public expenditure in general such that no growth in the proportion of GDP invested in libraries was possible. However, and in common with other service industries, productivity in libraries grew apace, as the number of staff employed declined and book stocks increased.

3.6 Developments in the library world which have occurred since 1986

The earlier study made reference to the diversity of library management organisations throughout Europe: Each state had a unique hierarchy and pattern of management responsibility for the various library sectors, which made the consistent measurement of activity and funding flows difficult. In retrospect, it is seen that the organisation and funding of libraries will always be undergoing constant change. Different structures are always evolving to suit the local demands of the time. Hence, such change can be seen as development:

- New premises have been built for the Bibliothèque de France. It has consumed substantial investment, principally in respect of the building and furnishing costs but also in respect of additional staff.

- The British Library made significant investment in new premises.

- Libraries in Spain and Portugal have grown both in terms of availability and size of collections in the latter half of the 1980s. For instance the average numbers of books in library collections in Spain and Portugal have increased by 7.8% and 6.7% per annum respectively compared to the European Union annual average increase of 1.4%.

Such changes relate to a dynamic organisation of libraries in Europe, providing some solace to offset the continuing difficulties in measuring the relative change which has occurred in the intervening period since the previous study took place.

3.7 Maturity of library definitions

The difficulty of obtaining both activity and financial data relating to a sector where the responsibility is split over more than one government department / ministry continues to occur. Where such divisions of responsibilities exist there are often no centrally held statistics. The number of instances of such split responsibilities and resultant absences of centrally collated library statistics has not significantly reduced since 1985. This problem, as manifested in Spain, was highlighted by Raman Abad in his paper presented at the International Federation of Librarians' Association (IFLA) conference held in Barcelona during August 1993:

> "In general we are in the presence of an overlapping of functions on the part of various administrations. This is manifested in the repetition of the same data in the various reports published within the same territory or in the absence of fundamental data, in cases where only one of the administrations within the territory is in charge of supplying them. In spite of the fact that the Autonomous Communities usually lump the cultural and educational domains together and that many of them have their own legislation in which library systems operating in the Community are defined, there are very few cases where overall statistical reports are produced."

This problem has also been encountered by UNESCO, where a number of their statistics state that they refer to part of the library sector, for instance university libraries only, excluding all other institutions of tertiary education. In Italy the Ministry for Cultural and Environmental Assets is responsible for the university libraries founded before the unification of Italy, and the Ministry for University and Scientific Research is responsible for the remaining university libraries. Public libraries statistics were held locally, if at all. It requires a significant effort in organising central collection.

The lack of standard definitions of financial terms relating to libraries, which encumbered the original study team, referred to in paragraph 3.2, continued to hamper the collation of financial data for the current study. For instance some national statistical frameworks differentiate between capital and revenue expenditure and others do not; some consider the acquisition of stock to be capital expenditure and others treat this item as revenue expenditure (See Appendix 2, paragraph 1.3 point 6). The quality and quantity of data supplied is often influenced by the level at which the budgets are held and the relationship of the budget holders to the collators of statistics.

The most comprehensive returns of data received related to the National Library sector while the returns relating to School Libraries were extremely sparse.

As a result of the difficulties experienced in the original study a number of revisions were made to the survey questionnaire relating to:

- Mobile and Static Service Points - a combined definition was used;

- Library Staff - The definition of "support" staff was developed;

- Total Expenditure - the distinction between "Revenue" and "Capital" costs was abandoned;

- Expenditure relating to the Acquisition of Stock - the definition was clarified;

- Expenditure relating to Information Technology - the item of expenditure was included as a separate heading;

- Sources of Income - the breakdown was simplified and the distinction between "central" as opposed to "local" government funding discontinued.

3.8 Mobile and Static Service Points

The original study sought the respective the number of static and mobile service for all sectors. Only Public Libraries provide mobile service points, and the questionnaires were therefore amended to incorporate mobile with all static points.

The data had shown that the provision of mobile libraries was a matter of policy rather than average population density. For instance, in Denmark and the United Kingdom there were approximately 14 and 12 mobile service points per million population respectively; in the Netherlands, Portugal and France there was roughly half this level of provision; while in Greece there were approximately two mobile service points per million population.

3.9 Library Staff

The original questionnaires asked for the number of staff (expressed as full-time equivalents, assuming a normal working week to be 40 hours) employed in the provision of library services under the following three categories:

- Trained Librarians;

- Other Library Staff;

- Other Support Staff.

The problem relating to varying interpretations of "Trained Librarians" is discussed below. The other two categories of "Other Library Staff" and "Other Support Staff" have been amalgamated because many of the respondents to the first survey appeared unable to differentiate between them. Furthermore, the number of support staff will depend upon the structure of the library administration and that of its responsible government department/ministry. Therefore, it is an estimation of the number of "Trained Librarians" employed which is of particular interest to this study.

3.10 <u>Trained Librarians</u>

Paragraph 3.2 refers to the original study's findings concerning the general acceptance of the definitions regarding activity data, and the practicability of applying these to existing national statistical frameworks. The study found that these problems still exist. For instance, there remains a divergence of opinion as to the interpretation of "Trained Librarians". The survey notes of guidance, which correspond with the UNESCO and ISO definitions, state that "Trained Librarians" are:

> "All members of staff who have received a general training in librarianship or information science. The training may be by formal methods or by means of an extended period of work in a library under supervision."

When validating the returned data, and during some of the study visits, it became apparent that some states and sectors only included those members of staff with a university degree in librarianship, some included graduates of any discipline and some also included members of staff with a diploma in librarianship (See Appendix 2, paragraph 1.3 point 5). These different interpretations of "Trained Librarians" may well reflect the standing or status of the library profession within that country, for instance:

ITALY:
"It is estimated that Italian libraries between them employ some 25,000 staff, around 12,000 of whom are qualified. However, librarianship is not yet a recognised profession in Italy, legally regulated with a national register of librarians. Many libraries do not require any qualification in librarianship when recruiting."
Report on Library Information Services and Products in the Italian Market, Martin Rose, British Council.

GREECE:
"The lack of recognition of the profession of Librarianship is reflected by the absence of a separate grading structure within the civil service. Until this is changed librarians occupy clerical posts with no professional status and promotion inevitably means a move into another field in which their professional expertise is not used."
Libraries and Information Profile - Greece, British Council Libraries Department.

IRELAND:
"An Chomhairle was glad to learn at the end of the year that University College, Dublin, was finalising a proposal for the inclusion of Information Studies in the Bachelor of Science Degree Course from October 1992. An Chomhairle has, for many years, stressed the need to

promote a graduate-based library profession in Ireland and it welcomes this development at University College, Dublin."
44th Annual Report, Year ended December 1991, An Chomhairle Leabarlanna.

SWEDEN:
"All training of librarians and documentalists in Sweden takes place at the School of Library and Information Science, in Borås near Gothenburg. The study program is tailored for all work in all types of libraries as well as related areas of cultural and information sectors. To be admitted to the course one must have completed upper-secondary school education and two years of further studies. About 220 librarians annually graduate from the two-year program."
Libraries in Sweden, Thomas Lidman.

3.11 Total Expenditure

Previously recipients of the questionnaires were asked to separate revenue (or current) and capital expenditure. From the returns provided by those who were able to distinguish between these two types of expenditure, there emerged a number of differing interpretations of both revenue and capital expenditure. It became clear that a number of inconsistencies were inherent in the funding structures which precluded the determination of standard headings in a survey of this kind.

In order not to replicate these inconsistencies the new questionnaires requested the TOTAL expenditure incurred by the library sector for each year. An ensuing memorandum concerning capital expenditure was an optional section, to be completed only where reliable data were available. Those states which were able to complete this memorandum were asked to indicate in a specified box whether the figures relating to capital expenditure had been included in the Total expenditure figures. This approach proved more successful than that used previously. However, it was not possible to create estimates of capital expenditure from the returns received. Given that the interpretation of "capital investment" is so inconsistent throughout Europe the results would not be reliable. (See Appendix 2, paragraph 1.3 point 6).

3.12 Expenditure relating to the Acquisition of Stock

Acquisition of new stock represents the second largest item of expenditure, after the cost of library staff, for all library sectors (see paragraph 4.3). The previous survey asked respondents to report their acquisition expenditure within the following three categories:

- Books;

- Current Periodicals;

- Other Materials.

While the total expenditure on the acquisition of stock appears to be one of the few financial statistics available, few respondents were able to breakdown the costs across the three categories. Therefore, the revised questionnaires requested the total Acquisition Cost only.

An indication of the relative expenditure on the different types of materials purchased was inferred from the numbers held in collections and the annual additions to the collection.

3.13 Expenditure relating to Information Technology

Expenditure on Information Technology equipment and systems maintenance has been difficult to monitor. Developments in technology throughout the decade have seen equipment costs reducing substantially, allowing Information Technology benefits to accrue for the same real cost during the period. However, the breakdown of such expenditure within national summary reports has been too hazardous a base upon which to establish the trends within this study. The application of Information Technology and Systems within libraries in the European Union are the subject of a separate report, study reference EUR 14660 EN January 1992 *"The state of the art of the application of new information technologies in libraries and their impact on library functions."* This report is comprised of 12 individual reports relating to each Member State.

3.14 Sources of Income

Respondents to the first survey were asked to show their income received under five headings:

- Central Taxes / Grants;

- Local Taxes / Grants;

- Private Sources;

- Fees and Charges;

- Other Income.

A number of respondents were unable to provide such detailed returns, particularly in respect of distinguishing between central and local government funding. For those able to distinguish between these two sources, no uniform pattern emerged, reflecting the differing organisational responsibilities for library sectors within the member states of the European Union. For instance, in the UK the Department of National Heritage has overall responsibility for public libraries, but these are administered by various tiers of local government, depending on their location within the country. In France, the local responsibility is similarly organised, but the central funding sources are difficult to trace through more than one ministry, and a third or regional tier, vested in the various Departments. The principal aim was to establish the overall level of public funding which libraries attract rather than measuring a possibly spurious difference between central and local government sources. Therefore, the subsequent survey simply asked for "Government/Municipal Funding".

Income received from "Private Sources" proved to be so insignificant in the original study that this source was included in "Other Income" and the notes of guidance were amended accordingly.

Wherever possible, the above amendments have been applied to the original study data set so that trends were traced on consistent definitions throughout the ten year study period.

CHAPTER 4

FINANCIAL RESULTS

4.1 <u>Overall Library Expenditure</u>

The average annual library expenditure shown in ECUs for the two five year periods, 1981-1985 and 1986-1990, expressed at 1990 constant prices, increased by 1.9% per annum. Within this overall increase, individual library sector changes in expenditure varied considerably, as table 5 below shows.

Table 5:

ANNUAL AVERAGE LIBRARY EXPENDITURE FOR THE PERIODS 1981-1985 AND 1986-1990

Sector	1981-1985 (Million ECUs)	% of Total	1986-1990 (Million ECUs)	% of Total	Annualised Change (% pa)
National	401.2	5.7%	423.6	6.8%	1.1%
Higher Education	946.1	13.3%	1,079.7	16.9%	2.7%
Other Major Non-Specialised	266.5	4.1%	281.0	3.3%	1.1%
School	965.8	17.9%	981.9	14.1%	0.3%
Special	531.5	9.5%	607.2	10.7%	2.7%
Public	2,924.9	49.5%	3,263.3	48.2%	2.2%
TOTAL	6,036.0	100 %	6,636.7	100 %	1.9%

These total expenditures are equivalent to 17.85 and 19.52 ECUs per head of population resident in the European Union (as shown in Figure 3 Chapter 1).

The increase in expenditure for the Higher Education sector, from some 920 million ECUs in 1981 to 1,145 million ECUs expressed at 1990 constant prices represents an annual increase of 2.5% and reflects the higher number entering tertiary education. Substantial costs will have arisen to provide expanded premises and staff to meet this increased demand. In addition, the need to maintain the content of the Higher Education Libraries' book stock will have exerted further pressure on expenditure levels as institutions have endeavoured to keep pace with technological developments.

The increase in expenditure for the National Library sector, from some 399 million ECUs in 1981 to 433 million ECUs in 1990, both figures are expressed at 1990 constant prices, equates to an increase of 0.9% per annum over the ten year study period, may be explained in part by the substantial costs incurred by the United Kingdom and France for new or refurbished premises.

The meagre increase in spending for School Libraries reflects the reduced number of pupils, with a corresponding reduction in the number of service points and staff. However, the estimates for School Library expenditure are based upon relatively poor data (see paragraph 2.5).

Expenditure relating to Public Libraries increased from some 2,812 million ECUs in 1981 to 3,338 million ECUs in 1990, where both figures are expressed at 1990 constant prices, representing an annual average increase of 1.9% over the decade.

Table 5 shows that expenditure relating to the Public Library sector has increased by 2.2% per annum relative to the retail price index. However, Figure 6, below, plots Public Library expenditure as a percentage of Gross Domestic Product.

Figure 6:

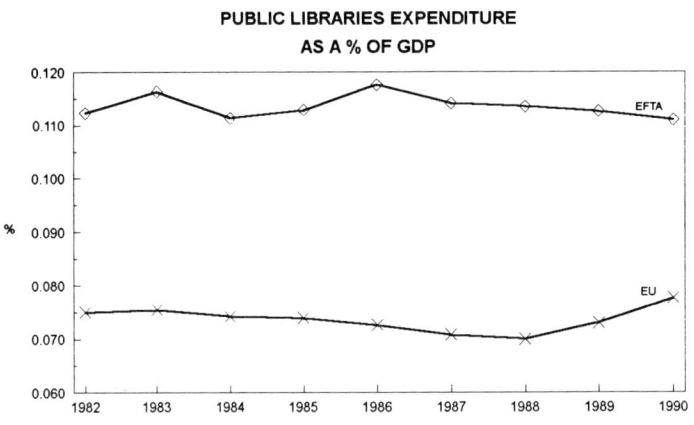

For the first quinquennium, the annual average was 0.075% and for the second 0.073%. Some 58% of public library expenditure is spent on staff and as Figure 3 (paragraph 1.4ii) shows salaries have grown faster than the rate for consumer prices in the later half of the decade. As a result investment in Public Libraries in real terms has not increased. Thus while total library expenditure, as a percentage of Gross Domestic Product has remained constant throughout the decade, the resources have been channelled to the various library sectors in differing proportions.

4.2   Staffing Expenditure

Table 6:

ANNUAL AVERAGE STAFFING COSTS

Sector	1981-1985 (Million ECUs)	1986-1990 (Million ECUs)	Annualised Change (% pa)
National	228.4	240.8	1.1%
Higher Education	540.5	609.9	2.4%
Other Major Non-Specialised	161.7	171.0	1.2%
School	583.2	592.9	0.3%
Special	318.0	365.2	2.8%
Public	1,694.7	1,853.2	1.8%
TOTAL	3,526.5	3,833.0	1.7%

Annual average staffing costs have increased by 1.7% per annum compared with the total expenditure increase for the same period of 1.9%. However, the unit cost per employee has increased by 6.1% from 15,230 to 16,160 ECUs over the two five year periods, which may reflect the higher number of "Trained Librarians" recorded in the second quinquennium. See Chapter 5 for the overall and sector staffing numbers.

4.3 Expenditure on the acquisition of stock

Table 7 shows the expenditure relating to the acquisition of stock increased by 2% per annum and remained the second largest item within the library budget representing some 21% of total annual average expenditure for the two five year periods. Over the ten year period this figure increased from some 1,254 million ECUs in 1981 to 1,443 million ECus, expressed at 1990 constant prices, equating to an annual average increase of 1.6%.

The annual average stock of books and bound periodicals in School Libraries only increased by 0.3% per annum over the two five year periods (see paragraph 5.2), which is reflected in the constrained expenditure on acquisitions (a slight increase of 0.3% per annum) for this sector. There was, however, an increase in the number of loans per head of sector population from 11.06 to 11.33.

Public Libraries account for approximately 49% of total expenditure and hold some 44% of the total book stock. However, the consumption on acquisitions has not really changed in real terms over the decade. Public Libraries' budgets have evidently been constrained. Within overall Public Libraries spending staffing expenditure has increased in real terms by 1.8% per annum, but acquisition expenditure has increased by 2.2% per annum. The question arises as to whether the traditional role of providing a general choice in the book stock available to the population at large is a goal which Public Libraries are continuing to pursue. Without an emphasis on such expenditure it seems probable that choice to the users has been insufficient to maintain the level of usage. This is reflected in the decline in the annual average number of consultations per book in Public Libraries from 3.5 to 3.0 and the number of consultations per 1000 population from 5,354 to 5,352 (Table 15, paragraph 5.6, shows the number of consultations per 1000 population for each library sector).

Table 7:

ANNUAL AVERAGE ACQUISITION EXPENDITURE

Sector	1981-1985 (Million ECUs)	% of Sector Expenditure	1986-1990 (Million ECUs)	% of Sector Expenditure	% Change (p.a.)
National	67.216	16.8%	71.971	17.0%	1.4%
Higher Education	295.544	31.2%	341.031	31.6%	2.9%
Other Major Non-Specialised	56.215	21.1%	59.610	21.2%	1.2%
School	218.323	22.6%	221.774	20.0%	0.3%
Special	125.649	23.6%	144.857	24.1%	2.9%
Public	523.453	17.9%	584.282	19.4%	2.2%
TOTAL	1,286.400	21.3%	1,423.527	21.4%	2.0%

The increase in acquisition expenditure of 2.9% per annum for the Higher Education sector is in line with the overall increase in total expenditure for the sector. The comparatively smaller increase in acquisition expenditure for the National library sector of 1.4% per annum is less than the overall increase in total acquisition expenditure of 2% per annum. This may be partly accounted for by the increase in premises costs incurred by the French and British National Libraries (the British Library reported a reduction in acquisition expenditure in its 1990 Annual Report), and the role of national libraries as deposit libraries.

4.4 Income for Library Services

Figure 7:

The sources of income and their respective proportions for all libraries 1986-1990

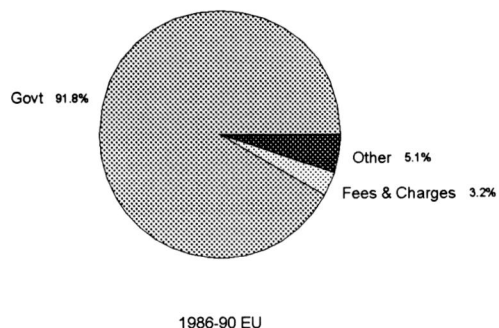

1986-90 EU

Figure 7 shows the proportions of library funding for the years 1986-1990 which mirrored those of the previous quinquennia. Although in accounting terms income should meet expenditure, if the budgets for libraries are to balance, a difference arises from year to year relating either to an accumulation to, or use of balances. This study assumes that income and expenditure will balance in each year.

Table 8:

ANNUAL AVERAGE FEES AND CHARGES RECEIVED BY LIBRARIES

Sector	1981-1985 (Million ECUs)	% age of Total Income	1986-1990 (Million ECU)	% age of Total Income	Annualised Change % pa
National	6.489	1.62%	7.035	1.66%	1.6%
Higher Education	27.049	2.86%	32.171	2.98%	3.6%
Other Major Non-Specialised	8.474	3.18%	8.929	3.18%	1.3%
School	31.215	3.23%	31.727	3.23%	0.3%
Special	16.832	3.17%	19.238	3.17%	2.7%
Public	90.158	3.08%	110.793	3.40%	4.2%
TOTAL	180.216	2.99%	209.894	3.16%	1.4%

Public Libraries - Sources of Funding

Figure 8:   **Figure 9:**

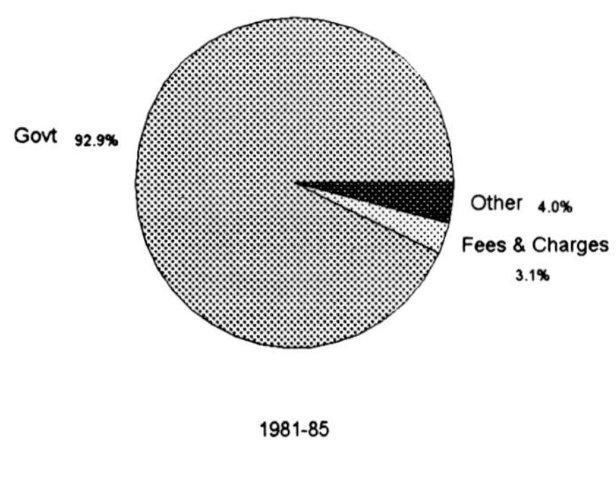

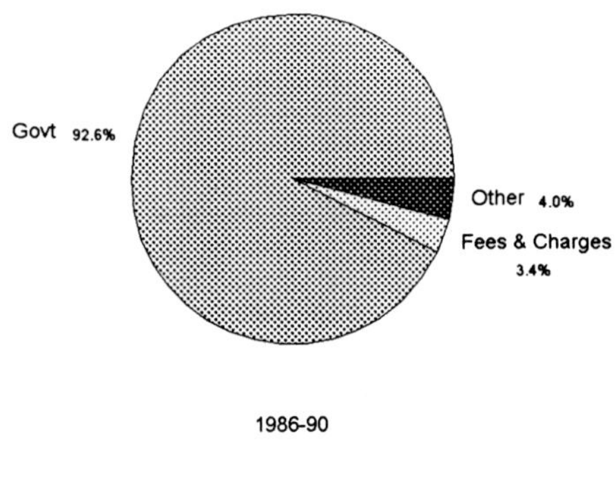

1981-85   1986-90

- 30 -

Fees and charges as a proportion of total income have increased slightly from an average of 2.99% for the first quinquennium to 3.16% for the second quinquennium However, the the income received from fees and charges in the Public Library sector increased from some 86 million ECUs in 1981 to 1,118 million ECUs in 1990, where both figures are expressed at 1990 constant prices. This represents an annual average increase of 3.6% over the decade compared to that of total fees and charges received of 2.5% increase per annum. As a result the proportion of fees and charges for public libraries has increased from 3.08% to 3.4%, reflecting an emergent "market philosophy", perhaps encouraged by a restraint on government funding as reflected in figures 8 and 9.

4.5 Remaining Expenditure Items

Figure 10:
The principal items of expenditure and their respective proportions for all library sectors 1986-1990

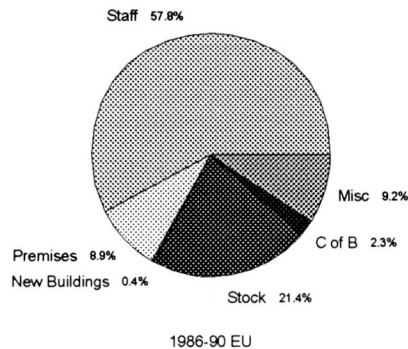

Note : C of B = Cost of Borrowing

Figure 10 depicts the annual average patterns of spending for the period 1986-1990 which mirrors that of the previous quinquennium. However, new buildings / refurbishment of the National Library sector has increased marginally from 2.9% to 3.0% of their budgets. This may reflect the major investment being undertaken in France and the UK in respect of new and refurbished premises.

While the proportion of overall budget accounted for by premises related expenditure remained constant during the decade (9%), premise related expenditure per library service point increased from an annual average for the period 1981-85 of 5,990 ECUs to 6,432 ECUs for the period 1986-90, representing an increase of 1.4% per annum.

The above are based upon a high proportion of estimated data, reflecting the continuing sparsity of consistent information about expenditure, other than that for staffing and acquisition costs.

CHAPTER 5

ACTIVITY DATA

5.1 The Provision of Library Services

Table 9:

AVERAGE NUMBER OF SERVICE POINTS FOR THE FIVE YEAR PERIODS 1981-1985 AND 1986-1990

SECTOR	1981-85 Service Points	1986-90 Service Points	Annualised Change
National	45	48	1.1%
Higher Education	4,421	4,874	2.0%
Other Major Non-Specialised	260	257	-0.2%
School	33,251	33,215	-
Special	4,997	5,806	3.0%
Public	45,488	51,681	2.6%
TOTAL	88,461	95,880	1.6%

The number of service points is a measure of the access which users have to libraries and the observed number has increased markedly (average increase of 1.6% per annum) over the average for the first quinquennium in the 1980s. Part of the dynamics shown in the Table 9 above is explained by the reclassification of major libraries to the administrations of the National libraries (France) and the returns for the national library sectors for Denmark and Germany record an increase in the number of service points. Part stems from the decline in school populations, and the passing of the "continuing education bulge" into the Higher Education sector. The growth in Special Libraries may reflect the growing importance of these information resources to the expanding service industries, which continued to develop in importance in the European economy during the latter part of the decade. However, the principal reason for the apparent growth is due to better reporting in the latter half of the decade.

Thus, in overall terms the number of service points per head of population improved from an annual average of 3,820 to 3,550 over the decade. Figure 11, overleaf, shows the annual average population per service point in the EU, excepting Greece, for the second quinquennium (see Appendix 6 notes relating to Greece).

Figure 11:

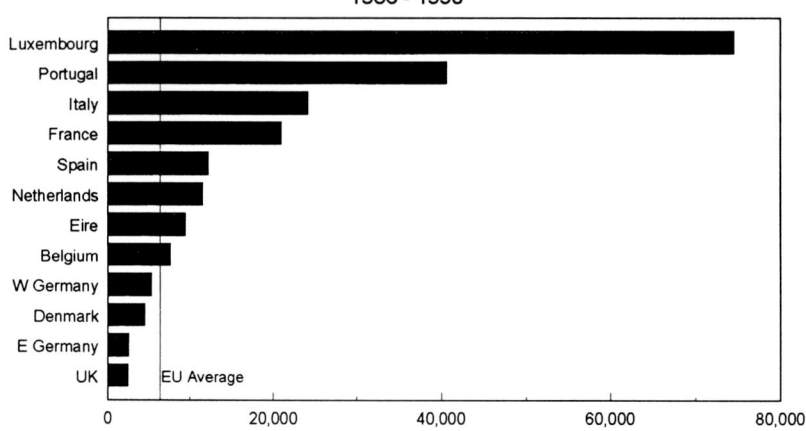

5.2 Book Stocks

Most respondents (95%) were able to report both the number of volumes in their collections and the respective annual additions. These returns show that book stocks for all sectors other than Schools continued to grow throughout the second half of the decade, but at a slower rate than during the previous five years. This restraint in growth is reflected in the reduction of the proportion which acquisition of stock represents of total library expenditure.

Volumes held by the Higher Education sector increased from 245 million in 1981 to 300 million in 1990, representing an annual average increase of 2.3% per annum during the ten year period.

For the Public Library sector the number of volumes in collections increased from 526 million in 1981 to 623 million in 1990, representing an annual average increase of 1.9% per annum.

The differing rates of increase in book stocks between library sectors are further evidenced by the changing proportions of total book stock which each sector represents (See Table 10). The Institutes of Higher Education now account for more than one fifth of total library book stocks in the European Union. For instance, the average number of volumes per service point in the Higher Education sector for the years 1986-1990 was 58,150 compared to that for the for the Public Library sector of 11,767.

Table 10:

ANNUAL AVERAGE NUMBER OF VOLUMES IN COLLECTIONS

Sector	1981-1985 (Millions)	% of Total	1986-1990 (Millions)	% of Total	Annualised Change
National	86.866	6.0 %	92.604	6.6%	1.3%
Higher Education	249.742	19.6 %	283.425	20.3%	2.6%
Other Major Non-Specialised	58.433	3.6 %	61.455	4.4%	1.0%
School	198.029	18.4 %	201.161	14.4%	0.3%
Special	127.126	8.9 %	149.632	10.7%	3.3%
Public	552.242	43.5 %	608.111	43.5%	1.9%
TOTAL	1,272.438	100 %	1,396.388	100%	1.9%

5.3 Current Periodicals

The total count of periodicals amounted to 7.2 millions. However, as experienced in the previous study, it has proven difficult to differentiate between titles and volumes in most countries. Table 11, below, provides an overview of activity:

Table 11:

ANNUAL AVERAGE COLLECTIONS OF CURRENT PERIODICALS

Sector	1981-1985 (Millions)	% of Total	1986-1990 (Millions)	% of Total	Annualised Change
National	0.599	8.9 %	0.660	9.1 %	2.0%
Higher Education	1.737	25.2 %	1.836	25.4 %	1.1%
Other Major Non-Specialised	1.706	24.7 %	1.710	23.6 %	0.1%
School	0.029	0.4 %	0.029	0.4 %	0.0%
Special	1.758	25.5 %	1.884	26.3 %	1.4%
Public	1.073	15.6 %	1.118	15.0%	0.8%
TOTAL	6.902	100 %	7.239	100%	1.0%

5.4 Audio Visual Material

The EU data relating to the two five year periods are not been comparable for the following reasons :

1　The statistical definition of "Audio-visual" materials in collections is clear but open to interpretation in the most convenient manner to suit the format in which the local statistics are held.

2　A number of reclassifications of stock items appear to have occurred within the study period. For instance, the National Library in the Former Federal Republic of Germany reports a substantial decrease between the years 1984 and 1985, reducing from 5.266 million items to 0.283 millions. These figures have been validated by the relevant contact.

Table 12:

ANNUAL AVERAGE NUMBER OF AUDIO VISUAL MATERIALS IN LIBRARY COLLECTIONS

Sector	1990 (Millions)
National	3.264
Higher Education	5.219
Other Major Non-Specialised	1.100
School	5.996
Special	5.285
Public	26.695
TOTAL	47.559

The Public Libraries, as reported in the original study, hold over half of the audio-visual materials contained within library collections (56%). They have experienced considerable growth in the number of issues of audio-visual materials over the latter part of the decade. In the UK 0.23 audio-visual issues per head of population were made in 1980 compared with 0.48 in 1990 representing an average annual increase of 7.6%.

5.5 Staff Numbers

Table 13:

AVERAGE ANNUAL NUMBER OF STAFF EMPLOYED

Sector	1981-1985 (Thousands)	1986-1990 (Thousands)	% Change p.a.
National	9.500	9.644	0.3%
Higher Education	34.544	37.798	1.8%
Other Major Non-Specialised	10.318	10.751	0.8%
School	39.216	39.379	0.1%
Special	19.587	21.437	1.8%
Public	118.399	118.218	0.0%
TOTAL	231.565	237.227	0.5%

The annual average number of staff employed for the two quinquennia has increased by 5,662 (0.5% per annum). The number of staff employed within the Higher Education Library sector has increased in line with the expansion of this sector to mirror the education bulge, and it is gratifying to note the importance of libraries in meeting demand.

The slight reduction in staff in the Public Library sector reflects the constraints on expenditure, but it also demonstrates an increase in productivity.

The ratio of Trained Librarians to Other Library Staff has decreased between the two quinquennia from 1:2.47 to 1:2.28. For while the total number of staff has increased by 0.5% per annum, the number of Trained Librarians has increased by an average of 1.7% per annum and the number of "Other Library Staff" have marginally decreased. Table 14 shows the number of Trained Librarians in each sector and the ratio of Trained Librarians to Other Staff.

Table 14:

ANNUAL AVERAGE NUMBER OF TRAINED LIBRARIANS

Sector	1981-1985 Trained Librarians	Ratio to Other Staff	1986-1990 Trained Librarians	Ratio to Other Staff
National	3,087	1 : 2.1	3,343	1 : 1.9
Higher Education	10,145	1 : 2.4	12,218	1 : 2.1
Other Major Non-Specialised	2,916	1 : 2.5	2,808	1 : 2.8
School	4,769	1 : 7.2	4,789	1 : 7.2
Special	7,002	1 : 1.8	8,375	1 : 1.6
Public	38,879	1 : 2.0	41,068	1 : 1.9
TOTAL	66,798	1 : 2.5	72,600	1 : 2.3

The number of books per Trained Librarian has increased from an annual average of 19,050 (for the years 1981-1985) to 19,230 (for the years 1986-1990), providing another indication of increased productivity.

Whilst the number of Trained Librarians has increased, the number of "Other Library Staff" has decreased marginally from an annual average of 164,800 to 164,600 for the two quinquennia, equating to a drop of 0.02% per annum. This may be partly due to the clarification of the definitions of staff now employed (see paragraphs 3.9 and 3.10). However, a number of states are increasing the number of places available for students of librarianship and information systems, thus increasing the number of suitably qualified staff.

5.6 Library Users

The annual average number of registered borrowers per thousand population has increased from 301 to 313 (0.8% per annum) over the two five year periods. This figure should, however be treated with some caution since the understanding of what constitutes a registered borrower / user can vary considerably. Also the number of users can be influenced by how often the libraries, particularly Public Libraries, update their records. For instance a registered borrower may have moved out of the area and registered with a library in a new location without having cancelled the previous membership.

Furthermore there is the distinction between a registered user and an active user of the library facilities. This is highlighted by the UK figure of 581 registered users per thousand population for the Public Library sector (compared to 118 for the previous quinquennium). This figure has been taken from Len England's work "Borrowing Books" which found from survey data that 58% of the UK population hold a library card.

The average annual number of consultations per thousand population for the individual sectors for the two quinquennia are shown in Table 15 below:

Table 15:

LIBRARY CONSULTATIONS PER THOUSAND POPULATION

Sector	Consultations (millions) 1981-1985	Consultations per 1000 Pop	Consultations (millions) 1986-1990	Consultations per 1000 Pop	*Annualised Change %*
National	11.892	35.2	12.083	35.5	*0%*
Higher Education	88.518	261.8	101.262	297.8	*2.6%*
Other Major Non-Specialised	17.436	51.65	18.131	53.33	*3.2%*
School	803.592	2,376.3	803.954	2,364.3	*-0.1%*
Special	18.091	53.5	19.953	58.7	*1.9%*
Public	1,810.564	5,353.9	1,819.866	5,351.9	*0%*
TOTAL	2,750.093	8,132.2	2,775.249	8,161.6	*0%*

Consultations per thousand population have been used in Table 15 rather than "Registered Borrowers" since they provide a more reliable basis for comparison. The differing interpretations relating to "Registered Borrowers" are discussed above and within the individual Country Profiles (See Appendices 6 and 2, paragraph 1.3iv).

CHAPTER 6

EUROPEAN FREE TRADE AGREEMENT STATES

6.1 The context of EFTA countries within this study

Information about the EFTA states was not included in the previous study and contacts were asked primarily to collate data relating to 1986-1990. As a secondary issue, they were asked to provide data relating to the first half of the decade if these were easily retrievable. Many respondents, particularly within the Scandinavian states were able to provide data relating to the whole decade. The Nordic Statistical Secretariat publish data relating to book stocks, additions, loans, staff and finance for the research libraries in Denmark, Finland, Iceland, Norway and Sweden. Estimated data for non-respondents relating to 1981-1985 has therefore been heavily based upon the Scandinavian experience, and may be biased accordingly.

6.2 Summary of financial results

The average annual library expenditure for the two quinquennia for the EFTA states increased from 44.17 to 47.09 ECUs (1990 constant prices) per head of population. This compares with a change from 17.85 to 19.52 ECUs for the European Union states. However, the cost of living is substantially higher in the majority of EFTA states than that of the average in the European Union.

The average annual expenditure per capita for libraries within the EFTA states increased by 1.3% per annum compared with a per capita increase of 1.5% recorded in the European Union.

Table 16:
ANNUAL AVERAGE LIBRARY EXPENDITURE 1981-85 AND 1986-90

Sector	1981-1985 (Million ECUs)	% of Total	1986-1990 (Million ECUs)	% of Total	Annualised Change (p.a.)
National	32.42	2.3%	38.74	2.6%	3.6%
Higher Education	225.64	15.9%	265.02	17.5%	3.5%
Other Major Non-Specialised	96.67	6.7%	97.71	6.4%	0.4%
School	299.99	21.1%	255.34	16.8%	-3.2%
Special	113.42	8.0%	118.62	7.8%	0.9%
Public	652.16	45.9%	740.01	48.8%	2.6%
TOTAL	1,419.31	100%	1,515.44	100%	2.8%

The above average increase in the National Library sector expenditure may due to the following factors:

1 In Finland the National Library is also the University of Helsinki Library and costs have been difficult to apportion between the sectors.

2 The construction of a new building to house the combined National and University of Iceland Library in Reykjavik presents a similar problem.

3   The National Library in Liechtenstein, because of the size of the country, also serves as a public library and a special library. Data have not been disaggregated across the three sectors.

Table 17:
AVERAGE ANNUAL STAFFING LEVELS AND EXPENDITURE

Sector	1981-1985 (Million ECUs)	No. of Staff	1986-1990 (Million ECUs)	No. of Staff	Annual % Change ECU	Annual % Change No.
National	20.565	861	23.514	913	2.7%	1.2%
Higher Education	135.071	3,803	157.412	4,246	3.1%	2.2%
Other Major Non-Specialised	60.087	3,554	61.447	3,560	0.5%	0.0%
School	183.908	11,620	157.040	9,922	-3.1%	-3.2%
Special	67.018	3,233	70.128	3,407	0.9%	1.1%
Public	359.810	19,653	408.982	20,987	2.6%	1.3%
TOTAL	826.459	42,724	878.553	43,035	1.2%	0.2%

The number of staff employed within the library service in the EFTA states has increased by 0.1% per annum, with the School sector recording a substantial reduction in numbers of 3.2% per annum, equating to a difference of 26,870 between the average number of staff employed within the School Libraries for the two quinquennia. This reduction reflects the decline in pupil numbers and the number of school library service points over the two quinquennia. The overall increase in the number of staff employed is less than that reported for the EU states of 0.5% per annum.

The average annual costs per member of staff in the EFTA states for the two five year periods were respectively 19,340 and 20,420 ECUs at 1990 constant prices. The significantly higher unit costs for EFTA states over those for the European Union (15,230 and 16,160 ECUs respectively) simply reflect the higher cost of living.

Table 18:
ANNUAL AVERAGE EXPENDITURE INCURRED IN THE ACQUISITION OF STOCK

Sector	1981-1985 (Million ECUs)	% of Total Expenditure	1986-1990 (Million ECUs)	% of Total Expenditure	Change (% pa)
National	3.126	9.6%	3.903	10.2%	4.5%
Higher Education	55.292	24.5%	65.576	24.7%	3.1%
Other Major Non-Specialised	19.213	20.1%	19.523	20.0%	0.3%
School	60.683	20.2%	50.987	20.0%	-3.4%
Special	27.269	24.0%	28.590	24.1%	1.0%
Public	127.402	19.5%	143.274	19.4%	2.4%
TOTAL	292.985	21.5%	311.854	20.6%	1.3%

Over the decade, expenditure relating to the acquisition of stock has increased from 234 million ECUs in 1981 to 309 million ECUs in 1990, both figures are expressed at 1990 constant prices. This represents an annual average increase of 0.9% per annum over the decade, which suggests that the cost of stock acquisition has grown at a lesser rate amongst the EFTA states than within the European Union (0.9% compared with 1.6% per annum). Otherwise the pattern of expenditure within the overall budget is similar to the distribution observed within the EU.

Hence, the relative budget proportions for all Library sectors allocated to stock acquisition in the EFTA states accords with that of the average for the European Union states (21%).

3   Activity Data

AVAILABILITY OF LIBRARIES

The average population per square kilometre was 24 for the EFTA states, compared with an EU average of 143 per square kilometre. Of the countries participating in the current study, population per square kilometre ranged from 365 in the Netherlands to 2 in Iceland. Relative sparsity, therefore, is the main determinant of the demand for, and the size of, libraries. Figure 12 below shows the Public Library service points per thousand population for the individual EFTA states. Figure 11, paragraph 5.1 depicts the number of Public Library service points for the EU states.

Figure 12:

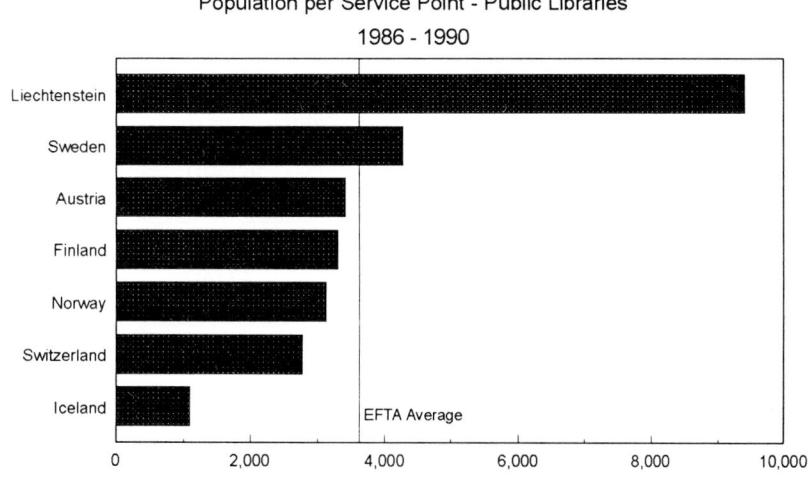

Table 19:

AVERAGE NUMBER OF SERVICE POINTS FOR THE TWO QUINQUENNIA 1981-1985 AND 1986-1990

Sector	1981-85 Service Points	% of Total	1986-90 Service Points	% of Total	Annualised Change
National	12	0.04%	11	0.04%	-1.4%
Higher Education	1,308	4.35%	1,361	4.87%	0.8%
Other Major Non-Specialised	111	0.37%	112	0.40%	0.1%
School	18,085	60.09%	15,857	56.80%	-2.6%
Special	880	2.92%	931	3.33%	1.1%
Public	9,701	32.23%	9,646	34.55%	-0.1%
TOTAL	30,097	100%	27,917	100%	-1.5%

The average number of service points per head of population is lower for the EFTA states than for the European Union states (1,150 compared to 3,550 respectively), reflecting the substantially lower population density of many of these states. Legislation relating to the provision of public libraries amongst the EFTA states also has a bearing. For instance:

SWEDEN:
Each of the 284 municipalities in Sweden must provide a public library service. Each municipality is free to determine its own library policy and priorities and the consequent level of service provision. More than half of the municipalities in Sweden serve populations of less than 20,000 demonstrating that many libraries serve scattered populations.

NORWAY:
Each municipality must, by statute, provide a public library service, either alone or in conjunction with a neighbouring municipality. In addition, County libraries supplement the activities of Public and School libraries in Norway.

These differences in legislation are mirrored by the lower number of service points per administrative unit amongst the EFTA states than in the European Union. There was an average of 1 service point per administrative unit amongst the EFTA states compared to 5.9 within the European Union.

Table 20:

AVERAGE NUMBER OF VOLUMES IN COLLECTIONS

Sector	1981-1985 (Millions)	% of Total	1986-1990 (Millions)	% of Total	Annualised Change
National	11.250	3.8 %	12.593	4.0 %	1.3%
Higher Education	58.202	19.7 %	67.491	21.3 %	3%
Other Major Non-Specialised	26.499	9.0 %	27.012	8.5 %	0.4%
School	58.701	19.8 %	50.099	15.9 %	-3.1%
Special	24.280	8.2 %	25.605	8.1 %	1.1%
Public	116.827	39.5 %	133.258	42.2 %	2.1%
TOTAL	295.760	100 %	316.058	100 %	1.3%

The number of volumes within library collections increased from 289 million in 1981 to 316 million in 1990, representing an annual average increase of 1.3% per annum over the decade, resulting in a slower rate of growth than that observed among the European Union states of 1.7% per annum throughout the decade.

There was an average of 9.2 books per head of EFTA population during the first half of the decade, which by the second half had grown to 9.8. Relative to the European Union (5.9), these reflect higher units of provision, but also arise simply because the average library caters for a smaller catchment population in the EFTA states, but seeks to maintain a commensurate standard of choice.

Usage

The average number of registered borrowers per thousand population for the EFTA states has increased by 2.4% per annum from 289 for the years 1981-1985 to 325 for 1986-1990. The annual average increase in registered borrowers is substantially higher than that relating to the EU states of 0.8%.

The number of registered borrowers per thousand population in the Public Library sector has increased by 1.1% per annum from 107 to 113 for the two five year periods. The corresponding averages for the EU states were 196 and 205 respectively, representing an annual increase of 0.9%. The figures for the EU states are distorted by the differing interpretations of "Registered Borrowers". (See paragraph 5.3 and Appendix 2, paragraph 1.3).

The number of consultations per head of population in Public Libraries has increased slightly in the EFTA states from 6.0 to 6.14 books per head of population (0.5% per annum), compared to a constant level of usage throughout the decade for the EU states of 5.4 books per head of population. This suggests that while the ratio of registered borrowers per thousand population may prove inconsistent as a result of disparate interpretations, the level of usage of Public Library facilities throughout Europe is fairly consistent. Table 21 provides an analysis of consultations per 1,000 head of population for the individual library sectors.

The choice of books available, particularly within the Public Library sector, appears to be greater in the EFTA states than in the EU states perhaps reflecting diseconomies of scale due to low population density and small average size of library authorities. The average number of consultations per book in the Public Library sector in the EFTA states were 2.3 for the first quinquennia and 2.1 for the second quinquennia; compared to the corresponding EU averages of 5.0 and 4.6.

Table 21

CONSULTATIONS PER THOUSAND POPULATION

Sector	1981-1985 Consultations (millions)	Consultations per 1000 Pop	1986-1990 Consultations (millions)	Consultations per 1000 Pop	*Annualised Change % (No. of Consultations)*
National	1.186	37	1.187	37	*0%*
Higher Education	7.004	2,779	8.828	3,512	*4.7%*
Other Major Non-Specialised	8.373	369	8.373	369	*0%*
School	61.082	10,068	60.000	9,905	*-0.4%*
Special	3.136	147	3.268	153	*0.8%*
Public	191.213	5,950	197.730	6,145	*0.7%*
TOTAL	271.994	8,464	279.385	8,682	*0.5%*

CHAPTER 7

THE WAY FORWARD

7.1 <u>The need for standardisation</u>

The original study cited three major difficulties encountered during the survey period :

"1. It was not usual practice to include financial breakdowns in the same surveys used nationally to collect activity based data relating to libraries. Consequently the figures drawn from different sources were inconsistent, leading to implausible unit costs."

2. There were no commonly held standards defining the forms of account.

3. Responsibility for libraries often crosses several government Departments/ Ministries, each with their own priorities for identifying the costs of such activities."

The recommendations proposed as a consequence of these are shown at Appendix 7.

Similar problems were encountered during the subsequent study. As with the previous survey, the quality and quantity of "Activity" data were far superior to that of the "Financial" Data.

Where inconsistencies/anomalies relating to "Activity" data occurred these tended to be associated with the actual method of counting the item, e.g. Current Periodicals or Audio Visual Materials, rather than misinterpretations of its definition. (See Appendix 2 paragraph 1.3 which discusses the inconsistencies /anomalies which occurred relating to Current Periodicals, Audio Visual Materials, Staff, and Loans) Inconsistencies relating to the interpretation of Registered Borrowers/Library Users are discussed in paragraph 5.6 Differing methods of counting items of stock may also occur with microforms and manuscripts.

There are working parties established by IFLA and ISO to refine the definitions employed for library statistics; perhaps their remit should be extended to include recommended methods of counting the physical numbers of items in their collections and other "Activity" statistics in order to facilitate international comparisons.

The problem of identifying the complete range of library costs, particularly where the "Financial" data are kept separately from the "Activity" data was identified during the original study and continued to exist during the subsequent study. For instance the premises related costs of libraries belonging to the Higher Education and School library sectors are often subsumed within the overall premises costs of the educational establishment to which they belong. Any apportionment of costs to the libraries may be made on an inconsistent basis and by those with insufficient knowledge of library operations and management

Expenditure relating to staff and the acquisition of stock are the items most commonly held "Financial" statistics, however, there are varying interpretations relating to both of these items of expenditure. For instance some returns for staff expenditure included direct staffing costs only, while others included all or some of the associated indirect staffing costs. Some returns relating to the acquisition of stock included binding costs and others did not. In order to facilitate international library comparisons a set of definitions for recording financial information for each of the principal items of expenditure (listed below) is urgently required:

    Staff

    Premises operating costs

    New buildings/refurbishment

    Acquisition of Stock

    Cost of Borrowing

    Miscellaneous expenditure

International comparisons of library finances are only meaningful if the total expenditure figures, rather than differentiating between Revenue and Capital expenditure, are used. For while the definitions of revenue and capital expenditure are acknowledged, the treatment of specific items such as the acquisition of stock and furniture may vary substantially from country to country and between library sectors. (See Appendix 2, paragraph 1.3 point 6).

7.2   <u>Any other data which would be of assistance</u>

Data relating to the additions of stock have proved to be unreliable and not as abundant as those other "Activity" data requested in the surveys. This information would be useful to identify the priorities which libraries place upon the constituent materials which comprise their collections. However, data relating to the number and type of acquisitions are not always maintained. Where such information is collected some data represents the GROSS additions and others the NET additions to the library collections. GROSS additions encompasses the total number of materials added to the collection during the year whether they were purchased or donated. (See Appendix 3 Notes of Guidance point xi.). NET additions deduct losses from collections due to wastage or any other means. As discussed in paragraph 7.1 guidance needs to be provided in respect of recording such data in order that meaningful international comparisons might be generated. In this context, a forum on the most useful indicators of performance which could be derived from available data might take place.

7.3   <u>Maintaining the momentum initiated by these studies</u>

If the negotiating position of libraries within the Government public spending round is to be strengthened then timely and accurate information relating to both "Financial" and "Activity" data are required. Furthermore, meaningful international comparisons may further support national or local bids for additional funding.

In order to maintain the existing role of libraries and to ensure that the present level of funding is maintained, if not increased given the relative constraints identified within this study, the European Commission should consider commissioning a similar exercise either annually or biennially. The ease with which contacts are able to provide the required information will improve if they know that this exercise is to become a regular, rather than an ad hoc, exercise.

7.4   Study proposals

In conclusion the study recommends that the European Commission considers the following points :

1. That the collection of library statistics by the European Commission becomes a regular practice, either annually or biennially, so that information is both timely and consistent. More frequent collection is needed to maintain the development of systems for keeping consistent information which fall into abeyance over longer periods.

2. The benefits of preparing national data to ISO standards and definitions might be recommended by the European Commission to all its Member States.

3. A recognised agency or organisation might be jointly appointed by the European Commission and UNESCO to undertake future surveys thus eliminating any duplication of survey effort, and enhancing the information attached to the collection of international statistics.

4. The European Commission might wish to publicise in Member States the apparent constraints on the resources available to libraries, as suggested by the study. The closer link between library resources and education programmes might be highlighted as a demonstration of the vital importance of libraries in the cultural development of the European Union.

5. That a review of possible performance measures be undertaken for general use by subscribing states. In this context the European Commission may wish to consider holding a forum on the subject.

6. That ISO and IFLA be asked to consider amending the detailed definition and guidance notes relating to the questions asked in this study where apparent inconsistencies in returned data arose (see Appendix 2.3).

APPENDIX 1

Study Specification

PROLIB/ECON

Library Economics in the European Union

Member States - Update

APPENDIX 1
PROLIB/ECON

LIBRARY ECONOMICS IN THE EC MEMBER STATES - UPDATE

Study Specifications

1. Objectives of the Study

The present study is designed to update and complement a previous study through an extension of the 5 year period originally covered to provide coverage for the decade 1980-1990. Comparable data to that of the first study will be collected for the new period on the volume of library activities and their associated costs in the Member States in order to enable comparison, improved statistics and an updated analysis of policies and economics of the library service. This update is relevant in respect of planning of activities in the libraries field in the context of the IVth R&TD Framework Programme.

For this purpose, the starting point of the investigation will remain the framework and definitions of UNESCO, as used in the previous study.

2. Work to be carried out

The work to be carried out and the methodology to be followed is described in the proposal of the contractor (sections 1 to 5), which is appended to and forms part of these study specifications.

For the purposes of constructing the data model for the 10 year period envisaged, the contractor will make use of the same data (updated where necessary) as was used in the previous study. Any estimation should be framed within reasonable limits of error which are explained (preferably not superior to 20%).

The study will cover the 12 Member States of the European Community and attempt to cover also the other countries comprising the European Economic Area. The number of countries to be visited in order to obtain and discuss the data to be collected, their collection practices etc. shall be as proposed by the contractor.

A Proposal to Undertake
a Study of Library Economics
in the European Community

The following proposal seeks to update information collated five years ago to measure the scale and scope of libraries activities within the European Community. The previous study reference LIB1-ECON was published as EUR Report No. 11546.

The methodology suggested for updating the previous study includes a review of existing data sources as well as the undertaking of direct surveys, so as to examine the development of the economic status of libraries within the European Economic Community and to take the opportunity to collect information from other states covered by the European Economic Area Agreement. This "update" will provide a statistical profile covering the inclusive years 1986 to 1990, but as much information as are available for subsequent years will also be collated.

The Institute of Public Finance (IPF) undertook the previous study, and personnel engaged then will also be working on this updating exercise, thereby lending their direct experience to the progress of an otherwise difficult area in which to gain consistency in statistical measurement. The study will use the same UNESCO definitions as previously to describe the relevant libraries sectors. The intention is to commence the study as soon as possible, with the aim of finalising our report by the end of October, 1993. This timetable will depend upon making significant progress with contacts established in the survey states. The proposal is structured as follows:

1. Aims, issues and methods;
2. The study team;
3. The study specification;
4. Timetable.

1. AIMS, ISSUES & METHODS:

1.1 The libraries activities of the community states were first measured in a consistent manner in 1986/87. At the time of undertaking this first study (LIB1-ECON) many difficulties were encountered concerning the consistency and completeness of information about library provisions and costs. Such difficulties had been (and continue to be) encountered by UNESCO. There was no suggestion by the researchers, or by DG XIII in commissioning the original study, that the adoption of common definitions should be pursued by all states without reference to their local management practices. However, it was hoped that some sympathy for the benefits of standardisation would derive from the attractions of being able to review individual circumstances in the context of the wider sphere of international activities; and, for this to be undertaken effectively, there needed to be some subscription to the use of standard forms of accounting for information. In this respect, it was also desirable that the International Standards Organisation (ISO) and indeed the professional accountancy bodies would take an interest in the development of definitions to facilitate the interpretation of public and private sector activities. Unfortunately such developments have been slow in evolving and it will be necessary to construct the revised series of statistics in a careful manner. However, more up-to-date information will assist each member state to evaluate their own provisions against the background of a consistent benchmark for national and sector comparisons. The renewal of such data will also provide fresh material for debating libraries policies and focus the debate within contemporary measures. For instance, the former West German statistics need now to incorporate the figures for the East following the unification of Germany. Where trends are discernible some commentary will be possible on the likely impact of policy initiatives which may have taken place during the period. The opportunity also arises to extend the survey to those other states comprising the European Economic Area Agreement and this will provide valuable information for gauging their activities against existing member states.

1.2 It is envisaged that the study will fall into various distinct but partially concurrent stages:

1.3 A renewal of the network of contacts will be made in preparation for the survey phase of the study. This work will be essential in establishing efficient lines of communication and professional understandings both for the undertaking of the study and in considering the results. The network of contacts are, to a great degree, the consumers of its findings. They will need to be appraised of the survey objectives so as to boost their participation and effect good response rates. However, their understanding of their own national sources of information need to be fully explored and at the time of making contact, we will request existing published sources of data and their comments on their usefulness.

1.4 An appraisal of common or consistent factors within the published sources for the respective states will be undertaken. A review of their literature will be made to refine the questionnaire design and detailed definitions for later use in the survey phase. The UNESCO definitions of the library sectors remain unchanged since the last study, but it is in the definition of the data items (fiscal as well as activity based) that some change may have occurred during the past five years. This is certainly the case on the definition of financial forms of account for private sector operations in Europe, and we will liaise closely with the Fédération des Experts Comptables Européens (FEE) in this respect.

1.5 The survey stage will be conducted in two steps, designed to assist respondents:

   1. We shall attempt to construct the relevant data from the available published sources and those supplied by contacts and draft these into the questionnaires. These "prepared" statistics will then form a framework about which we will ask respondents to check the given data, and "fill-in" gaps. We will also take the opportunity of representing their data for the previous quinquennial (those data to which the first study referred), so that they can check these, and also

have regard to the consistency of the later figures in the context of a reliable time series.

    2. Upon receipt of the survey returns from each respondent, we will carry out appropriate validation checks for plausibility and consistency. Verification profile reports will then be sent back to our contacts, together with follow-up requests for corrections, when the supplied data fail the check processes.

1.6 The experience gained from the previous study tends to confirm the need to visit contacts in many of the states. We propose to defer the making of arrangements for such visits until after we have generated the "prepared statistics" and not received suitable replies in correspondence. However, we will need to follow-up non-response with visits at an early stage, and provisional appointments will be made at the time of confirming the contacts network, but only carried out if necessary. <u>We do not propose to visit those other "European Economic Area Agreement" states (excepting perhaps those which can demonstrate good practices where more detailed discussions can provide useful material).</u>

1.7 Close co-operation with UNESCO will be followed throughout the study and we will provide their statistics division with as much information deriving from the study which might usefully add to their own data holding. Such collaboration justifies the use of their established definitions of the library sectors which are described in detail in our previous report (Appendix 2 - Page 67, "A study of library economics in the European Communities - EUR 11546 EN). The relevant libraries sectors are:-

    1. National;
    2. Other Major Non-Specialised;
    3. Public (or "Popular");
    4. Higher Education;
    5. School;
    6. Specialised.

The available data from UNESCO are specified in Section 3.

2. THE STUDY TEAM

2.1 The Director of Research for this Study will be Phillip Ramsdale, who co-ordinated the previous study. He is Managing Director of IPF, which is a company wholly owned by the Chartered Institute of Public Finance and Accountancy. Through this association, IPF can rely upon an extensive professional identity amongst the public sector in Europe, and Phillip Ramsdale has undertaken several exchanges with European states on statistical matters.

2.2 It is intended that he will be assisted by Josephine Blower and Yvonne Clarke in administering the study. Yvonne Clarke is the Head of IPF's surveys division and Josephine Blower is the Manager of Research. Both have extensive experience in large scale data collection and interpretation studies. Data processing will be undertaken by Tim Ramsdale and Anne Taylor who are used to processing data where the significance of plausibility needs to be regarded.

2.3 The type of study described in this proposal would benefit from involving independent assessments at various stages to verify the quality of the work and indeed advise on the interpretation of the results. In this respect we would wish to involve John Sumsion, who was formerly Director of Public Lending Right and currently directs the Library Information and Statistics Unit at Loughborough University.

2.4 The resources of IPF include more than 30 full-time staff and a network of more than 80 contract staff. Throughout the period of this study it would be possible to maintain the momentum of the exercise by the use of alternative staff if necessary, but this proposal is based upon involving the above named individuals. Any variation in personnel dedicated to the study would be by prior agreement of the Commission.

3. STUDY SPECIFICATIONS

3.1 The first "benchmark" collation of statistics of the library economics within the European Communities complemented the overall response to the resolution (adopted 27/9/85) of the Council of Ministers to undertake a series of studies covering library activities. This follow-up study should therefore aim to:

   a) collect data on the volume of Library activities and their associated costs within the member states of the EEC (including the former East Germany) and the other countries subscribing to the European Economic Area Agreement:

   Austria
   Switzerland
   Sweden
   Norway
   Iceland
   Finland
   Liechtenstein

   b) appraise the existing statistical framework and review the action taken by member states since the last study was undertaken.

   c) update the findings of the previous study (covering the period 1981-1986) allowing trends over the complete decade (1981-1990) to be considered.

3.2 In pursuance of these aims the following Terms of Reference are set out for the guidance of the study:

   a) Collect data, estimates, and information from existing sources following established leads; visiting selected sources; and exploring and developing professional contacts.

   b) Place primary emphasis on completing the "database update" for existing member states of the community, but ensure that such data collated for the other countries provide sufficient specificity of coverage, consistency and currency to allow comparisons to be made.

   c) Compare the findings with those of the previous study covering the period 1981-1986. For this part of the study countries outside the Community will be presented separately.

   d) Interpret results in report format containing:
   - A commentary on the various statistical frameworks employed;
   - Comparative statistics (Graphic);
   - Assessment of library activities in economic context;
   - Appraisal of problem areas and suggestions for overcoming these;
   - Documentation of sources;
   - Statistical appendix (i.e. data tabulation); and
   - Methodological appendix.

   e) Provide a computerised archive.

3.3 The following headings show the basic data matrix for libraries to be constructed in the study:

   a) The <u>Nations</u> covered will all be either members of the EEC or those listed at 3.1(a), above.

   b) The Library <u>Sectors</u> (UNESCO defined) will identify separately "National"; "Other major non-specialised"; "Public"; and "Higher Education" based libraries. If possible the "School" library sector will also be separately identified but "Special" libraries may simply be noted according to consistency of data held by the subject states.

   c) The analysis of <u>Expenditure</u> will concentrate on the revenue cost consequences of operating these library sectors. Where capital expenditure (investment in infrastructure) is known, this will be reported. However, the revenue accounts will portray gross expenditure, income and net expenditure. An attempt will be made to identify such expenditure on individual items like employees, premises and acquisitions but a robust definition of "Total Expenditure" will be developed for reporting purposes.

d) The <u>Volume</u> of library services will be demonstrated by showing the number of staff employed (professional and others); the number of service points and administrative units managing these; and the size and composition of acquisitions to library stocks, particularly books and periodicals.

e) The time <u>Trends</u> in the above data will be examined by expressing the findings over a period of years (either consecutive, or in stepped series) to provide longitudinal context.

3.4　The study documentation will be prepared in the English language but survey forms and guidance notes will be developed by the Contractor in the following languages: English, French, Spanish, German, Italian, Greek, Swedish.

3.5　The definitions will follow a logic designed to complement the established UNESCO classifications and elements, and will build on those employed in the previous study. However the following simplifications in definition will be attempted:

- No separation of staff numbers or costs under "support" or "administrative" headings will be used;

- The distinction between expenditure incurred in one year and "capitalised" and the total value of infrastructure costs incurred during the year will be made so as to arrive at an overall consistent definition of total (revenue + capital) expenditure.

3.6　Reports on progress of the study will be made at two monthly intervals or at times when departures from the timetable set out at paragraph 4.2 are encountered.

3.7　Data available from UNESCO prior to the study's commencement include coverage of the sectors in general terms as follows:

National libraries	1986	and	1989
Non-specialised libraries	1986	and	1989
Public libraries	1986	and	1989
University libraries	1987	and	1990
School libraries	1987	and	1990
Special libraries	1985		

There are, however, various anomalies which will need to be investigated. For instance, the special libraries data for Greece refer to 1984 instead of 1985; the public libraries data for Spain refer to 1988 instead of 1989. More detailed information on the UNESCO database is available for those countries which have responded to their questionnaires but more up-to-date data with less specificity exist when drawn from published sources, e.g. Scandinavian states. UNESCO have also suspended the survey of special libraries and it is understood that their data for school libraries are extremely poor. The contractor will provide UNESCO with a complete audit of the above data based on the findings of this study together with data items which derive.

APPENDIX 2

METHODOLOGY USED IN THIS STUDY

1.1   **Study Phases**

1.2   **Econometric Data**

1.3   **Technical differences and standardisation**

1.4   **Methodology used to create grossed (estimated) data**

1.5   **Repricing of financial data**

1.6   **Study Data Set**

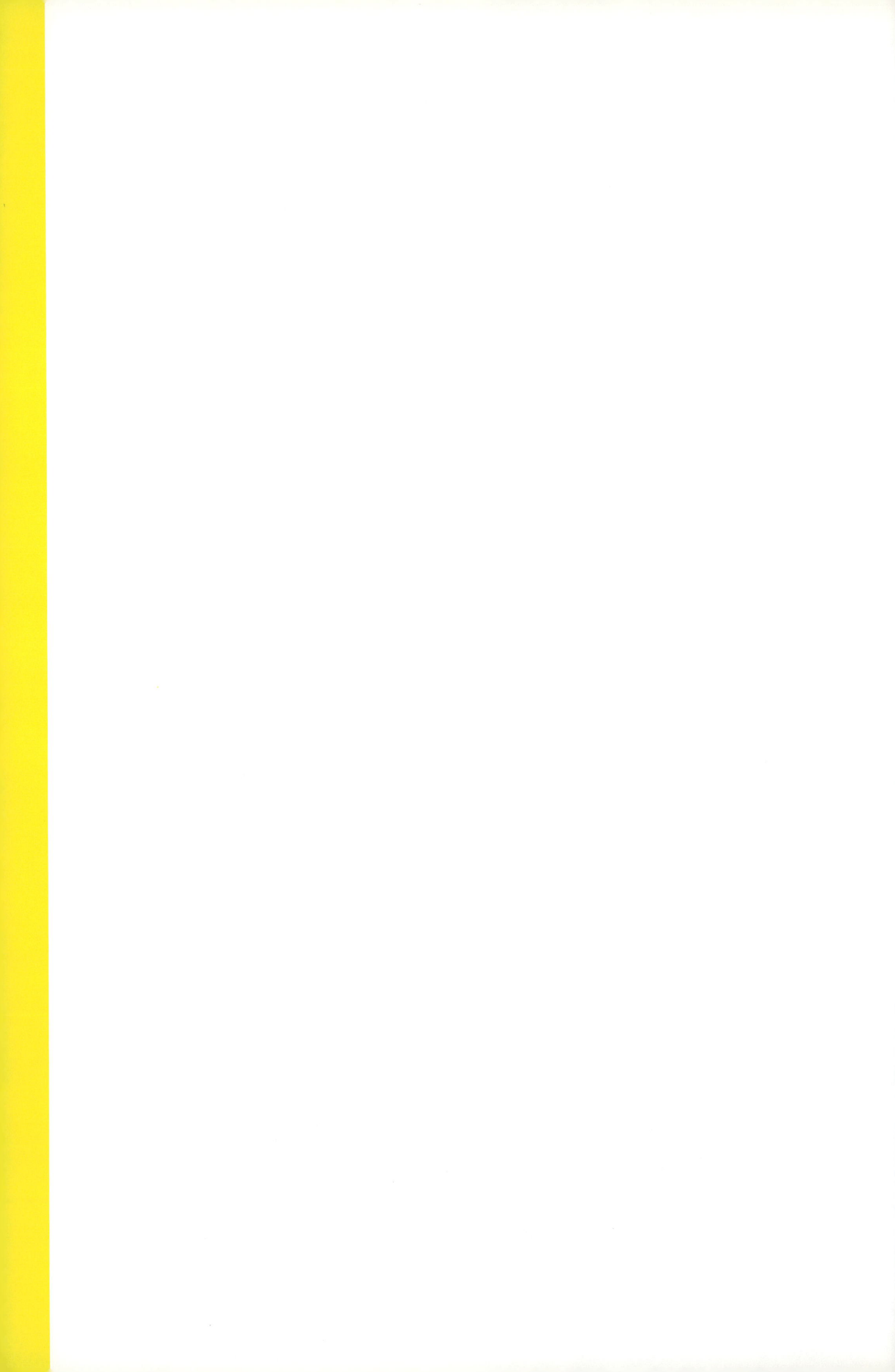

APPENDIX 2

METHODOLOGY USED IN THIS STUDY

1.1 <u>Study Phases</u>

The principal phases of the study were:

(i) Establishing and renewing contacts for each sector in each state;

(ii) Designing of the questionnaires and notes of guidance;

(iii) Validation of the returned data and creation of grossed data for non-respondents;

(iv) Undertaking of study visits;

(v) Analysing data and preparing the statistical profiles; and

(vi) Reporting the findings

The study timetable is shown at paragraph 1 7.

(i) Establishing and renewing contacts

During May, June and July 1993 all respondents to the original study were contacted, to request their assistance in this subsequent work. A thorough literature search was undertaken and local contacts were asked if there were any publications of which they were aware which would enable the study team to partly complete the statistical profile within each questionnaire before their despatch. Further data from the original data set and extracts from the UNESCO statistics were included in the pro forma prior to their being sent to the respective contacts in each state. This approach was adopted as a means of assisting those responsible for the completion of the questionnaire by establishing the framework for the individual library sector and providing guidance as to the reasonableness of the data.

Throughout the summer months of 1993 the original network of respondents was substantially increased by securing further contacts in a number of previously non-responding sectors within the European Union member states. Additional contacts were made with interested parties within the EFTA states. A complete list of those who were contacted during this study is shown at Appendix 6 Country Profiles.

(ii) Design of the questionnaires and notes of guidance

The format and presentation of the questionnaire for the current study were revised in order to encompass the whole decade and to include the revisions to the questions which were discussed in Chapter 3. The layout was designed to aid the compiler by listing the questions in logical groupings. Different type faces were employed for the pre-printed data to indicate their sources.

The survey instructions emphasised that the primary concern was the collection of data relating to the years 1986-1990. Recipients of the questionnaires were asked to validate the information contained within the document relating to this period, and to address any omissions wherever possible. As a secondary concern they were invited to raise any queries regarding the data for the period 1981-1985.

The questionnaires contained 185 data cells for the years 1986-1990, (105 relating to activity and 85 relating to financial data). This represented a reduction of 18% in the number of cells, compared with the original study questionnaires, which contained 225 data cells for the preceding 5 year period. In theory the shorter questionnaire would reduce inconsistencies, and ease the task of checking and completing the survey.

(iii) Validation of returned data and the creation of grossed data for non-respondents

Any inconsistencies which arose were checked with the suppliers of the data. Where national publications rather than completed questionnaires were supplied, the transposed data were returned to the contacts for verification.

During the study visits data were validated and checked for reasonableness by the calculation of selected ratios using the preliminary data set.

The findings of the study were monitored throughout the study to resolve apparent anomolies.

Where respondents were unable to provide data, whether activity or financial, grossed or estimated data based upon the accumulated proportions of the sum of returned data received were calculated. Separate totals for the EU and EFTA states were maintained throughout the grossing process. The grossing or estimating processes are exemplified at paragraph 1.4 below.

(iv) Study Visits

The majority of contacts were able to provide reasonably robust data relating to the particular sectors for which they were responsible. However, a few respondents experienced some difficulties in completing the questionnaires, particularly where a number of ministries or departments were responsible for a particular sector. It was sometimes difficult to ascertain which of these, if any, had the primary responsibility to provide a national perspective for the library sector involved. In order to establish such an overall perspective the study team visited the respective ministries/departments and contacts in France, Belgium, Italy, Portugal and Spain.

1.2 Econometric Data

Supplementary data were collated in order that the library data might be set in the wider European economic perspective, and also to create grossed or estimated data for those sectors where no real data were available or where the returned data were not sufficient. The use of these "econometric benchmark" data for estimation purposes is discussed in paragraphs 1.4 These data related to:

♦ Population by age bands;

♦ ECU exchange rates for all the national currencies included in the study expressed as equated annual averages;

- Consumer Price Indices; and

- National Gross Domestic Products for all states included in the study.

These additional data were drawn from "Eurostat" and United Nations publications and some of the national statistical bureaux of the EFTA states (see Appendix 5).

Excepting some specifications, which are discussed later, population age bands were used for creating the grossed data for most of the respective library sectors:

SECTOR	AGE RANGE
National	Total Population
Institutes of Higher Education Libraries	20-24 Population Age Band
Other Major Non-Specialised Libraries	Total Population
School Libraries	5-19 Population Age Band
Special Libraries	15-64 Population Age Band
Public (or Popular)	Total Population

These were the same bases used in the original 1981-1985 research, thus ensuring consistent treatment across the two studies.

The sector populations for the European Union and EFTA states for 1981-1990 are shown at Appendix 5. Also shown are the annual average ECU exchange rates compared with the national currencies and consumer price indices.

1.3 Technical differences and Standardisation

When collating data from 19 individual states there will inevitably occur national differences concerning both the interpretation of terminology and the detail of data collected. The principal examples of varying interpretations and subsequent recording of the data were:

(i) Current Periodicals

(ii) Audio-Visual Materials

(iii) Registered Borrowers

(iv) Loan Transactions

(v) Trained Librarians

(vi) Capital and Revenue Expenditure.

The definitions employed for the study survey accord with those of UNESCO and the ISO 2789.

(i) Current Periodicals

"The number of periodical titles received by the Library during the year of account." (See paragraph 5.3).

From the completed study questionnaires and data transposed from national publications it became apparent that some states and sectors counted the number of "Unique Titles" whilst others counted the overall number of volumes; i.e. if "Public Money and Management" is a quarterly publication then some library authorities would count this publication as one while others might record it as four current periodicals.

The grossed estimates for this study are based on the number of volumes available. The ratio of current periodicals to book stocks for the two quinquennia for the EU states are 1: 184 and 1:192 respectively (an increase of 0.9% per annum).

(ii) Audio-Visual Materials

"These include non-book, non-microform library materials which require the use of special equipment in order to be seen and/or heard; e.g. records, tapes, compact discs, motion pictures, video tapes, slides and transparencies." (See paragraph 5.4).

While the above definition, is relatively clear as to what constitutes library material to be included in this category, there appears to be differing methods of counting this category of stock.

(iii) Registered Borrowers

"Those persons registered with the library in order that they may borrow material from the library for use outside the library confines. Please count the number of persons registered in the specified year, do not confuse this term with that of "Library users" who are persons making use of ANY of the library services and not specifically the borrowing of materials." (See paragraph 5.6).

Whilst the definition of a registered borrower is clear, the reliability and "age" of these records within libraries varies considerably. For instance, within such records there is no distinction between an "active" registered borrower who makes use of the library facilities and those who do not. The proportion of "active" registered borrowers to those who do not make use of the facilities will be influenced by the frequency with which the library updates its records and identifies those registered borrowers who have not made use of the facilities for over 12 months. For instance if a public library updates its registered borrowers records every five years, then during that time registered borrowers, may have moved out of the area and registered with a library in their new location but have not cancelled their previous library registration. Thus the number of registered borrowers may be "artificially" inflated.

(iv) Loan Transactions

"Direct lending transaction of a document to a user, including registered loans within a library." (See paragraph 5.6 Table 16)

As with the definition of Current Periodicals and Audio Visual materials the above ISO definition is relatively clear and succinct. However, local practices in compiling these figures vary considerably. Specific guidance is required to clarrify which isssues should be included in such counts and which should be excluded. For instance :

a) Inter library loans should not be included.

b) Renewals should be included. However, a limit should be placed upon the number of renewals counted for a particular item where the loan periods are 24 hours or less.

c) Withdrawals from stock should be excluded from the count.

d) Where issues of stock are made to institutions such as playgroups the initial issue made at the library service point should be included. However, any subsequent "sub-issues / loans" which the institution might make should be excluded.

e) Loans of uncatalogued materials should be included.

There are no standard loan periods within lindividual library sectors which impacts on the number of laons made by individual libraries.

(v) Trained Librarians

"All members of staff who have received training in librarianship or information science. The training may be by formal methods or by means of an extended period of work in a library under supervision." (see paragraphs 3.10 and 5.5)

The UNESCO and ISO 2789 definitions do not correspond completely with one another since UNESCO differentitates between those staff with formal qualifications in librarianship and those who have received training while in-situ.

a) Trained librarians holding an official diploma in librarianship.

b) Trained librarians who have received their training in the form of an extended period of work in a library under supervision.

While the ISO 2789 standard defines a trained librarian as :

"Person employed in a library who has received training in librarianship and/or information science."

A subsequent note states that :

"The training may be by formal methods or by m,eans of an extended period of work of a professional nature in a library under supervision."

Local responses to the trained librarian staff category are influenced by their staff by their individual personal record systems, including the grading systems and the status afforded to Librarians within each sector and country.

(vi) Capital and Revenue Expenditure

The study covers librraies which are principally financed by either the public or private sector, and, therefore, the financial data are not presented in a similar format on a national basis, much less on an international basis. The European Commission Fourth Council Directive of 25 July 1978 (78/660/EEC) provides a standard form of accounts for private companies within the EU but has not issued comparable guidance for the public sector.

Both UNESCO and ISO 2789 categorize the following expenditure heads under revenue or current and expenditure :

Revenue : Employees

Acquisitions

Other (including binding, rent, services, depreciation).

Capital : Sites and buildings

Other

The definition of capital expenditure employed for this study centres upon the funding of capital expenditure :

"Any payments made on major spending funded either from Internal Capital Funds of the Administration or from borrowings from external sources."

While staffing costs are universally considered to be revenue or current expenditure, the treatment of other items such as the acquisition of stock and refurbishment of premises is not consistent throughout Europe. Paragraph 3.11 concludes that it was niot possible to create estimates of capital investment from the data returned and that given the inconsistency of interpretation of this terminology throughout Europe the results would not be reliable.

1.4 Methodology used to create grossed (estimated) data

Grossed expenditure data were created as follows:

(i) The totals of returned expenditure were calculated for each EU and EFTA state.

(ii) The total book stocks were matched to the returned financial data for each EU and EFTA state.

(iii) The total expenditure observed in step 1 were divided by the respective book stock sums so matched in step 2. The result was then multiplied by the book stocks for those states and sectors for which financial data were unavailable, thus providing an estimated total expenditure figure. The total book stock figure, rather than sector population, was used as the non-financial denominator, as the actual returns received showed that there is a much stronger correlation between book stock and expenditure than between population and expenditure. It would appear that the level of provision varies considerably and does not seem to be significantly related to population. Appendix 2.2 shows that there is a much stronger correlation between book stock and expenditure than that of population and expenditure.

(iv) Using the sum of total expenditure generated in the first step, the distribution was observed over the following subjective headings:

- Staff Expenses;

- Premises and Operating Expenses;

- Cost of New Buildings / Refurbishment;

- Cost of Acquisition of Stock;

- Cost of Borrowing;

- Miscellaneous Expenditure

(v) These relative proportions were then applied to the estimated total expenditure figures which were generated in step 3.

(vi) Unit costs or ratios based upon the relevant sector populations were then computed from the data deriving from the previous steps. Such unit measures were then applied to the sector population of non-responding states.

(vii) Where data were available for some years but not others, the estimates for the missing information were made by interpolation. In such cases the interpolated data took precedence over the "per capita estimates" derived from step 6.

In this manner, a complete data framework was built-up and general trends discovered. However, because of the variability in the estimates from year to year, the overall conclusions concerning trends are more reliably based upon the averages for the two quinquennia.

1.5 Repricing of financial data

In order to provide a uniform basis for comparisons of library income and expenditure data, the respective national currency figures were repriced using national consumer price indices and annual ECU exchange rates. Therefore, unless stated otherwise, all financial figures quoted in this report are shown in ECUs and at constant 1990 prices.

The financial data quoted in the previous study were repriced to 1985 constant prices. In this report, these have been revised and are quoted for comparative purposes at 1990 constant prices.

The annual average ECU exchange rates and Consumer Price Indices are shown at Appendix 5.

1.6 Study Data Set

Profiles deriving from the application of this methodology to the assembled data were prepared and sent to each correspondent for information and verification.

APPENDIX 2.2

The relationship between book stocks and library expenditure, and population and library expenditure

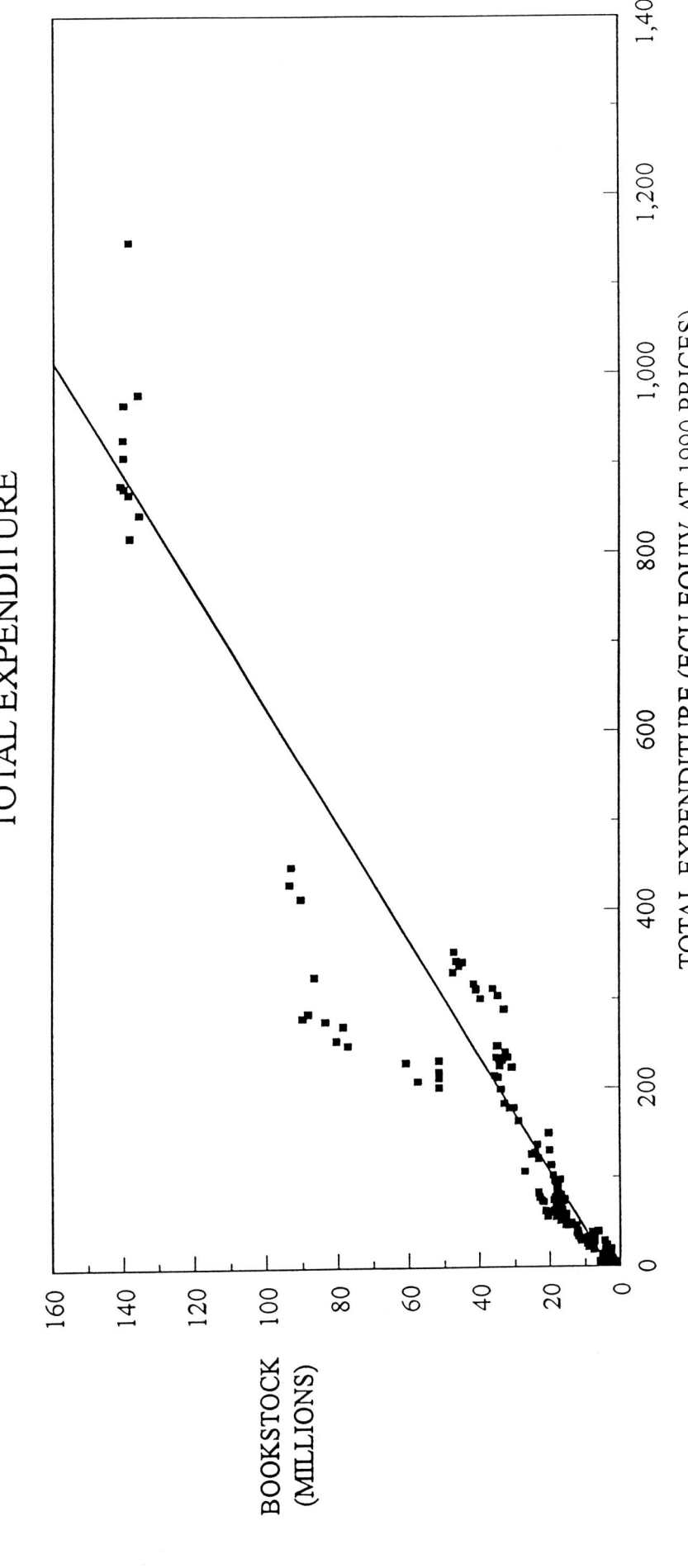

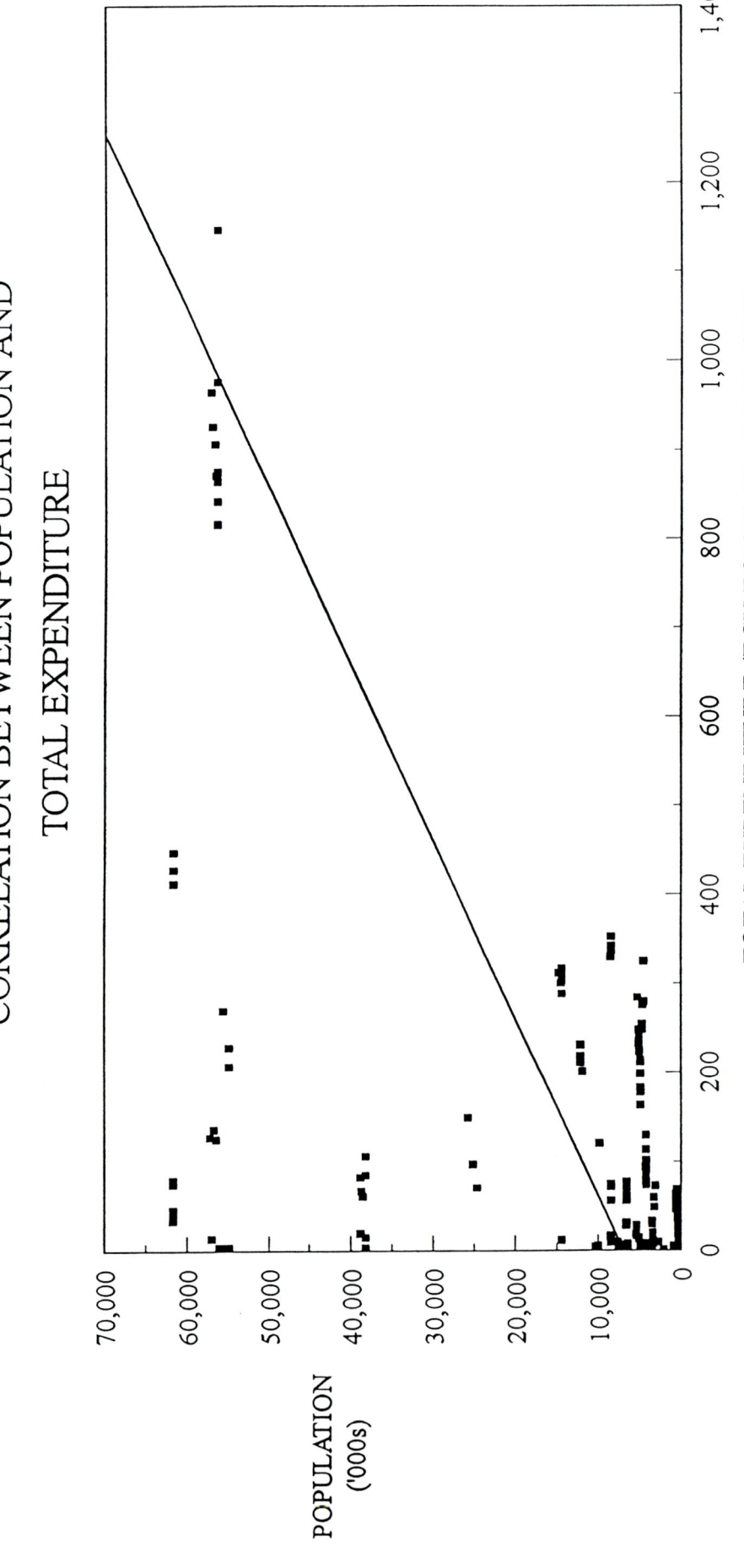

APPENDIX 2.3

INCONSISTENCIES IN STANDARD DEFINITIONS

Inconsistencies in standard definitions which were observed from the survey and published data.

1. Other Major Non-Specialised Libraries:

    Definition = "Non-Specialised Libraries of a learned character which are neither libraries of institutes of higher education nor national libraries, though they may fulfil the functions of a national library for a specified geographical area".

    The UNESCO data for this sector in Denmark records five administrative units in 1989. The Statens Biblioteksjeneste confirmed that these are in fact, university libraries.

2. University and Special Libraries

    ISO definition = "Library primarily serving students and teachers in universities and other institutions of education at the third level, which may also serve as a public library".

    UNESCO definition = "Libraries of institutions of higher education primarily serving students and teachers in universities and other institutions of education at the third level. They may be open to the general public as well. A distinction should be made between:

    i) The main or central university library, or a group of libraries which may be located separately but having one and the same director.

    ii) Libraries attached to university institutes or departments but which are not under the direction of or administered by the main or central university library.

    iii) Libraries attached to institutions of higher education which are not part of a university.

    Some states only include university libraries within their UNESCO returns. While some of the Scandinavian national publications refer to libraries of tertiary education as special libraries.

3. Current Periodicals

    ISO definition = Continuous series under the same title published at regular or irregular intervals, over an indefinite period; individual issues in the series being numbered consecutively or each issue being dated.

    The variance in returns for those items of stock suggest that some respondents counted the number of unique titles while others counted the overall number of volumes.

4   Audio-Visual Materials

ISO definition = "Non-microform, non-electronic document which requires the use of special equipment to be seen and/or heard".

As with current periodicals the returns and published data suggest that a number of approaches to counting these materials exist.

5   Registered Borrowers

ISO definition = "Person or organisation registered with a library in order to use its documents within or away from the library".

To enable more meaningful comparisons of usage to be generated a clear distinction between "active" and "non-active" users needs to be made. For those libraries which do not regularly update their registered borrowers will have inflated records.

6   Loan Transactions

ISO definition = "Direct lending transaction of a document to a user, including registered loans within a library".

Local practices for compiling these figures vary considerably. Specific guidance is required in respect of which loans should be included in the count and which should be omitted. For instance, renewals should be included but withdrawals from stock and inter-library loans should be excluded.

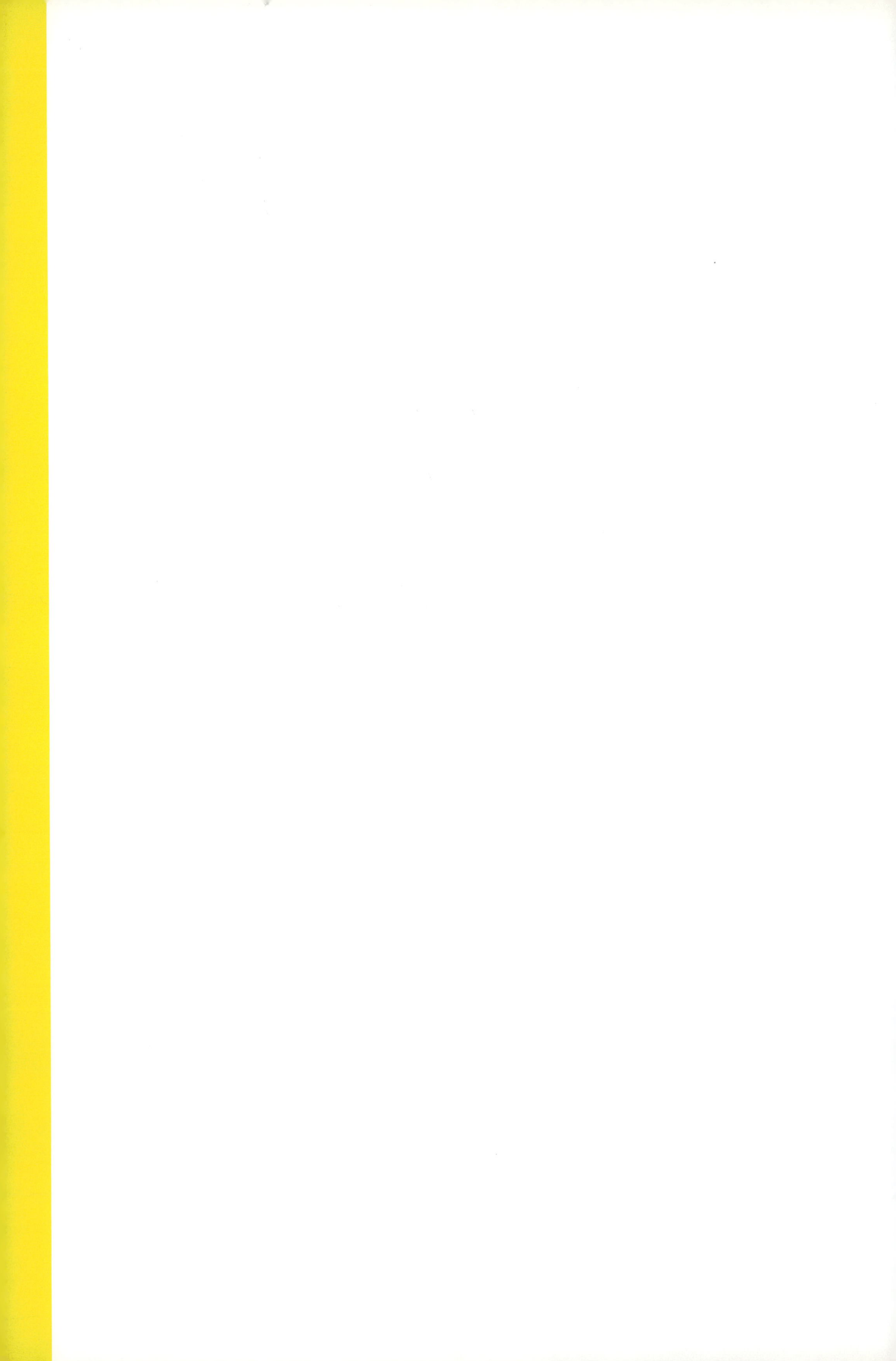

APPENDIX 3

NOTES OF GUIDANCE PRESENTED IN:

English
French
German
Greek
Italian
Spanish
Swedish

SURVEY QUESTIONNAIRES FOR THE SIX LIBRARY SECTORS

Sector:
1. National
2. Higher Education
3. Other Major Non-Specialised
4. School
5. Special
6. Public

NOTES OF GUIDANCE

LIBRARY SECTORS

The 6 library sectors included in this study correspond directly to the UNESCO definitions, namely:

NATIONAL LIBRARIES :
Libraries which, irrespective of their title, are responsible for acquiring and conserving copies of significant publications produced in the country and functioning as a "deposit" library, either by law or other arrangement, and normally compiling a national bibliography.

LIBRARIES OF INSTITUTIONS OF HIGHER EDUCATION :
Libraries primarily serving students and teachers in universities and other institutions of education at the third level.

OTHER MAJOR NON-SPECIALISED LIBRARIES :
Non-specialised libraries of a learned character which are neither libraries of institutions of higher education nor national libraries, though they may fulfil the functions of a national library for a specified geographical area.

SCHOOL LIBRARIES :
Those attached to all types of schools and colleges below the third level of education, and serving primarily the pupils and teachers of such schools and colleges, even though they may also be open to the general public.

SPECIAL LIBRARIES :
Those maintained by an association, government service, parliament, research institution (excluding university institutes), learned society, professional association, museum, business firm, industrial enterprise, chamber of commerce etc., or other organised group, the greater part of their collections covering a specific field or subject, e.g. natural sciences, social sciences, agriculture, chemistry, medicine, economics, engineering, law, history.

PUBLIC LIBRARIES :
Those which serve the population of a community or region free of charge or for a nominal fee; they may serve the general public or special categories of users such as children, members of the armed forces, hospital patients, prisoners, workers and employees.

QUESTIONS 1 AND 2 (Collections)

Question 1 asks for the total number of materials held by the library, both in stock and out on loan at 31 December of each year. If the stock count corresponds to a different date, please note this on the questionnaire.

Question 2 asks for the gross number of acquisitions made by the library during that year; i.e. all acquisitions of materials including those to replace losses due to non-returns, old age or other forms of wastage.

DEFINITIONS
i) YEAR:
If the period of account for which you hold statistics does not correspond to calendar years, then please make your returns under that year which covers the majority of the period to which your accounts relate to. For example, if your records cover the year from 1 April to 31 March, for your year 1 April 1986 to 31 March 1987 enter these into the space for the year ending 1986, since the majority of your accounting period (9 months) relates to the calendar year 1986. Would you then mark on the questionnaire that your accounting period is 1 April to 31 March.

If your accounts refer to the period 1 July to 30 June, e.g. 1 July 1986 to 30 June 1987, then enter this period in the calendar year ending 1986 and annotate the questionnaire accordingly. Should your accounting year start and finish at some other point in the year, then allocate your accounting year to the calendar year which covers the majority of your accounting period, as in the above examples.

ii) **ADMINISTRATIVE UNIT :**
Any group of libraries, or an independent library, under a single director or a single administration.

iii) **SERVICE POINT :**
A designated place or area providing a service for library users. Independent libraries, central libraries and branch libraries (both static and mobile library vans, ships' libraries etc.) are considered as service points provided that they serve their users directly and not through a third party. Thus "static" points are those which provide a service from a fixed point; and "mobile" are those in a vehicle which moves to various locations to enable potential users to make use of the library service. The library van itself represents one service point; the stops which it makes on its round DO NOT constitute mobile service points. Vans which are used solely for the transportation of material from one library to another DO NOT constitute mobile service points.

iv) **COLLECTION :**
All library materials provided by the library for its users. Statistics relating to library collections should cover only the following documents available to users, including an allowance for materials on loan:

v) **BOOKS AND BOUND PERIODICALS :**
"Books" should be counted by volume. In this context, a volume includes reproduced material (except microforms) forming a physical unit of any printed work contained in one binding or portfolio. "Periodicals" are numbered consecutively or each issue is dated. Annuals are included; but monographic series are defined as a continuous series over an indefinite period where individual issues in the series are excluded. Bound periodicals should be counted as physical units. Unbound periodicals (not current) should be included in the count as if they were collected into bound physical units. Newspapers are included and should be counted in volumes or parcels.

vi) **CURRENT PERIODICAL TITLES :**
The number of periodical titles received by the Library during the year of account.

vii) **MANUSCRIPTS :**
Any original hand written or drawn work contained in one binding or portfolio.

viii) **MICROFORMS :**
Micro printed reproductions of original works or publications including micro reduced film copies of manuscripts.

ix) **AUDIO-VISUAL MATERIALS :**
These include non-book, non-microform library materials which require the use of special equipment in order to be seen and/or heard; e.g. records, tapes, cassettes, compact discs, motion pictures, video tapes, slides and transparencies.

x) **OTHER MATERIAL :**
Those items which are stocked by libraries for reference by users, such as maps, charts, art prints, photographs and dioramas etc., but excluding books, periodicals, manuscripts, microforms and audio-visual materials.

xi) **ADDITIONS :**
The number of all additions made to collections during the year which were to be made available to users. This should show the total number of additions before deducting losses from collections due to discarding, wastage or misplacement. Please include any additions whether by purchase, donation, exchange or any other method of gain to the collection. However, only include additions for the categories of materials as listed in the categories on the questionnaire (i.e. Books, Periodicals, Manuscripts, Microforms, Audio-Visual and Other).

xii) LIBRARY USERS : <u>National Libraries Only</u>
Any persons utilising the services of the library(ies) in the year of account.

xiii) LIBRARY CONSULTATIONS : <u>National Libraries Only</u>
The number of formal requests for assistance.

xiv) REGISTERED BORROWERS :
Those persons registered with the library in order that they may borrow material from the library for use outside the library confines. Please count only the number of persons registered in the specified year; do not confuse this term with that of "Library users", who are persons making use of ANY of the library services and not specifically the borrowing of materials.

xv) LOAN TRANSACTIONS :
This should be calculated by the number of works loaned out and copies supplied in place of loans; i.e. books, periodicals and manuscripts loaned out, counted by the number of volumes, and the number of copies produced to take place of original materials, counted by volumes.

xvi) LENGTH OF OCCUPIED SHELVING :
Length of shelving, in metres, of the collection available to users.

xvii) SECTOR POPULATION SERVED :
The total number of potential users in the geographic or subject area served by the library(ies); e.g. for PUBLIC libraries this will be the total number of inhabitants in the administrative area; for libraries serving institutions of HIGHER EDUCATION the "sector population" will be the number of students and teachers served. As a general rule, with the exception of PUBLIC, NATIONAL and OTHER NON-SPECIALISED libraries, confine the estimate of "sector population" to the potential number of primary users of the libraries excluding the general public at large, even though the latter may use the facilities from time to time.

QUESTION 4

xviii) TRAINED LIBRARIANS :
All members of staff who have received a general training in librarianship or information science. The training may be by formal methods or by means of an extended period of work in a library under supervision.

xix) OTHER LIBRARY STAFF :
Please include all staff who are under the direct supervision of the Director(s) of the Library(ies) who are employed on library functions AND staff required to service the proper running of the library(ies) but who are not necessarily under the direct supervision of the Director(s), i.e. support staff. This may include accountants and other "support staff", part of whose time is spent on library matters for the administration, either as employees of that administration or on a contract basis.

QUESTION 5 : Financial Statistics

xx) EXPENDITURE :
Expenditure relates to the TOTAL estimated expenditure for the library sector for the financial year. This expenditure should be shown as far as possible under the following headings:

xxi) STAFF :
This figure includes salaries, overtime payments, pension contributions paid by employers, training costs, travel and subsistence expenses and other staff emoluments relating to all staff working within the library sector. You should also include your best estimate of the apportioned staff and other premises/computing/legal/accounting and other support heads incurred by the administration on the library SECTOR outside the direct supervision of the Director(s) of the Library(ies).

xxii) PREMISES AND OPERATING COSTS :
All items relating to the running costs of the library, such as rents; property taxes, cleaning materials, energy costs, repairs and maintenance etc. Please exclude the cost of staff, which should be included in the "STAFF" category. Please do not include the cost of outstanding borrowing incurred on library premises, which should be included in "COST OF BORROWING".

xxiii) NEW BUILDINGS/REFURBISHMENT :
Relates to significant expenditure on material improvements to the fabric of existing library premises or the construction of a new building.

xxiv) ACQUISITIONS OF STOCK :
Relates to spending on the acquisition of materials in order to enhance the collection available to users. Please do not include the cost of purchases of equipment for use by the library administration/ management (this should be included under "MISCELLANEOUS EXPENDITURE").

xxv) COST OF BORROWING :
The repayment of loans and leasing agreements entered into by the library SECTOR.

xxvi) MISCELLANEOUS :
All other expenditure incurred towards the cost of running the library SECTOR during the year and which is not specifically detailed in the above categories.

xxvii) INCOME :
All receipts received during the year of account used to offset the cost of the library SECTOR.

xxviii) GOVERNMENT/MUNICIPAL FUNDING (TAXES/GRANTS) :
Any monies received from central or local government, whether in the form of a grant or contribution to the maintenance of the library SECTOR.

xxix) FEES AND CHARGES :
All trading income received by the library(ies) administration during the year of account.

xxx) OTHER INCOME :
Any other income during the year which is not directly specified in the above categories. Examples would include proceeds from the sales of assets; transfers of monies between different administrations made during the year of account; interest earned on bank balances; private donations or sponsorship income.

xxxi) CAPITAL EXPENDITURE :
(i.e. Investments in new libraries or refurbishments)
Any payments made on major spending funded either from Internal Capital Funds of the Administration or from borrowings from external sources.

xxxii) OTHER CAPITAL EXPENDITURE :
All other capital expenditure incurred towards the cost of providing the library service and which is not specifically included in the above categories.

xxxiii) OUTSTANDING DEBT :
The accumulated amount borrowed to finance Capital expenditure which remains unpaid at the end of the year.

NOTES A TITRE D'INFORMATION

SECTEURS DES BIBLIOTHEQUES
Les six bibliothèques dans cette étude correspondent très exactement aux définitions données a l'UNESCO, à savoir.

LES BIBLIOTHEQUES NATIONALES:
Les bibliothèques qui, indépendamment de leur titre sont responsables de l'acquisition et de la préservation des copies de documents importants produits dand le pays et qui fonctionnent auusi comme bibliothèques de dépôt, suivant la loi ou à cause d'autres arrangements et normalement compile une bibliographie à l'echelle nationale.

LES BIBLIOTHEQUES D'INSTITUTS D'ENSEIGNMENT SUPERIEUR:
Ce sont des bibliothèques qui sont essentiellement au service des étudiants et des enseignants dans les universités ou tout autres instituts d'enseignement du troisième échellon.

AUTRES BIBLIOTHEQUES PRINCIPALES NON-SPECIALISEES:
Ce sont les bibliothèques non spécialisées d'un charactère éducatif qui sont ni des bibliothèques d'instituts d'enseignement supérieur, ni des bibliothèques nationales bien qu'elles puissent faire fonction de bibliothèque nationale dans une région bien spécifique.

LES BIBLIOTHEQUES SCOLAIRES:
Les bibliothèques attachées à tous les écoles, lycées, colleges en basse du troisième niveau d'éducation et qui servent essentiellement les étudians et les enseignants des écoles, lycées, colleges etc. pareil quand même ils seraient ouvertes au public general.

LES BIBLIOTHEQUES SPECIALISEES:
Ceci s'adresse aux bibliothèques reliées à une association, à un departement gouvernemental, au parlement, un institut de recherche (à l'exception des universités), des sociétés éducatives, des associations professionnelles, des musées, des entreprises, des Chambres de Commerce, ect. ou de toute autre organisation dont la plus grande partie de leur collection couvre un sujet ou domaine spécifique tel que les sciences naturelles, les sciences sociales, l'agriculture, la chimie, la médecine, l'économie, l'engineering, le droit ou l'histoire.

LES BIBLIOTHEQUES MUNICIPALES:
Ceci s'adresse aux bibliothèques qui desservent la population d'une communauté ou d'une région gratuitement ou pour une somme nominale; elles peuvent desservir le public en général ou des sections particulières de la population comme les enfants, l'armée, les patients des hopitaux, les prisoniers, les travailleurs et employés,

QUESTION 1 ET 2 (Collections)

La première question concerne le nombre total des ouvrages/documents que la bibliothèque a en stock ou bien en prêt au 31 Décembre de chaque année. Si 'la prise de stock' correspond à une date différente, veuillez, s'il vous plaît en faire mention sur le questionnaire.

La deuxième question concerne le nombre des acquisitions faites par la bibliothèque au cours de la même année; à savoir toutes les acquisitions d'ouvrages/documents avant la soustraction des pertes dues aux ouvrages qui n'ont pas été retournés ou ceux qui doivent être remplacés à cause de leur âge ou parce qu'ils sont endommagés.

DEFINITIONS

i) L'ANNEE:
Si la période pour laquelle vous tenez vos comptes et sur laquelle vous basez vos statistiques ne correspond pas au calendrier, veuillez s'il vous plait faire votre entrée dans l'espace correspondant à l'année qui couvre la plus grande partie de votre année comptable. Par example, si vous tenez vos comptes du premier Avril 1986 ou 31 Mars 1987, faites votre entrée pour l'année 1986, étant donné que la majorité de votre année comptable (9 mois) correspond au calendrier 1986. Pourriez-vous mentionner sur le questionnaire les dates de votre année comptable - ex: 1 Avril - 31 Mars.

Si votre année va du premier Juillet au 30 Juin, par example 1 Juillet 1986 au 30 Juin 1987, faites votre entrée pour l'année 1986 et faites en note sur le questionnaire. Si votre année comptable commence et finit à d'autres dates, faites votre entrée pour l'année qui correspond à la majorité de votre année comptable comme dans les examples donné ci-dessus.

ii) LA DIVISION ADMINISTRATIVE
Tout groupe de bibliothèques ou une bibliothèque indépendante sous la direction d'un seul directeur ou d'une seule unité administrative.

iii) RECEPTION
Un espace destiné au service des usagers. Les bibliothèques indépendantes, les bibliothèques centrales et leurs différentes branches (à la fois statiques et mobiles, les bibliobus, les bibliothèques de bateaux etc.) sont considérées comme points de service tant qu'elles assurent le service elles-mêmes et non pas par l'intermédiare d'un tiers. Les points 'statiques' sont donc ceux qui offrent un véhicule se déplacant dans différentes localités faisant en sorte que l'usager puisse avoir accès à leurs services. C'est le bibliobus lui-même qui représente un point de service mobile; Le nombre d'arrêts que le bibliobus fait en route sur ses tournées NE CONSTITUE PAS comme receptions mobiles. Les bibliobus qui sont utilisés seulement pur le transport de matériel d'une bibliothèque à l'autre NE CONSISTUTE PAS comme receptions mobiles.

iv) COLLECTION
Tous les ouvrages/documents sont fournis par la bibliothèque pour ses usagers. Les statistiques concernant les collections devraient seulement couvrir les documents accessibles aux usagers en tenants compte des ouvrages/documents en prêt:

v) LIVRES ET REVUES PERIODIQUES RELIEES
Les livres devraient être comptés par volume. A ce contexte un volume est un ouvrage composé d'une unité comprenant tout ouvrage imprimé inclu dans une reliure ou un portfolio. Les périodiques sont définis comme une série continue sur une periode indéfinie ou les publications dans la série sont numérotées successivement ou chaque publication est datée. Les publications annuelles sont inclues dans cette définition, mais les monographes sont exclus. Les périodiques reliés devraient être compté à l'unité. Les périodiques non reliées (pas actuelles) devraient inclus en plus comme en unités reliées Les journaux y sont inclus et devraient être comptés par volumes ou paquets.

vi) TITRES DES ABONNEMENTS EN COURS
Le nombre des titres des publications périodiques reçues par la bibliothèque durant leur année comptable.

vii) LES MANUSCRITS
Tout ouvrage écrit ou dessiné à la main contenu dans une reliure ou un portfolio est considéré être un manuscrit.

viii) MICROFORMES
Les reproductions micro-imprimées d'ouvrages originaux ou publications. Veuillez inclure les copies filmiques micro réduit de manuscrits.

ix) MATERIEL AUDIO-VISUEL
Comprenant ouvrages/documents qui ne se présentent pas sous la forme de livres ou microformes et demandent l'utilisation d'un équipement spécial de manière à l'écouter ou le regarder: par example, disques, cassettes, compactes, films, videos, diapositives.

x) AUTRES MATERIAUX
Tout ce qui est stocké par les bibliothèques et utilisé comme référence par l'usager: cartes, photos, gravures, graphiques, dioramas ... a l'exclusion des livres, ouvrages périodiques, manuscrits, microformes et matériel audio-visuel.

xi) ADDITIONS
Le nombre de toutes les additions faites à la collection durant l'année et qui auraient dû être mises à la disposition de l'usager durant l'année. Ce nombre devrait représenter le nombre total des additions avant les déductions dues aux pertes soient par l'élimination de certains ouvrages de la collection, les ouvrages endommagés ou égarés. Veuillez inclure toutes les additions résultant d'achats, donations, échanges ou toutes autres sources d'acquisition. Néanmoins, prenez soin de n'inclure que les additions qui correspondent aux catégories du questionnaire (à savoir, livres, périodiques, manuscrits, microfilms, audio-visuel et autre).

QUESTION 3

xii) LES USAGERS: Bibliothèques nationales seulement
Toute personne qui à utilisé les services offerts par la bibliotheque durant l'année comptable

xiii) CONSULTATIONS: Bibliothèques nationales seulement
Le nombre des demandes d'assistance rédigées officiellement.

xiv) ABONNES DE LA BIBLIOTHEQUE
Tous les lecteurs présents sur le registre afin de pouvoir emprunter des ouvrages pour leur usage personnel à l'exterieur de la bibliothèque. Ne compter que le nombre des lecteurs enregistrés pour l'année en question. Ne confondez pas ce terme avec les 'usagers' qui représentent les personnes utilisant n'importe quelle des facilités offertes par la bibliothèque et non pas seulement l'emprunt d'ouvrages/documents/materiaux.

xv) TRANSACTIONS D'EMPRUNTS
Le nombre des emprunts devraient être calculé suivant le nombre des ouvrages empruntés et le nombre de copies fourni en place d'emprunts ex. livre, périodiques et manuscrits, en prêt. Faîtes ce compte du numéro de volumes et du noméro de reproductions mis en place des matériaux originaux - comptez par volumes;

xvi) LA LONGUEUR DES RAYONS DE RANGEMENT ACTUELLEMENT UTILISES
La longueur des étagères en mètres de la collection à la disposition de l'usager.

xvii) LE SECTION DE LA POPULATION DESSERVIE
Le nombre total des usagers qui existent potentiellement dans une région ou pur l'un des centres d'intérêt couverts par la(les) bibliothèque(s): par example, pour les bibliothèques municipales, ce sera le nombre total des habitants dans le district d'aministratif, pour les bibliothèques desservant des instituts D'ENSEIGNEMENT SUPERIEUR, le 'Secteur Population' sera représenté par le nombre des étudiants et enseignants attachés à cet(s) institut(s) qui sont servis. En règle générale, à l'exception des bibliothèques nationales, municipales et autres bibliothèques non-spécialisées, il vaut mieux pour estimer le 'Secteur Population' se limiter au nombre possible des usagers de base de la bibliothèque et exclure le grand public, même si le public utilise la bibliothèque et ses services de temps en temps.

QUESTION 4

xviii) PERSONNEL DE BIBLIOTHEQUE QUALIFIE
Tous les membres du personnel qui ont suivi une formation générale de bibliothécaire ou dans les sciences de l'information. La formation a pu être faite suivant des méthodes formelles ou par une période prolongée de formation sur le tas sous supervision dans un bibliothèque.

xix) AUTRE PERSONNEL DE BIBLIOTHEQUE
Veuillez inclure tout le personnel sous la supervision du directeur(trice) de la(les) bibliothèque(s), qui est employé dans la bibliothèque y compris le personnel nécessaire au maintien des services, mais qui no sont pas nécessairement sous la supervision du directeur; ex. personnel de soutien; ceci peut comprendre les comptables et tout autre personnel d'administration ou travaillant soit en tant qu'employés de cette administration ou temporairement sous contrat.

QUESTION 6 STATISTIQUES FINANCIERS

xx) DEPENSES
Dépenses concernant le TOTAL des dépenses estimées pour le SECTEUR des bibliothèques pour l'année en revue. Ces dépenses devraient être présentées sous les titres suivants:

xxi) PERSONNEL
Cette figure comprend: les salaires, les heures supplémentaires, les contributions sociales (retraite) payées par les employeurs, les frais de formation, le frais de déplacement, le indemnitées de subsistence, et tous autres honoraires concernant le personnel travaillant dans le secteur bibliothècaire. Veuillez inclure votre meilleur estimation de personnel assigné et d'autre locaux/informatique/legal/comptabilité et d'autre têtes de service de soutien encource par l'administration sur le secteur de bibliothèque que n'est pas dirigé par le directeur(s) de la bibliothèque.

xxii) DEPENSE LIEES AUX LOCAUX ET LEUR OPERATION

Toutes les dépenses concernant le coût du maintien des locaux: loyers, taxes foncières, produits d'entretien, dépenses en électricité (énergie en général), réparations et maintien. Veuillez exclure les dépenses concernant le personnel; celles-ci devraient figurer dans la catégorie 'PERSONNEL'. Veuillez ne pas inclure le coût des emprunts associés aux locaux des bibliothèques. Ceux-ci devraient figurer sous la reburique: COUT DES EMPRUNTS FONCIERS.

xxiii) NOUVEAUX LOCAUX ET REMISE A NEUF
Concerne les dépenses importantes destinées à l'amélioration de la structure des locaux existants ou la construction de nouveaux locaux.

xxiv ACQUISITIONS NOUVELLES
Dépenses destinées à l'acquisition d'ouvrages ayant pour but d'améliorer la collection à la disposition des usagers. Veuillez ne pas inclure le coût de l'acquisition d'équipement destiné à l'administration/management (ces dépenses devraient figurer sous le rubrique 'FRAIS DIVERS')

xxv) COUT DES EMPRUNTS FONCIERS
Le remboursement des emprûnts et des baux en cours dans le SECTEUR des bibliothèques.

xxvi) FRAIS DIVERS
Toutes autres dépenses liées aux frais d'exploitation dans le secteur, durant l'année et qui ne figurent pas dans les autres catégories.

xxvii) REVENU
Tous les revenus reçus durant l'année comptables et qui ont été utilisés pour compenser les depenses dans le SECTEUR des bibliothèques.

xxviii) FINANCEMENT GOUVERNEMENTAL/MUNICIPAL (IMPÔTS/BOURSES)
A inclure tous les financements reçus des gouvernements locaux ou du gouvernement central que ce soit sous forme de bourse ou d'une contribution au maintien de secteur.

xxix) HONORAIRES
Tous les revenus de nature commerciale reçus par l'administration de la bibliothèque durant l'année comptable.

xxx) AUTRES REVENUS
Tous autres revenus durant l'année qui ne soient pas directement liés aux catégories indiquées ci-dessus; les examples pourraient inclure: revenus dus à vente de biens, transferts de sommes entre différentes administrations effectués durant l'année en revue; intérêts gagnés de soldes bancaires, dons privés et sponsors.

xxxi) DEPENSE EN CAPITAL (D'EQUIPMENT)
(à savoir, investissements dans une ou des nouvelle(s) bibliothèque(s) ou remise à neuf.)
Toutes dépenses majeures, financées soit par des fonds capitaux internes à l'administration ou d'emprunts de source externes à l'organisation.

xxxii) AUTRES DEPENSES MAJEURES (D'EQUIPMENT)
Tous autres dépenses majeures concernant les dépenses accrues de manière à rendre possible l'existence et fonctionnement d'un secteur bibliothécaire et qui ne sont pas inclues dans les catégories ci-dessus.

xxxiii) DETTES EN SUSPENS
Le montant des emprunts accumulés pur financer les dépenses majeures et qui sont encore impayées à la fin de l'année.

ANMERKUNGEN ZUR ORIENTIERUNG

Bücherei-Sektoren

Die 6 Bibliotheks-Sektoren, die in dieser Studie enthalten sind, stimmen genau mit den UNESCO-Definitionen überein:

NATIONALE BIBLIOTHEKEN

Bibliotheken, die unabhängig von ihrer Bezeichnung für den Erwerb und die Erhaltung von Exemplaren wichtiger Publikationen, die im Lande erstellt wurden, verantwortlich sind und die als "Aufbewahrungs"-Büchereien agieren, entweder von Rechts wegen oder durch andere Vereinbarung und die normalerweise eine nationale Bibliographie zusammentragen.

BIBLIOTHEKEN VON EINRICHTUNGEN DER HOCHSCHULEN:

Bibliotheken, die primär den Studenten und Lehrern in Universitäten und anderen Einrichtungen der Hochschulen dienen.

ANDERE GRÖSSERE NICHTSPEZIALISIERTE BIBLIOTHEKEN

Nichtspezialisierte Büchereien von wissenschaftlicher Art, die weder Büchereien von Hochschulen noch staatliche Büchereien sind, jedoch die Aufgaben von staatlichen Büchereien in einer bestimmten geographischen Region erfüllen.

SCHULBIBLIOTHEKEN

Bibliotheken, die an alle Arten von Schulen und Bildungsanstalten unter dem Hochschulniveau angebunden sind und primär den Schülern und Lehrern derartiger Schulen und Bildungsanstalten dienen, auch wenn sie der allgemeinen Öffentlichkeit zur Verfügung stehen dürfen.

SPEZIELLE BIBLIOTHEKEN

Büchereien, die von einer Vereinigung, der Regierung, dem Parlament, einer Forschungseinrichtung (Universitätseinrichtungen ausgeschlossen), einer wissenschaftlichen Gesellschaft, einem Fachverband, einem Museum, einem Handelsunternehmen, einem industriellen Unternehmen, einer Handelskammer, etc. oder von einem anderen organisierten Konsortium unterhalten werden, und deren größter Teil des Bestandes spezielle Gebiete oder Fächer wie z.B. Naturwissenschaften, Sozialwissenschaften, Landwirtschaft, Chemie, Medizin, Wirtschaftswissenschaften, Ingenieurwissenschaften, Rechtswissenschaften und Geschichte beinhalten.

ÖFFENTLICHE BIBLIOTHEKEN

Büchereien, die der Bevölkerung einer Gemeinde oder einer Region unentgeltlich oder für eine geringe Gebühr zur Verfügung stehen; sie mögen der allgemeinen Öffentlichkeit oder einer speziellen Benutzerkategorie wie z.B. Kindern, Angehörigen der Steitkräfte, Krankenhauspatienten, Häftlingen, Arbeitern und Angestellten dienen.

FRAGEN 1 UND 2 (SAMMLUNGEN)

Frage 1 fragt nach der Gesamtzahl von Material, das am 31. Dezember jedes Jahres im Besitz der Bibliothek ist, sowohl im Bestand als auch momentan im Verleih. Falls die Bestandzählung mit einem anderen Datum übereinstimmt, ist dies bitte auf dem Fragebogen zu kennzeichnen.

Frage 2 fragt nach der Gesamtzahl von Erwerbungen der Bibliothek während dieses Jahres: dies bedeutet alle Neuerwerbungen von Materialien inklusive denen, die dem Ersatz von nicht zurückgegebenem Material, verschlissenem Material oder anderen Arten des Verbrauchs dienen.

DEFINITIONEN

I) JAHR

Falls der Zeitraum der Berechnung, den Sie in die Statistik einbeziehen, nicht mit den Kalenderjahren übereinstimmt, schließen Sie bitte die Zurückerstattung in das Jahr ein, welches den größten Zeitraum beinhaltet, auf den sich Ihre Berechnung bezieht.

Zum Beispiel: wenn Ihre Registrierungen das Jahr vom 1. April bis zum 31. März beinhalten, dann tragen Sie bitte das Jahr vom 1. April 1986 bis zum 31. März 1987 in das Feld ein für das Jahr, das 1986 endet, da der größte Teil Ihres Untersuchungszeitraums (9 Monate) sich auf das Kalenderjahr 1986 bezieht. Kennzeichnen Sie dann bitte auf dem Fragebogen, daß Ihr Berechnungszeitraum der 1. April bis 31. März ist.

Falls Ihre Berechnungen sich auf den Zeitraum vom 1. Juli bis 30. Juni beziehen, z.B. 1. Juli 1986 bis 30. Juni 1987, dann tragen Sie die Periode bitte in das Kalenderjahr ein, die 1986 endet und kennzeichnen Sie den Fragebogen entsprechend.

Sollte Ihr Rechnungsjahr zu unterschiedlichen Zeitpunkten des Jahres anfangen und enden, dann ordnen Sie bitte das Rechnungsjahr dem Kalenderjahr zu, das den größten Teil des Berechnungszeitraums beinhaltet, wie in den oben angegebenen Beispielen.

II) VERWALTUNGSEINHEIT

Jede Gruppe von Büchereien oder eine unabhängige Bibliothek unter einem Leiter oder einer Verwaltung.

III) DIENSTSTELLE

Ein bestimmter Ort oder eine bestimmte Gegend, die einen Dienst für Büchereibenutzer bereitstellt. Unabhängige Büchereien, Zentralbüchereien und Zweigbüchereien (sowohl stationäre Büchereien als auch mobile Büchereifahrzeuge und Schiffsbüchereien etc.) werden als Dienststellen bezeichnet, vorausgesetzt sie dienen unmittelbar und nicht durch Dritte den Benutzern. Stationäre Stellen sind solche, die einen Dienst von einem Ort aus bereitstellen und mobile Stellen sind solche, die in einem Fahrzeug sind, das sich zu verschiedenen Orten bewegt, um potentiellen Benutzern die Möglichkeit zu geben, die Büchereidienste zu nutzen. Die Büchereifahrzeuge stellen selbst eine Dienststelle dar; die Zahl der Haltepunkte auf der Fahrt bilden keine mobilen Dienststellen. Die Fahrzeuge, die nur dem Transport von Material von einer Bücherei zu einer anderen dienen, bilden keine mobilen Dienststellen.

IV) SAMMLUNG

Das gesamte Büchereimaterial, das die Bibliothek dem Benutzer zur Verfügung stellt. Statistiken, die sich auf die Büchereisammlung beziehen, sollten nur die folgenden Dokumente beinhalten, die dem Benutzer zur Verfügung stehen, inklusive des Materials, das verliehen ist.

V) BÜCHER UND GEBUNDENE MAGAZINE

Bücher sollten als Bände gezählt werden. Ein Band beinhaltet reproduziertes Material (außer microforms), das eine physische Einheit von jedem gedruckten Werk in einer Bindung oder einer Mappe bildet. Magazine werden als eine kontinuierliche Serie über einen unbegrenzten Zeitraum definiert, in der individuelle Ausgaben in der Serie fortlaufend numeriert sind oder jede Ausgabe ein Datum erhält. Jahrbücher sind eingeschlossen, aber monographische Serien sind ausgenommen. Gebundene Magazine sollten als eine physische Einheit gezählt werden. Ungebundene Magazine (nicht fortlaufend) sollten so in die Zählung eingeschlossen werden, als wenn sie in physischen Einheiten gebunden wären. Zeitungen sind eingeschlossen und sollten in Bänden oder Paketen gezählt werden.

VI) LAUFENDE MAGAZINTITEL

Die Anzahl der Magazintitel, die von der Bücherei während des Berechnungsjahres erhalten werden.

VII) MANUSKRIPTE

Jedes original handschriftlich oder gezeichnete Werk, das in einem Band oder einer Mappe enthalten ist.

VIII) MICROFORMS

Mikrogedruckte Reproduktionen von Originalwerken oder Publikationen einschließlich Mikrofilmkopien von Manuskripten

IX) AUDIOVISUELLE MATERIALIEN

Diese enthalten Nicht-Buch -, Nicht-mikroform-Materialien, die die Benutzung von speziellen Geräten erfordern, um gehört oder gesehen zu werden; z.B. Schallplatten, Bänder, Kassetten, Compact Disks, Filme, Videobänder, Dias und Transparente.

X) ANDERES MATERIAL

Gegenstände, die von der Bücherei als Nachschlagewerke für Benutzer aufbewahrt werden, wie z.B. Karten, Tabellen, Kunstdrucke, Fotographien und Schaubilder; ausgenommen sind Bücher, Magazine, Manuskripte, Microforms und "audio-visuelle" Materialien.

XI) ZUGÄNGE

Die Zahl aller Zugänge zur Sammlung während des Jahres, die dem Benutzer zugänglich gemacht werden. Dies sollte die gesamte Zahl von Zugängen anzeigen, vor Abzug von Verlusten von Sammlungen durch Verlegung, Wegwerfen und Abnutzung.

Bitte nennen Sie jeden Zugang durch Kauf, Schenkung, Austausch oder jede andere Form von Erwerb zur Sammlung. Jedoch nennen Sie nur in Kategorien von Materialien, die als Kategorien in den Fragebögen angegeben sind (Bücher, Magazine, Manuskripte, Microforms, audio-visuelle Materialien und andere).

FRAGE 3

XII BÜCHEREIBENUTZER: <u>NUR STAATLICHE BÜCHEREIEN</u>

Jede Person, die die Dienste der Bücherei(en) im Jahr der Berechnung nutzt.

XIII) BÜCHEREI KONSULTATIONEN:

<u>NUR STAATLICHE BÜCHEREIEN</u>: Zahl der formellen Anfragen nach Hilfe.

XIV) REGISTRIERTE LEIHER:

Personen, die in der Bibliothek registriert sind, um Material aus der Bücherei auszuleihen und es außerhalb der Bibliothek zu benutzen. Bitte zählen Sie nur die Zahl der Personen, die im speziellen Jahr registriert sind. Verwechseln Sie nicht diesen Begriff mit den "Büchereibenutzern", die irgendeinen Büchereidienst nutzen und nicht spezielle Materialien ausleihen.

XV) LEIHTRANSAKTIONEN:

Dies sollte aus der Zahl von ausgeliehenen Werken und gelieferten Exemplaren stellvertretend für Leihgaben errechnet werden; das bedeutet: Bücher, Magazine und Manuskripte, die ausgeliehen sind, werden an Hand von Bänden und Exemplaren gezählt, die stellvertretend für Originalmaterialien, die in Bänden gezählt werden, produziert wurden.

XVI) LÄNGE DER BESETZTEN REGALE

Länge der Regale der den Benutzern zur Verfügung stehenden Sammlung in Metern.

XVII) SEKTOREN DER VERSORGTEN BEVÖLKERUNG

Gesamtzahl der potentiellen Benutzer in der geographischen oder betreffenden Region, die von der Bücherei versorgt wird: z.B. für öffentliche Büchereien ist dies die Gesamtzahl von Einwohnern in der betreffenden Gegend: für Büchereien, die Hochschulen dienen, ist die "Sektorbevölkerung" die Zahl der Studenten und Lehrer, die versorgt werden. Als generelle Regel, mit Ausnahme von öffentlichen staatlichen und nicht spezialisierten Büchereien, begrenze die Schätzung der "Sektorbevölkerung" auf die potentielle Zahl der primären Benutzer der Büchereien und schließe die allgemeine Öffentlichkeit aus, auch wenn diese die Einrichtung von Zeit zu Zeit benutzt.

FRAGE 4

XVIII) GESCHULTE BIBLIOTHEKARE

Alle Angestellten, die eine allgemeine Ausbildung in Bilbiothekswissenschaften oder Informationswissenschaften erhalten haben. Die Ausbildung kann durch formelle Methoden oder durch eine lange Tätigkeit in einer Bibliothek unter Aufsicht erfolgen.

XIX) ANDERES PERSONAL DER BÜCHEREI

Bitte nennen Sie alle Angestellten, die unter unmittelbarer Aufsicht des Leiters der Bibliothek stehen, die für Büchereifunktionen angestellt sind und Angestelte, deren Dienste für den reibungslosen Ablauf des Büchereibetriebes benötigt werden und nicht unbedingt unter unmittelbarer Aufsicht des Leiters stehen, d.h. Hilfsangestellte sind. Dies darf Buchhalter und andere Hilfsangestellte beinhalten, die Teile ihrer Zeit mit Büchereiverwaltungsaufgaben verbringen; entweder als Angestellte der Verwaltung oder auf vertraglicher Basis.

FRAGE 5   FINANZ-STATISTIK

XX) AUSGABEN

Ausgaben beziehen sich auf die gesamten geschätzten Ausgaben für den Büchereisektor im Finanzjahr. Diese Ausgaben sollten soweit wie möglich unter den folgenden Rubriken aufgeführt werden:

XXI) MITARBEITER

Diese Summe enthält Gehälter, Überstundenbezahlung, Rentenbeiträge, die vom Arbeitnehmer gezahlt werden, Ausbildungskosten, Reise- und Unterhaltskosten und andere Angestelltenlöhne für alle Angestellten, die im Büchereisektor arbeiten. Sie sollten auch Ihre beste Schätzung der anteilmäßigen Personalkosten nennen, die für die Verwaltung von Gebäuden, Computern durch Rechtsfragen und Verwaltungsaufgaben auf dem Büchereisektor außerhalb der unmittelbaren Direktion der Bücherei entstehen.

XXII) GEBÄUDE- UND BETRIEBSKOSTEN

Alle Posten wie Mieten, Grundsteuern, Reinigungsmaterialien, Energiekosten, Reparatur- und Wartungskosten etc., die sich auf die Betriebskosten der Bücherei beziehen. Bitte schließen Sie die Personalkosten aus, die in der "Angestellten"-Rubrik genannt werden. Bitte schließen Sie nicht ein die Kosten der Beleihung für Büroräume; diese sollten unter "Kosten der Beleihung" aufgeführt werden.

XXIII) NEUE GEBÄUDE; ERNEUERUNGEN

Diese beziehen sich auf Ausgaben für Verbesserungen an Gebäuden einer existierenden Bibliothek oder auf die Erstellung eines neuen Gebäudes.

XXIV) NEUERWERBUNGEN DES BESTANDES

Dies bezieht sich auf Ausgaben für den Erwerb von Material, um die den Benutzern zugängliche Sammlung zu erweitern. Bitte schließen Sie nicht ein die Kosten für den Kauf von Einrichtungen für die Verwaltung und das Management der Bibliothek (diese sollten bei "gemischten Ausgaben" aufgeführt werden).

XXV) KOSTEN DER BELEIHUNG

Die Rückzahlung von Kosten für Darlehen und für Mietverträge im Bibliothekssektor.

XXVI) GEMISCHTE KOSTEN

Alle anderen Ausgaben, die zu den Kosten des Betriebes der Bibliothek während des Jahres gehören, die nicht speziell bei den oben genannten Kategorien angegeben sind.

XXVII) EINKOMMEN

Alle Einnahmen während des Rechnungsjahres, die zum Ausgleich der Kosten des Büchereisektors benutzt werden.

XXVIII) REGIERUNGS/KOMMUNAL-UNTERSTÜTZUNG (STEUERN/ZUSCHÜSSE):

Alle Gelder, die in Form von Beihilfen oder Zuschüssen von der zentralen oder lokalen Regierung zum Unterhalt des Bibliothekssektors erhalten wurden.

XXIV) GEBÜHREN UND RECHNUNGEN

Alle Einkünfte durch Handel, die während des Rechnungsjahres von der Büchereiverwaltung erhalten wurden.

XXX) ANDERE EINKÜNFTE

Alle anderen Einkünfte während des Jahres, die nicht in den oben genannten Kategorien spezifiziert sind. Beispiele sind: Gewinne aus dem Verkauf von Betriebskapital, Transfer von Geldern zwischen verschiedenen Verwaltungen während des Rechnungsjahres; Zinsen, die auf Bankkonten eingenommen wurden; private Spenden und Sponsoreneinkünfte.

XXXI) HAUPTAUSGABEN (INVESTITIONEN IN NEUE BIBLIOTHEKEN ODER ERNEUERUNGEN)

Alle Zahlungen, die für große Ausgaben durchgeführt wurden, unterstützt entweder von internationalen Kapitalfonds oder durch Anleihen bei externen Geldquellen.

XXXII) ANDERE HAUPTAUSGABEN

Alle anderen Hauptausgaben für den Unterhalt des Büchereisektors, die nicht speziell unter den anderen Sektoren genannt wurden.

XXXIII) NICHT BEZAHLTE SCHULDEN

Die Summe der Gelder, die geliehen wurden und am Ende des Jahres noch nicht zurückgezahlt waren.

ΕΠΕΞΗΓΗΜΑΤΙΚΕΣ ΣΗΜΕΙΩΣΕΙΣ

<u>ΚΑΤΗΓΟΡΙΕΣ ΒΙΒΛΙΟΘΗΚΩΝ</u>
Υπάρχουν 6 διαφορετικές κατηγορίες βιβλιοθηκών και οι 6 αντιστοιχούν στους όρους της UNESCO.

ΕΘΝΙΚΕΣ ΒΙΒΛΙΟΘΗΚΕΣ:
Σ'αυτή τη κατηγορία υπάγονται οι βιβλιοθήκες που άσχετα από το τίτλο τους, είναι υπεύθυνες για τη αγορά και φύλαξη αντιτύπων όλων των σημαντικών εκδόσεων της χώρας και που είτε με νομοθετική ή άλλη ειδική ρύθμιση λειτουργούν ως "αποθεματικές" εθνικές βιβλιοθήκες.

ΒΙΒΛΙΟΘΗΚΕΣ ΑΝΩΤΑΤΩΝ ΕΚΠΑΙΔΕΥΤΙΚΩΝ ΙΔΡΥΜΑΤΩΝ:
Εξυπηρετούν κατ'αρχήν φοιτητές και καθηγητές των πανεπιστημίων και άλλων ιδρυμάτων τριτοβάθμιας εκπαίδευσης.

ΑΛΛΕΣ ΣΗΜΑΝΤΙΚΕΣ ΜΗ ΕΙΔΙΚΕΣ ΒΙΒΛΙΟΘΗΚΕΣ:
Πρόκειται για βιβλιοθήκες που διαθέτουν πλούσια συλλογή βιβλίων χωρίς να είναι βιβλιοθήκες ανωτάτων εκπαιδευτικών ιδρυμάτων ούτε εθνικές βιβλιοθήκες, ακόμη και αν ορισμένες εκτελούν χρέη εθνικής βιβλιοθήκης σε μία δεδομένη γεωγραφική περιοχή.

ΣΧΟΛΙΚΕΣ ΒΙΒΛΙΟΘΗΚΕΣ:
Πρόκειται για αυτές που εξυπηρετούν την πρωτοβάθμια, δευτεροβάθμια και κολλεγιακή εκπαίδευση και που μπορούν να είναι ανοικτές στο ευρύτερο κοινό.

ΕΙΔΙΚΕΣ ΒΙΒΛΙΟΘΗΚΕΣ:
Θεωρούνται οι βιβλιοθήκες η λειτουργία των οποίων εξασφαλίζεται από συλλόγους, κυβερνητικές υπηρεσίες, κοινοβούλια, ινστιτούτα ερευνών (εκτός από πανεπιστημιακά ιδρύματα), επιστημονικές εταιρίες, βιομηχανικές επιχειρήσεις, εμπορικά επιμελητήρια κλπ ή άλλες οργανωμένες ομάδες. Το μεγαλύτερο μέρος των συλλογών τους αφορά μία συγκεκριμένη επιστήμη ή θέμα π.χ. φυσικές επιστήμες, κοινωνιολογία, γεωργία, χημεία, ιατρική, οικονομικές επιστήμες, μηχανολογία, νομικά, ιστορία.

ΔΗΜΟΣΙΕΣ ΒΙΒΛΙΟΘΗΚΕΣ:
Θεωρούνται οι βιβλιοθήκες που εξυπηρετούν τον πληθυσμό ενός δήμου ή κοινότητας σε δωρεάν βάση ή με κάποια τυπική επιβάρυνση. Μπορεί, επίσης, να εξυπηρετούν το ευρύτερο κοινό ή ειδικές κατηγορίες χρηστών όπως παιδιά, στρατιωτικούς, νοσηλευόμενους σε νοσοκομεία, κρατούμενους φυλακών, εργαζόμενους και εργοδότες.

<u>ΕΡΩΤΗΣΕΙΣ 1η ΚΑΙ 2η (Συλλογές)</u>
Η πρώτη ερώτηση αφορά το σύνολο του υλικού της βιβλιοθήκης είτε δανειζομένου είτε όχι, στις 31 Δεκεμβρίου καθ'έτους. Αν το σύνολο αντιστοιχεί σε διαφορετική ημερομηνία, παρακαλούμε σημειώστε το στο ερωτηματολόγιο.

Η δεύτερη ερώτηση αφορά το σύνολο του καινούργιου υλικού που προμηθεύτηκε η βιβλιοθήκη με οποιοδήποτε τρόπο στη διάρκεια του έτους, π.χ. όλο το καινούργιο υλικό χωρίς να περιλαμβάνονται τα αντικαταστημένα.

ΟΡΙΣΜΟΙ

i) ΕΤΟΣ:
Αν η περίοδος υπολογισμού που λαμβάνετε υπόψη σας για τις στατιστικές σας δεν αντιστοιχεί σε ημερολογιακό έτος, σας παρακαλούμε, να αναφέρετε το έτος που καλύπτει το μεγαλύτερο διάστημα της περιόδου αυτής και να προσδιορίσετε στο ερωτηματολόγιο την πραγματική χρονική περίοδο που καλύπτουν οι στατιστικές σας. Για παράδειγμα, αν τα στοιχεία σας αναφέρονται σε έτη που αρχίζουν από τον Απρίλιο ενός έτους εώς το Μάρτιο του επομένου, τότε αρχίστε την εγγραφή των δεδομένων σας από το ημερολογιακό έτος που περιλαμβάνει τους πρώτους εννεά μήνες αυτής της περιόδου και σημειώστε στο ερωτηματολόγιο "1η Απριλίου/31 Μαρτίου".

Εάν τα στοιχεία που έχετε αφορούν περίοδο που αρχίζει από την 1η Ιουλίου μέχρι τις 31 Ιουνίου του επομένου έτους, οι απαντήσεις σας πρέπει να αφορούν το προηγούμενο έτος και να αναφερθείτε το επόμενο μόνο αν, πράγματι, καλύπτει το μεγαλύτερο διάστημα της περιόδου που καλύπτουν οι πίνακές σας.

ii) ΔΙΟΙΚΗΤΙΚΗ ΜΟΝΑΔΑ:
Είναι κάθε ανεξάρτητη βιβλιοθήκη ή ομάδα βιβλιοθηκών μ'έναν επικεφαλή ή μία διοικητική αρχή.

iii) ΣΗΜΕΙΑ ΕΞΥΠΗΡΕΤΗΣΗΣ:
Κάθε βιβλιοθήκη, είτε είναι ανεξάρτητη είτε τμήμα μιάς ευρύτερης διοικητικής μονάδας, έχει τη δυνατότητα να εξυπηρετεί τους χρήστες της σε κάποιο ιδιαίτερο χώρο. "Σημεία εξυπυρέτησης" θεωρούνται οι ανεξάρτητες βιβλιοθήκες, κεντρικές και παραρτήματα, σε σταθερή ή μεταχινούμενη θέση (φορτηγά, πλοίο ή τραίνο) που εξυπηρετούν απευθείας τους χρήστες. Τα σημεία όπου σταματούν τα οχήματα βιβλιοθήκες δεν υπολογίζονται ως σημεία εξυπηρέτησης. "ΣΤΑΘΕΡΑ" σημεία θεωρούνται αυτά που εξυπηρετούν τους χρήστες σε μία συγκεκριμένη θέση και "ΚΙΝΗΤΑ" τα οχήματα που μεταχινούνται για την εξυπηρέτηση των χρηστών. Τα οχήματα που μεταχινούνται μόνον για τη μεταφορά υλικού από τη μιά βιβλιοθήκη στη άλλη, δεν θεωρούνται "ΚΙΝΗΤΑ" σημεία εξυπηρέτησης.

iv) ΣΥΛΛΟΓΗ:
Κάθε είδος εγγράφων που διαθέτει η βιβλιοθήκη για τους χρήστες της. Οι στατιστικές που αφορούν τις συλλογές πρέπει να καλύπτουν μόνο τις εξής κατηγορίες εγγράφων συμπεριλαμβανομένων των εγγράφων που δανείζει η βιβλιοθήκη.

v) ΒΙΒΛΙΑ ΚΑΙ ΒΙΒΛΙΟΔΕΤΗΜΕΝΑ ΠΕΡΙΟΔΙΚΑ:
Τα "Βιβλία" υπολογίζονται κατά τόμο. Στη δεδομένη περίπτωση, ο τόμος περιλαμβάνει κάθε αναπαραγόμενο υλικό (εκτός από τα μιχροαντίτυπα) που αποτελεί μια ανεξάρτητη μονάδα εγγράφων που είναι βιβλιοδετημένα ή περιέχονται σε ειδικό φάκελο. "Περιοδικά" θεωρούνται οι δημοσιεύσεις που εκδίδονται με τον ίδιο τίτλο, σε συνεχή σειρά και για αόριστη χρονική περίοδο σε τακτά ή μη χρονικά διαστήματα. Τα περιοδικά πρέπει να υπολογίζονται με βάση τον αριθμό των διαθέσιμων τίτλων. Στην κατηγορία αυτή περιλαμβάνονται οι εφημερίδες που πρέπει να υπολογίζονται σε τόμους ή φακέλους.

vi) ΤΙΤΛΟΙ ΠΕΡΙΟΔΙΚΩΝ:
Τίτλοι περιοδικών που ελήφθησαν στο τρέχον έτος από τη βιβλιοθήκη.

vii) ΧΕΙΡΟΓΡΑΦΑ:
Κάθε πρωτότυπο έγγραφο που έχει συνταχθεί ή σχεδιασθεί με το χέρι και που είναι βιβλιοδετημένο ή περιέχεται σε ειδικό φάκελο.

viii) ΜΙΚΡΟΑΝΤΙΤΥΠΑ:
Πρόκειται για την επανέκδοση σε μικρές διαστάσεις πρωτότυπων εγγράφων καθώς και μικροφίλμ χειρογράφων.

ix) ΟΠΤΙΚΟΑΚΟΥΣΤΙΚΑ ΥΛΙΚΑ:
Πρόκειται για υλικό βιβλιοθήκης εκτός από βιβλία και μικροέντυπα, που η χρησιμοποίησή του προυποθέτει ειδικούς εξοπλισμούς π.χ. δίσκοι, μαγνητοταινίες, κασσέτες, κινηματογραφικές ταινίες, βιντεοταινίες, φωτεινές διαφάνειες, κλπ.

x) ΑΛΛΟ ΥΛΙΚΟ:
Είναι όλα τα είδη που διαθέτουν οι βιβλιοθήκες για την ενημέρωση των χρηστών τους όπως χάρτες, γραφικές παραστάσεις, αντίγραφα πινάκων, φωτογραφίες και φωτεινές προβολές, κλπ, εκτός από βιβλία, περιοδικά, χειρόγραφα, μικροαντίτυπα και οπτικοακουστικό υλικό.

xi) ΠΡΟΣΘΗΚΕΣ:
Πρέπει να αναφέρονται συνολικά δηλαδή, όλες οι προσθήκες που γίνονται στις συλλογές κατά τη διάρκεια του έτους για την εξυπηρέτηση των χρηστών πριν αφαιρεθούν οι απώλειες που οφείλονται στη διαλογή και την ταξινόμηση. Σας παρακαλούμε να συμπεριλάβετε κάθε προσθήκη που αυξάνει το περιεχόμενο της συλλογής είτε αυτή γίνεται με αγορά, δωρεά, ανταλλαγή ή οποιοδήποτε άλλο τρόπο. Σημειώσετε όμως μόνον τις προσθήκες που αφορούν τις κατηγορίες των ειδών που προβλέπει το ερωτηματολόγιο (π.χ. βιβλία και βιβλιοδετημένα περιοδικά, χειρόγραφα, μικροαντίτυπα, οπτικοακουστικό υλικό, κλπ.)

ΕΡΩΤΗΣΗ 3η

xii) ΧΡΗΣΤΕΣ ΒΙΒΛΙΟΘΗΚΗΣ: Η κατηγορία αυτή αφορά μόνον τις Εθνικές Βιβλιοθήκες. Είναι τα άτομα που χρησιμοποιούν τις υπηρεσίες της βιβλιοθήκης ή των βιβλιοθηκών κατά τη διάρκεια του έτους αναφοράς.

xiii) ΑΙΤΗΣΕΙΣ ΒΟΗΘΕΙΑΣ:
Αριθμός ατόμων που ζητούν βοήθεια για την ανεύρεση υλικού.

xiv) ΕΓΓΕΓΡΑΜΜΕΝΟΙ ΔΑΝΕΙΖΟΜΕΝΟΙ:
Είναι άτομα εγγεγραμμένα στη βιβλιοθήκη με το δικαίωμα να δανείζονται τα έγγραφα της συλλογής και να τα χρησιμοποιούν εκτός βιβλιοθήκης. Υπολογίστε μόνο τον αριθμό των εγγεγραμμένων κατά τη διάρκεια του συγκεκριμένου έτους, αποφεύγοντας σύγχυση του όρου αυτού με τον όρο "χρήστες βιβλιοθήκης" που αφορά οποιοδήποτε άτομο που χρησιμοποιεί τις υπηρεσίες της βιβλιοθήκης.

xv) ΣΥΝΑΛΛΑΓΕΣ ΔΑΝΕΙΣΜΟΥ:
Πρέπει να μετρηθούν με βάση τον αριθμό των αιτήσεων που έλαβε και διεκπεραίωσε η βιβλιοθήκη και όχι με βάση τον αριθμό των έργων που δανείσθηκαν εκτός βιβλιοθήκης. Σας παρακαλούμε να σημειώσετε το συνολικό αριθμό των δανεισμών που έγιναν κατά τη διάρκιεα του έτους αναφοράς.

xvi)   ΜΗΚΟΣ ΡΑΦΙΩΝ:
       Μήκος ραφιών πού φέρουν βιβλία κλπ, σε μέτρα.

xvii) ΕΞΥΠΗΡΕΤΟΥΜΕΝΟΣ ΠΛΗΘΥΣΜΟΣ:
       Είναι ο συνολικός αριθμός των πιθανών χρηστών στη περιφέρεια μιάς βιβλιοθήκης, π.χ. για τις ΔΗΜΟΣΙΕΣ ΒΙΒΛΙΟΘΗΚΕΣ ο αριθμός αυτός αφορά το σύνολο των κατοίκων της διοικητικής περιφέρειας, για τις βιβλιοθήκες ανώτατων εκπαιδευτικών ιδρυμάτων το σύνολο των φοιτητών και των καθηγητών. Γενικά, εκτός από τις ΔΗΜΟΣΙΕΣ, ΕΘΝΙΚΕΣ και ΑΛΛΕΣ ΜΗ ΕΙΔΙΚΕΣ βιβλιοθήκες, οι εκτιμήσεις σας πρέπει να περιοριστούν στον αριθμό των κυριότερων πιθανών χρηστών αποκλείοντας το ευρύτερο κοινό έστω και αν κάνει καμιά φορά χρήση των υπηρεσιών της βιβλιοθήκης.

Ερώτηση 4η

xviii) ΕΚΠΑΙΔΕΥΜΕΝΟΙ ΒΙΒΛΙΟΘΗΚΑΡΙΟΙ:
       Πρόκειται για όλους τους υπαλλήλους που εργάζονται σε βιβλιοθήκη και που έχουν εκπαιδευθεί στον τομέα της βιβλιοθηκονομίας ή σε άλλες επιστήμες πληροφόρησης. Η εκπαίδευσή τους μπορεί να έγινε σε επίσημη ειδική σχολή ή με παρατεταμένες περιόδους μαθητείας σε βιβλιοθήκη κάτω από την εποπτεία ειδικών.

xviii) ΑΛΛΑ ΜΕΛΗ ΤΟΥ ΠΡΟΣΩΠΙΚΟΥ:
       Πρόκειται για το προσωπικό των βιβλιοθηκών που ασχολείται με βιβλιοθηκονομικά καθήκοντα κάτω από τη διεύθυνση της βιβλιοθήκης. Στην περίπτωση που το προσωπικό αυτό ασχολείται και με άλλα καθήκοντα (μη βιβλιοθηκονομίας) σας παρακαλούμε να εκτιμήσετε τις καθαρά βιβλιοθηκονομικές τους υπηρεσίες σε ισοδύναμο χρόνο πλήρους απασχόλησης.

Ερώτηση 6η   ΟΙΚΟΝΟΜΙΚΕΣ ΣΤΑΤΙΣΤΙΚΕΣ

xx)   ΔΑΠΑΝΕΣ:
       Είναι οι συνολικές εκτιμήσεις των ετήσιων δαπανών της βιβλιοθήκης. Αυτές οι εκτιμήσεις θα πρέπει να καταχωρηθούν όσο το δυνατό με μεγαλύτερη ακρίβεια στις ακόλουθες κατηγορίες δαπανών.

xxi)   ΔΑΠΑΝΕΣ ΠΡΟΣΩΠΙΚΟΥ:
       Πρόκειται για δαπάνες που αφορούν το προσωπικό, μισθοί, πληρωμή υπερωριών, εργοδοτικές εισφορές συνταξιοδότησης, δαπάνες επιμόρφωσης, δαπάνες ταξιδιού και διαμονής και κάθε άλλη αποζημίωση που αφορά το προσωπικό της σχετικής κατηγορίας βιβλιοθήκης. Επίσης πρέπει να περιλάβετε τις δαπάνες για εκείνο το προσωπικό που δεν υπάγεται στη διεύθυνση της βιβλιοθήκης αλλά που χρησιμοποιείται και χρηματοδοτείται από τη βιβλιοθήκη, π.χ. δικηγόροι, λογιστές, μηχανογράφοι, κλπ.

xxii) ΔΑΠΑΝΕΣ ΚΤΙΡΙΑΚΩΝ ΕΓΚΑΤΑΣΤΑΣΕΩΝ ΚΑΙ ΛΕΙΤΟΥΡΓΙΑΣ:
       Αφορούν το κόστος διαχείρισης των κτιρίων της βιβλιοθήκης: ενοίκια, φόρους ακίνητης περιουσίας, είδη καθαρισμού, ενέργεια, επισκευές και συντήρηση κλπ. Αποκλείονται οι δαπάνες για το προσωπικό (που πρέπει να περιληφθούν στην "Ερώτηση 4η") και τα οφειλόμενα δάνεια που έχουν συναφθεί από τη βιβλιοθήκη (και που πρέπει να καταχωρηθούν στις "Δαπάνες Δανεισμού Χρήματος").

xxiii)   ΚΑΙΝΟΥΡΓΙΑ ΚΤΙΡΙΑ/ΑΝΑΚΑΙΝΗΣΕΙΣ:
         Αφορούν δαπάνες οικοδόμησης καινούργιων κτιρίων ή επεκτάσεων ή σημαντικών αναχαινήσεων.

xxiv)   ΑΓΟΡΩΝ ΒΙΒΛΙΩΝ:
         Αφορούν τις δαπάνες αγορών για τη αύξηση των συλλογών. Παρακαλούμε μη συμπεριλάβετε τις δαπάνες για τη αγορά των εξοπλισμών (μηχανημάτων κλπ) και που προορίζονται για τη διεύθυνση και λειτουργία της βιβλιοθήκης (αυτές πρέπει να καταχωρηθούν στη κατηγορία "ΔΙΑΦΟΡΕΣ ΔΑΠΑΝΕΣ".

xv)   ΔΑΠΑΝΕΣ ΔΑΝΕΙΣΜΟΥ ΧΡΗΜΑΤΟΣ:
         Αφορούν τις εξοφλήσεις δανείων, και επίσης τις δαπάνες ενοικιάσεως κτιρίων που μπορεί να έχουν συναφθεί από τη σχετική κατηγορία βιβλιοθήκης.

xvi)   ΔΙΑΦΟΡΕΣ ΔΑΠΑΝΕΣ:
         Αφορούν όλες τις υπόλοιπες δαπάνες που έχουν σχέση με τη διαχείρηση και τη λειτουργία της βιβλιοθήκης κατά τη διάρκεια του έτους και που δεν περιλαμβάνονται στις προηγούμενες κατηγορίες.

xxvii)   ΕΣΟΔΑ:
         Είναι το σύνολο των εσόδων που εισπράττονται κατά τη διάρκεια του έτους αναφοράς και που προορίζονται για τη κάλυψη των δαπανών των διαφορετικών κατηγοριών βιβλιοθηκών.

xxviii) ΚΥΒΕΡΝΗΤΙΚΕΣ/ΤΟΠΙΚΕΣ ΧΡΗΜΑΤΟΔΟΤΗΣΕΙΣ (ΦΟΡΟΙ/ΕΠΙΧΟΡΗΓΗΣΕΙΣ):
         Αφορούν οποιαδήποτε χρηματοδότηση από τη κεντρική ή τοπική διοίκηση, είτε σαν επιχορήγηση ή σαν εισφορά για τις δαπάνες των διαφορετικών κατηγοριών βιβλιοθηκών.

xxix)   ΔΙΚΑΙΩΜΑΤΑ ΚΑΙ ΕΠΙΒΑΡΥΝΣΕΙΣ:
         Αφορούν όλα τα έσοδα απο δανεισμούς του υλικού κατά τη διάρκεια του έτους.

xxx)   ΑΛΛΑ ΕΣΟΔΑ:
         Αφορούν οποιαδήποτε άλλα έσοδα που δεν υπάγονται στις προηγούμενες κατηγορίες, όπως π.χ. εισπράξεις από πωλήσεις αγαθών, μεταβιβάσεις χρηματικών ποσών μεταξύ διαφόρων διοχήσεων κατά τη διάρκεια του οικονομικού έτους αναφοράς, από τόκους καταθέσεων, ιδιωτικές δωρεές ή ιδιωτικές πηγές.

xxxi)   ΚΕΦΑΛΑΙΟΥΧΙΚΕΣ ΔΑΠΑΝΕΣ:
         (π.χ. επενδύσεις σε καινούργιες βιβλιοθήκες ή ανακαινήσεις)
         Αφορούν οποιαδήποτε πληρωμή που γίνεται για τις κυριότερες δαπάνες που χρηματοδοτούνται είτε από εσωτερικά κεφαλαιουχικά κονδύλια της Διοίκησης είτε από δάνεια εξωτερικών πηγών.

xxxii)   ΑΛΛΕΣ ΔΑΠΑΝΕΣ ΚΕΦΑΛΑΙΟΥ:
         Αφορούν οποιεσδήποτε άλλες κεφαλαιουχικές δαπάνες που γίνονται για το σχετικό τομέα βιβλιοθηκών και που δεν καταχωρίζονται στις παραπάνω κατηγορίες.

xxxiii) ΤΡΕΧΟΝ ΧΡΕΟΣ:
         Πρόκειται για το συνολικό ποσό που δανείστηκε η βιβλιοθήκη για τη χρηματοδότηση κεφαλαιουχικών δαπανών, και η εξόφληση των οποίων δεν έχει γίνει ως το τέλος του έτους.

NOTE ESPLICATIVE DELLE DEFINIZIONI UTILIZZATE

BIBLIOTECA

BIBLIOTECHE NAZIONALI
Tali biblioteche, independentemente dalla denominazione, sono responsibili dell'acquisto e della conservazione di copie di tutte le pubblicazioni significative che escono nel paese in questione, fungendo altresi' da biblioteche di "deposito" ai sensi di disposizioni di legge o simili e eventualmente denominate "nazionali".

BIBLIOTECHE DI ISTITUTI DI ISTRUZIONE SUPERIORE
Trattasi di biblioteche che servono principalmente studenti E personale docente a livello universitario a di altri istituti di istruzione superiore.

ALTRE IMPORTANTI BIBLIOTECHE NON SPECIALIZZATE
Trattasi di biblioteche a carattere accademico peraltro non comprese nella categoria delle biblioteche di istituti di istruzione superiore o di quelle nazionali, benche possano svolgere le funzioni delle biblioteche nazionali per un'area geografica determinata.

BIBLIOTECHE SCOLASTICHE
Sono destinate principalmente a studenti E insegnanti di tutti i tipi di istituti scolastici al di sotto del livello universitario o superiore benche possano essere aperte al pubblico.

BIBLIOTECHE SPECIALIZZATE
Trattasi delle biblioteche mantenute da associazioni, servizi governativi o parlamentari, istituti di ricerca (esclusi quelli universitari), accademie, associazioni professionali, musei, imprese commerciali e industriali, camere di commercio ecc. o qualsiasi altro gruppo organizzato, limitate in gran parte a determinanti settori o soggetti (scienze naturali, scienze sociali, agricoltura, chimica, medicina, economia, ingegneria, diritto, storia)

BIBLIOTECHE PUBBLICHE
Biblioteche destinate a servire la popolazione di una comunita o regione gratuitamente o dietro correispettivi nominali. Tali biliotheche possono servire il grande pubblico ovvero particolari categorie di utenti come ad esempio bambini, membri delle forze armate, degenti ospedalieri, carcerati, operai, imprenditori.

DOMANDE 1 E 2 (RACCOLTA)

La domanda N. 1 chiede del numero totale di materiali tenuti dalle biblioteche sia quello in magazzino che quello fuori in prestito al 31 dicembre di ogni anno. Se il conto inventari corrisponde a una data diversa, annotatelo sul questionario.

La domanda N. 2 chiede del numero lordo di acquisiti effettuati dalle biblioteche in quell'anno, cioè, tutti gli acquisti di materiali inclusi quelli che vanno a sostituire perdite dovute a materiale non restituito, quello vecchio e altri tipi di spreco.

DEFINIZIONI

i) ANNI:
Se il periodo contabile utilizzato per le vostre statistiche non corrisponde ad anni di calendario, si prega di riportare i dati sotto l'anno comprendente la maggior parte del periodo a cui si riferiscono i resoconti, indicando sul questionario il periodo effettivamente coperto dalle statistiche. Ad esempio, se i dati si riferiscono ad un periodo annuale calcolato dal mese di aprile al marzo successivo, i dati vanno registrati in base all'anno di calendario comprendenti i primi nove mesi del periodo succitato, mentre il questionario deve recare l'indicazione "aprile/marzo".

Se i resoconti si referiscono al periodo luglio-fine giugno dell'anno successivo, registrare i dati sotto l'anno precedente, e utilizzare quello seguente soltanto se quest'ultimo comprende una percentuale maggiore del periodo coperto dai dati.

ii) UNITÀ AMMINISTRATIVA:
Una biblioteca indipendente o un gruppo di bilioteche sottoposte a un unico direttore o ad un' unica amministrazione.

iii) PUNTO DI SERVIZIO:
Qualsiasi biblioteca presso la quale venga fornito, in sede separata, un servizio agli utenti. Le biblioteche indipendenti, le biblioteche centrali a quelle distaccate (furgoni statici e mobili, biblioteche di bordo) vengono considerate punti di servizio, purchè gli utenti vengano serviti direttamente. I punti "statici" sono dunque quelli che forniscono un servizio a partire da un punto fisso; quelli "mobili" sono costituiti da un veicolo che si sposta in varie località in funzione degli utenti. Le fermate di una biblioteca su ruote non sono considerate punti di servizio. Gli eventuali veicoli utilizzati esclusivamente per il trasporto di materiale fra i diversi edifici di una biblioteca non vanno compresi fra i punti di servizi "mobili".

iv) RACCOLTA:
Tutti i materiali di bilioteca a disposizione degli utenti. Le relative statistiche dovrebbero comprendere soltanto le seguenti categorie di materiale a disposizione degli utenti, compreso il materiale in prestito: -

v) LIBRI E PERIODICI RILEGATI:
I "libri" vanno conteggiati per volume. In questo contesto, un volume comprende materiale riprodotto (microforme eccettuate) constituente una unità fisica di opera stampata contenuta in una copertina o raccoglitore. I "periodici" vanno conteggiati per titolo in una serie continua di pubblicazioni che vengano acquisite per un periodo di tempo indeterminato, benchè tali acquisizioni possano verificarsi a intervalli regolari o irregolari. Gli annuari sono inclusi, ma le serie mongrafiche sonon escluse. I periodici rilegati vanno conteggiati come signole unità fisiche rilegate. Includere i giornali ed altre pubblicazioni datate o numerate che escono con frequenza annuale o anche minore.

vi) TITOLI PERIODICI CORRENTI:
Devono essere indicati dal numero di periodici ricevuti dalla biblioteca nell'anno di conteggio.

vii) MANOSCRITTI:
Qualsiasi manoscritto a disegno originale contenuto in una rilegatura o raccoglitore.

viii) MICROFORME:
Riproduzione microstampate di opere o pubblicazioni originali, comprese le copie microfilmate di manoscritti.

ix) MATERIALI AUDIOVISIVI:
Comprendono materiali di bilioteca che non costituiscono libri o microforme, e richiedono per la visualizzazione o l'ascolto l'impiego di apparecchiature speciali, come ad esempio dischi fonografici, nastri magnetici, cassette, cds, pellicole cinematografiche, nastri video, diapositive, veline ecc.

x) ALTRI MATERIALI:
Tutti gli altri materiali raccolti dalle biblioteche e destinati alla consultazione da parte degli utenti, come carte geografiche e topografiche, riproduzione, fotografie, diorama ecc., escludendo libri, periodici, manoscritti, microforme e materiali audiovisivi.

xi) ACQUISIZIONI:
Trattasi di tutte le acquisizioni effetuate durante l'anno a beneficio degli utenti, senza dedurre le perdite dovute a eliminazione o distruzioni di materiali. Includere qualsiasi tipo di aggiunta che sia stata fatta tramite acquisto, donazione, scambio o qualsiasi altro metodo di acquisizione. Includere, tuttavia, solo le aggiunte per le categorie deil materiali elencati nelle categorie del questionario (cioè: libri, periodici, manoscritti, microforme, audio visivi e altri.)

Domanda N. 3

xii) UTENTI DELLE BIBLIOTECHE: Soltanto le Biblioteche Nazionali
Chiunque utilizzi i servizi delle biblioteche durante l'anno di contaggio.

xiii) CONSULTAZIONI BIBLIOTECARIE:
Trattasi solo di Biblioteche nazionali. Il numero delle richeiste formali di assistenza

xiv) UTENTI ESTERNI:
I scritti su apposito registro e autorizzati al prestito dei materiali all'esterno della biblioteca. Conteggiare soltanto i soggetti registrati nell'anno specificato, e non confondere la categoria con quella degli "utenti della biblioteca", che costituiscono tutti coloro che utilizzano i servizi.

xv) TRANSAZIONI DI PRESTITO:
Vanno conteggiate in base al numero di richieste ricevute (e soddisfatte) anziche semplicemente in base al numero delle opere prestate. Indicare il numero totale delle transazioni soddisfatte nel corso dell'anno.

xvi) LUNGHEZZA DEGLI SCAFFALI OCCUPATI
Indicare la lunghezza, in metri, degli scaffali occupati dalla raccolta messa a disposizione degli utenti.

xvii) POPOLAZIONE SETTORIALE SERVITA:
Il numero totale degli utenti potenziali nell'aria geografica o tematica servita dalle biblioteche: ad esempio, nel caso di biblioteche PUBBLICHE, si tratterà della popolazione totale dell'area amministrativa di competenza; per biblioteche al servizio di istituti di ISTRUZIONE SUPERIORE, la "popolazione settoriale" sarà costituita dal numero degli studenti e insegnanti interessati. In via generale, eccesion fatta per le biblioteche PUBBLICHE, NAZIONALI e ALTRE NON SPECIALIZZATE, limitare la stima della "popolazione settoriale" al numero potenziale degli utenti primari delle biblioteche ad esclusione del pubblico generale, anche se quest'ultimo può utilizzare saltuariamente i servizi.

Domanda No. 4

xviii) PERSONALE SPECIALIZZATO:
Tutto il personale della biblioteca dotato di formazione professionale in materiale di biblioteconomia o scienza dell' informazione. La formazione può essere a carattere scolastico effettuata direttamente secondo il metodo dell'apprendistato.

xix) ALTRO PERSONALE DI BIBLIOTECA:
Va compreso tutto il rimanente personale, alle dipendenze del o dei direttori, che esercita funzioni di biblioteca e personale addizionli necessari per assicurare il buon funzionamento delle biblioteche, ma che non sone alle dirette dipendenze dei direttori delle medesime. Può trattarsi di contabili e d'altro personale adibito a servizi di sostegno, la cui attività lavorativa interessa parzialmente le biblioteche sotto il profilo amministrativo, direttamente o su contratto.

Domanda N. 5 - Statistiche Finanziarie

xx) SPESA:
Si riferisce al totale della spesa stimata per la gestione del settore biblioteche durante l'anno. Queste spese andrebbero per quanto possibile riportate nelle categorie seguenti:

xxi) PERSONALE DELLA BIBLIOTECA:
Comprende retribuzioni, pagamenti per lavoro straordinario, contributi di sicurezza sociale a carico del datore di lavoro, costi di formazione, spese di viaggio e soggiorno ed altri emolumenti corrisposti al personale impiegato per lo svolgimento di attività relative a funzioni di biblioteca. Dovrebbe comprendere la stima più attendibile del costo attribuibile per il personale nonchè spese generali per infrastrutture/elaborazione elettronica/azioni legali/contabilità/ed altre spese di sostegno incorse dall'amministrazione per il SETTORE biblioteche, non alle dirette dipendenze del direttore o dei direttori delle biblioteche.

xxii) SPESA PER LE INFRASTRUTTURE:
Comprende il costo di gestione della sede delle biblioteche: affitti; imposte fondiarie; materiali di pulizia; costi energetici; riparazioni e manutenzzione ecc. Si prega di escludere i costi per il personale che dovrebbero essere invece compresi nella categoria "PERSONALE", e anche di non includere il costo di mutui contratti per spese infrastrutturali, che dovrebbero essere compresi nella categoria "ONERI E RIMBORSO PRESTITI".

xxiii) NUOVI EDIFICI/RISTRUTTURAZIONI:
Si riferisce alle principali spese per le migliorie sostanziali alle strutture di biblioteche già esistenti o per la costruzione di nuovi edifici.

xxiv) SPESE PER ACQUISIZIONI:
Si riferisce alle spese per acquisizioni di materiali entrati a far parte delle raccolte a disposizione degli utenti. Escludere invece il costo relativo ad acquisti di apparecchiature destinate ad atttività di amministrazione/gestione delle biblioteche (da comprendersi nella voce "SPESE MISCELLANEE").

xxv) ONERI E RIMBORSO PRESTITI:
Si riferisce al rimborso di capitale e interesse per prestiti contratti in riferimento a beni delle biblioteche.

xxvi) SPESE MISCELLANEE:
Tutte le altre spese sostenute per la gestione del settore biblioteche durante l'anno.

xxvii) INTROITI TOTALI:
Tutte le somme ricevute nel corso dell'anno a fronte dei costi del SETTORE biblioteche.

xxviii) FONDI GOVERNATIVI/MUNCIPALI (Tasse/Sussidi)
Qualsiasi somma ricevuta dal governo centrale o locale, sia nella forma di sussidio o contributo al sostenimento del settore bibliotecario.

xxix) TARIFFE E ADDEBITI
Si intendono, tutte le entrate commerciali ottenute dall'amministrazione delle biblioteche durante l'anno contabile.

xxx) ALTRE ENTRATE
Qualsiasi altro tipo di entrata riscontrata durante l'anno, non specificata direttamente nelle categorie sopraccitate, tra cui: il ricavato dalle vendite di capitale, trasferimento di denaro tra amministrazioni durante l'anno contabile, interessi bancari maturati, donazioni private o sponsorizzazioni.

xxxi) SPESE D'INVESTIMENTO
Es:. investimenti in nuove biblioteche o per ristrutturazioni.
Qualsiasi pagamento effettuato per spese principali stanziate da Fondi d'Investimento Interni dell'amministrazione o da prestiti da fonti esterne.

xxxii) ALTRE SPESE D'INVESTIMENTO
Tutte le altre spese d'investimento incorse a seguito della fornitura del settore biblioteche non specificate nei settori soppraccitati.

xxxiii) DEBITO RIMANENTE:
L'ammontare dei prestiti contratti per il finanziamento di spese in conto capitale non ancora rimborsato all fine dell'anno.

NOTAS DE DIRECCION

SECTORES DE LA BIBLIOTECA
Los 6 sectores de la biblioteca incluidos en este estudio corresponden directamente a las definiciones de la UNESCO, particularmente:

BIBLIOTECAS NACIONALES:
Bibliotecas que, a pesar de su titulo, son responsables de la adquisicion y conservacion de copias de publicaciones significantes producidas en este pais y que funcionan como biblioteca 'deposito', sea por ley u otros acuerdos, y que normalmente compilan una bibliografia nacional.

BIBLIOTECAS DE INSTITUCIONES DE EDUCACION ELEVADA:
Bibliotecas que primordialmente asisten a estudiantes y profesores en universiadades y otras instituciones de tercer grado.

OTRAS BIBLIOTECAS MAYORES NO-ESPECIALIZADAS:
Bibliotecas no-especializadas de caracter instruido que no sean bibliotecas de instituciones de educaion elevada ni bibliotecas nacionales, pero que pueden cumplir las funciones de una biblioteca nacional para un sector geografico especifico.

BIBLIOTECAS DE COLEGIOS:
Aquellas adjunta a todo tipos de colegios y escuelas por debajo del tercer grado de educacion y asisten primordialmente a los estudiantes y profesores de tales colegios y escuelas, aunque estas puedan ser utilizadas por el publico en general.

BIBLIOTECAS ESPECIALES:
Aquellas sostenidas por una asociacion, administracion publica, parlamento, institucion de investigacion (excluyendo instituciones universitarias), sociedad instructora, asociacion profesional, museo, compañia de negocios, empresa industrial, camara de comercio, etc u otro grupo organisado, la cual la mayor parte de sus colecciones cubren un tema o campo especifico, p.e. ciencias naturales, ciencias sociales, agricultura, quimica, medicina, economias, ingenieria, derechos, historia.

BIBLIOTECAS PUBLICAS:
Aquellas que asisten a la poblacion de una comunidad o region, gratuitamente o bajo una cuota nominal; pueden servir al publico en general o categorias especiales de usuarios tales como niños, miembros de las fuerzas armadas, pacientes hospitalizados, presos, obreros y empleados.

PREGUNTAS 1 Y 2 (Coleccionee)
Pregunta No. 1 solicita el numero total de materiales mantenidos por la biblioteca tanto en existencia como en prestamo, en el 31 de diciembre de cada año. Si el inventario corresponde a fecha distinta, por favor anotenla en el cuestionario.

Pregunta No.2 solcita el numero grueso de adquisiciones hechas por la biblioteca durante ese año, es decir todas las adquisiciones de materiales incluyendo aquellas de reemplazos por perdidas a causa de no-devolucion, antigüedad u otras formas de desgaste.

DEFINICIONES

i) Año

Si su periodo de cuentas (estadisticas) no corresponden al año del calendario, por favor haga su respuesta bajo el año que cubra la mayoria del periodo al cual sus cuentas se refieren. Por ejemplo, si sus estadisticas cubren el año correspondiente del 1 de abril al 31 de mazo, si su año fuese el 1 de abril de 1986 al 31 de marzo de 1987 anoten estos en el espacio para el año que finaliza 1986, ya que la mayoria de su periodo de cuentas (9 meses) se relaciona con el año del calendario de 1986. Tambien anoten en su cuestionario que el periodo de cuentas es del 1 abril al 31 de marzo.

Si sus cuentas se refieren al periodo 1 de julio al 30 de junio, p.e. 1 de julio de 1986 al 30 de junio de 1987, anoten este periodo en el año del calendario en el que finaliza 1986 y tambien conforme al cuestionario. Si su año de cuentas comienza y termina en diferentes puntos del año, entonces asigne su año de cuentas al año del calendario que mas mayoritariamente cubra su periodo de cuentas, tal como queda entendido por los ejemplos superiores.

ii) UNIDAD ADMINISTRATIVA:

Cualquier grupo de bibliotecas, o biblioteca independiente, bajo un director unico o administracion unica.

iii) PUNTO DE SERVICIO:

Lugar designado o area que proporciona un servicio a los usuarios de la biblioteca, Bibliotecas independientes, bibliotecas centrales y sucursales (tanto estaticas como moviles) son consideradas como puntos de servicio, mientras que estas asistan a sus usuarios directamente y no por medio de una tercera persona. Por lo tanto, puntos 'estaticos' son aquellos que proporcionan un servicio desde un punto fijo; y ' moviles' son aquellos que desde un vehiculo se mueve hacia varias localizaciones para facilitar posibles usuarios hacer uso del servicio bibliotecario. El vehiculo bibliotecario como tal representa un punto de servicio; el numero de paradas que hace en sus viajes NO constituyen puntos des servicios moviles. Vehiculos utilizados unicamente para el transporte de materiales entre una biblioteca y otra NO constituyen puntos de servicios moviles.

iv) COLECCION:

Todo material bibliotecario a disposicion de los usuarios de la biblioteca. Estadisticas relacionadas a las colecciones bibliotecarias deben solo cubrir los siguientes documentos disponibles a los usuarios incluyendo una concesion para materiales en prestamo:-

v) **LIBROS Y PERIODICOS ENCUADERNADOS:**
'Libros' deben ser contados por volumen. En este contexto, un volumen incluye material reproducido (excepto microformas), formando una unidad fisica de cualquier obra impresa contenida en un encuadernado o carpeta.

'Periodicos' son definidos como series continua sobre un periodo indefinido donde copias individuales en las series son numeradas consecutivamente o donde cada copia es fechada. Anuarios quedan incluidos; pero series monograficas quedan excluidas. Periodicos encuadernados deben ser contados como unidades fisicas. Periodicos no encuadernados (no corrientes) deben ser incluidos en la cuenta como si fuesen coleccionados en unidades fisicas encuadernadas. Los diarios quedan incluidos y deben ser contados en volumenes o paquetes.

vi) **TITULOS DE PERIODICOS CORRIENTES:**
El numero de titulos de periodicos recibido por la Biblioteca durante el año en cuenta.

vii) **MANUSCRITOS:**
Cualquier obra original escrita o dibujada a mano contenida en una encuadernacion o carpeta.

viii) **MICROFORMAS:**
Reproducciones micro-impresa de obras o publicaciones originales incluyendo copias de peliculas micro-reducida de manuscritos.

ix) **MATERIALES AUDIO-VISUAL:**
Estos incluyen materiales de biblioteca que no sean libros ni microformas y que requieran uso de equipo especial para poder ser visto y/o oido; p.e. discos, cintas, cassettes, discos compactos, peliculas de cine, cintas video, diapositivas y transparencias.

x) **OTRO MATERIAL:**
Aquellos articulos provistos por bibliotecas para uso de referencia tales como mapas, cartas graficas, grabados, fotografias, dioramas, etc. pero excluyendo libros, periodicos, manuscritos, microformas y materiales audio-visual.

xi) **ADICIONES:**
El numero de adiciones hechas a las colecciones durante el año en que estas fueron puestas a disposicion de los usuarios. Esto debe enseñar el numero total de adiciones antes de que se deduzca perdidas de las colecciones por desecho, desgaste o extravio. Por favor incluyan todas las adiciones ya sean por compra, donacion, intercambio o por cualquier otro modo de ganancia a la coleccion. Sin embargo, solo incluya adiciones para las categorias de materiales enumeradas en las categorias del cuestionario (es decir, Libros, Periodicos, Manuscritos, Microformas, Audio-visual y Otros).

PREGUNTA 3

xii) USUARIOS DE LA BIBLIOTECA: Bibliotecas Nacionales unicamente
Cualiquier persona utilisando los servicios de la biblioteca/s en el año en cuenta.

xiii) CONSULTAS A LA BIBLIOTECA: Bibliotecas Nacionales unicamente
El numero de solicitudes formales de asistencia.

xiv) PRESTATARIOS REGISTRADOS:
Aquellas personas registradas con la biblioteca en orden de que puedan alquilar material de la misma para uso externo de los limites bibliotecarios. Por favor cuenten solamente el numero de personas registradas en el año especificado; no confundir este termino con el de 'usuarios de la biblioteca' ya que estas son personas que utilizan CUALQUIERA de los servicios de la biblioteca y no especificamente el prestamo de materiales.

xv) TRAMITACION DE PRESTAMOS:
Esto debe calcularse segun el numero de obras prestadas y de copias provistas en su lugar; es decir libros, periodicos y manuscritos prestados deben ser contados por el numero de volumenes y el numero des copias producidas para tomar el lugar de los materiales originales contados por volumenes.

xvi) LONGITUD DE ESTANTERIAS OCUPADAS:
Longitud de estanterias, en metros, de la coleccion disponible a usuarios.

xvii) SECTOR DE POBLACION ATENDIDA:
El numero total de posibles usuarios, en el area geografico o tematico, asistidos por la biblioteca/s; p.e. para bibliotecas PUBLICAS esto seria el numero total de habitantes en el area administrativo; para bibliotecas asistiendo a instituciones de EDUCAION ELEVADA, el 'sector de poblacion' seria el numero de estudiantes y profesores asistidos. Como regla general, con la excepcion de bibliotecas PUBLICAS, NACIONALES y OTRAS NO-ESPECIALIZADAS, limitan el calculo del 'sector de poblacion' al numero posible de usuarios primarios de las bibliotecas, excluyendo al publico en general, aunque estos ultimos utilizen las facilidades de vez en cuando.

PREGUNTA 4

xviii) BIBLIOTECARIOS FORMADOS:
Todos los miembros del personal que haya recibido una formacion general en bibliotecaria o ciencia informativa. La formacion puede ser por metodos formales o por medio de periodos extensivos de trabajo en una biblioteca bajo vigilancia profesional

xix) OTROS EMPLEADOS DE LA BIBLIOTECA:
Por favor incluya todo el personal que estan bajo la vigilancia directa del Director/es de la Biblioteca/s y que estan empleados para funciones bibliotecarias Y tambien el personal requerido para servir propiamente a la biblioteca/s pero que no estan necesariamenta bajo la vigilancia directa del Director/es, es decir el personal de soporte. Esto puede incluir a contadores y otro 'personal de apoyo', los cuales pasan parte del tiempo en asuntos de la biblioteca para la administracion, bien como empleados de tal administracion o por contrato.

PREGUNTA 5 ESTADISTICAS ECONOMICAS

xx) GASTOS:
Gastos relacionados al presupuesto de gastos TOTAL del sector bibliotecario para el ano financiero. Este gasto debe justificarse lo mas posible bajo los siguientes titulares:

xxi) PERSONAL:
Esta cifra incluye salarios, pagos de horas extras, cotizacion de la empresa para las pensiones, costes de formacion profesional, gastos de viajes y subsistencia, y otros emolumentos de personal relacionado a todos los empleados que trabajan dentro del sector bibliotecario. Debe tambien incluir su mejor calculo acerca del personal repartido y de otros encabezamientos como edificios/ordenadores/legal/contadores y otras mantenciones incurridas por la administracion del SECTOR de la biblioteca que queda fuera de la vigilancia directa del Director/es de la Biblioteca/s.

xxii) LOCALES Y GASTOS DE FUNCIONAMIENTO:
Todos los articulos relacionados con los gastos de funcionamiento de la biblioteca, tales como rentas; impuestos de propiedad; materiales de limpieza; gastos de energia; reparacion y mantenimiento, etc.
Por favor excluya el gasto del personal ya que este debe ser incluido en la categoria de 'PERSONAL'. Por favor no incluya el coste de prestamos pendientes incurridos en los edificios de la biblioteca, esto debe ser incluido en ' GASTOS DE PRESTAMOS'.

xxiii) NUEVOS EDIFICIOS/RENOVACION:
Se relaciona a gastos significantes a mejoras materiales a la estructura de edificio/s bibliotecario/s existente o a la construccion de un nuevo edificio.

xxiv) ADQUISICIONES DE RESERVA:
Se relaciona a gastos en la adquisicion de materiales para realzar la coleccion disponible a los usuarios. Por favor no incluya el coste de compras de equipo para uso de la administracion/gestion (esto debe ser incluido bajo 'GASTOS DIVERSOS').

xxv) GASTOS DE PRESTAMOS:
La devolucion de prestamos y acuerdos de arrendamiento establecidos por el SECTOR bibliotecario.

xxvi) DIVEROS:
Todo otros gastos incurridos para el coste de funcionamiento de SECTOR bibliotecario durante el año y que no estan especificamente detallados en las categorias superiores.

xxvii) INGRESOS:
Todo los recibos del año en cuenta utilizado para compensar el coste del SECTOR bibliotecario.

xxviii) FONDOS GUVERNAMENTALES/MUNICIPALES (IMPUESTOS/CONCESIONES):
Dineros recibido del gobierno central o local, sea en forma de concesion o contribucion al mantenimiento del SECTOR bibliotecario.

xxix) CUOTAS Y COBROS:
Todo ingreso comercial recibido por la administracion de la biblioteca/s durante el año en cuenta.

xxx) OTROS INGRESOS:
Cualquier otro ingreso habido durante al año que no este directamente especificado en las categorias superiores, p.e. intergros de ventas de bienes; transferencias de dineros entre diferentes administraciones durante el año en cuenta; interes obtenido en saldos bancarios; donaciones privadas o ingresos patrocinados.

xxxi) GASTOS DE CAPITAL:
(es decir, inversiones en bibliotecas nuevas o renovaciones)
Cualquier pago de gastos mayores extraidos de los Fondos del Capital Interno de la Administracion o de prestamos de fuentes externas.

xxxii) OTROS GASTOS DE CAPITAL:
Todo otro gasto de capital incurrido en el coste del suministro del sector de la biblioteca y que no esta especificamente incluido en los sectores superiores.

xxxiii) DEUDAS PENDIENTES:
El total acumulado de prestamo para financiar los gastos de Capital que quedan por pagar al final del año.

VÄGLEDNING FÖR BESVARANDET AV ENKÄTEN

BIBLIOTEKESSEKTORER

De 6 bibliotekssektorer inkluderade i denna undersökning motsvarar exakt UNESCOs definitioner, nämligen:

NATIONELLA BIBLIOTEK:

Bibliotek som, oavsett namn, är ansvariga för att anskaffa och bevara exemplar av betydande publikationer producerade i landet, och vilka fungerar som "källbibliotek", antingen enligt lag eller genom annat arrangemang och tjänar normalt som nationella bibliografier.

INSTITUTIONSBIBLIOTEK FÖR HÖGRE UTBILDNING

Bibliotek som huvudsakligen betjänar studerande och lärare vid universitet och andra institutioner för utbildning på högre nivå.

ÖVRIGA BETYDANDE ICKE-SPECIALISERADE BIBLIOTEK

Icke-specialiserade bibliotek av vetenskaplig karaktär, vilka varken är institutionsbibliotek för högre utbildning eller nationella bibliotek, även om de kan fylla ett nationalbiblioteks funktioner för ett specifikt geografiskt område.

SKOLBIBLIOTEK:

Bibliotek knutna till alla typer av skolor, utom skolor för högre utbildning, och vilka huvudsakligen betjänar elever och lärare i sådana skolor, även om de också kan vara öppna för allmänheten.

SPECIALBIBLIOTEK:

Bibliotek upprätthållna av en sammanslutning, statligt serviceorgan, riksdag, forskningsinstitut (utom universitetsinstitut), vetenskaplig förening, yrkessammanslutning, museum, affärsföretag, industriföretag, handelskammare, etc eller annan organiserad grupp, vars samlingar till största delen täcker ett speciellt område eller ämne t.ex. naturvetenskap, socialkunskap, lantbruksvetenskap, kemi, medicin, ekonomi, ingenjörsvetenskap, rättsvetenskap, historia.

OFFENTLIGA BIBLIOTEK/LÄNS-STADS-FOLKBIBLIOTEK

Sådana som betjänar befolkningen i en kommun eller region utan att ta ut avgift eller för en nominell avgift; de kan betjäna allmänheten eller särskilda kategorier såsom barn, medlemmar av försvaret, sjukhuspatienter, fängelseinterner, arbetare och anställda.

där enstaka exemplar i serien är numrerade i löpande ordning eller varje nummer är daterat. Årsskrifter skall inkluderas men monografiska serier räknas ej. Inbundna tidskriftsårgångar skall räknas som fysiska enheter. Lösnummer av icke aktuella tidskrifter bör räknas som om de vore samlade i fysiska enheter. Dagstidningar är också inkluderade och bör räknas i volymer eller paket.

vi) **AKTUELLA TIDSKRIFTSTITLAR:**
Antalet tidskriftstitlar biblioteket erhåller under redovisningsåret.

vii) **MANUSKRIPT:**
Alla handskrivna eller ritade arbeten i original inrymda i ett band eller en mapp.

viii) **MIKROFICHE:**
Mikrotryckta reproduktioner av originalarbeten eller publikationer inklusive mikrofilmade kopior av manuskript.

xi) **AUDIO-VISUELLT MATERIAL:**
Detta innefattar material vilket inte är i bokform eller mikroformat och som fordrar särskild utrustning för att ses och/eller höras, t.ex. grammofonskivor, band, kassetter, CD-skivor, filmer, videoband, diabilder och material för overheadprojektor.

x) **ÖVRIGT MATERIAL:**
Sådana artiklar vilka biblioteket tillhandahåller som referensmaterial som kartor, tabeller och diagram, konstreproduktioner, fotografier, diorama etc, men ej böcker, tidskrifter, manuskript, mikrofiche och audio-visuellt material.

xi) **TILLSKOTT:**
Alla tillskott under året vilka var tillgängliga för låntagare. Detta bör visa det totala antalet tillskott innan avdrag gjorts för förluster p.g.a. utrangering och svinn. Var god inkludera alla tillskott vare sig genom inköp, donation, utbyte eller genom andra metoder till gagn för samlingen. Inkludera emellertid endast tillskott för kategorier angivna i enkäten (böcker, tidskrifter, manuskript, mikrofiche, audio-visuella och övrigt).

FRÅGA 3

xii) **LÅNTAGARE: Endast nationalbibliotek**
Alla personer som använder sig av de tjänster biblioteket(en) tillhandahåller under redovisningsåret.

xiii) **FÖRFRÅGNINGAR TILL BIBLIOTEKET:**
Endast nationella bibliotek: Antalet formella önskemål om hjälp.

xiv) **REGISTRERADE LÅNTAGARE:**
Personer registrerade hos biblioteket för att låna material från biblioteket för användning annorstädes. Var god räkna endast de personer registrerade under det specificerade året; förväxla inte denna term med "låntagare", vilka är personer som använder sig av bibliotekets alla tjänster och inte endast hemlån.

xxii) **LOKALER OCH DRIFTSKOSTNADER:**
Alla poster som gäller driften av biblioteket såsom hyror, fastighetsskatt, rengöringsmateriel, energikostnader, reparationer och underhåll etc. Ta inte upp kostnader för personal, vilka bör ingå i "PERSONAL"kategorin. Var god inkludera inte heller kostnader för obetalda lån för bibliotekslokaler. Dessa bör införas under LÅNEKOSTNADER.

xxiii) **NYA BYGGNADER/RENOVERINGAR:**
Detta gäller betydande utgifter för materiella förbättringar av konstruktionen av existerande biblioteks lokal(er) eller för uppförandet av en ny byggnad.

xxiv) **ANSKAFFNING AV LAGER:**
Gäller anskaffandet av material(böcker etc) för att förbättra samlingen tillgänglig för låntagare. Var god inkludera ej kostnader för inköp av utrustning för bibliotekets administration (detta bör införas under DIVERSE utgifter)

xxv) **LÅNEKOSTNADER:**
Ränta och amortering på lån och leasing-överenskommelser för biblioteksSEKTORN.

xxvi) **DIVERSE:**
Alla andra utgifter för driften av biblioteksSEKTORN under året och vilka ej är specificerade i ovanstående kategorier.

xxvii) **INTÄKTER**
Alla inkomster under räkenskapsåret och som använts för att bestrida utgifterna för biblioteksSEKTORN.

xxviii) **STATS/KOMMUN BIDRAG (SKATTER/ANSLAG):**
Alla penningmedel erhållna från stat eller kommun, vare sig i form av anslag eller bidrag för underhåll av biblioteksSEKTORN.

xxix) **AVGIFTER:**
Alla inkomster biblioteket erhåller inom bibliotekets lokaler t.ex. böter, ev. försäljning.

xxx) **ÖVRIGA INTÄKTER:**
Alla andra inkomster under året vilka ej är direkt specificerade i ovanstående kategorier. Exempel kan inkludera intäkter från försäljning av tillgångar, överföring av medel mellan olika administrationer, ränteinkomster på bankmedel, privata donationer eller inkomster från sponsorer.

xxxi) **KAPITALUTGIFTER:**
(dvs investeringar i nya bibliotek eller renoveringar)
Alla betydande utgifter finansierade antingen med interna kapitaltillgångar från administrationen eller med lån från external källor.

xxxii) **ÖVRIGA KAPITALUTGIFTER:**
Alla andra kapitalutgifter för att täcka kostnader för bibliotekssektorn och vilka ej är inkluderade i ovanstående kategorier.

SECTOR 1 : NATIONAL LIBRARIES

PLEASE REFER TO THE ACCOMPANYING NOTES OF GUIDANCE

NAME OF COUNTRY _____

For your guidance and background information, we have included the data which we have already collated from various sources and our previous study. **Our primary concern is to collect data relating to 1986 - 1990.** However should you have any queries about the data relating to 1981-1985 please raise these with us. The figures in *italics* represent estimates made in our previous study; the shaded figures represent figures from UNESCO sources; and the figures in **bold** type have been taken from your national publications. Please fill in the gaps and verify the pre-printed data.

Question 1

i) Number at year end:

	1981	1982	1983	1984	1985	1986	1987	1988	1989	1990
ii) Administrative Units										
iii) Service Points										
iv) Collections :										
v) Books & Bound Periodicals										
vi) Current Periodical Titles										
vii) Manuscripts										
viii) Microforms										
ix) Audio-visual										
x) Other Material										

Question 2

xi) Additions (GROSS) during the year

	1981	1982	1983	1984	1985	1986	1987	1988	1989	1990
ii) Administrative Units										
iii) Service Points										
iv) Collections :										
v) Books & Bound Periodicals										
vii) Manuscripts										
viii) Microforms										
ix) Audio-visual										
x) Other Material										

Question 3

General information concerning usage and capacity

	1981	1982	1983	1984	1985	1986	1987	1988	1989	1990
xii) Library Users										
xiii) Library Consultations										
xvi) Length of Occupied Shelving(Metres)										
xvii) Sector Population served										

Question 4

Library employees expressed as FTE

	1981	1982	1983	1984	1985	1986	1987	1988	1989	1990
xviii) Trained Librarians										
xix) Other Library Staff										

PLEASE TURN OVER

Question 5 *National Library Expenditure & Income* *PLEASE INCLUDE ALL EXPENDITURE INCURRED DURING THE YEAR OF ACCOUNT*

(Expressed in National currency, outturn prices.)

	1981	1982	1983	1984	1985	1986	1987	1988	1989	1990
xx) **EXPENDITURE**										
xxi) Staff										
xxii) Premises and Operating Costs										
xxiii) New Buildings \ Refurbishment										
xxiv) Acquisition of stock										
xxv) Cost of Borrowing										
xxvi) Miscellaneous										
TOTAL EXPENDITURE										

	1981	1982	1983	1984	1985	1986	1987	1988	1989	1990
xxvii) **INCOME**										
xxviii) Government \ Municipal Funding										
xxix) Fees & Charges										
xxx) Other Income										
TOTAL INCOME										

MEMORANDUM :

If it is possible to differentiate between capital and revenue expenditure please complete the following :

If these costs are included above please tick this box ☐

	1981	1982	1983	1984	1985	1986	1987	1988	1989	1990
xxxi) CAPITAL EXPENDITURE										
xxiii) New Buildings \ Refurbishment										
xxiv) Acquisition of stock										
xxxii) Other Capital Expenditure										
TOTAL CAPITAL										
xxxiii) OUTSTANDING DEBT										

(i.e. borrowing remaining to be paid at the end of the year)

Name of Person Completing this form : _____   Telephone No. & Extension : _____

Address (including Department) : _____

THANK-YOU FOR YOUR HELP IN COMPLETING THIS FORM.

SECTOR 2 : LIBRARIES IN INSTITUTIONS OF HIGHER EDUCATION

NAME OF COUNTRY _____

PLEASE REFER TO THE ACCOMPANYING NOTES OF GUIDANCE

For your guidance and background information, we have included the data which we have already collated from various sources and our previous study. **Our primary concern is to collect data relating to 1986 - 1990.** However should you have any queries about the data relating to 1981-1985 please raise these with us. The figures in *italics* represent estimates made in our previous study; the shaded figures represent figures from UNESCO sources; and the figures in **bold** type have been taken from your national publications. Please fill in the gaps and verify the pre-printed data.

Question 1

i) Number at year end:

	1981	1982	1983	1984	1985	1986	1987	1988	1989	1990
ii) Administrative Units										
iii) Service Points										

iv) Collections :

	1981	1982	1983	1984	1985	1986	1987	1988	1989	1990
v) Books & Bound Periodicals										
vi) Current Periodical Titles										
vii) Manuscripts										
viii) Microforms										
ix) Audio-visual										
x) Other Material										

Question 2

xi) Additions (GROSS) during the year

	1981	1982	1983	1984	1985	1986	1987	1988	1989	1990
ii) Administrative Units										
iii) Service Points										

Question 3

	1981	1982	1983	1984	1985	1986	1987	1988	1989	1990
v) Books & Bound Periodicals										
vii) Manuscripts										
viii) Microforms										
ix) Audio-visual										
x) Other Material										

General information concerning usage and capacity

	1981	1982	1983	1984	1985	1986	1987	1988	1989	1990
xiv) Registered Borrowers										
xv) Loan Transactions to Users										
xvi) Length of Occupied Shelving (Metres)										
xvii) Sector Population served										

Question 4

Library employees expressed as FTE

	1981	1982	1983	1984	1985	1986	1987	1988	1989	1990
xviii) Trained Librarians										
xix) Other Library Staff										

PLEASE TURN OVER

Question 5

Institutions of Higher Education Library Expenditure & Income

PLEASE INCLUDE ALL EXPENDITURE INCURRED DURING THE YEAR OF ACCOUNT

(Expressed in National currency, outturn prices.)

	1981	1982	1983	1984	1985	1986	1987	1988	1989	1990
xx) EXPENDITURE										
xxi) Staff										
xxii) Premises and Operating Costs										
xxiii) New Buildings / Refurbishment										
xxiv) Acquisition of stock										
xxv) Cost of Borrowing										
xxvi) Miscellaneous										
TOTAL EXPENDITURE										

	1981	1982	1983	1984	1985	1986	1987	1988	1989	1990
xxvii) INCOME										
xxviii) Government \ Municipal Funding										
xxix) Fees & Charges										
xxx) Other Income										
TOTAL INCOME										

MEMORANDUM :

If it is possible to differentiate between capital and revenue expenditure please complete the following :

If these cost are included above please tick this box ☐

	1981	1982	1983	1984	1985	1986	1987	1988	1989	1990
xxxi) CAPITAL EXPENDITURE										
xxiii) New Buildings / Refurbishment										
xxiv) Acquisition of stock										
xxxii) Other Capital Expenditure										
TOTAL CAPITAL										

xxxiii) OUTSTANDING DEBT
(i.e. borrowing remaining to be paid at the end of the year)

Name of Person Completing this form : _____   Telephone No. & Extension : _____

Address (including Department) : _____

THANK-YOU FOR YOUR HELP IN COMPLETING THIS FORM.

SECTOR 3 : OTHER MAJOR NON-SPECIALISED LIBRARIES
PLEASE REFER TO THE ACCOMPANYING NOTES OF GUIDANCE

NAME OF COUNTRY _____

For your guidance and background information, we have included the data which we have already collated from various sources and our previous study. **Our primary concern is to collect data relating to 1986-1990.** However, should you have any querries about the data relating to 1981-1985 please raise these with us. The figures in italics represent estimates made in our previous study; the shaded figures represent figures from UNESCO sources; and, the figures in BOLD type have been taken from your national publications. Please fill in the gaps and verify the pre-printed data.

Question 1

i) Number at year end:

	1981	1982	1983	1984	1985	1986	1987	1988	1989	1990
ii) Administrative Units										
iii) Service Points										
iv) Collections :										
v) Books & Bound Periodicals										
vi) Current Periodical Titles										
vii) Manuscripts										
viii) Microforms										
ix) Audio-visual										
x) Other Material										

Question 2

xi) Additions (GROSS) during the year

	1981	1982	1983	1984	1985	1986	1987	1988	1989	1990
ii) Administrative Units										
iii) Service Points										
iv) Collections :										
v) Books & Bound Periodicals										
vii) Manuscripts										
viii) Microforms										
ix) Audio-visual										
x) Other Material										

Question 3

General information concerning usage and capacity

	1981	1982	1983	1984	1985	1986	1987	1988	1989	1990
xiv) Registered Borrowers										
xv) Loan Transaction to Users										
xvi) Length of Occupied Shelving (Metres)										
xvii) Sector Population served										

Question 4

Library employees expressed as FTE

	1981	1982	1983	1984	1985	1986	1987	1988	1989	1990
xviii) Trained Librarians										
xix) Other Library Staff										

PLEASE TURN OVER

Question 5

Major Non-Specialised Library Expenditure & Income
(Expressed in National currency, outturn prices.)

PLEASE INCLUDE ALL EXPENDITURE INCURRED DURING THE YEAR OF ACCOUNT

xx) EXPENDITURE

	1981	1982	1983	1984	1985	1986	1987	1988	1989	1990
xxi) Staff										
xxii) Premises: Operating Costs										
xxiii) New Buildings \ Refurbishment										
xxiv) Acquisition of stock										
xxv) Cost of Borrowing										
xxvi) Miscellaneous										
TOTAL EXPENDITURE										

xxvii) INCOME

	1981	1982	1983	1984	1985	1986	1987	1988	1989	1990
xxviii) Government \ Municipal Funding										
xxix) Fees & Charges										
xxx) Other Income										
TOTAL INCOME										

MEMORANDUM :

If it is possible to differentiate between capital and revenue expenditure please complete the following :

If these costs are included above please tick this box ☐

	1981	1982	1983	1984	1985	1986	1987	1988	1989	1990
xxxi) CAPITAL EXPENDITURE										
xxiii) New Buildings \ Refurbishment										
xxiv) Acquisition of stock										
xxxii) Other Capital Expenditure										
TOTAL CAPITAL										

xxxiii) OUTSTANDING DEBT
(i.e. borrowing remaining to be paid at the end of the year)

Name of Person Completing this form : _____ Telephone No. & Extension : _____

Address (including Department) : _____

THANK-YOU FOR YOUR HELP IN COMPLETING THIS FORM.

SECTOR 4 : SCHOOL LIBRARIES
PLEASE REFER TO THE ACCOMPANYING NOTES OF GUIDANCE

NAME OF COUNTRY _____

For your guidance and background information, we have included the data which we have already collated from various sources and our previous study. **Our primary concern is to collect data relating to 1986-1990.** However, should you have any queries about the data relating to 1981-1985 please raise these with us. The figures in italics represent estimates made in our previous study; the shaded figures represent figures from UNESCO sources; and, the figures in BOLD type have been taken from your national publications. Please fill in the gaps and verify the pre-printed data.

Question 1

i) *Number at year end:*

	1981	1982	1983	1984	1985	1986	1987	1988	1989	1990
ii) Administrative Units										
iii) Service Points										
iv) Collections :										
v) Books & Bound Periodicals										
vi) Current Periodical Titles										
vii) Manuscripts										
viii) Microforms										
ix) Audio-visual										
x) Other Material										

Question 2

xi) *Additions (GROSS) during the year*

	1981	1982	1983	1984	1985	1986	1987	1988	1989	1990
ii) Administrative Units										
iii) Service Points										
iv) Collections :										
v) Books & Bound Periodicals										
vii) Manuscripts										
viii) Microforms										
ix) Audio-visual										
x) Other Material										

Question 3

General information concerning usage and capacity

	1981	1982	1983	1984	1985	1986	1987	1988	1989	1990
xiv) Registered Borrowers										
xv) Loan Transaction to Users										
xvi) Length of Occupied Shelving (Metres)										
xvii) Sector Population served										

Question 4

Library employees expressed as FTE

	1981	1982	1983	1984	1985	1986	1987	1988	1989	1990
xviii) Trained Librarians										
xix) Other Library Staff										

PLEASE TURN OVER

Question 5   *School Library Expenditure & Income*   PLEASE INCLUDE ALL EXPENDITURE INCURRED DURING THE YEAR OF ACCOUNT

(Expressed in National currency, outturn prices.)

	1981	1982	1983	1984	1985	1986	1987	1988	1989	1990
xx) EXPENDITURE										
xxi) Staff										
xxii) Premises: Operating Costs										
xxiii) New Buildings \ Refurbishment										
xxiv) Acquisition of stock										
xxv) Cost of Borrowing										
xxvi) Miscellaneous										
TOTAL EXPENDITURE										

	1981	1982	1983	1984	1985	1986	1987	1988	1989	1990
xxvii) INCOME										
xxviii) Government \ Municipal Funding										
xxix) Fees & Charges										
xxx) Other Income										
TOTAL INCOME										

MEMORANDUM :

If it is possible to differentiate between capital and revenue expenditure please complete the following :

If these costs are included above please tick this box ☐

	1981	1982	1983	1984	1985	1986	1987	1988	1989	1990
xxxi) CAPITAL EXPENDITURE										
xxiii) New Buildings \ Refurbishment										
xxiv) Acquisition of stock										
xxxii) Other Capital Expenditure										
TOTAL CAPITAL										

xxxiii) OUTSTANDING DEBT
(i.e. borrowing remaining to be paid at the end of the year)

Name of Person Completing this form :   _____   Telephone No. & Extension :   _____

Address (including Department) :   _____

THANK-YOU FOR YOUR HELP IN COMPLETING THIS FORM.

SECTOR 5 : SPECIAL LIBRARIES

PLEASE REFER TO THE ACCOMPANYING NOTES OF GUIDANCE

NAME OF COUNTRY _____

For your guidance and background information, we have included the data which we have already collated from various sources and our previous study. **Our primary concern is to collect data relating to 1986 - 1990.** However should you have any queries about the data relating to 1981-1985 please raise these with us. The figures in *italics* represent estimates made in our previous study; the shaded figures represent figures from UNESCO sources; and the figures in **bold** type have been taken from your national publications. Please fill in the gaps and verify the pre-printed data.

Question 1

i) *Number at year end:*

	1981	1982	1983	1984	1985	1986	1987	1988	1989	1990
ii) Administrative Units										
iii) Service Points										
iv) Collections :										
v) Books & Bound Periodicals										
vi) Current Periodical Titles										
vii) Manuscripts										
viii) Microforms										
ix) Audio-visual										
x) Other Material										

Question 2

xi) *Additions (GROSS) during the year*

	1981	1982	1983	1984	1985	1986	1987	1988	1989	1990
ii) Administrative Units										
iii) Service Points										
iii) Collections :										
v) Books & Bound Periodicals										
vii) Manuscripts										
viii) Microforms										
ix) Audio-visual										
x) Other Material										

Question 3

General information concerning usage and capacity

	1981	1982	1983	1984	1985	1986	1987	1988	1989	1990
xiv) Registered Borrowers										
xv) Loan Transactions to Users										
xvi) Length of Occupied Shelving(Metres)										
xvii) Sector Population served										

Question 4

Library employees expressed as FTE

	1981	1982	1983	1984	1985	1986	1987	1988	1989	1990
xviii) Trained Librarians										
xix) Other Library Staff										

PLEASE TURN OVER

Question 5

Special Library Expenditure & Income

PLEASE INCLUDE ALL EXPENDITURE INCURRED DURING THE YEAR OF ACCOUNT

(Expressed in National currency, outturn prices.)

	1981	1982	1983	1984	1985	1986	1987	1988	1989	1990
xx) EXPENDITURE										
xxi) Staff										
xxii) Premises and Operating Costs										
xxiii) New Buildings \ Refurbishment										
xxiv) Acquisition of stock										
xxv) Cost of Borrowing										
xxvi) Miscellaneous										
TOTAL EXPENDITURE										

	1981	1982	1983	1984	1985	1986	1987	1988	1989	1990
xxvii) INCOME										
xxviii) Government \ Municipal Funding										
xxix) Fees & Charges										
xxx) Other Income										
TOTAL INCOME										

MEMORANDUM:

If it is possible to differentiate between capital and revenue expenditure please complete the following :

If these costs are included above please tick this box ☐

	1981	1982	1983	1984	1985	1986	1987	1988	1989	1990
xxxi) CAPITAL EXPENDITURE										
xxiii) New Buildings \ Refurbishment										
xxiv) Acquisition of stock										
xxxii) Other Capital Expenditure										
TOTAL CAPITAL										
xxxiii) OUTSTANDING DEBT										

(i.e. borrowing remaining to be paid at the end of the year)

Name of Person Completing this form : _____   Telephone No. & Extension : _____

Address (including Department) : _____

THANK-YOU FOR YOUR HELP IN COMPLETING THIS FORM.

SECTOR 6 : PUBLIC LIBRARIES
PLEASE REFER TO THE ACCOMPANYING NOTES OF GUIDANCE

NAME OF COUNTRY _____

For your guidance and background information, we have included the data which we have already collated from various sources and our previous study. **Our primary concern is to collect data relating to 1986 - 1990.** However should you have any queries about the data relating to 1981-1985 please raise these with us. The figures in *italics* represent estimates made in our previous study; the shaded figures represent figures from UNESCO sources; and the figures in **bold** type have been taken from your national publications. Please fill in the gaps and verify the pre-printed data.

Question 1

i) *Number at year end:*

	1981	1982	1983	1984	1985	1986	1987	1988	1989	1990	1991
ii) Administrative Units											
iii) Service Points											
iv) Collections :											
v) Books & Bound Periodicals											
vi) Current Periodical Titles											
vii) Manuscripts											
viii) Microforms											
ix) Audio-visual											
x) Other Material											

Question 2

xi) *Additions (GROSS) during the year*

	1981	1982	1983	1984	1985	1986	1987	1988	1989	1990	1991
ii) Administrative Units											
iii) Service Points											
iv) Collections :											
v) Books & Bound Periodicals											
vii) Manuscripts											
viii) Microforms											
ix) Audio-visual											
x) Other Material											

Question 3

General information concerning usage and capacity

	1981	1982	1983	1984	1985	1986	1987	1988	1989	1990	1991
xiv) Registered Borrowers											
xv) Loan Transactions to Users											
xvi) Length of Occupied Shelving (Metres)											
xvii) Sector Population served											

Question 4

Library employees expressed as FTE

	1981	1982	1983	1984	1985	1986	1987	1988	1989	1990	1991
xviii) Trained Librarians											
xix) Other Library Staff											

PLEASE TURN OVER

Question 5

Public Library Expenditure & Income
(Expressed in National currency, outturn prices.)

PLEASE INCLUDE ALL EXPENDITURE INCURRED DURING THE YEAR OF ACCOUNT

xx) EXPENDITURE

	1981	1982	1983	1984	1985	1986	1987	1988	1989	1990	1991
xxi) Staff											
xxii) Premises and Operating Costs											
xxiii) New Buildings \ Refurbishment											
xxiv) Acquisition of stock											
xxv) Cost of Borrowing											
xxvi) Miscellaneous											
TOTAL EXPENDITURE											

xxvii) INCOME

	1981	1982	1983	1984	1985	1986	1987	1988	1989	1990	1991
xxviii) Government \ Municipal Funding											
xxix) Fees & Charges											
xxx) Other Income											
TOTAL INCOME											

MEMORANDUM :

If it is possible to differentiate between capital and revenue expenditure please complete the following :

If these costs are included above please tick this box ☐

	1981	1982	1983	1984	1985	1986	1987	1988	1989	1990	1991
xxxi) CAPITAL EXPENDITURE											
xxiii) New Buildings \ Refurbishment											
xiv) Acquisition of stock											
xxxii) Other Capital Expenditure											
TOTAL CAPITAL EXPENDITURE											

xxxiii) OUTSTANDING DEBT
(i.e. borrowing remaining to be paid at the end of the year)

Name of Person Completing this form : _____   Telephone No. & Extension : _____

Address (including Department) : _____

THANK-YOU FOR YOUR HELP IN COMPLETING THIS FORM.

APPENDIX 4

STUDY DATA SETS

ACTIVITY DATA

Administrative Units
Service Points
Collections = Books & Bound Periodicals
Collections = Current Periodical Titles
Collections = Manuscripts
Collections = Microforms
Collections = Audiovisuals
Collections = Other Material
Library Users
Library Consultations

FINANCIAL DATA

All Sectors Estimated Average Expenditure and Income per annum (1986-90)

All Sectors Estimated Average Expenditure and Income per annum (1981-85)

National Libraries Estimated Average Expenditure and Income per annum (1986-90)

National Libraries Estimated Average Expenditure and Income per annum (1981-85)

Higher Education Estimated Libraries Average Expenditure and Income per annum (1986-90)

Higher Education Estimated Libraries Average Expenditure and Income per annum (1981-85)

Other Major Non-Specialised Libraries Estimated Average Expenditure and Income per annum (1986-90)

Other Major Non-Specialised Libraries Estimated Average Expenditure and Income per annum (1981-85)

School Libraries Estimated Average Expenditure and Income per annum (1986-90)
School Libraries Estimated Average Expenditure and Income per annum (1981-85)
Special Libraries Estimated Average Expenditure and Income per annum (1986-90)
Special Libraries Estimated Average Expenditure and Income per annum (1981-85)
Public Libraries Estimated Average Expenditure and Income per annum (1986-90)
Public Libraries Estimated Average Expenditure and Income per annum (1981-85)

Administrative Units

Sector 1 — NATIONAL

	1981	1982	1983	1984	1985	1986	1987	1988	1989	1990	1981–85 Average	1986–90 Average	81/85 – 86/90 Year on Year Increase	Decade: Year on Year Increase
AUSTRIA	(1)	(1)	(1)	(1)	(1)	1	1	1	1	1	1	1	0.0%	0.0%
BELGIUM	(1)	(1)	(1)	(1)	(1)	(1)	(1)	(1)	(1)	(1)			0.0%	0.0%
DENMARK	(1)	(1)	(1)	(1)	(1)								0.0%	0.0%
EAST GERMANY	(2)	(2)	(2)	(2)	(2)	2	3	3	(3)	3	2	3	7.0%	4.6%
EIRE	1	1	1	1	1	1	1	1	1	1	1	1	0.0%	0.0%
FINLAND	1	1	1	1	1	1	1	1	1	1	1	1	0.0%	0.0%
FRANCE	1	1	1	1	1	1	1	1	1	1	1	1	0.0%	0.0%
GREECE	1	1	1	1	1	1	1	1	1	1	1	1	0.0%	0.0%
ICELAND	1	1	1	1	1	1	1	1	1	1	1	1	0.0%	0.0%
ITALY	(2)	(2)	(2)	(2)	(2)	(2)	(2)	(2)	(2)	(2)	2	2	0.0%	0.0%
LIECHTENSTEIN	(1)	(1)	(1)	(1)	(1)	1	1	1	1	1			0.0%	0.0%
LUXEMBOURG	1	1	1	1	1	1	1	1	1	1	1	1	0.0%	0.0%
NETHERLANDS	(1)	(1)	(1)	(1)	(1)	1	1	1	(1)	(1)			0.0%	0.0%
NORWAY	1	1	1	1	1	1	1	1	1	1	1	1	0.0%	0.0%
PORTUGAL	2	2	2	2	2	1	1	1	1	1	2	1	–12.9%	–7.4%
SPAIN	(1)	(1)	(1)	(1)	(1)								0.0%	0.0%
SWEDEN	(1)	(1)	(1)	(1)	(1)								0.0%	0.0%
SWITZERLAND	3	3	3	3	3	3	3	3	3	3	3	3	0.0%	0.0%
UK	3	6	7	7	7	7	7	7	7	7	7	7	0.0%	0.0%
WEST GERMANY														
EU TOTAL	24	23	24	24	24	23	24	24	24	24	24	24	0.0%	0.0%
EFTA TOTAL	7	7	7	7	7	7	7	7	7	7	7	7	0.0%	0.0%
EUROPE TOTAL	31	30	31	31	31	30	31	31	31	31	31	31	0.0%	0.0%

Sector 2 — HIGHER EDUCATION

	1981	1982	1983	1984	1985	1986	1987	1988	1989	1990	1981–85 Average	1986–90 Average	81/85 – 86/90 Year on Year Increase	Decade: Year on Year Increase
AUSTRIA	(21)	(21)	(21)	(21)	(21)	(21)	(21)	21	(21)	21	21	21	0.0%	0.0%
BELGIUM	14	14	14	14	14	16	16	16	16	16	14	16	2.7%	1.5%
DENMARK	14	14	14	14	14	(19)	(19)	19	18	18	14	19	5.8%	2.8%
EAST GERMANY	(29)	(29)	(29)	29	(28)	(28)	28	(28)	(28)	(28)	29	28	–0.6%	–0.4%
EIRE	15	15	15	15	15	(15)	(15)	(15)	(15)	(15)	15	15	0.0%	0.0%
FINLAND	30	30	30	30	30	30	30	30	30	30	30	30	0.0%	0.0%
FRANCE	61	61	61	61	61	62	63	64	67	67	61	65	1.2%	1.0%
GREECE	(39)	(39)	(39)	(39)	(39)	(39)	(39)	(39)	(39)	(39)	39	39	0.0%	0.0%
ICELAND	(1)	(1)	1	(1)	(1)	1	1	1	1	1	1	1	0.0%	0.0%
ITALY	10	10	10	10	10	10	11	10	10	10	10	10	0.4%	0.0%
LIECHTENSTEIN	(1)	(1)	(1)	(1)	(1)	(1)	(1)	(1)	(1)	(1)			0.0%	0.0%
LUXEMBOURG	1	1	1	1	1	1	1	1	1	1	1	1	0.0%	0.0%
NETHERLANDS	690	739	734	(721)	653	617	561	520	477	(477)	707	530	–5.6%	–4.0%
NORWAY	(89)	(89)	(89)	89	(86)	88	85	92	99	99	88	92	0.8%	1.2%
PORTUGAL	177	183	187	138	(171)	126	191	192	229	204	171	188	1.9%	1.6%
SPAIN	332	408	440	473	505	538	(596)	596	(567)	567	432	573	5.8%	6.1%
SWEDEN	(15)	(15)	(15)	15	15	15	15	26	25	32	15	23	8.5%	8.6%
SWITZERLAND	(12)	(12)	(12)	12	(12)	12	12	12	12	12	12	12	0.0%	0.0%
UK	215	215	215	215	215	216	215	215	215	215	215	215	0.0%	0.0%
WEST GERMANY	159	146	166	168	157	167	168	175	182	(182)	159	175	1.9%	1.5%
EU TOTAL	1,756	1,874	1,925	1,898	1,883	1,854	1,923	1,890	1,864	1,867	1,867	1,874	0.1%	0.5%
EFTA TOTAL	169	169	169	169	166	166	165	183	189	196	168	180	1.3%	1.7%
EUROPE TOTAL	1,925	2,043	2,094	2,067	2,049	2,020	2,088	2,073	2,053	2,035	2,036	2,054	0.2%	0.6%

Figures in parentheses are grossed.

Administrative Units

Sector 3 – OTHER NON-MAJOR SPEC

	1981	1982	1983	1984	1985	1986	1987	1988	1989	1990	1981–85 Average	1986–90 Average	81/85 – 86/90 Year on Year Increase	Decade: Year on Year Increase
AUSTRIA	(8)	(8)	(8)	(8)	(8)	(8)	(8)	(8)	8	(8)	8	8	0.0%	0.0%
BELGIUM	(5)	(5)	(5)	(5)	(5)	(5)	(5)	(5)	(5)	5	5	5	0.0%	0.0%
DENMARK	0	0	0	0	0	0	0	0	0	0	0	0	0.0%	0.0%
EAST GERMANY	(93)	(93)	(93)	(93)	(93)	(93)	(93)	(93)	(93)	(91)	93	93	-0.1%	-0.2%
EIRE	2	2	2	2	2	2	2	2	2	2	2	2	0.0%	0.0%
FINLAND	0	0	0	0	0	0	0	0	0	0	0	0	0.0%	0.0%
FRANCE	(1)	(1)	(1)	(1)	(1)	1	1	1	1	1	1	1	0.0%	0.0%
GREECE	(5)	(5)	(5)	(5)	(5)	(5)	(5)	(5)	5	(5)	5	5	0.0%	0.0%
ICELAND	0	0	0	0	0	0	0	0	0	0	0	0	0.0%	0.0%
ITALY	(33)	(33)	(33)	(33)	(33)	33	(33)	(34)	34	(34)	33	34	0.4%	0.3%
LIECHTENSTEIN	0	0	0	0	0	0	0	0	0	0	0	0	0.0%	0.0%
LUXEMBOURG	0	0	0	0	0	0	0	0	0	0	0	0	0.0%	0.0%
NETHERLANDS	6	6	6	6	5	5	4	4	3	(3)	6	4	-8.1%	-7.4%
NORWAY	0	0	0	0	0	0	0	0	0	0	0	0	0.0%	0.0%
PORTUGAL	(24)	(24)	(24)	(24)	24	22	(22)	(22)	(22)	(22)	24	22	-1.7%	-1.0%
SPAIN	(13)	(13)	(13)	(13)	(13)	(13)	(13)	(13)	(13)	13	13	13	0.0%	0.0%
SWEDEN	(54)	(54)	(54)	(54)	(54)	(54)	54	54	28	(28)	54	43	-4.5%	-7.8%
SWITZERLAND	(33)	(33)	(54)	(33)	(33)	33	33	34	34	34	33	34	0.4%	0.3%
UK	(26)	(26)	(26)	(26)	(26)	(26)	(26)	(26)	(26)	(26)	26	26	0.0%	0.0%
WEST GERMANY	31	31	30	32	29	31	32	32	30	(30)	31	31	0.3%	-0.4%
EU TOTAL	239	239	238	240	236	236	236	237	234	232	238	235	-0.3%	-0.3%
EFTA TOTAL	95	95	95	95	95	95	95	96	68	68	95	84	-2.3%	-3.6%
EUROPE TOTAL	334	334	333	335	331	331	331	333	302	300	333	319	-0.9%	-1.2%

Sector 4 – SCHOOLS

	1981	1982	1983	1984	1985	1986	1987	1988	1989	1990	1981–85 Average	1986–90 Average	81/85 – 86/90 Year on Year Increase	Decade: Year on Year Increase
AUSTRIA	(165)	(165)	(165)	(165)	(165)	(165)	(165)	(165)	(165)	(163)	165	165	0.0%	-0.1%
BELGIUM	(122)	(122)	(122)	(122)	(122)	(122)	(122)	(122)	(122)	122	122	122	0.0%	0.0%
DENMARK	(275)	(275)	(275)	(275)	(275)	(275)	(275)	(275)	(275)	(275)	275	275	0.0%	0.0%
EAST GERMANY	(368)	(368)	(368)	(368)	(368)	(368)	(368)	(368)	(368)	(360)	368	366	-0.1%	-0.2%
EIRE	(31)	(31)	(31)	(31)	(31)	(31)	(31)	(31)	(31)	(31)	31	31	0.0%	0.0%
FINLAND	(5,200)	(5,200)	(5,200)	5,200	(5,200)	5,200	5,340	(5,439)	(5,439)	5,439	5,200	5,371	0.7%	0.5%
FRANCE	(732)	(732)	(732)	(732)	(732)	(732)	(732)	(732)	(732)	(732)	732	732	0.0%	0.0%
GREECE	(129)	(129)	(129)	(129)	(129)	(129)	(129)	(129)	(129)	(129)	129	129	0.0%	0.0%
ICELAND	(37)	(37)	(37)	(37)	37	39	47	68	75	78	37	61	10.7%	8.6%
ITALY	(776)	(776)	(776)	(776)	(776)	(776)	(776)	(776)	(776)	(776)	776	776	0.0%	0.0%
LIECHTENSTEIN	(1)	(1)	(1)	(1)	(1)	(1)	(1)	(1)	(1)	(1)	1	1	0.0%	0.0%
LUXEMBOURG	(4)	(4)	(4)	(4)	(4)	(4)	(4)	(4)	(4)	(4)	4	4	0.0%	0.0%
NETHERLANDS	(198)	(198)	(198)	(198)	(198)	(198)	(198)	(198)	(198)	(198)	198	198	0.0%	0.0%
NORWAY	(3,789)	(3,789)	(3,789)	3,789	3,658	3,521	3,383	3,523	3,437	3,383	3,763	3,449	-1.7%	-1.3%
PORTUGAL	712	719	599	677	677	758	635	668	768	675	677	701	0.7%	-0.6%
SPAIN	626	(626)	(626)	(626)	(626)	(626)	(626)	(626)	(626)	(626)	626	626	0.0%	0.0%
SWEDEN	(5,483)	(5,451)	(5,419)	5,387	(5,355)	(5,323)	(5,291)	(5,259)	5,226	(5,194)	5,419	5,259	-0.6%	-0.6%
SWITZERLAND	(138)	(138)	(138)	(138)	(138)	(138)	(138)	(138)	(138)	(137)	138	138	0.0%	-0.1%
UK	(120)	(120)	(120)	(120)	(120)	(120)	(120)	(120)	(120)	(120)	120	120	0.0%	0.0%
WEST GERMANY	(729)	(729)	(729)	(729)	(729)	(729)	(729)	(729)	(729)	(729)	729	729	0.0%	0.0%
EU TOTAL	4,822	4,829	4,709	4,787	4,787	4,868	4,745	4,778	4,878	4,777	4,787	4,809	0.1%	-0.1%
EFTA TOTAL	14,813	14,781	14,749	14,717	14,554	14,387	14,365	14,593	14,481	14,395	14,723	14,444	-0.4%	-0.3%
EUROPE TOTAL	19,635	19,610	19,458	19,504	19,341	19,255	19,110	19,371	19,359	19,172	19,510	19,253	-0.3%	-0.3%

Figures in parentheses are grossed.

Administrative Units

Sector 5 SPECIAL

	1981	1982	1983	1984	1985	1986	1987	1988	1989	1990	1981–85 Average	1986–90 Average	81/85 – 86/90 Year on Year Increase	Decade: Year on Year Increase
AUSTRIA	(255)	(255)	(255)	(255)	(255)	(255)	(255)	(255)	(255)	(257)	255	255	0.0%	0.1%
BELGIUM	(97)	(97)	(97)	(97)	(97)	(97)	(97)	(97)	(97)	97	97	97	0.0%	0.0%
DENMARK	15	15	15	15	15	15	15	15	15	(15)	15	15	0.0%	0.0%
EAST GERMANY	(558)	(558)	(558)	(558)	(558)	(558)	(558)	(558)	(558)	(550)	558	556	-0.1%	-0.2%
EIRE	(21)	(21)	(21)	(21)	(21)	(21)	(21)	(21)	(21)	(21)	21	21	0.0%	0.0%
FINLAND	19	19	19	27	27	26	26	26	26	26	22	26	3.2%	3.5%
FRANCE	(523)	(523)	(523)	(523)	(523)	(523)	(523)	(523)	(523)	(523)	523	523	0.0%	0.0%
GREECE	(94)	(94)	(94)	(94)	(94)	(94)	(94)	(94)	(94)	(94)	94	94	0.0%	0.0%
ICELAND	(23)	(23)	(23)	(23)	(23)	(23)	(23)	(23)	24	(24)	23	23	0.3%	0.5%
ITALY	(25)	(25)	(25)	(25)	(25)	(25)	(25)	(25)	(25)	(25)	25	25	0.0%	0.0%
LIECHTENSTEIN	0	0	0	0	0	0	0	0	0	0	0	0	0.0%	0.0%
LUXEMBOURG	(4)	(4)	(4)	(4)	(4)	(4)	(4)	(4)	(4)	(4)	4	4	0.0%	0.0%
NETHERLANDS	545	673	695	638	699	705	690	658	630	(602)	650	657	0.2%	1.1%
NORWAY	(125)	(128)	(131)	(134)	149	154	164	147	138	128	133	146	1.8%	0.3%
PORTUGAL	166	188	126	98	202	239	191	244	275	229	156	236	8.6%	3.6%
SPAIN	464	500	602	704	805	907	1,106	1,305	(1,250)	1,196	615	1,153	13.4%	11.1%
SWEDEN	(22)	(26)	(30)	(34)	38	38	38	61	69	57	30	53	11.9%	11.2%
SWITZERLAND	(225)	(225)	(225)	(225)	(225)	(225)	(225)	(225)	(225)	(227)	225	225	0.0%	0.1%
UK	(541)	(541)	(541)	(541)	(541)	(541)	(541)	(541)	(541)	(541)	541	541	0.0%	0.0%
WEST GERMANY	584	525	573	608	629	809	822	797	799	(801)	584	806	6.7%	3.6%
EU TOTAL	3,637	3,764	3,874	3,926	4,213	4,538	4,687	4,882	4,832	4,698	3,883	4,727	4.0%	2.6%
EFTA TOTAL	669	676	683	698	717	721	731	737	737	719	689	729	1.1%	0.8%
EUROPE TOTAL	4,306	4,440	4,557	4,624	4,930	5,259	5,418	5,619	5,569	5,417	4,571	5,456	3.6%	2.6%

Sector 6 PUBLIC

	1981	1982	1983	1984	1985	1986	1987	1988	1989	1990	1981–85 Average	1986–90 Average	81/85 – 86/90 Year on Year Increase	Decade: Year on Year Increase
AUSTRIA	2,190	(2,161)	(2,132)	2,172	2,292	2,042	2,081	2,080	2,054	1,997	2,189	2,051	-1.3%	-1.0%
BELGIUM	39	39	39	39	39	39	39	39	38	38	39	39	-0.2%	-0.3%
DENMARK	247	247	249	250	(250)	(250)	250	250	250	250	249	250	0.1%	0.1%
EAST GERMANY	(911)	(911)	(911)	(911)	(911)	(911)	(911)	(911)	(911)	(911)	911	911	0.0%	0.0%
EIRE	31	31	31	31	31	31	31	31	31	31	31	31	0.0%	0.0%
FINLAND	(445)	(445)	(445)	445	445	445	445	445	444	444	445	445	0.0%	-0.0%
FRANCE	(1,068)	(1,107)	(1,141)	(1,200)	(1,269)	(1,366)	1,462	(1,522)	1,581	1,641	1,157	1,514	5.5%	4.9%
GREECE	(51)	(51)	(51)	(51)	(51)	(51)	(51)	(51)	(51)	(51)	51	51	0.0%	0.0%
ICELAND	241	240	238	235	234	233	231	215	212	205	238	219	-1.6%	-1.8%
ITALY	(106)	(106)	(106)	(106)	(106)	(108)	(106)	(106)	(106)	(106)	106	106	0.0%	0.0%
LIECHTENSTEIN	(3)	(3)	(3)	(3)	(3)	3	(3)	(3)	3	(3)	3	3	0.0%	0.0%
LUXEMBOURG	2	2	2	2	2	2	(2)	2	2	(2)	2	2	0.0%	0.0%
NETHERLANDS	469	468	471	471	470	473	502	597	605	606	470	557	3.4%	2.9%
NORWAY	(463)	(461)	(459)	(457)	(455)	453	449	448	446	446	459	448	-0.5%	-0.4%
PORTUGAL	112	109	178	119	148	194	159	122	173	167	133	163	4.1%	4.5%
SPAIN	1,357	1,688	1,843	1,998	2,152	2,307	2,307	2,982	(3,133)	3,285	1,808	2,803	9.2%	10.3%
SWEDEN	(394)	(392)	(390)	(388)	(386)	384	383	381	377	377	390	380	-0.5%	-0.5%
SWITZERLAND	45	45	(46)	(46)	46	(46)	(46)	(46)	(46)	(46)	46	46	0.2%	0.2%
UK	166	166	166	166	166	166	166	166	167	167	166	166	0.0%	0.1%
WEST GERMANY	116	116	116	116	118	(116)	(116)	(116)	(116)	(116)	116	116	0.0%	0.0%
EU TOTAL	4,675	5,041	5,304	5,460	5,711	6,012	6,102	6,895	7,164	7,371	5,238	6,709	5.1%	5.2%
EFTA TOTAL	3,781	3,747	3,713	3,746	3,861	3,606	3,638	3,618	3,582	3,518	3,770	3,592	-1.0%	-0.8%
EUROPE TOTAL	8,456	8,788	9,017	9,206	9,572	9,618	9,740	10,513	10,746	10,889	9,008	10,301	2.7%	2.8%

Figures in parentheses are grossed.

Administrative Units

	1981	1982	1983	1984	1985	1986	1987	1988	1989	1990	1981–85 Average	1986–90 Average	81/85 – 86/90 Year on Year Increase	Decade: Year on Year Increase
ALL SECTORS														
AUSTRIA	2,640	2,611	2,582	2,622	2,742	2,492	2,531	2,530	2,504	2,447	2,639	2,501	-1.1%	-0.8%
BELGIUM	278	278	278	278	278	280	280	280	279	279	278	280	0.1%	0.0%
DENMARK	552	552	554	555	555	560	560	560	559	559	554	560	0.2%	0.1%
EAST GERMANY	1,961	1,961	1,961	1,961	1,960	1,960	1,961	1,961	1,961	1,943	1,961	1,957	-0.0%	-0.1%
EIRE	101	101	101	101	101	101	101	101	101	101	101	101	0.0%	0.0%
FINLAND	5,695	5,695	5,695	5,703	5,703	5,702	5,842	5,941	5,940	5,940	5,698	5,873	0.6%	0.5%
FRANCE	2,386	2,425	2,459	2,518	2,587	2,685	2,782	2,843	2,905	2,965	2,475	2,836	2.8%	2.4%
GREECE	319	319	319	319	319	319	319	319	319	319	319	319	0.0%	0.0%
ICELAND	303	302	300	297	296	297	303	308	313	309	300	306	0.4%	0.2%
ITALY	952	952	952	952	952	952	953	953	953	953	952	953	0.0%	0.0%
LIECHTENSTEIN	6	6	6	6	6	6	6	6	6	6	6	6	0.0%	0.0%
LUXEMBOURG	12	12	12	12	12	12	12	12	12	12	12	12	0.0%	0.0%
NETHERLANDS	1,909	2,085	2,105	2,035	2,026	1,999	1,956	1,978	1,914	1,887	2,032	1,947	-0.9%	-0.1%
NORWAY	4,467	4,468	4,469	4,470	4,349	4,215	4,082	4,211	4,121	4,057	4,445	4,137	-1.4%	-1.1%
PORTUGAL	1,192	1,224	1,115	1,057	1,223	1,340	1,199	1,249	1,468	1,298	1,162	1,311	2.4%	1.0%
SPAIN	2,794	3,237	3,526	3,816	4,103	4,392	4,649	5,523	5,590	5,688	3,495	5,168	8.1%	8.2%
SWEDEN	5,969	5,939	5,909	5,879	5,849	5,815	5,782	5,782	5,724	5,687	5,909	5,758	-0.5%	-0.5%
SWITZERLAND	454	454	455	455	455	455	455	456	456	457	455	456	0.1%	0.1%
UK	1,071	1,071	1,071	1,071	1,071	1,072	1,071	1,071	1,072	1,072	1,071	1,071	0.0%	0.0%
WEST GERMANY	1,626	1,553	1,621	1,660	1,667	1,859	1,874	1,856	1,863	1,865	1,625	1,863	2.8%	1.5%
EU TOTAL	15,153	15,770	16,074	16,335	16,854	17,531	17,717	18,706	18,996	18,941	16,037	18,378	2.8%	2.5%
EFTA TOTAL	19,534	19,475	19,416	19,432	19,400	18,962	19,001	19,234	19,064	18,903	19,451	19,037	-0.4%	-0.4%
EUROPE TOTAL	34,687	35,245	35,490	35,767	36,254	36,513	36,718	37,940	38,060	37,844	35,489	37,415	1.1%	1.0%

Administrative Units per 1000 Population

	1981	1982	1983	1984	1985	1986	1987	1988	1989	1990	1981–85 Average	1986–90 Average	81/85 – 86/90 Year on Year Increase	Decade: Year on Year Increase
European Union														
Sector 1	0.00	0.00	0.00	0.00	0.00	0.00	0.00	0.00	0.00	0.00	0.00	0.00	-0.1%	-0.0%
Sector 2	0.01	0.01	0.01	0.01	0.01	0.01	0.01	0.01	0.01	0.01	0.01	0.01	-0.0%	0.5%
Sector 3	0.00	0.00	0.00	0.00	0.00	0.00	0.00	0.00	0.00	0.00	0.00	0.00	-0.4%	-0.4%
Sector 4	0.01	0.01	0.01	0.01	0.01	0.01	0.01	0.01	0.01	0.01	0.01	0.01	-0.0%	-0.1%
Sector 5	0.01	0.01	0.02	0.02	0.02	0.02	0.02	0.02	0.02	0.02	0.01	0.02	3.9%	2.0%
Sector 6	0.01	0.01	0.02	0.02	0.02	0.02	0.02	0.02	0.02	0.02	0.02	0.02	5.0%	5.2%
All Sectors	0.04	0.05	0.05	0.05	0.05	0.05	0.05	0.05	0.06	0.06	0.05	0.05	2.7%	2.5%
EFTA														
Sector 1	0.00	0.00	0.00	0.00	0.00	0.00	0.00	0.00	0.00	0.00	0.00	0.00	-0.0%	-0.1%
Sector 2	0.01	0.01	0.01	0.01	0.01	0.01	0.01	0.01	0.01	0.01	0.01	0.01	1.3%	1.6%
Sector 3	0.00	0.00	0.00	0.00	0.00	0.00	0.00	0.00	0.00	0.00	0.00	0.00	-2.4%	-3.7%
Sector 4	0.46	0.46	0.46	0.46	0.45	0.45	0.45	0.45	0.45	0.44	0.46	0.45	-0.4%	-0.4%
Sector 5	0.02	0.02	0.02	0.02	0.02	0.02	0.02	0.02	0.02	0.02	0.02	0.02	1.1%	0.7%
Sector 6	0.12	0.12	0.12	0.12	0.12	0.11	0.11	0.11	0.11	0.11	0.12	0.11	-1.0%	-0.9%
All Sectors	0.61	0.61	0.60	0.60	0.60	0.59	0.59	0.60	0.59	0.58	0.61	0.59	-0.5%	-0.4%
Europe Total														
Sector 1	0.00	0.00	0.00	0.00	0.00	0.00	0.00	0.00	0.00	0.00	0.00	0.00	-0.1%	-0.0%
Sector 2	0.01	0.01	0.01	0.01	0.01	0.01	0.01	0.01	0.01	0.01	0.01	0.01	0.1%	0.6%
Sector 3	0.00	0.00	0.00	0.00	0.00	0.00	0.00	0.00	0.00	0.00	0.00	0.00	-1.0%	-1.2%
Sector 4	0.05	0.05	0.05	0.05	0.05	0.05	0.05	0.05	0.05	0.05	0.05	0.05	-0.4%	-0.3%
Sector 5	0.01	0.01	0.01	0.01	0.01	0.01	0.01	0.02	0.03	0.03	0.01	0.01	3.5%	2.6%
Sector 6	0.02	0.02	0.02	0.02	0.03	0.03	0.03	0.03	0.03	0.03	0.02	0.03	2.6%	2.8%
All Sectors	0.09	0.10	0.10	0.10	0.10	0.10	0.10	0.10	0.10	0.10	0.10	0.10	1.0%	0.9%

Service Points

Sector 1
NATIONAL

	1981	1982	1983	1984	1985	1986	1987	1988	1989	1990	1981–85 Average	1986–90 Average	81/85 – 86/90 Year on Year Increase	Decade: Year on Year Increase
AUSTRIA													0.0%	0.0%
BELGIUM	(1)	(1)	(1)	(1)	(1)	(1)	(1)	(1)	(1)	(1)			0.0%	0.0%
DENMARK	1	1	1	1	1	1	1	1	1	1	1	1	19.1%	16.7%
EAST GERMANY	(6)	(6)	(6)	(6)	(6)	(6)	(6)	(6)	(6)	4			0.7%	1.7%
EIRE	2	2	2	2	2	2	2	2	2	(7)	2	2	0.0%	0.0%
FINLAND										2			0.0%	0.0%
FRANCE	1	1	1	1	1	1	1	1	1	1	1	1	0.0%	0.0%
GREECE													0.0%	0.0%
ICELAND	(1)	(1)	(1)	(1)	(1)	(1)	(1)	(1)	(1)	(1)			0.0%	0.0%
ITALY	2	2	2	2	2	2	2	2	2	2	2	2	0.0%	0.0%
LIECHTENSTEIN	(1)	(1)	(1)	(1)	(1)	(1)	(1)	(1)	(1)	(1)			0.0%	0.0%
LUXEMBOURG	1	1	1	1	1	1	1	1	1	1	1	1	0.0%	0.0%
NETHERLANDS	4	4	4	4	4	4	4	4	4	4	4	4	0.0%	0.0%
NORWAY	(3)	(3)	(3)	3	(2)	3	3	3	3	(1)	3	3	–6.5%	–4.4%
PORTUGAL	1	1	1	1	1	1	1	1	1	1	1	1	0.0%	0.0%
SPAIN	3	3	3	3	3	3	2	2	2	2	3	3	–7.8%	–4.4%
SWEDEN	(4)	(4)	(4)	(4)	(4)	4	4	4	4	4	(4)	4	0.0%	0.0%
SWITZERLAND	(1)	(1)	(1)	(1)	(1)	1	1	1	1	1	(1)	1	0.0%	0.0%
UK	16	16	16	16	16	16	16	16	16	16	16	16	0.0%	0.0%
WEST GERMANY	6	6	6	6	6	8	8	8	8	8	6	8	5.9%	3.2%
EU TOTAL	**45**	**45**	**45**	**45**	**45**	**46**	**48**	**47**	**49**	**50**	**45**	**48**	**1.1%**	**1.2%**
EFTA TOTAL	**12**	**12**	**12**	**12**	**11**	**11**	**11**	**11**	**11**	**11**	**12**	**11**	**–1.4%**	**–1.0%**
EUROPE TOTAL	**57**	**57**	**57**	**57**	**56**	**57**	**57**	**58**	**60**	**61**	**57**	**59**	**0.6%**	**0.8%**

Sector 2
HIGHER EDUCATION

	1981	1982	1983	1984	1985	1986	1987	1988	1989	1990	1981–85 Average	1986–90 Average	81/85 – 86/90 Year on Year Increase	Decade: Year on Year Increase
AUSTRIA	(193)	(202)	(206)	(209)	(218)	(221)	(217)	(209)	(243)	(248)	206	228	2.1%	2.8%
BELGIUM	140	140	140	140	140	140	140	140	140	140	140	140	0.0%	0.0%
DENMARK	25	25	25	25	25	(19)	(19)	19	18	18	25	19	–5.7%	–3.6%
EAST GERMANY	(504)	(504)	(504)	504	(504)	(504)	504	(504)	(504)	(504)	504	504	0.0%	0.0%
EIRE	38	39	37	35	36	33	33	34	36	33	37	34	–1.8%	–1.6%
FINLAND	(499)	(499)	(499)	(499)	(499)	499	499	498	500	457	499	491	–0.3%	–1.0%
FRANCE	184	184	184	184	185	192	195	195	195	200	184	195	1.2%	0.9%
GREECE	(70)	(70)	(70)	(70)	(70)	(70)	(70)	(70)	(70)	(70)	70	70	0.0%	0.0%
ICELAND	(17)	(17)	(17)	(17)	(17)	17	18	18	18	18	17	18	0.9%	0.6%
ITALY	(10)	(10)	(10)	(10)	(10)	(10)	(10)	(10)	(10)	(10)	10	10	0.0%	0.0%
LIECHTENSTEIN	1	1			1	(1)	(1)	(1)	(1)	(1)	1	1	0.0%	0.0%
LUXEMBOURG	1,016	1,059	1,043	(1,039)	(1,039)	(1,039)	(1,039)	(1,039)	(1,039)	(1,039)	1,039	1,039	–0.0%	0.2%
NETHERLANDS	(200)	(200)	(200)	200	(200)	200	204	221	217	210	200	210	1.0%	0.5%
NORWAY	177	183	187	138	171	169	227	257	320	264	171	247	7.6%	4.5%
PORTUGAL	626	730	879	1,029	1,178	1,327	(1,378)	1,428	(1,228)	1,028	888	1,278	7.5%	5.7%
SPAIN	(134)	(134)	(134)	134	(134)	134	139	128	136	142	134	136	0.3%	0.6%
SWEDEN	(249)	(249)	(249)	(249)	(263)	(263)	(270)	(280)	(287)	(290)	252	278	2.0%	1.7%
SWITZERLAND	860	860	860	860	860	(864)	(860)	(860)	(860)	(860)	860	861	0.0%	0.0%
UK	491	491	491	491	491	453	463	486	488	(490)	491	476	–0.6%	–0.0%
WEST GERMANY														
EU TOTAL	**4,142**	**4,296**	**4,431**	**4,526**	**4,710**	**4,821**	**4,939**	**5,043**	**4,909**	**4,657**	**4,421**	**4,874**	**2.0%**	**1.3%**
EFTA TOTAL	**1,293**	**1,302**	**1,306**	**1,309**	**1,332**	**1,335**	**1,348**	**1,355**	**1,402**	**1,366**	**1,308**	**1,361**	**0.8%**	**0.6%**
EUROPE TOTAL	**5,435**	**5,598**	**5,737**	**5,835**	**6,042**	**6,156**	**6,287**	**6,398**	**6,311**	**6,023**	**5,729**	**6,235**	**1.7%**	**1.1%**

Figures in parentheses are grossed.

Service Points

Sector 3 – OTHER NON-MAJOR SPEC.

	1981	1982	1983	1984	1985	1986	1987	1988	1989	1990	1981–85 Average	1986–90 Average	81/85 – 86/90 Year on Year Increase	Decade: Year on Year Increase
AUSTRIA	(6)	(6)	(6)	(6)	(6)	(6)	(6)	(6)	(6)	(6)	6	6	0.0%	0.0%
BELGIUM	6	6	6	6	6	6	6	6	6	6	6	6	0.0%	0.0%
DENMARK	0	0	0	0	0	0	0	0	0	0	0	0	0.0%	0.0%
EAST GERMANY	(105)	(105)	(105)	(105)	(105)	(105)	(105)	(105)	(105)	(103)	105	105	-0.1%	-0.2%
EIRE	4	4	4	4	4	4	4	4	4	4	4	4	0.0%	0.0%
FINLAND	0	0	0	0	0	0	0	0	0	0	0	0	0.0%	0.0%
FRANCE	(1)	(1)	(1)	(1)	(1)	(1)	(1)	(1)	(1)	(1)	1	1	0.0%	0.0%
GREECE	6	6	6	6	6	6	6	6	6	6	6	6	0.0%	0.0%
ICELAND	0	0	0	0	0	0	0	0	0	0	0	0	0.0%	0.0%
ITALY	(33)	(33)	(33)	(33)	(33)	33	(33)	(34)	34	(34)	33	34	0.4%	0.3%
LIECHTENSTEIN	0	0	0	0	0	0	0	0	0	0	0	0	0.0%	0.0%
LUXEMBOURG	0	0	0	0	0	0	0	0	0	0	0	0	0.0%	0.0%
NETHERLANDS	6	6	6	6	5	5	5	5	5	5	6	5	-2.9%	-2.0%
NORWAY	0	0	0	0	0	0	0	0	0	0	0	0	0.0%	0.0%
PORTUGAL	(26)	(26)	(26)	(26)	28	22	(22)	(22)	(22)	(22)	26	22	-3.3%	-1.8%
SPAIN	15	15	15	15	15	(15)	(15)	(15)	(15)	(15)	15	15	0.0%	0.0%
SWEDEN	(72)	(72)	(72)	(72)	(72)	(72)	(72)	(72)	(72)	(72)	72	72	0.0%	0.0%
SWITZERLAND	(33)	(33)	(33)	(33)	(33)	33	33	34	34	34	33	34	0.4%	0.3%
UK	(23)	(23)	(23)	(23)	(23)	(23)	(23)	(23)	(23)	(23)	23	23	0.0%	0.0%
WEST GERMANY	37	37	37	37	37	37	38	38	36	(36)	37	37	0.0%	-0.3%
EU TOTAL	262	262	262	262	261	257	258	259	257	255	262	257	-0.4%	-0.3%
EFTA TOTAL	111	111	111	111	111	111	111	112	112	112	111	112	0.1%	0.1%
EUROPE TOTAL	373	373	373	373	372	368	369	371	369	367	373	369	-0.2%	-0.2%

Sector 4 – SCHOOLS

	1981	1982	1983	1984	1985	1986	1987	1988	1989	1990	1981–85 Average	1986–90 Average	81/85 – 86/90 Year on Year Increase	Decade: Year on Year Increase
AUSTRIA	(438)	(438)	(438)	(438)	(438)	(438)	(438)	(438)	(438)	(432)	438	437	-0.1%	-0.2%
BELGIUM	(923)	(923)	(923)	(923)	(923)	(923)	(923)	(923)	(923)	(923)	923	923	0.0%	0.0%
DENMARK	(1,900)	(1,900)	(1,900)	(1,900)	(1,900)	(1,900)	(1,900)	(1,900)	(1,900)	(1,900)	1,900	1,900	0.0%	0.0%
EAST GERMANY	(974)	(974)	(974)	(974)	(974)	(974)	(974)	(974)	(974)	(952)	974	970	-0.1%	-0.3%
EIRE	(453)	(453)	(453)	(453)	(453)	(453)	(453)	(453)	(453)	(453)	453	453	0.0%	0.0%
FINLAND	(5,340)	(5,340)	(5,340)	(5,340)	(5,340)	(5,340)	5,340	5,439	5,439	5,439	5,340	5,399	0.2%	0.2%
FRANCE	(5,533)	(5,533)	(5,533)	(5,533)	(5,533)	(5,533)	(5,533)	(5,533)	(5,533)	(5,533)	5,533	5,533	0.0%	0.0%
GREECE	(974)	(974)	(974)	(974)	(974)	(974)	(974)	(974)	(974)	(974)	974	974	0.0%	0.0%
ICELAND	(37)	(37)	(37)	(37)	37	39	47	68	75	78	37	61	10.7%	8.6%
ITALY	8,920	(8,920)	(8,920)	(8,920)	(8,920)	(8,920)	(8,920)	(8,920)	(8,920)	(8,920)	8,920	8,920	0.0%	0.0%
LIECHTENSTEIN	(2)	(2)	(2)	(2)	(2)	(2)	(2)	(2)	(2)	(2)	2	2	0.0%	0.0%
LUXEMBOURG	(32)	(32)	(32)	(32)	(32)	(32)	(32)	(32)	(32)	(32)	32	32	0.0%	0.0%
NETHERLANDS	(1,493)	(1,493)	(1,493)	(1,493)	(1,493)	(1,493)	(1,493)	(1,493)	(1,493)	(1,493)	1,493	1,493	0.0%	0.0%
NORWAY	(3,789)	(3,789)	(3,789)	3,789	3,655	3,521	3,383	3,523	3,437	3,383	3,762	3,449	-1.7%	-1.3%
PORTUGAL	712	719	599	677	677	779	916	693	892	707	677	797	3.3%	-0.1%
SPAIN	(626)	(626)	(626)	(626)	(626)	(626)	(626)	(626)	(626)	(626)	626	626	0.0%	0.0%
SWEDEN	(9,024)	(8,634)	(8,244)	(7,854)	(6,947)	(6,561)	(6,368)	(6,368)	(5,905)	(5,515)	8,141	6,143	-5.5%	-5.3%
SWITZERLAND	(365)	(365)	(365)	(365)	(365)	(365)	(365)	(365)	(365)	(361)	365	364	0.0%	-0.1%
UK	5,384	5,292	5,240	5,187	5,086	5,086	5,086	5,086	5,086	(5,086)	5,238	5,086	-0.6%	-0.6%
WEST GERMANY	(5,508)	(5,508)	(5,508)	(5,508)	(5,508)	(5,508)	(5,508)	(5,508)	(5,508)	(5,508)	5,508	5,508	0.0%	0.0%
EU TOTAL	33,432	33,347	33,175	33,200	33,099	33,201	33,338	33,115	33,314	33,107	33,251	33,215	-0.0%	-0.1%
EFTA TOTAL	18,995	18,605	18,215	17,825	16,784	16,286	15,943	16,203	15,661	15,210	18,085	15,857	-2.6%	-2.4%
EUROPE TOTAL	52,427	51,952	51,390	51,025	49,883	49,487	49,281	49,318	48,975	48,317	51,335	49,072	-0.5%	-0.5%

Figures in parentheses are grossed.

Service Points

Sector 5 SPECIAL

	1981	1982	1983	1984	1985	1986	1987	1988	1989	1990	1981–85 Average	1986–90 Average	81/85 – 86/90 Year on Year Increase	Decade: Year on Year Increase
AUSTRIA	(312)	(312)	(312)	(312)	(312)	(312)	(312)	(312)	(312)	(314)	312	312	0.0%	0.1%
BELGIUM	(121)	(121)	(121)	(121)	(121)	(121)	(121)	(121)	(121)	(121)	121	121	0.0%	0.0%
DENMARK	(179)	(179)	(179)	(179)	(179)	(179)	(179)	(179)	(179)	181	179	179	0.0%	0.1%
EAST GERMANY	(682)	(682)	(682)	(682)	(682)	(682)	(682)	(682)	(682)	(671)	682	680	-0.1%	-0.2%
EIRE	(38)	(38)	(38)	(38)	(38)	(38)	(38)	(38)	(38)	(38)	38	38	0.0%	0.0%
FINLAND	(60)	(64)	(69)	(78)	(82)	(83)	(87)	(86)	(98)	(97)	71	90	5.1%	5.5%
FRANCE	(654)	(654)	(654)	(654)	(654)	(654)	(654)	(654)	(654)	(654)	654	654	0.0%	0.0%
GREECE	(118)	(118)	(118)	(118)	(118)	(118)	(118)	(118)	(118)	(118)	118	118	0.0%	0.0%
ICELAND	(2)	(3)	(3)	(3)	(4)	(4)	(5)	(6)	(7)	(8)	3	6	14.9%	16.7%
ITALY	(25)	(25)	(25)	(25)	(25)	(25)	(25)	(25)	(25)	(25)	25	25	0.0%	0.0%
LIECHTENSTEIN	0	0	0	0	0	0	0	0	0	0	0	0	0.0%	0.0%
LUXEMBOURG	(5)	(5)	(5)	(5)	(5)	(5)	(5)	(5)	(5)	0	5	5	0.2%	1.0%
NETHERLANDS	677	819	856	784	869	869	850	811	777	742	801	810	1.6%	0.5%
NORWAY	(134)	(137)	(141)	(144)	162	162	172	157	148	140	144	156	14.4%	7.8%
PORTUGAL	166	188	126	98	319	395	(343)	291	405	327	179	352	12.6%	9.4%
SPAIN	612	602	717	832	948	1,063	(1,296)	1,528	(1,451)	1,375	742	1,343	3.6%	2.8%
SWEDEN	(72)	(74)	(76)	(78)	80	80	69	99	114	92	76	91	0.0%	0.1%
SWITZERLAND	(275)	(275)	(275)	(275)	(275)	(275)	(275)	(275)	(275)	(277)	275	275	0.0%	0.0%
UK	(676)	(676)	(676)	(676)	(676)	(676)	(676)	(676)	(676)	(676)	676	676	0.0%	0.0%
WEST GERMANY	776	776	776	776	776	809	822	797	799	(801)	776	806	0.8%	0.4%
EU TOTAL	4,729	4,883	4,973	4,988	5,410	5,634	5,809	5,925	5,930	5,734	4,997	5,806	3.0%	2.2%
EFTA TOTAL	855	865	876	890	915	917	920	935	954	928	880	931	1.1%	0.9%
EUROPE TOTAL	5,584	5,748	5,849	5,878	6,325	6,551	6,729	6,860	6,884	6,662	5,877	6,737	2.8%	2.0%

Sector 6 PUBLIC

	1981	1982	1983	1984	1985	1986	1987	1988	1989	1990	1981–85 Average	1986–90 Average	81/85 – 86/90 Year on Year Increase	Decade: Year on Year Increase
AUSTRIA	2,038	(2,129)	(2,221)	2,313	(2,081)	(2,081)	2,081	2,080	2,494	2,374	2,156	2,222	0.6%	1.7%
BELGIUM	1,667	1,652	1,587	1,544	1,517	1,416	1,315	1,269	1,209	1,151	1,593	1,272	-4.4%	-4.0%
DENMARK	1,177	1,173	1,162	1,159	(1,151)	(1,148)	1,148	1,106	1,057	1,031	1,164	1,098	-1.2%	-1.5%
EAST GERMANY	(6,139)	(6,139)	(6,139)	(6,139)	(6,139)	(6,139)	(6,139)	(6,139)	(6,139)	(6,139)	6,139	6,139	0.0%	0.0%
EIRE	374	373	376	380	381	384	382	362	356	359	377	369	-0.4%	-0.5%
FINLAND	(2,013)	(1,943)	(1,873)	1,803	1,755	1,754	1,500	1,437	1,405	1,383	1,877	1,496	-4.4%	-4.1%
FRANCE	(1,278)	(1,354)	1,462	(1,486)	(1,572)	(2,156)	2,740	(2,740)	(2,740)	(2,740)	1,430	2,623	12.9%	8.8%
GREECE	(51)	(51)	(51)	(51)	(51)	(51)	(51)	(51)	(51)	(51)	51	51	0.0%	0.0%
ICELAND	249	248	245	243	242	241	240	225	222	215	245	229	-1.4%	-1.6%
ITALY	(2,366)	(2,366)	(2,366)	(2,366)	(2,366)	(2,366)	(2,366)	(2,366)	(2,366)	(2,366)	2,366	2,366	0.0%	0.0%
LIECHTENSTEIN	(3)	(3)	(3)	(3)	(3)	3	(3)	(3)	3	(3)	3	3	0.0%	0.0%
LUXEMBOURG	5	5	5	5	5	5	5	5	(5)	(5)	5	5	0.0%	0.0%
NETHERLANDS	1,050	1,070	1,082	1,204	1,205	1,210	1,263	1,270	1,288	1,265	1,122	1,259	2.3%	2.1%
NORWAY	(1,482)	(1,461)	(1,440)	(1,419)	(1,398)	1,377	1,373	1,339	1,334	1,292	1,440	1,343	-1.4%	-1.5%
PORTUGAL	174	171	240	181	344	317	270	192	239	234	222	250	2.4%	3.3%
SPAIN	1,938	2,136	2,243	2,350	2,457	2,564	(2,885)	3,206	(3,421)	3,635	2,225	3,142	7.1%	7.2%
SWEDEN	(1,975)	(1,975)	(1,975)	(1,975)	(1,975)	(1,975)	(1,975)	(1,975)	1,975	(1,975)	1,975	1,975	0.0%	0.0%
SWITZERLAND	(1,896)	(1,948)	(2,009)	(2,052)	(2,113)	(2,201)	(2,290)	(2,378)	(2,467)	(2,555)	2,004	2,378	3.5%	3.4%
UK	16,747	16,939	17,617	18,611	18,561	20,228	20,938	21,947	22,771	23,463	17,695	21,869	4.3%	3.6%
WEST GERMANY	10,666	11,093	11,147	11,220	11,363	11,529	11,386	11,378	10,929	(10,962)	11,098	11,237	0.2%	0.3%
EU TOTAL	43,632	44,522	45,477	46,696	47,112	49,514	50,886	52,031	52,571	53,401	45,488	51,681	2.6%	2.3%
EFTA TOTAL	9,656	9,707	9,766	9,808	9,567	9,632	9,462	9,437	9,900	9,797	9,701	9,646	-0.1%	0.2%
EUROPE TOTAL	53,288	54,229	55,243	56,504	56,679	59,146	60,348	61,468	62,471	63,198	55,189	61,326	2.1%	1.9%

Figures in parentheses are grossed.

Service Points

ALL SECTORS	1981	1982	1983	1984	1985	1986	1987	1988	1989	1990	1981-85 Average	1986-90 Average	81/85 - 86/90 Year on Year Increase	Decade: Year on Year Increase
AUSTRIA	2,988	3,088	3,184	3,279	3,056	3,059	3,055	3,046	3,494	3,375	3,119	3,206	0.6%	1.4%
BELGIUM	2,858	2,843	2,778	2,735	2,708	2,607	2,506	2,460	2,400	2,342	2,784	2,463	-2.4%	-2.2%
DENMARK	3,282	3,278	3,267	3,264	3,256	3,248	3,245	3,206	3,158	3,134	3,269	3,198	-0.4%	-0.5%
EAST GERMANY	8,410	8,410	8,410	8,410	8,410	8,410	8,410	8,410	8,410	8,376	8,410	8,403	-0.0%	-0.0%
EIRE	909	909	910	912	914	914	912	893	889	889	911	899	-0.3%	-0.2%
FINLAND	7,913	7,847	7,782	7,721	7,677	7,678	7,427	7,461	7,443	7,377	7,788	7,477	-0.8%	-0.8%
FRANCE	7,651	7,727	7,835	7,859	7,948	8,537	9,124	9,124	9,124	9,129	7,804	9,008	2.9%	2.0%
GREECE	1,220	1,220	1,220	1,220	1,220	1,220	1,220	1,220	1,220	1,220	1,220	1,220	0.0%	0.0%
ICELAND	306	306	303	301	301	302	311	318	323	320	303	315	0.7%	0.5%
ITALY	11,356	11,356	11,356	11,356	11,356	11,356	11,356	11,357	11,357	11,357	11,356	11,357	0.0%	0.0%
LIECHTENSTEIN	7	7	7	7	7	7	7	7	7	7	7	7	0.0%	0.0%
LUXEMBOURG	44	44	44	44	44	44	44	44	44	44	44	44	0.0%	0.0%
NETHERLANDS	4,246	4,451	4,484	4,530	4,615	4,620	4,654	4,622	4,606	4,548	4,465	4,610	0.6%	0.8%
NORWAY	5,608	5,590	5,573	5,555	5,417	5,282	5,134	5,242	5,138	5,027	5,549	5,161	-1.4%	-1.2%
PORTUGAL	1,256	1,288	1,179	1,121	1,538	1,683	1,779	1,456	1,879	1,555	1,276	1,670	5.5%	2.4%
SPAIN	3,820	4,112	4,483	4,855	5,227	5,597	6,202	6,805	6,743	6,681	4,499	6,406	7.3%	6.4%
SWEDEN	11,281	10,893	10,505	10,117	9,212	8,826	8,627	8,646	8,206	7,800	10,402	8,421	-4.1%	-4.0%
SWITZERLAND	2,819	2,871	2,932	2,975	3,050	3,138	3,234	3,333	3,429	3,518	2,929	3,330	2.6%	2.5%
UK	23,706	23,806	24,432	25,373	25,222	26,893	27,599	28,608	29,432	30,124	24,508	28,531	3.1%	2.7%
WEST GERMANY	17,484	17,911	17,965	18,038	18,181	18,344	18,225	18,215	17,768	17,805	17,916	18,071	0.2%	0.2%
EU TOTAL	86,242	87,355	88,363	89,717	90,637	93,472	95,276	96,420	97,030	97,204	88,463	95,880	1.6%	-1.3%
EFTA TOTAL	30,922	30,602	30,286	29,955	28,720	28,272	27,795	28,053	28,040	27,424	30,097	27,917	-1.5%	-1.3%
EUROPE TOTAL	117,164	117,957	118,649	119,672	119,357	121,744	123,071	124,473	125,070	124,628	118,560	123,797	0.9%	0.7%

Service Points per 1000 Population

European Union	1981	1982	1983	1984	1985	1986	1987	1988	1989	1990	1981-85 Average	1986-90 Average	81/85 - 86/90 Year on Year Increase	Decade: Year on Year Increase
Sector 1	0.00	0.00	0.00	0.00	0.00	0.00	0.00	0.00	0.00	0.00	0.00	0.00	1.0%	1.2%
Sector 2	0.01	0.01	0.01	0.01	0.01	0.01	0.01	0.01	0.01	0.01	0.01	0.01	1.9%	1.3%
Sector 3	0.00	0.00	0.00	0.00	0.00	0.00	0.00	0.00	0.00	0.00	0.00	0.00	-0.5%	-0.3%
Sector 4	0.10	0.10	0.10	0.10	0.10	0.10	0.10	0.10	0.10	0.10	0.10	0.10	-0.1%	-0.1%
Sector 5	0.01	0.01	0.01	0.01	0.02	0.02	0.02	0.02	0.02	0.02	0.01	0.02	2.9%	2.1%
Sector 6	0.13	0.13	0.13	0.14	0.14	0.15	0.15	0.15	0.16	0.16	0.13	0.15	2.5%	2.2%
All Sectors	0.26	0.26	0.26	0.27	0.27	0.27	0.28	0.28	0.29	0.29	0.26	0.28	1.5%	1.3%

EFTA	1981	1982	1983	1984	1985	1986	1987	1988	1989	1990	1981-85 Average	1986-90 Average	81/85 - 86/90 Year on Year Increase	Decade: Year on Year Increase
Sector 1	0.00	0.00	0.00	0.00	0.00	0.00	0.00	0.00	0.00	0.00	0.00	0.00	-1.4%	-1.0%
Sector 2	0.04	0.04	0.04	0.04	0.04	0.04	0.04	0.04	0.04	0.04	0.04	0.04	0.8%	0.5%
Sector 3	0.00	0.00	0.00	0.00	0.00	0.00	0.00	0.00	0.00	0.00	0.00	0.00	0.1%	0.0%
Sector 4	0.59	0.58	0.57	0.55	0.52	0.51	0.50	0.50	0.49	0.47	0.56	0.49	-2.6%	-2.5%
Sector 5	0.03	0.03	0.03	0.03	0.03	0.03	0.03	0.03	0.03	0.03	0.03	0.03	1.1%	0.8%
Sector 6	0.30	0.30	0.30	0.31	0.30	0.30	0.29	0.29	0.31	0.30	0.30	0.30	-0.1%	0.1%
All Sectors	0.96	0.95	0.94	0.93	0.89	0.88	0.86	0.87	0.87	0.85	0.94	0.87	-1.5%	-1.4%

Europe Total	1981	1982	1983	1984	1985	1986	1987	1988	1989	1990	1981-85 Average	1986-90 Average	81/85 - 86/90 Year on Year Increase	Decade: Year on Year Increase
Sector 1	0.00	0.00	0.00	0.00	0.00	0.00	0.00	0.00	0.00	0.00	0.00	0.00	0.5%	0.7%
Sector 2	0.01	0.02	0.02	0.02	0.02	0.02	0.02	0.02	0.02	0.02	0.02	0.02	1.6%	1.1%
Sector 3	0.00	0.00	0.00	0.00	0.00	0.00	0.00	0.00	0.00	0.00	0.00	0.00	-0.3%	-0.2%
Sector 4	0.14	0.14	0.14	0.14	0.13	0.13	0.13	0.13	0.13	0.13	0.14	0.13	-1.0%	-0.9%
Sector 5	0.02	0.02	0.02	0.02	0.02	0.02	0.02	0.02	0.02	0.02	0.02	0.02	2.7%	2.0%
Sector 6	0.14	0.15	0.15	0.15	0.15	0.16	0.16	0.16	0.17	0.17	0.15	0.16	2.0%	1.9%
All Sectors	0.32	0.32	0.32	0.32	0.32	0.33	0.33	0.33	0.34	0.34	0.32	0.33	0.8%	0.7%

Collections: Books & Bound Periodicals

Sector 1 NATIONAL	1981	1982	1983	1984	1985	1986	1987	1988	1989	1990	1981–85 Average	1986–90 Average	81/85 – 86/90 Year on Year Increase	Decade: Year on Year Increase
AUSTRIA	(2,372,802)	(2,403,901)	(2,435,000)	(2,468,099)	(2,497,198)	2,535,449	2,552,633	2,581,645	2,617,950	2,652,693	2,435,000	2,588,074	1.2%	1.2%
BELGIUM	2,761,630	2,804,476	2,839,345	2,882,553	2,889,945	(3,167,458)	(3,444,972)	(3,722,486)	4,000,000	(4,277,514)	2,835,590	3,722,486	5.6%	5.0%
DENMARK	2,500,000	2,500,000	2,500,000	2,700,000	2,700,000	2,750,000	2,800,000	2,715,000	3,347,679	3,447,148	2,580,000	3,011,965	3.1%	3.6%
EAST GERMANY	(10,911,000)	(10,911,000)	(10,911,000)	(10,911,000)	(10,911,000)	10,911,000	(11,234,501)	11,558,000	(11,881,499)	12,204,998	10,911,000	11,558,000	1.2%	1.3%
EIRE	(790,000)	(790,000)	(790,000)	(790,000)	(790,000)	808,000	720,000	730,000	740,000	750,000	790,000	749,600	-1.0%	-0.6%
FINLAND	1,741,565	1,787,900	1,815,000	1,861,900	1,904,000	1,949,300	1,996,000	2,041,000	2,085,300	2,133,700	1,822,073	2,041,060	2.3%	2.3%
FRANCE	12,350,000	12,350,000	12,350,000	12,350,000	12,350,000	12,350,000	12,350,000	12,350,000	12,350,000	12,350,000	12,350,000	12,350,000	0.0%	0.0%
GREECE	2,500,000	2,500,000	2,500,000	2,500,000	2,500,000	2,500,000	(2,500,000)	(2,500,000)	2,500,000	(2,500,000)	2,500,000	2,500,000	0.0%	0.0%
ICELAND	(351,312)	(358,378)	(365,444)	(372,510)	379,576	385,718	392,494	399,494	406,066	414,906	365,444	399,736	1.8%	1.9%
ITALY	9,799,762	9,799,762	9,825,000	9,825,045	10,009,097	(9,852,098)	(9,904,430)	(9,956,764)	(10,009,098)	(10,061,432)	9,799,762	9,956,764	0.3%	0.3%
LIECHTENSTEIN	(150,000)	(150,000)	(150,000)	(150,000)	(150,000)	(150,000)	(150,000)	(150,000)	(150,000)	150,000	150,000	150,000	0.0%	0.0%
LUXEMBOURG	560,000	570,000	580,000	590,000	600,000	615,000	630,000	645,000	660,000	675,000	580,000	645,000	2.1%	2.1%
NETHERLANDS	1,721,000	1,798,000	1,837,000	1,919,000	2,006,000	2,094,000	2,183,000	2,294,000	2,482,000	(2,482,000)	1,856,200	2,307,000	4.4%	4.2%
NORWAY	(2,237,100)	(2,220,900)	(2,204,700)	2,069,000	(2,234,000)	2,399,000	2,213,000	2,432,000	2,030,000	1,988,000	2,193,140	2,212,400	0.2%	-1.3%
PORTUGAL	774,110	793,777	816,437	1,088,470	2,096,498	2,126,247	2,156,787	2,181,603	2,219,643	2,235,686	1,113,858	2,183,993	14.4%	12.5%
SPAIN	3,601,604	3,713,606	3,813,791	3,709,667	3,709,667	1,712,427	2,054,334	2,472,552	3,039,271	3,500,000	3,709,667	2,555,717	-7.2%	-0.3%
SWEDEN	(2,826,335)	(2,932,668)	(3,039,001)	3,145,334	(3,251,667)	3,358,000	3,424,000	3,550,000	3,677,000	3,125,100	3,039,001	3,426,820	2.4%	1.1%
SWITZERLAND	(1,245,423)	(1,245,423)	(1,245,423)	(1,245,423)	(1,245,423)	1,261,400	1,229,445	1,337,105	2,498,212	2,550,232	1,245,423	1,775,279	7.3%	8.3%
UK	(23,544,000)	(23,544,000)	(23,544,000)	(23,544,000)	(23,544,000)	(23,544,000)	(23,855,000)	24,166,000	24,679,500	25,193,000	23,544,000	24,287,500	0.6%	0.8%
WEST GERMANY	14,296,000	13,292,000	14,096,000	14,681,000	15,115,000	15,682,803	16,240,109	16,777,054	17,338,774	17,838,774	14,296,000	16,775,503	3.3%	2.5%
EU TOTAL	86,109,106	85,366,621	86,142,716	87,490,735	89,221,207	88,113,031	90,073,133	92,068,459	95,247,464	97,515,552	86,866,077	92,603,528	1.3%	1.4%
EFTA TOTAL	10,924,537	11,099,170	11,254,568	11,310,266	11,661,864	12,038,867	11,957,572	12,491,244	13,464,528	13,014,631	11,250,081	12,593,368	2.3%	2.0%
EUROPE TOTAL	97,033,643	96,465,791	97,397,284	98,801,001	100,883,071	100,151,898	102,030,705	104,559,703	108,711,992	110,530,183	98,116,158	105,196,896	1.4%	1.5%

Sector 2 HIGHER EDUCATION	1981	1982	1983	1984	1985	1986	1987	1988	1989	1990	1981–85 Average	1986–90 Average	81/85 – 86/90 Year on Year Increase	Decade: Year on Year Increase
AUSTRIA	11,235,183	11,743,422	12,005,731	12,193,649	12,702,992	12,902,207	12,654,716	12,167,812	14,135,611	14,477,691	11,976,195	13,267,607	2.1%	2.9%
BELGIUM	(5,988,084)	(5,988,084)	(5,988,084)	(5,988,084)	(5,988,084)	(5,988,084)	(5,988,084)	(5,988,084)	(5,988,084)	(5,988,084)	5,988,084	5,988,084	0.0%	0.0%
DENMARK	6,243,100	6,346,900	6,549,000	6,702,000	6,956,400	(6,856,401)	(7,336,523)	7,716,645	7,242,026	7,799,511	6,559,480	7,410,221	2.5%	2.5%
EAST GERMANY	(21,447,001)	(21,679,334)	(21,911,667)	22,144,000	(22,378,334)	(22,606,667)	22,841,000	(23,073,333)	(23,305,666)	(23,537,999)	21,911,667	23,073,333	1.0%	1.0%
EIRE	3,910,000	4,082,000	4,259,000	4,325,000	4,440,000	4,619,000	4,756,000	4,893,000	4,989,000	5,018,000	4,203,200	4,855,000	2.9%	2.8%
FINLAND	7,435,050	8,508,302	8,954,000	9,308,973	10,511,763	10,898,938	11,305,132	11,701,489	12,054,059	12,265,675	8,943,618	11,645,058	5.4%	5.7%
FRANCE	17,700,000	17,900,000	18,000,000	18,000,000	18,100,000	18,300,000	18,500,000	19,000,000	19,500,000	20,000,000	17,940,000	19,060,000	1.2%	1.4%
GREECE	(6,482,356)	(6,482,356)	(6,482,356)	(6,482,356)	(6,482,356)	(6,482,356)	(6,482,356)	(6,482,356)	(6,482,356)	(6,482,356)	6,482,356	6,482,356	0.0%	0.0%
ICELAND	(197,000)	(208,000)	(219,000)	(230,000)	(241,000)	252,000	264,000	274,000	285,000	296,000	219,000	274,200	4.6%	4.6%
ITALY	(6,006,501)	(6,006,501)	5,867,107	5,999,569	6,152,826	(5,982,551)	5,812,276	(5,727,138)	(5,642,000)	5,642,000	6,006,501	5,761,193	-0.6%	-0.7%
LIECHTENSTEIN	(29,772)	(29,772)	(29,772)	(29,772)	(29,772)	(29,772)	(29,772)	(29,772)	(29,772)	(29,506)	29,772	29,719	-0.0%	-0.1%
LUXEMBOURG	(268,673)	(268,673)	(268,673)	(268,673)	(268,673)	(268,673)	(268,673)	(268,673)	(268,673)	(268,673)	268,673	268,673	0.0%	0.0%
NETHERLANDS	17,536,000	18,748,000	19,584,000	(18,622,667)	20,633,000	21,004,000	22,177,000	22,502,000	23,370,000	(24,238,000)	19,024,733	22,658,200	3.6%	3.7%
NORWAY	(7,240,499)	(7,404,666)	(7,568,833)	7,733,000	(7,912,000)	8,091,000	8,375,000	8,374,000	8,887,000	8,718,000	7,571,800	8,489,000	2.3%	2.1%
PORTUGAL	1,957,393	1,760,203	1,738,692	1,434,544	(1,722,708)	2,110,015	3,784,150	3,512,943	4,902,291	5,080,276	1,722,708	3,697,935	16.5%	11.2%
SPAIN	8,461,493	10,446,827	11,284,138	12,121,449	12,958,760	13,796,070	(14,539,688)	15,283,308	(15,666,717)	16,050,125	11,054,533	15,067,182	6.4%	7.4%
SWEDEN	(13,719,001)	(14,267,334)	(14,815,667)	15,364,000	15,694,000	16,217,000	16,833,000	18,035,000	18,243,000	18,654,000	14,772,000	17,596,400	3.6%	3.5%
SWITZERLAND	(14,534,001)	(14,534,001)	(14,534,001)	14,534,001	(15,310,570)	15,310,570	15,743,020	16,313,309	16,712,530	16,867,612	14,689,315	16,189,408	2.0%	1.7%
UK	(77,161,000)	(77,161,000)	(77,161,000)	(77,161,000)	(77,161,000)	(77,161,000)	80,329,000	83,497,000	86,664,000	89,832,000	77,161,000	83,496,600	1.6%	1.7%
WEST GERMANY	71,419,000	66,901,000	70,760,000	73,256,000	74,759,000	80,116,688	82,955,846	86,234,935	88,306,810	(90,417,786)	71,419,000	85,606,373	3.7%	2.7%
EU TOTAL	244,580,601	243,770,878	249,853,717	252,505,342	257,999,141	265,393,505	275,770,397	284,179,415	291,427,623	300,354,810	249,741,936	283,425,150	2.6%	2.3%
EFTA TOTAL	54,390,506	56,695,497	58,127,004	59,393,395	62,402,097	63,701,485	65,204,640	68,895,382	70,346,972	71,308,484	58,201,700	67,491,393	3.0%	3.1%
EUROPE TOTAL	298,971,107	300,466,375	307,980,721	311,898,737	320,401,238	329,094,990	340,975,037	351,074,797	361,774,595	371,663,294	307,943,636	350,916,543	2.6%	2.4%

Figures in parentheses are grossed.

Collections: Books & Bound Periodicals

	1981	1982	1983	1984	1985	1986	1987	1988	1989	1990	1981-85 Average	1986-90 Average	81/85 – 86/90 Year on Year Increase	Decade: Year on Year Increase
Sector 3 – OTHER NON–MAJOR SPEC														
AUSTRIA	(1,544,000)	(1,544,000)	(1,544,000)	(1,544,000)	(1,544,000)	(1,544,000)	(1,544,000)	(1,544,000)	(1,544,000)	(1,544,000)	1,544,000	1,544,000	0.0%	0.0%
BELGIUM	(1,401,501)	(1,401,501)	(1,401,501)	(1,401,501)	(1,401,501)	(1,401,501)	(1,401,501)	(1,401,501)	(1,401,501)	(1,401,501)	1,401,501	1,401,501	0.0%	0.0%
DENMARK	0	0	0	0	0	0	0	0	0	0			0.0%	0.0%
EAST GERMANY	(26,351,980)	(26,351,980)	(26,351,980)	(26,351,980)	(26,351,980)	(26,351,980)	(26,351,980)	(26,351,980)	(26,351,980)	(25,971,276)	26,351,980	26,275,839	-0.1%	-0.2%
EIRE	(317,200)	(317,200)	(317,200)	(317,200)	(317,200)	317,200	319,910	322,827	325,663	328,300	317,200	322,780	0.3%	0.4%
FINLAND	0	0	0	0	0	0	0	0	0	0			0.0%	0.0%
FRANCE	(400,000)	(400,000)	(400,000)	(400,000)	(400,000)	400,000	400,000	400,000	400,000	400,000	400,000	400,000	0.0%	0.0%
GREECE	(1,399,049)	(1,399,049)	(1,399,049)	(1,399,049)	(1,399,049)	(1,399,049)	(1,399,049)	(1,399,049)	(1,399,049)	(1,399,049)	1,399,049	1,399,049	0.0%	0.0%
ICELAND	0	0	0	0	0	0	0	0	0	0			0.0%	0.0%
ITALY	(3,557,337)	(3,836,630)	4,115,923	4,260,417	4,953,802	6,777,000	7,056,293	(7,335,586)	7,394,000	(7,673,293)	4,144,822	7,247,234	11.8%	8.9%
LIECHTENSTEIN	0	0	0	0	0	0	0	0	0	0			0.0%	0.0%
LUXEMBOURG	0	0	0	0	0	0	0	0	0	0			0.0%	0.0%
NETHERLANDS	(1,944,000)	(1,944,000)	(1,944,000)	(1,944,000)	1,593,000	1,640,000	(1,232,250)	(1,113,625)	995,000	(876,375)	1,873,800	1,171,450	-9.0%	-8.5%
NORWAY	0	0	0	0	0	0	0	0	0	0			0.0%	0.0%
PORTUGAL	(2,682,980)	(2,682,980)	(2,682,980)	(2,682,980)	(2,682,980)	2,682,980	2,854,493	2,360,170	2,826,432	1,995,026	2,682,980	2,543,820	-1.1%	-3.2%
SPAIN	(646,309)	(646,309)	(646,309)	(646,309)	(646,309)	(646,309)	(646,309)	(646,309)	(646,309)	(646,309)	646,309	646,309	0.0%	0.0%
SWEDEN	(18,035,000)	(18,035,000)	(18,035,000)	(18,035,000)	(18,035,000)	(18,035,000)	(18,035,000)	(18,035,000)	18,035,000	(18,035,000)	18,035,000	18,035,000	0.0%	0.0%
SWITZERLAND	(6,767,811)	(6,844,099)	(6,920,387)	(6,996,675)	(7,072,963)	7,149,251	7,328,307	7,595,932	7,635,087	7,454,405	6,920,387	7,432,596	1.4%	1.1%
UK	(8,025,735)	(8,025,735)	(8,025,735)	(8,025,735)	(8,025,735)	(8,025,735)	(8,025,735)	(8,025,735)	(8,025,735)	(8,025,735)	8,025,735	8,025,735	0.0%	0.0%
WEST GERMANY	11,189,250	10,827,000	11,104,000	11,477,000	11,349,000	12,028,711	12,428,811	11,868,514	11,849,208	11,931,703	11,189,250	12,021,349	1.4%	0.7%
EU TOTAL	57,915,341	57,832,384	58,388,677	58,906,171	59,120,556	61,670,465	62,116,131	61,225,296	61,614,877	60,648,567	58,432,626	61,455,067	1.0%	0.5%
EFTA TOTAL	26,346,811	26,423,099	26,499,387	26,575,675	26,651,963	26,728,251	26,907,307	27,174,932	27,214,087	27,033,405	26,499,387	27,011,596	0.4%	0.3%
EUROPE TOTAL	84,262,152	84,255,483	84,888,064	85,481,846	85,772,519	88,398,716	89,023,438	88,400,228	88,828,964	87,681,972	84,932,013	88,466,664	0.8%	0.4%
Sector 4 SCHOOLS														
AUSTRIA	(2,267,311)	(2,267,311)	(2,267,311)	(2,267,311)	(2,267,311)	(2,267,311)	(2,267,311)	(2,267,311)	(2,267,311)	(2,239,971)	2,267,311	2,261,843	-0.0%	-0.1%
BELGIUM	(8,577,760)	(8,577,760)	(8,577,760)	(8,577,760)	(8,577,760)	(8,577,760)	(8,577,760)	(8,577,760)	(8,577,760)	(8,577,760)	8,577,760	8,577,760	0.0%	0.0%
DENMARK	(17,920,000)	(18,575,000)	(19,829,000)	(19,350,000)	19,926,844	20,428,305	20,929,966	21,431,627	21,933,288	22,434,949	19,120,129	21,431,627	2.3%	2.5%
EAST GERMANY	(5,047,916)	(5,047,916)	(5,047,916)	(5,047,916)	(5,047,916)	(5,047,916)	(5,047,916)	(5,047,916)	(5,047,916)	(4,930,971)	5,047,916	5,024,527	-0.1%	-0.3%
EIRE	(4,211,885)	(4,211,885)	(4,211,885)	(4,211,885)	(4,211,885)	(4,211,885)	(4,211,885)	(4,211,885)	(4,211,885)	(4,211,885)	4,211,885	4,211,885	0.0%	0.0%
FINLAND	(4,986,001)	(5,257,334)	(5,528,667)	5,800,000	6,250,000	6,700,000	7,010,000	(6,885,334)	(7,156,667)	7,428,000	5,564,400	7,036,000	4.8%	4.5%
FRANCE	(51,390,388)	(51,390,388)	(51,390,388)	(51,390,388)	(51,390,388)	(51,390,388)	(51,390,388)	(51,390,388)	(51,390,388)	(51,390,388)	51,390,388	51,390,388	0.0%	0.0%
GREECE	(9,048,632)	(9,048,632)	(9,048,632)	(9,048,632)	(9,048,632)	(9,048,632)	(9,048,632)	(9,048,632)	(9,048,632)	(9,048,632)	9,048,632	9,048,632	0.0%	0.0%
ICELAND	(130,851)	(130,851)	(130,851)	(130,851)	130,851	145,072	189,233	301,606	332,054	358,368	130,851	265,267	15.2%	11.8%
ITALY	15,620,203	(15,620,203)	(15,620,203)	(15,620,203)	(15,620,203)	(15,620,203)	(15,620,203)	(15,620,203)	(15,620,203)	(15,620,203)	15,620,203	15,620,203	0.0%	0.0%
LIECHTENSTEIN	(9,256)	(9,256)	(9,256)	(9,256)	(9,256)	(9,256)	(9,256)	(9,256)	(9,256)	(9,183)	9,256	9,241	-0.0%	-0.1%
LUXEMBOURG	(296,356)	(296,356)	(296,356)	(296,356)	(296,356)	(296,356)	(296,356)	(296,356)	(296,356)	(296,356)	296,356	296,356	0.0%	0.0%
NETHERLANDS	13,868,150	13,868,150	13,868,150	13,868,150	13,868,150	(13,868,150)	(13,868,150)	(13,868,150)	(13,868,150)	(13,868,150)	13,868,150	13,868,150	0.0%	0.0%
NORWAY	(6,645,000)	(6,645,000)	(6,645,000)	6,645,000	6,703,000	6,703,000	6,501,000	6,849,000	7,022,838	6,858,000	6,656,600	6,804,768	0.4%	0.4%
PORTUGAL	1,658,000	1,871,000	1,821,667	2,253,870	2,495,704	2,558,656	2,601,284	2,904,116	3,357,221	2,899,532	2,020,048	2,864,162	7.2%	6.4%
SPAIN	(2,268,000)	(2,268,000)	(2,268,000)	(2,268,000)	(2,268,000)	(2,268,000)	(2,268,000)	(2,268,000)	(2,268,000)	(2,268,000)	2,268,000	2,268,000	0.0%	0.0%
SWEDEN	(46,760,000)	(44,740,000)	(42,720,000)	40,700,000	36,000,000	34,000,000	33,000,000	33,000,000	30,600,000	(28,580,000)	42,184,000	31,836,000	-5.5%	-5.3%
SWITZERLAND	(1,889,294)	(1,889,294)	(1,889,294)	(1,889,294)	(1,889,294)	(1,889,294)	(1,889,294)	(1,889,294)	(1,889,294)	(1,873,175)	1,889,294	1,886,070	-0.0%	-0.1%
UK	(51,396,241)	(51,396,241)	(51,396,241)	(51,396,241)	(51,396,241)	(51,396,241)	(51,396,241)	(51,396,241)	(51,396,241)	(51,396,241)	51,396,241	51,396,241	0.0%	0.0%
WEST GERMANY	(15,163,113)	(15,163,113)	(15,163,113)	(15,163,113)	(15,163,113)	(15,163,113)	(15,163,113)	(15,163,113)	(15,163,113)	(15,163,113)	15,163,113	15,163,113	0.0%	0.0%
EU TOTAL	196,466,644	197,334,644	198,539,311	198,492,514	199,310,992	199,875,605	200,416,804	201,224,387	202,179,153	202,106,180	198,028,821	201,161,044	0.3%	0.3%
EFTA TOTAL	62,687,713	60,939,046	59,190,379	57,441,712	53,249,712	51,803,933	50,866,094	51,201,801	49,277,420	47,346,897	58,701,712	50,099,189	-3.1%	-3.1%
EUROPE TOTAL	259,154,357	258,273,690	257,729,690	255,934,226	252,560,704	251,679,538	251,283,988	252,426,188	251,456,573	249,452,877	256,730,533	251,260,233	-0.4%	-0.4%

Figures in parentheses are grossed.

- 136 -

Collections: Books & Bound Periodicals

	1981	1982	1983	1984	1985	1986	1987	1988	1989	1990	1981-85 Average	1986-90 Average	81/85 - 86/90 Year on Year Increase	Decade: Year on Year Increase
Sector 5														
SPECIAL														
AUSTRIA	(8,111,401)	(8,111,401)	(8,111,401)	(8,111,401)	(8,111,401)	(8,111,401)	(8,111,401)	(8,111,401)	(8,111,401)	(8,167,029)	8,111,401	8,122,527	0.0%	0.1%
BELGIUM	(3,441,375)	(3,441,375)	(3,441,375)	(3,441,375)	(3,441,375)	(3,441,375)	(3,441,375)	(3,441,375)	(3,441,375)	(3,441,375)	3,441,375	3,441,375	0.0%	0.0%
DENMARK	1,563,000	1,654,000	1,676,000	1,819,000	1,808,000	(2,536,945)	(3,265,690)	3,994,835	3,876,625	3,735,206	1,704,000	3,481,900	15.4%	10.2%
EAST GERMANY	(17,748,145)	(17,748,145)	(17,748,145)	(17,748,145)	(17,748,145)	(17,748,145)	(17,748,145)	(17,748,145)	(17,748,145)	(17,465,423)	17,748,145	17,691,601	-0.1%	-0.2%
EIRE	(131,000)	(131,000)	(131,000)	(131,000)	(131,000)	(131,000)	(131,000)	(131,000)	(131,000)	(131,000)	131,000	131,000	0.0%	0.0%
FINLAND	1,565,281	1,662,174	1,786,574	2,037,187	2,128,945	2,194,701	2,261,412	2,241,538	2,550,845	2,519,350	1,836,024	2,353,587	5.1%	5.4%
FRANCE	(18,600,504)	(18,600,504)	(18,600,504)	(18,600,504)	(18,600,504)	(18,600,504)	(18,600,504)	(18,600,504)	(18,600,504)	(18,600,504)	18,600,504	18,600,504	0.0%	0.0%
GREECE	(3,342,517)	(3,342,517)	(3,342,517)	(3,342,517)	(3,342,517)	(3,342,517)	(3,342,517)	(3,342,517)	(3,342,517)	(3,342,517)	3,342,517	3,342,517	0.0%	0.0%
ICELAND	(62,817)	(68,830)	(76,346)	(86,367)	(101,398)	(116,429)	(131,460)	146,491	176,554	(206,617)	79,152	155,510	14.5%	14.1%
ITALY	4,631,526	4,631,526	4,105,118	4,688,442	5,101,020	(5,218,394)	(5,335,768)	(5,453,142)	(5,570,516)	(5,687,890)	4,631,526	5,453,142	3.3%	2.3%
LIECHTENSTEIN	0	0	0	0	0	0	0	0	0	0	0	0	0.0%	0.0%
LUXEMBOURG	(131,849)	(131,849)	(131,849)	(131,849)	(131,849)	(131,849)	(131,849)	(131,849)	(131,849)	(131,849)	131,849	131,849	0.0%	0.0%
NETHERLANDS	10,790,000	12,317,000	13,010,000	12,039,000	13,761,000	14,635,000	15,071,000	14,765,000	14,992,000	(15,517,250)	12,383,400	14,996,050	3.9%	4.1%
NORWAY	3,102,800	3,174,600	3,248,400	3,318,200	3,390,000	3,713,000	3,797,000	3,637,000	3,470,047	3,749,000	3,246,400	3,653,200	2.4%	2.1%
PORTUGAL	2,253,065	2,246,535	2,000,231	1,804,417	2,573,000	2,935,018	2,708,711	3,203,962	4,237,172	3,354,630	2,175,450	3,287,899	8.6%	4.5%
SPAIN	9,080,277	10,785,449	12,327,259	13,869,069	15,410,878	16,952,688	18,604,380	20,258,072	19,263,725	18,271,378	12,294,586	18,669,649	8.7%	8.1%
SWEDEN	(3,737,000)	(3,791,000)	(3,845,000)	(3,899,000)	3,953,000	4,127,000	4,252,000	3,742,000	4,394,000	4,223,000	3,845,000	4,147,600	1.5%	1.4%
SWITZERLAND	(7,161,776)	(7,161,776)	(7,161,776)	(7,161,776)	(7,161,776)	(7,161,776)	(7,161,776)	(7,161,776)	(7,161,776)	(7,213,769)	7,161,776	7,172,175	0.0%	0.1%
UK	(19,240,126)	(19,240,126)	(19,240,126)	(19,240,126)	(19,240,126)	(19,240,126)	(19,240,126)	(19,240,126)	(19,240,126)	(19,240,126)	19,240,126	19,240,126	0.0%	0.0%
WEST GERMANY	31,302,000	30,913,000	30,343,000	31,706,000	32,246,000	39,300,836	39,993,412	41,275,921	42,175,398	(43,074,875)	31,302,000	41,164,088	5.6%	3.6%
EU TOTAL	122,255,384	125,183,026	126,097,122	128,561,444	133,535,414	144,214,397	147,614,877	151,584,448	152,750,952	151,994,023	127,126,478	149,631,699	3.3%	2.4%
EFTA TOTAL	23,741,055	23,969,781	24,227,497	24,613,911	24,846,520	25,424,397	25,715,049	25,040,206	25,764,576	26,078,765	24,279,753	25,604,599	1.1%	1.0%
EUROPE TOTAL	145,996,439	149,152,807	150,324,619	153,175,355	158,381,934	169,638,794	173,329,926	176,624,654	178,515,528	178,072,788	151,406,231	175,236,298	3.0%	2.2%
Sector 6														
PUBLIC														
AUSTRIA	(5,863,485)	(6,122,577)	(6,381,669)	(6,640,761)	6,899,853	6,915,870	7,441,939	7,225,002	7,450,296	8,195,315	6,381,669	7,445,684	3.1%	3.8%
BELGIUM	18,374,564	20,747,940	21,681,833	22,480,946	23,266,721	24,802,740	26,033,169	27,679,535	28,894,340	29,678,316	21,306,401	27,417,620	5.2%	5.5%
DENMARK	30,739,000	31,857,000	32,588,000	33,407,000	34,122,476	34,684,874	35,079,153	34,923,622	34,709,047	34,285,411	32,542,695	34,736,421	1.3%	1.2%
EAST GERMANY	(66,486,847)	(66,486,847)	(66,486,847)	(66,486,847)	(66,486,847)	(66,486,847)	(66,486,847)	(66,486,847)	(66,486,847)	(66,486,847)	66,486,847	66,486,847	0.0%	0.0%
EIRE	7,148,969	7,424,522	7,720,843	7,969,366	8,188,340	8,426,271	9,212,654	9,403,655	9,570,082	10,979,927	7,690,414	9,518,516	4.4%	4.9%
FINLAND	(25,713,815)	(26,801,413)	(27,899,011)	28,976,609	30,249,890	31,454,699	32,787,849	33,852,981	34,879,914	35,502,195	27,928,148	33,651,528	3.6%	3.6%
FRANCE	57,324,000	60,732,000	63,951,000	67,196,000	71,073,209	(74,773,605)	78,474,000	(81,999,000)	(85,524,000)	(89,049,000)	64,055,242	81,963,921	5.1%	5.0%
GREECE	7,486,000	7,486,000	7,486,000	7,485,988	7,486,000	7,486,000	(7,486,000)	(7,486,000)	(7,486,000)	(7,486,000)	7,485,998	7,486,000	0.0%	0.0%
ICELAND	1,338,189	1,385,307	1,426,603	1,504,811	1,556,997	1,640,707	1,670,777	1,678,713	1,733,826	1,767,952	1,442,381	1,698,395	3.3%	3.1%
ITALY	(80,029,921)	(80,029,921)	(80,029,921)	(80,029,921)	(80,029,921)	(80,029,921)	(80,029,921)	(80,029,921)	(80,029,921)	(80,029,921)	80,029,921	80,029,921	0.0%	0.0%
LIECHTENSTEIN	(17,665)	(18,332)	(18,999)	(19,666)	(20,333)	21,000	(21,666)	(22,333)	23,000	(23,667)	18,999	22,333	3.3%	3.3%
LUXEMBOURG	(612,888)	(612,888)	(612,888)	(612,888)	(612,888)	(612,888)	(612,888)	(612,888)	(612,888)	(612,888)	612,888	612,888	0.0%	0.0%
NETHERLANDS	32,976,000	34,722,000	36,112,000	37,177,000	38,564,000	39,572,000	40,921,000	40,766,000	40,916,000	41,515,000	35,910,200	40,738,000	2.6%	2.6%
NORWAY	(15,978,750)	(16,300,000)	(16,621,250)	(16,942,500)	(17,263,750)	38,564,000	18,278,000	18,364,000	18,556,000	18,870,000	16,621,250	18,330,800	2.0%	1.9%
PORTUGAL	6,265,984	6,564,606	7,546,139	3,497,065	4,139,887	4,782,708	3,896,787	4,202,000	4,688,000	3,371,000	5,602,736	4,188,095	-5.7%	-6.7%
SPAIN	12,148,473	13,946,662	14,485,153	15,922,737	17,360,322	19,697,000	21,485,516	23,274,031	(25,240,788)	27,207,544	14,772,669	23,380,976	9.6%	9.4%
SWEDEN	(41,380,250)	(42,059,000)	(42,737,750)	(43,416,500)	(44,095,250)	44,774,000	45,713,000	46,550,000	47,226,000	47,489,000	42,737,750	46,350,400	1.6%	1.5%
SWITZERLAND	20,538,545	21,093,498	21,755,224	22,221,972	22,886,154	(23,843,713)	(24,801,273)	(25,758,832)	(26,716,392)	(27,673,951)	21,699,079	25,758,832	3.5%	3.4%
UK	136,126,000	138,799,000	139,187,000	141,373,000	140,536,000	140,573,797	140,715,878	140,518,108	138,977,708	136,359,300	139,204,200	139,428,958	0.0%	0.0%
WEST GERMANY	70,028,935	73,485,184	75,660,048	78,315,740	85,221,639	88,151,001	90,338,799	93,392,812	92,934,686	95,797,905	76,542,309	92,123,041	3.8%	3.5%
EU TOTAL	525,747,561	542,894,570	553,527,672	561,954,528	577,088,250	590,079,852	600,772,602	610,774,419	616,070,287	622,859,059	552,242,520	608,111,204	1.9%	1.9%
EFTA TOTAL	110,830,699	113,780,127	116,830,506	119,722,819	122,972,227	126,234,989	130,695,504	133,451,861	136,385,428	139,522,080	116,827,276	133,257,972	2.7%	2.6%
EUROPE TOTAL	636,578,260	656,674,697	670,358,178	681,677,347	700,060,477	716,314,641	731,468,106	744,226,280	752,455,715	762,381,139	669,069,796	741,369,176	2.1%	2.0%

Figures in parentheses are grossed.

Collections: Books & Bound Periodicals

	1981	1982	1983	1984	1985	1986	1987	1988	1989	1990	1981-85 Average	1986-90 Average	81/85 - 86/90 Year on Year Increase	Decade: Year on Year Increase
ALL SECTORS														
AUSTRIA	31,394,182	32,192,612	32,745,112	33,223,221	34,022,755	34,276,238	34,572,000	33,897,171	36,126,569	37,276,699	32,715,576	35,229,735	1.5%	1.9%
BELGIUM	40,544,914	42,961,136	43,909,898	44,772,219	45,565,388	47,378,918	48,886,881	50,810,741	52,303,060	53,364,550	43,550,711	50,548,826	3.0%	3.1%
DENMARK	58,965,100	60,932,900	63,142,000	63,978,000	65,513,520	67,356,525	69,411,532	70,781,729	71,108,665	71,702,225	62,506,304	70,072,135	2.3%	2.2%
EAST GERMANY	147,992,889	148,225,222	148,457,555	148,689,888	148,922,222	149,154,555	149,710,389	150,266,221	150,822,053	150,597,514	148,457,555	150,110,146	0.2%	0.2%
EIRE	16,509,054	16,956,607	17,429,928	17,744,481	18,078,425	18,513,356	19,351,459	19,692,367	19,967,610	21,419,112	17,343,699	19,788,781	2.7%	2.9%
FINLAND	41,441,692	44,017,123	45,973,212	47,984,649	51,044,598	53,197,728	55,340,393	56,722,342	58,526,785	59,848,920	46,092,263	56,727,233	4.2%	4.2%
FRANCE	157,764,892	161,372,892	164,691,892	167,936,892	171,914,101	175,814,497	179,714,892	183,739,892	187,764,892	191,789,892	164,736,134	183,764,813	2.2%	2.2%
GREECE	30,258,554	30,258,554	30,258,554	30,258,542	30,258,554	30,258,554	30,258,554	30,258,554	30,258,554	30,258,554	30,258,552	30,258,554	0.0%	0.0%
ICELAND	2,080,169	2,151,366	2,218,244	2,324,539	2,409,822	2,539,926	2,647,964	2,800,304	2,933,500	3,043,843	2,236,828	2,793,107	4.5%	4.3%
ITALY	119,645,250	119,924,543	119,303,413	120,423,597	121,866,869	123,480,165	123,758,891	124,122,754	124,265,738	124,714,739	120,232,734	124,068,457	0.6%	0.5%
LIECHTENSTEIN	206,693	207,360	208,027	208,694	209,361	210,028	210,694	211,361	212,028	212,356	208,027	211,293	0.3%	0.3%
LUXEMBOURG	1,869,766	1,879,766	1,889,766	1,899,766	1,909,766	1,924,766	1,939,766	1,954,766	1,969,766	1,984,766	1,889,766	1,954,766	0.7%	0.7%
NETHERLANDS	78,835,150	83,397,150	86,355,150	85,569,817	90,425,150	92,813,150	95,452,400	95,308,775	96,623,150	98,496,775	84,916,483	95,738,850	2.4%	2.5%
NORWAY	35,204,149	35,745,186	36,288,183	36,707,700	37,502,750	38,581,000	39,185,000	39,656,000	39,865,838	40,183,000	36,289,190	39,490,168	1.7%	1.5%
PORTUGAL	15,591,532	15,919,101	16,606,146	12,761,346	15,710,777	17,195,824	18,002,192	18,364,794	21,330,760	18,936,150	15,317,780	18,765,904	4.1%	2.2%
SPAIN	36,206,156	41,806,853	44,824,650	48,537,231	52,353,936	55,072,494	59,598,228	64,200,272	66,124,810	67,943,356	44,745,765	62,587,832	6.9%	7.2%
SWEDEN	126,457,586	125,825,002	125,192,418	124,559,834	121,028,917	120,511,000	121,257,000	122,912,000	122,175,000	120,106,100	124,612,751	121,392,220	-0.5%	-0.6%
SWITZERLAND	52,138,850	52,768,091	53,506,105	54,049,141	55,566,180	56,616,004	58,153,115	60,058,248	62,613,291	63,633,144	53,605,273	60,214,360	2.4%	2.2%
UK	315,493,102	318,166,102	318,554,102	320,740,102	319,903,102	319,940,899	323,561,980	326,843,210	328,983,310	330,046,402	318,571,302	325,875,160	0.5%	0.5%
WEST GERMANY	213,398,298	210,581,297	217,126,181	224,598,853	233,853,752	250,443,152	257,119,690	264,712,349	267,767,989	274,224,156	219,911,672	262,853,467	3.6%	2.8%
EU TOTAL	1,233,074,657	1,252,382,123	1,272,549,215	1,287,910,734	1,316,275,560	1,349,346,655	1,376,766,834	1,401,056,424	1,419,290,356	1,435,478,191	1,272,438,458	1,396,387,692	1.9%	1.7%
EFTA TOTAL	288,921,321	292,906,720	296,129,341	299,057,778	301,784,383	305,931,922	311,346,166	316,255,426	322,453,011	324,304,062	295,759,908	316,058,117	1.3%	1.3%
EUROPE TOTAL	1,521,995,978	1,545,288,843	1,568,678,556	1,586,968,512	1,618,059,943	1,655,278,577	1,688,113,000	1,717,311,850	1,741,743,367	1,759,782,253	1,568,198,366	1,712,445,809	1.8%	1.6%

Collections: Books & Bound Periodicals per 1000 Population

	1981	1982	1983	1984	1985	1986	1987	1988	1989	1990	1981-85 Average	1986-90 Average	81/85 - 86/90 Year on Year Increase	Decade: Year on Year Increase
European Union														
Sector 1	254.74	252.55	254.84	258.83	263.36	258.63	264.40	269.21	281.76	287.84	256.87	272.37	1.2%	1.4%
Sector 2	723.57	721.17	739.17	747.01	761.54	778.98	809.49	830.94	862.09	886.58	738.49	833.62	2.5%	2.3%
Sector 3	171.34	171.09	172.74	174.27	174.51	181.02	182.33	179.02	182.27	179.02	172.79	180.73	0.9%	0.5%
Sector 4	581.23	583.79	587.36	587.22	588.31	586.67	588.31	588.38	598.08	596.57	585.58	591.60	0.2%	0.3%
Sector 5	361.68	370.34	373.05	380.34	394.16	423.30	433.30	443.23	451.86	448.65	375.91	440.07	3.2%	2.4%
Sector 6	1,555.37	1,608.10	1,637.55	1,662.48	1,703.40	1,732.00	1,763.49	1,785.90	1,822.43	1,838.54	1,632.96	1,788.47	1.8%	1.9%
All Sectors	3,647.92	3,705.04	3,764.71	3,810.15	3,885.27	3,960.60	4,041.32	4,096.69	4,198.49	4,237.20	3,762.62	4,106.86	1.8%	1.7%
EFTA														
Sector 1	339.94	345.38	350.21	351.95	362.89	374.62	372.09	388.69	418.98	402.30	350.07	391.34	2.3%	1.9%
Sector 2	1,692.49	1,764.21	1,808.76	1,848.17	1,941.79	1,982.22	2,029.00	2,081.61	2,189.01	2,204.22	1,811.08	2,097.21	3.0%	3.0%
Sector 3	819.84	822.22	824.59	826.96	829.34	831.71	837.28	845.61	846.83	835.63	824.59	839.41	0.4%	0.2%
Sector 4	1,950.68	1,896.26	1,841.85	1,787.43	1,656.99	1,612.00	1,582.82	1,583.26	1,533.38	1,463.54	1,826.64	1,557.00	-3.1%	-3.1%
Sector 5	738.76	745.88	753.90	765.92	773.16	791.14	800.18	779.19	801.73	806.12	755.52	795.67	1.0%	1.0%
Sector 6	3,448.76	3,540.54	3,635.46	3,725.46	3,828.57	3,928.10	4,066.80	4,152.67	4,243.96	4,312.78	3,635.36	4,140.88	2.6%	2.5%
All Sectors	8,990.47	9,114.48	9,214.76	9,305.89	9,390.73	9,519.79	9,688.27	9,841.03	10,033.89	10,024.60	9,203.27	9,821.52	1.3%	1.2%
Europe Total														
Sector 1	262.14	260.61	263.12	266.92	271.98	268.63	273.68	279.47	293.67	297.82	264.95	282.65	1.3%	1.4%
Sector 2	807.69	811.73	832.03	842.61	863.80	882.70	914.61	938.37	977.28	1,001.44	831.57	942.88	2.5%	2.4%
Sector 3	227.64	227.62	229.33	230.93	231.24	237.10	238.79	236.28	239.96	236.26	229.35	237.68	0.7%	0.4%
Sector 4	700.12	697.74	696.27	691.42	680.90	675.05	674.03	674.69	679.27	672.14	693.29	675.04	-0.5%	-0.5%
Sector 5	394.42	402.94	406.11	413.81	428.99	455.00	464.83	472.09	482.23	479.81	408.86	470.81	2.9%	2.2%
Sector 6	1,719.75	1,774.04	1,811.01	1,841.59	1,887.35	1,921.30	1,962.04	1,989.20	2,032.65	2,054.21	1,806.75	1,991.88	2.0%	2.0%
All Sectors	4,111.75	4,174.68	4,237.87	4,287.28	4,362.26	4,439.78	4,528.09	4,590.10	4,705.07	4,741.68	4,234.77	4,600.94	1.7%	1.6%

- 138 -

Collections: Current Periodical Titles

	1981	1982	1983	1984	1985	1986	1987	1988	1989	1990	1981–85 Average	1986–90 Average	81/85 – 86/90 Year on Year Increase	Decade: Year on Year Increase
Sector 1														
NATIONAL														
AUSTRIA	(9,751)	(9,947)	(10,143)	(10,339)	(10,535)	10,731	11,064	11,136	11,337	11,517	10,143	11,157	1.9%	1.9%
BELGIUM	(10,974)	(10,974)	(10,974)	(10,974)	(10,974)	(10,974)	(10,974)	(10,974)	(10,974)	(10,974)	10,974	10,974	0.0%	0.0%
DENMARK	12,977	13,043	20,204	20,134	20,887	20,364	(31,841)	37,318	43,201	44,358	17,449	36,616	16.0%	14.6%
EAST GERMANY	(65,456)	(65,456)	(65,456)	(65,456)	(65,456)	(65,456)	(65,456)	(65,456)	(65,456)	65,456	65,456	65,456	0.0%	0.0%
EIRE	(2,200)	(2,200)	(2,200)	(2,200)	(2,200)	2,200	2,200	2,200	2,200	2,200	2,200	2,200	0.0%	0.0%
FINLAND	13,565	14,245	15,817	16,369	16,317	16,193	17,222	18,188	18,186	18,149	15,263	16,006	1.0%	3.3%
FRANCE	30,000	34,750	39,500	44,250	49,000	(49,000)	(49,000)	(49,000)	(49,000)	49,000	39,500	49,000	4.4%	5.6%
GREECE	(2,000)	(2,000)	(2,000)	(2,000)	(2,000)	(2,000)	(2,000)	(2,000)	(2,000)	(2,000)	2,000	2,000	0.0%	0.0%
ICELAND	(2,605)	(2,657)	(2,709)	(2,762)	(2,814)	(2,862)	(2,910)	2,962	(3,010)	(3,076)	2,709	2,964	1.8%	1.6%
ITALY	(52,344)	(52,344)	(52,344)	(52,344)	(52,344)	(52,344)	(52,344)	(52,344)	(52,344)	(52,344)	52,344	52,344	0.0%	0.0%
LIECHTENSTEIN	(250)	(250)	(250)	(250)	(250)	(250)	(250)	(250)	(250)	250	250	250	0.0%	0.0%
LUXEMBOURG	3,000	3,100	3,150	3,200	3,300	3,400	3,450	3,500	3,550	3,600	3,150	3,500	2.1%	2.0%
NETHERLANDS	22,600	22,900	24,500	28,150	30,200	31,300	32,300	39,200	37,000	(38,800)	25,670	35,720	6.8%	6.2%
NORWAY	(10,059)	(10,115)	(10,171)	(10,227)	(10,283)	10,339	11,282	11,064	6,024	10,563	10,171	9,854	–0.6%	0.5%
PORTUGAL	(3,945)	(3,945)	3,945	7,000	4,800	5,660	6,196	5,600	6,150	6,700	4,727	6,061	5.1%	6.1%
SPAIN	(23,803)	(36,268)	(34,059)	(31,377)	(31,377)	(31,377)	(31,377)	(31,377)	(31,377)	(31,377)	31,377	31,377	0.0%	3.1%
SWEDEN	(16,797)	(16,797)	(16,797)	(16,797)	(16,797)	25,001	20,895	12,411	12,700	12,877	16,797	16,797	–0.0%	–2.9%
SWITZERLAND	(7,320)	(7,577)	(7,834)	(8,091)	(8,348)	8,605	9,054	9,362	9,470	9,634	7,834	9,225	3.3%	3.1%
UK	(182,000)	(182,000)	(182,000)	(182,000)	(182,000)	182,000	(189,000)	196,000	(190,500)	185,000	182,000	188,500	0.7%	0.2%
WEST GERMANY	161,972	155,629	160,904	163,079	168,275	172,740	177,817	176,948	176,844	177,844	161,972	176,399	1.7%	1.0%
EU TOTAL	573,271	584,609	601,236	612,164	622,813	634,815	653,735	671,917	670,596	669,653	598,819	660,147	2.0%	1.7%
EFTA TOTAL	60,347	61,588	63,721	64,835	65,344	73,979	72,777	57,466	60,977	66,066	63,167	66,253	1.0%	1.0%
EUROPE TOTAL	633,618	646,197	664,957	676,999	688,157	708,794	726,532	729,383	731,573	735,719	661,986	726,400	1.9%	1.7%
Sector 2														
HIGHER EDUCATION														
AUSTRIA	51,310	50,934	53,895	52,415	53,371	53,545	51,766	47,015	56,416	55,900	52,385	52,928	0.2%	1.0%
BELGIUM	(30,000)	(30,000)	(30,000)	(30,000)	(30,000)	30,000	35,000	33,000	31,931	37,320	30,000	33,450	2.2%	2.5%
DENMARK	71,200	68,149	69,500	67,800	66,887	(71,794)	(76,701)	81,609	79,502	78,548	68,707	77,631	2.5%	1.1%
EAST GERMANY	(141,292)	(142,823)	(144,353)	(145,884)	(147,415)	(148,945)	(150,476)	(152,006)	(153,537)	(155,068)	144,353	152,006	1.0%	1.0%
EIRE	26,835	27,224	27,878	27,820	28,020	28,965	29,221	29,889	29,596	29,499	27,475	29,434	1.4%	1.1%
FINLAND	106,076	110,982	117,002	121,645	121,584	128,805	134,807	113,430	132,206	129,096	115,458	127,669	2.0%	2.2%
FRANCE	101,000	96,000	96,500	95,500	96,000	97,300	101,000	103,000	110,000	116,000	97,000	105,460	1.7%	1.6%
GREECE	(31,726)	(31,726)	(31,726)	(31,726)	(31,726)	(31,726)	(31,726)	(31,726)	(31,726)	(31,726)	31,726	31,726	0.0%	0.0%
ICELAND	(1,375)	(1,600)	(1,825)	(2,050)	(2,275)	2,500	2,800	3,200	3,400	3,060	1,825	3,060	10.9%	10.6%
ITALY	(193,795)	(193,795)	193,795	193,795	193,795	(193,795)	(193,795)	(193,795)	(193,795)	(193,795)	193,795	193,795	0.0%	0.0%
LIECHTENSTEIN	(196)	(196)	(196)	(196)	(196)	(196)	(196)	(196)	(196)	(194)	196	196	–0.0%	–0.1%
LUXEMBOURG	(800)	(800)	(800)	(800)	(800)	(800)	(800)	(800)	(800)	(800)	800	800	0.0%	0.0%
NETHERLANDS	188,000	191,000	182,000	(187,000)	176,700	173,700	181,500	179,900	181,600	(181,600)	184,940	179,660	–0.6%	–0.4%
NORWAY	(55,049)	(59,104)	63,159	(67,214)	(71,266)	75,324	76,632	77,632	85,664	91,543	63,159	81,359	5.2%	5.8%
PORTUGAL	(6,567)	(6,567)	(6,567)	(6,567)	(6,567)	(6,567)	(6,567)	(6,567)	(6,567)	(6,567)	6,567	6,567	0.0%	0.0%
SPAIN	63,873	88,234	100,681	113,128	125,575	138,020	(124,138)	110,525	(143,957)	177,659	98,298	138,860	7.2%	12.0%
SWEDEN	(135,205)	(130,713)	(126,221)	(121,729)	(117,237)	112,745	106,295	88,290	92,817	94,776	126,221	98,985	–4.7%	–3.9%
SWITZERLAND	(62,348)	(65,988)	(69,628)	(73,268)	(76,908)	80,548	82,170	84,168	91,468	119,236	69,628	91,518	5.6%	7.5%
UK	(484,000)	(484,000)	(484,000)	(484,000)	(484,000)	484,000	485,000	485,000	486,000	487,000	484,000	485,400	0.1%	0.1%
WEST GERMANY	369,587	369,843	372,818	372,679	371,008	392,819	396,498	406,095	404,216	(408,545)	369,587	401,635	1.7%	1.1%
EU TOTAL	1,708,675	1,730,161	1,732,418	1,756,499	1,758,493	1,798,431	1,812,422	1,813,912	1,853,227	1,904,127	1,737,249	1,836,424	1.1%	1.2%
EFTA TOTAL	411,559	419,517	431,926	438,517	442,840	453,663	454,866	413,931	462,167	494,145	428,872	455,714	1.2%	2.1%
EUROPE TOTAL	2,120,234	2,149,678	2,164,344	2,195,016	2,201,333	2,252,094	2,267,088	2,227,843	2,315,394	2,398,272	2,166,121	2,292,138	1.1%	1.4%

Figures in parentheses are grossed.

- 139 -

Collections: Current Periodical Titles

Sector 3 – OTHER NON-MAJOR SPEC.

	1981	1982	1983	1984	1985	1986	1987	1988	1989	1990	1981-85 Average	1986-90 Average	81/85 – 86/90 Year on Year Increase	Decade: Year on Year Increase
AUSTRIA	(34,458)	(34,458)	(34,458)	(34,458)	(34,458)	(34,458)	(34,458)	(34,458)	(34,458)	(34,458)	34,458	34,458	0.0%	0.0%
BELGIUM	(76,889)	(76,889)	(76,889)	(76,889)	(76,889)	(76,889)	(76,889)	(76,889)	(76,889)	(76,889)	76,889	76,889	0.0%	0.0%
DENMARK	0	0	0	0	0	0	0	0	0	0	0	0	0.0%	0.0%
EAST GERMANY	(588,105)	(588,105)	(588,105)	(588,105)	(588,105)	(588,105)	(588,105)	(588,105)	(588,105)	(579,609)	588,105	586,406	-0.1%	-0.2%
EIRE	(1,500)	(1,500)	(1,500)	(1,500)	(1,500)	1,500	1,501	1,503	1,498	1,499	1,500	1,500	0.0%	-0.0%
FINLAND	0	0	0	0	0	0	0	0	0	0	0	0	0.0%	0.0%
FRANCE	(2,310)	(2,318)	(2,326)	(2,334)	(2,342)	2,350	2,350	2,355	2,430	2,383	2,326	2,374	0.4%	0.3%
GREECE	(76,754)	(76,754)	(76,754)	(76,754)	(76,754)	(76,754)	(76,754)	(76,754)	(76,754)	(76,754)	76,754	76,754	0.0%	0.0%
ICELAND	0	0	0	0	0	0	0	0	0	0	0	0	0.0%	0.0%
ITALY	(443,210)	(443,210)	(443,210)	(443,210)	(443,210)	(443,210)	(443,210)	(443,210)	(443,210)	(443,210)	443,210	443,210	0.0%	0.0%
LIECHTENSTEIN	0	0	0	0	0	0	0	0	0	0	0	0	0.0%	0.0%
LUXEMBOURG	0	0	0	0	0	0	0	0	0	0	0	0	0.0%	0.0%
NETHERLANDS	(16,500)	(16,500)	(16,500)	(16,500)	16,500	16,800	(16,800)	(16,800)	(16,800)	(16,800)	16,500	16,800	0.4%	0.2%
NORWAY	0	0	0	0	0	0	0	0	0	0	0	0	0.0%	0.0%
PORTUGAL	(797)	(797)	(797)	(797)	(797)	(797)	(797)	(797)	(797)	(797)	797	797	0.0%	0.0%
SPAIN	(2,311)	(2,311)	(2,311)	(2,311)	(2,311)	(2,311)	(2,311)	(2,311)	(2,311)	2,311	2,311	2,311	0.0%	0.0%
SWEDEN	(402,493)	(402,493)	(402,493)	(402,493)	(402,493)	(402,493)	(402,493)	(402,493)	(402,493)	(402,493)	402,493	402,493	0.0%	0.0%
SWITZERLAND	(11,943)	(12,425)	(12,907)	(13,389)	(13,871)	14,353	15,543	15,980	16,523	16,280	12,907	15,736	4.0%	3.5%
UK	(440,304)	(440,304)	(440,304)	(440,304)	(440,304)	(440,304)	(440,304)	(440,304)	(440,304)	(440,304)	440,304	440,304	0.0%	0.0%
WEST GERMANY	56,835	55,481	56,074	57,209	58,576	60,570	60,725	64,250	64,597	(64,944)	56,835	63,017	2.1%	1.5%
EU TOTAL	1,705,515	1,704,169	1,704,770	1,705,913	1,707,288	1,709,560	1,709,748	1,713,278	1,713,695	1,705,500	1,705,531	1,710,362	0.1%	-0.0%
EFTA TOTAL	448,894	449,376	449,858	450,340	450,822	451,304	452,494	452,931	453,474	453,231	449,858	452,687	0.1%	0.1%
EUROPE TOTAL	2,154,409	2,153,545	2,154,628	2,156,253	2,158,110	2,160,864	2,162,240	2,166,209	2,167,169	2,158,731	2,155,389	2,163,049	0.1%	0.0%

Sector 4 – SCHOOLS

	1981	1982	1983	1984	1985	1986	1987	1988	1989	1990	1981-85 Average	1986-90 Average	81/85 – 86/90 Year on Year Increase	Decade: Year on Year Increase
AUSTRIA	(334)	(334)	(334)	(334)	(334)	(334)	(334)	(334)	(334)	(330)	334	333	-0.0%	-0.1%
BELGIUM	(675)	(675)	(675)	(675)	(675)	(675)	(675)	(675)	(675)	(675)	675	675	0.0%	0.0%
DENMARK	(363)	(363)	(363)	(363)	(363)	(363)	(363)	(363)	(363)	(363)	363	363	0.0%	0.0%
EAST GERMANY	(744)	(744)	(744)	(744)	(744)	(744)	(744)	(744)	(744)	(727)	744	741	-0.1%	-0.3%
EIRE	(332)	(332)	(332)	(332)	(332)	(332)	(332)	(332)	(332)	(332)	332	332	0.0%	0.0%
FINLAND	(735)	(775)	(815)	(855)	(921)	(988)	(1,033)	(1,015)	(1,055)	(1,095)	820	1,037	4.8%	4.5%
FRANCE	(4,046)	(4,046)	(4,046)	(4,046)	(4,046)	(4,046)	(4,046)	(4,046)	(4,046)	(4,046)	4,046	4,046	0.0%	0.0%
GREECE	(712)	(712)	(712)	(712)	(712)	(712)	(712)	(712)	(712)	(712)	712	712	0.0%	0.0%
ICELAND	(27)	(27)	(27)	(27)	(27)	(27)	(27)	(27)	(27)	(27)	27	27	0.0%	0.0%
ITALY	(4,289)	(4,289)	(4,289)	(4,289)	(4,289)	(4,289)	(4,289)	(4,289)	(4,289)	(4,289)	4,289	4,289	0.0%	0.0%
LIECHTENSTEIN	(1)	(1)	(1)	(1)	(1)	(1)	(1)	(1)	(1)	(1)	1	1	0.0%	0.0%
LUXEMBOURG	(23)	(23)	(23)	(23)	(23)	(23)	(23)	(23)	(23)	(23)	23	23	0.0%	0.0%
NETHERLANDS	(1,092)	(1,092)	(1,092)	(1,092)	(1,092)	(1,092)	(1,092)	(1,092)	(1,092)	(1,092)	1,092	1,092	0.0%	0.0%
NORWAY	(980)	(980)	(980)	(980)	(988)	(1,001)	(958)	(1,010)	(1,035)	(1,011)	982	1,003	0.4%	0.3%
PORTUGAL	(4,895)	(4,895)	(4,895)	(4,895)	(4,895)	(4,895)	(4,895)	(4,895)	(4,895)	(4,895)	4,895	4,895	0.0%	0.0%
SPAIN	(3,949)	(3,949)	(3,949)	(3,949)	(3,949)	(3,949)	(3,949)	(3,949)	(3,949)	(3,949)	3,949	3,949	0.0%	0.0%
SWEDEN	(6,894)	(6,596)	(6,298)	(6,000)	(5,307)	(5,012)	(4,865)	(4,865)	(4,511)	(4,213)	6,219	4,693	-5.5%	-5.3%
SWITZERLAND	(279)	(279)	(279)	(279)	(279)	(279)	(279)	(279)	(279)	(276)	279	278	-0.0%	-0.1%
UK	(4,046)	(4,046)	(4,046)	(4,046)	(4,046)	(4,046)	(4,046)	(4,046)	(4,046)	(4,046)	4,046	4,046	0.0%	0.0%
WEST GERMANY	(4,028)	(4,028)	(4,028)	(4,028)	(4,028)	(4,028)	(4,028)	(4,028)	(4,028)	(4,028)	4,028	4,028	0.0%	0.0%
EU TOTAL	29,194	29,194	29,194	29,194	29,194	29,194	29,194	29,194	29,194	29,177	29,194	29,191	-0.0%	-0.0%
EFTA TOTAL	9,250	8,992	8,734	8,476	7,857	7,642	7,497	7,531	7,242	6,953	8,662	7,373	-3.2%	-3.1%
EUROPE TOTAL	38,444	38,186	37,928	37,670	37,051	36,836	36,691	36,725	36,436	36,130	37,856	36,564	-0.7%	-0.7%

Figures in parentheses are grossed.

- 140 -

Collections: Current Periodical Titles

Sector 5 SPECIAL

	1981	1982	1983	1984	1985	1986	1987	1988	1989	1990	1981-85 Average	1986-90 Average	81/85 - 86/90 Year on Year Increase	Decade: Year on Year Increase
AUSTRIA	(100,421)	(100,421)	(100,421)	(100,421)	(100,421)	(100,421)	(100,421)	(100,421)	(100,421)	(101,110)	100,421	100,559	0.0%	0.1%
BELGIUM	(48,828)	(48,828)	(48,828)	(48,828)	(48,828)	(48,828)	(48,828)	(48,828)	(48,828)	(48,828)	48,828	48,828	0.0%	0.0%
DENMARK	28,000	24,900	32,500	30,000	35,200	(38,895)	(42,590)	46,762	46,762	44,572	30,120	43,821	7.8%	5.3%
EAST GERMANY	(219,727)	(219,727)	(219,727)	(219,727)	(219,727)	(219,727)	(219,727)	(219,727)	(219,727)	(216,227)	219,727	219,027	-0.1%	-0.2%
EIRE	(3,087)	(3,087)	(3,087)	(3,087)	(3,087)	(3,087)	(3,087)	(3,087)	(3,087)	(3,087)	3,087	3,087	0.0%	0.0%
FINLAND	15,525	16,149	16,574	20,055	23,888	24,254	24,667	27,603	26,500	27,842	18,438	26,153	7.2%	6.7%
FRANCE	(263,914)	(263,914)	(263,914)	(263,914)	(263,914)	(263,914)	(263,914)	(263,914)	(263,914)	(263,914)	263,914	263,914	0.0%	0.0%
GREECE	(47,425)	(47,425)	(47,425)	(47,425)	(47,425)	(47,425)	(47,425)	(47,425)	(47,425)	(47,425)	47,425	47,425	0.0%	0.0%
ICELAND	(4,877)	(4,877)	(4,877)	(4,877)	(4,877)	(4,877)	(4,877)	(4,877)	6,802	6,802	4,877	5,647	3.0%	3.8%
ITALY	(281,040)	(281,040)	(281,040)	(281,040)	(281,040)	(281,040)	(281,040)	(281,040)	(281,040)	(281,040)	281,040	281,040	0.0%	0.0%
LIECHTENSTEIN	0	0	0	0	0	0	0	0	0	0	0	0	0.0%	0.0%
LUXEMBOURG	(1,871)	(1,871)	(1,871)	(1,871)	(1,871)	(1,871)	(1,871)	(1,871)	(1,871)	(1,871)	1,871	1,871	0.0%	0.0%
NETHERLANDS	268,000	285,000	281,000	278,067	275,134	272,200	264,900	252,100	249,300	(246,500)	277,440	257,000	-1.5%	-0.9%
NORWAY	(37,283)	(38,249)	(39,215)	(40,181)	(41,147)	42,113	42,148	64,983	49,613	45,978	39,215	48,967	4.5%	2.4%
PORTUGAL	(4,895)	(4,895)	(4,895)	(4,895)	(4,895)	(4,895)	(4,895)	(4,895)	(4,895)	(4,895)	4,895	4,895	0.0%	0.0%
SPAIN	74,774	72,402	84,307	96,212	108,117	120,021	(146,969)	173,916	(172,795)	171,873	87,162	157,075	12.5%	9.7%
SWEDEN	(28,979)	(29,585)	(30,191)	(30,797)	(31,403)	27,094	26,638	36,658	40,138	29,518	30,191	32,009	1.2%	0.2%
SWITZERLAND	(88,665)	(88,665)	(88,665)	(88,665)	(88,665)	(88,665)	(88,665)	(88,665)	(88,665)	(89,308)	88,665	88,794	0.0%	0.1%
UK	(272,989)	(272,989)	(272,989)	(272,989)	(272,989)	(272,989)	(272,989)	(272,989)	(272,989)	(272,989)	272,989	272,989	0.0%	0.0%
WEST GERMANY	219,370	208,954	211,278	234,922	222,325	273,671	281,516	284,474	286,840	(289,206)	219,370	283,141	5.2%	3.1%
EU TOTAL	1,733,920	1,735,032	1,752,661	1,782,977	1,784,552	1,848,563	1,879,761	1,900,552	1,899,473	1,892,227	1,757,868	1,884,113	1.4%	1.0%
EFTA TOTAL	275,750	277,946	279,943	284,996	290,401	287,424	287,316	323,205	312,139	300,558	281,807	302,128	1.4%	1.0%
EUROPE TOTAL	2,009,670	2,012,978	2,032,604	2,067,973	2,074,953	2,135,987	2,167,077	2,223,757	2,211,612	2,192,785	2,039,676	2,186,242	1.4%	1.0%

Sector 6 PUBLIC

	1981	1982	1983	1984	1985	1986	1987	1988	1989	1990	1981-85 Average	1986-90 Average	81/85 - 86/90 Year on Year Increase	Decade: Year on Year Increase
AUSTRIA	(12,367)	(12,913)	(13,460)	(14,006)	(14,552)	(14,586)	(15,686)	(15,238)	(15,713)	(17,285)	13,460	15,704	3.1%	3.6%
BELGIUM	(226,724)	(226,724)	(226,724)	(226,724)	(226,724)	226,724	258,782	309,237	340,267	333,040	226,724	293,210	5.3%	4.4%
DENMARK	(122,659)	(122,659)	(122,659)	(122,659)	(122,659)	(122,659)	122,659	107,619	102,723	91,926	122,659	109,517	-2.2%	-3.2%
EAST GERMANY	(140,227)	(140,227)	(140,227)	(140,227)	(140,227)	(140,227)	(140,227)	(140,227)	(140,227)	(140,227)	140,227	140,227	0.0%	0.0%
EIRE	3,648	3,827	3,645	4,011	3,677	4,008	3,880	3,850	3,665	3,541	3,762	3,789	0.1%	-0.3%
FINLAND	(71,632)	(74,648)	77,664	80,680	83,696	86,712	84,379	87,771	93,336	93,428	77,664	89,125	2.6%	3.0%
FRANCE	3,057	3,660	4,703	4,966	5,253	(5,802)	(6,351)	(6,900)	(7,449)	(7,998)	4,328	6,900	9.6%	11.3%
GREECE	(15,573)	(15,573)	(15,573)	(15,573)	(15,573)	(15,573)	(15,573)	(15,573)	(15,573)	(15,573)	15,573	15,573	0.0%	0.0%
ICELAND	(2,822)	(2,922)	(3,009)	(3,174)	(3,284)	(3,460)	(3,524)	(3,541)	(3,657)	(3,729)	3,042	3,582	3.3%	3.1%
ITALY	(89,925)	(89,925)	(89,925)	(89,925)	(89,925)	(89,925)	(89,925)	(89,925)	(89,925)	(89,925)	89,925	89,925	0.0%	0.0%
LIECHTENSTEIN	(37)	(39)	(40)	(41)	(43)	(44)	(46)	(47)	(49)	(50)	40	47	3.4%	3.4%
LUXEMBOURG	(579)	(579)	(579)	(579)	(579)	(579)	(579)	(579)	(579)	(579)	579	579	0.0%	0.0%
NETHERLANDS	85,000	87,000	85,000	85,667	85,667	(85,667)	(85,667)	(85,667)	(85,667)	(85,667)	85,667	85,667	0.0%	0.1%
NORWAY	(45,645)	(45,645)	(45,645)	(45,645)	(45,645)	(45,645)	(45,645)	45,645	44,049	44,690	45,645	45,135	-0.2%	-0.2%
PORTUGAL	(15,914)	(15,914)	(15,914)	(15,914)	(15,914)	(15,914)	(15,914)	(15,914)	(15,914)	(15,914)	15,914	15,914	0.0%	0.0%
SPAIN	(106,353)	(106,353)	(106,353)	(106,353)	(106,353)	(106,353)	(106,353)	106,353	(121,985)	137,616	106,353	115,732	1.7%	2.9%
SWEDEN	(87,275)	(88,706)	(90,138)	(91,570)	(93,001)	(94,433)	96,413	98,178	99,604	(100,159)	90,138	97,757	1.6%	1.5%
SWITZERLAND	92,601	97,627	95,654	102,148	104,928	(101,673)	(104,755)	(107,837)	(110,919)	(114,001)	98,592	107,837	1.8%	2.3%
UK	166,853	169,661	173,326	182,805	173,161	177,456	167,878	136,867	122,479	136,009	173,161	148,098	-3.1%	-2.2%
WEST GERMANY	88,164	83,587	82,053	88,797	98,219	(94,840)	91,481	93,928	92,654	(93,215)	88,164	93,220	1.1%	0.6%
EU TOTAL	1,064,676	1,065,689	1,066,681	1,084,200	1,083,931	1,085,727	1,103,049	1,112,639	1,139,107	1,151,230	1,073,035	1,118,350	0.8%	0.9%
EFTA TOTAL	312,379	322,500	325,610	337,264	345,149	346,553	350,458	358,257	367,327	373,342	328,580	359,187	1.8%	2.0%
EUROPE TOTAL	1,377,055	1,388,189	1,392,291	1,421,464	1,429,080	1,432,280	1,453,507	1,470,896	1,506,434	1,524,572	1,401,616	1,477,538	1.1%	1.1%

Figures in parentheses are grossed.

Collections: Current Periodical Titles

	1981	1982	1983	1984	1985	1986	1987	1988	1989	1990	1981-85 Average	1986-90 Average	81/85 - 86/90 Year on Year Increase	Decade: Year on Year Increase
ALL SECTORS														
AUSTRIA	208,641	209,007	212,711	211,973	213,671	214,075	213,739	208,602	218,679	220,600	211,201	215,139	0.4%	0.6%
BELGIUM	394,090	394,090	394,090	394,090	394,090	394,090	429,148	479,603	509,564	507,728	394,090	464,026	3.3%	2.9%
DENMARK	235,199	229,114	245,228	240,958	245,996	260,075	274,154	273,195	272,551	259,767	239,298	267,948	2.3%	1.1%
EAST GERMANY	1,155,551	1,157,062	1,158,612	1,160,143	1,161,674	1,163,204	1,164,735	1,166,265	1,167,796	1,157,314	1,158,612	1,163,863	0.1%	0.0%
EIRE	37,602	38,170	38,442	38,750	38,818	40,092	40,221	40,861	40,378	40,158	38,356	40,342	1.0%	0.7%
FINLAND	207,533	216,799	227,872	239,604	246,406	256,952	262,008	240,100	271,283	269,610	227,643	259,991	2.7%	3.0%
FRANCE	404,327	404,688	410,989	415,010	420,555	422,412	426,661	429,215	436,839	443,341	411,114	431,694	1.0%	1.0%
GREECE	174,190	174,190	174,190	174,190	174,190	174,190	174,190	174,190	174,190	174,190	174,190	174,190	0.0%	0.0%
ICELAND	11,706	12,083	12,447	12,890	13,277	13,724	14,138	14,607	16,896	17,034	12,481	15,280	4.1%	4.3%
ITALY	1,064,603	1,064,603	1,064,603	1,064,603	1,064,603	1,064,603	1,064,603	1,064,603	1,064,603	1,064,603	1,064,603	1,064,603	0.0%	0.0%
LIECHTENSTEIN	484	486	487	488	490	491	493	494	496	495	487	494	0.3%	0.3%
LUXEMBOURG	6,273	6,373	6,423	6,473	6,573	6,873	6,723	6,773	6,823	6,873	6,423	6,773	1.1%	1.0%
NETHERLANDS	581,192	603,492	590,092	596,476	585,293	580,759	582,259	574,759	571,459	570,459	591,309	575,939	-0.5%	-0.2%
NORWAY	149,016	154,093	159,170	164,247	169,332	174,422	176,665	200,334	186,385	193,785	159,172	186,318	3.2%	3.0%
PORTUGAL	37,013	37,013	37,013	40,068	37,868	38,728	39,284	38,668	39,218	39,768	37,795	39,129	0.7%	0.8%
SPAIN	275,063	309,517	331,660	353,330	377,682	402,031	415,097	428,431	476,374	524,585	329,450	449,304	6.4%	7.4%
SWEDEN	677,643	674,890	672,138	669,386	666,238	666,778	657,699	642,893	652,263	644,036	672,059	652,734	-0.6%	-0.6%
SWITZERLAND	263,156	272,561	274,967	285,840	292,999	294,123	300,466	306,291	317,324	348,735	277,905	313,388	2.4%	3.2%
UK	1,550,192	1,553,000	1,556,665	1,566,144	1,556,500	1,560,795	1,559,017	1,535,206	1,516,318	1,525,348	1,556,500	1,539,337	-0.2%	-0.2%
WEST GERMANY	899,956	877,522	879,155	920,714	922,431	998,668	1,011,845	1,029,723	1,029,179	1,037,782	899,956	1,021,439	2.6%	1.6%
EU TOTAL	6,815,251	6,848,854	6,887,160	6,970,947	6,986,271	7,106,320	7,187,917	7,241,492	7,305,292	7,351,914	6,901,697	7,238,587	1.0%	0.8%
EFTA TOTAL	1,518,179	1,539,919	1,559,792	1,584,428	1,602,413	1,620,565	1,625,208	1,613,321	1,663,326	1,694,295	1,560,946	1,643,343	1.0%	1.2%
EUROPE TOTAL	8,333,430	8,388,773	8,446,952	8,555,375	8,588,684	8,726,885	8,813,125	8,854,813	8,968,618	9,046,209	8,462,643	8,881,930	1.0%	0.9%

Collections: Current Periodical Titles per 1000 Population

	1981	1982	1983	1984	1985	1986	1987	1988	1989	1990	1981-85 Average	1986-90 Average	81/85 - 86/90 Year on Year Increase	Decade: Year on Year Increase
European Union														
Sector 1	1.70	1.73	1.78	1.81	1.84	1.88	1.92	1.96	1.98	1.98	1.77	1.94	1.9%	1.7%
Sector 2	5.05	5.12	5.13	5.20	5.19	5.28	5.32	5.30	5.48	5.62	5.14	5.40	1.0%	1.2%
Sector 3	5.05	5.04	5.04	5.05	5.04	5.02	5.02	5.01	5.07	5.03	5.04	5.03	-0.1%	-0.0%
Sector 4	0.09	0.09	0.09	0.09	0.09	0.09	0.09	0.09	0.09	0.09	0.09	0.09	-0.1%	-0.0%
Sector 5	5.13	5.13	5.19	5.27	5.27	5.43	5.52	5.56	5.62	5.59	5.20	5.54	1.3%	1.0%
Sector 6	3.15	3.15	3.16	3.21	3.20	3.19	3.24	3.25	3.37	3.40	3.17	3.29	0.7%	0.8%
All Sectors	20.16	20.26	20.37	20.62	20.62	20.88	21.10	21.17	21.61	21.70	20.41	21.29	0.8%	0.8%
EFTA														
Sector 1	1.88	1.92	1.98	2.02	2.03	2.30	2.26	1.79	1.90	2.04	1.97	2.06	0.9%	0.9%
Sector 2	12.81	13.05	13.44	13.65	13.78	14.12	14.15	12.88	14.38	15.27	13.35	14.16	1.2%	2.0%
Sector 3	13.97	13.98	14.00	14.01	14.03	14.04	14.08	14.09	14.11	14.01	14.00	14.07	0.1%	0.0%
Sector 4	0.29	0.28	0.27	0.26	0.24	0.24	0.23	0.23	0.23	0.21	0.27	0.23	-3.2%	-3.2%
Sector 5	8.58	8.65	8.71	8.87	9.04	8.94	8.94	10.06	9.71	9.29	8.77	9.39	1.4%	0.9%
Sector 6	9.72	10.04	10.13	10.49	10.74	10.78	10.91	11.15	11.43	11.54	10.22	11.16	1.8%	1.9%
All Sectors	47.24	47.92	48.54	49.30	49.86	50.43	50.57	50.20	51.76	52.37	48.57	51.07	1.0%	1.2%
Europe Total														
Sector 1	1.71	1.75	1.80	1.83	1.86	1.90	1.95	1.95	1.98	1.98	1.79	1.95	1.8%	1.6%
Sector 2	5.73	5.81	5.85	5.93	5.93	6.04	6.08	5.95	6.25	6.46	5.85	6.16	1.0%	1.3%
Sector 3	5.82	5.82	5.82	5.83	5.82	5.80	5.80	5.79	5.85	5.82	5.82	5.81	-0.0%	-0.0%
Sector 4	0.10	0.10	0.10	0.10	0.10	0.10	0.10	0.10	0.10	0.10	0.10	0.10	-0.8%	-0.7%
Sector 5	5.43	5.44	5.49	5.59	5.59	5.73	5.81	5.94	5.97	5.91	5.51	5.87	1.3%	0.9%
Sector 6	3.72	3.75	3.76	3.84	3.85	3.84	3.90	3.93	4.07	4.11	3.78	3.97	1.0%	1.1%
All Sectors	22.51	22.66	22.82	23.11	23.15	23.41	23.64	23.67	24.23	24.37	22.85	23.86	0.9%	0.9%

Collections: Manuscripts

Sector 1 NATIONAL

	1981	1982	1983	1984	1985	1986	1987	1988	1989	1990	1981–85 Average	1986–90 Average	81/85 – 86/90 Year on Year Increase	Decade: Year on Year Increase
AUSTRIA	(85,703)	(87,429)	(89,155)	(90,881)	(92,607)	94,333	95,977	96,991	99,199	101,237	89,155	97,547	1.8%	1.9%
BELGIUM	36,940	36,955	36,969	36,982	37,000	(37,015)	(37,030)	(37,045)	(37,060)	(37,075)	36,969	37,045	0.0%	0.0%
DENMARK	151,628	151,628	151,628	151,628	151,628	151,628	151,628	144,000	154,694	156,189	151,628	151,628	-0.0%	0.3%
EAST GERMANY	(93,801)	(93,801)	(93,801)	(93,801)	(93,801)	(93,801)	(93,801)	(93,801)	(93,801)	(93,801)	93,801	93,801	0.0%	0.0%
EIRE	(60,000)	(60,000)	(60,000)	(60,000)	(60,000)	(60,000)	(60,000)	(60,000)	(60,000)	60,000	60,000	60,000	0.0%	0.0%
FINLAND	1,120	1,130	1,139	1,500	1,500	1,500	1,500	1,550	1,572	1,588	1,278	1,542	3.8%	4.0%
FRANCE	(242,846)	(242,846)	(242,846)	(242,846)	(242,846)	(242,846)	(242,846)	(242,846)	(242,846)	(242,846)	242,846	242,846	0.0%	0.0%
GREECE	(5,000)	(5,000)	(5,000)	(5,000)	(5,000)	(5,000)	(5,000)	(5,000)	(5,000)	(5,000)	5,000	5,000	0.0%	0.0%
ICELAND	(13,631)	(13,681)	(13,731)	(13,781)	13,831	13,881	13,931	13,981	14,301	14,081	13,731	14,035	0.4%	0.4%
ITALY	794,373	794,373	794,365	794,373	794,381	794,383	794,385	794,387	794,389	(794,391)	794,373	794,387	0.0%	0.0%
LIECHTENSTEIN	(2,721)	(2,721)	(2,721)	(2,721)	(2,721)	(2,721)	(2,721)	(2,721)	(2,721)	(2,721)	2,721	2,721	0.0%	0.0%
LUXEMBOURG	1,600	1,700	1,800	1,900	2,000	2,050	2,080	2,120	2,140	2,150	1,800	2,108	3.2%	3.3%
NETHERLANDS	7,000	7,000	7,000	7,000	7,000	7,029	7,036	7,045	7,063	7,079	7,000	7,050	0.1%	0.1%
NORWAY	(19,578)	(19,821)	(20,064)	(20,307)	(20,550)	(20,793)	(21,036)	21,279	21,520	21,766	20,064	21,279	1.2%	1.2%
PORTUGAL	14,556	14,966	18,418	18,745	19,208	21,668	22,707	22,972	23,056	23,536	17,179	22,788	5.8%	5.5%
SPAIN	35,247	35,283	35,377	35,302	35,302	22,802	22,830	22,860	22,438	22,039	35,302	22,594	-8.5%	-5.1%
SWEDEN	(83,174)	(83,174)	(83,174)	(83,174)	(83,174)	83,174	88,558	186,000	187,450	(187,450)	83,174	146,526	12.0%	9.4%
SWITZERLAND	(101,230)	(102,454)	(103,678)	(104,902)	(106,126)	107,350	107,846	110,914	111,022	44,906	103,678	96,408	-1.4%	-8.6%
UK	(211,000)	(211,000)	(211,000)	(211,000)	(211,000)	(211,000)	(213,000)	215,000	(282,500)	(350,000)	211,000	254,300	3.8%	5.8%
WEST GERMANY	124,000	124,000	123,000	123,000	126,000	128,139	129,552	130,803	131,544	132,544	124,000	130,516	1.0%	0.7%
EU TOTAL	1,777,991	1,778,552	1,781,204	1,781,577	1,785,166	1,777,361	1,781,865	1,777,879	1,856,531	1,926,650	1,780,898	1,824,063	0.5%	0.9%
EFTA TOTAL	307,157	310,410	313,662	317,266	320,509	323,752	331,569	433,436	437,785	373,749	313,801	380,058	3.9%	2.2%
EUROPE TOTAL	2,085,148	2,088,962	2,094,866	2,098,843	2,105,675	2,101,113	2,113,464	2,211,315	2,294,316	2,300,399	2,094,699	2,204,121	1.0%	1.1%

Sector 2 HIGHER EDUCATION

	1981	1982	1983	1984	1985	1986	1987	1988	1989	1990	1981–85 Average	1986–90 Average	81/85 – 86/90 Year on Year Increase	Decade: Year on Year Increase
AUSTRIA	(32,469)	(33,938)	(34,696)	(35,229)	(36,711)	(37,286)	(36,571)	(35,164)	(40,851)	(41,839)	34,611	38,342	2.1%	2.9%
BELGIUM	(10,368)	(10,368)	(10,368)	(10,368)	(10,368)	(10,368)	(10,368)	(10,368)	(10,368)	(10,368)	10,368	10,368	0.0%	0.0%
DENMARK	13,904	13,904	13,904	13,904	13,904	14,287	14,669	15,051	24,661	26,384	13,904	19,010	6.5%	7.4%
EAST GERMANY	(61,980)	(62,652)	(63,323)	(63,994)	(64,666)	(65,337)	(66,009)	(66,680)	(67,352)	(68,023)	63,323	66,680	1.0%	1.0%
EIRE	(4,102)	(4,102)	(4,102)	(4,102)	(4,102)	(4,102)	(4,102)	(4,102)	(4,102)	(4,102)	4,102	4,102	0.0%	0.0%
FINLAND	3,150	2,554	2,800	3,344	3,429	3,415	3,643	3,710	3,779	2,872	3,055	3,494	2.7%	-1.0%
FRANCE	(19,000)	(19,000)	(19,000)	(19,000)	(19,000)	(19,400)	(19,800)	(20,200)	(20,600)	21,000	19,000	20,200	1.2%	1.1%
GREECE	(10,317)	(10,317)	(10,317)	(10,317)	(10,317)	(10,317)	(10,317)	(10,317)	(10,317)	(10,317)	10,317	10,317	0.0%	0.0%
ICELAND	(569)	(601)	(633)	(665)	(696)	(728)	(763)	(792)	(824)	(855)	633	792	4.6%	4.6%
ITALY	76,084	76,084	75,022	76,549	76,681	76,830	76,979	(77,128)	(77,277)	(77,426)	76,084	77,128	0.3%	0.2%
LIECHTENSTEIN	(86)	(86)	(86)	(86)	(86)	(86)	(86)	(86)	(86)	(85)	86	86	-0.0%	-0.1%
LUXEMBOURG	(428)	(428)	(428)	(428)	(428)	(428)	(428)	(428)	(428)	(428)	428	428	0.0%	0.0%
NETHERLANDS	31,000	31,000	31,000	31,000	31,000	33,000	33,400	33,800	34,420	(34,600)	31,000	33,800	1.7%	1.2%
NORWAY	(510)	(510)	(510)	(510)	(510)	(510)	(510)	(510)	(510)	510	510	510	0.0%	0.0%
PORTUGAL	(59,200)	(59,200)	(59,200)	(59,200)	(59,200)	59,205	62,629	74,260	68,000	82,903	59,200	69,399	3.2%	3.8%
SPAIN	25,584	27,343	31,047	34,751	38,456	42,160	(45,966)	49,778	(75,549)	97,321	31,436	62,155	14.6%	16.0%
SWEDEN	(531,529)	(482,235)	(432,941)	(383,647)	(334,353)	285,059	282,213	149,872	187,149	87,882	432,941	198,435	-14.4%	-18.1%
SWITZERLAND	(283,753)	(283,753)	(283,753)	(283,753)	(283,753)	231,186	275,691	287,200	310,082	314,607	283,753	283,753	0.0%	1.2%
UK	(64,469)	(64,469)	(64,469)	(64,469)	(64,469)	(64,469)	(64,469)	(64,469)	(64,469)	(64,469)	64,469	64,469	0.0%	0.0%
WEST GERMANY	76,667	76,667	72,000	79,000	79,000	87,878	90,972	90,829	91,639	(93,511)	76,667	90,966	3.5%	2.2%
EU TOTAL	453,103	455,534	454,180	467,082	471,591	487,781	500,111	517,410	548,962	590,852	460,298	529,023	2.8%	3.0%
EFTA TOTAL	852,066	803,677	755,419	707,244	659,538	558,270	599,527	477,334	543,281	448,650	755,589	525,412	-7.0%	-6.9%
EUROPE TOTAL	1,305,169	1,259,211	1,209,599	1,174,326	1,131,129	1,046,051	1,099,638	994,744	1,092,243	1,039,502	1,215,887	1,054,436	-2.8%	-2.5%

Figures in parentheses are grossed.

Collections: Manuscripts

Sector 3 – OTHER NON-MAJOR SPEC

	1981	1982	1983	1984	1985	1986	1987	1988	1989	1990	1981–85 Average	1986–90 Average	81/85 – 86/90 Year on Year Increase	Decade: Year on Year Increase
AUSTRIA	(191)	(191)	(191)	(191)	(191)	(191)	(191)	(191)	(191)	(191)	191	191	0.0%	0.0%
BELGIUM	16,241	16,241	16,241	16,241	16,241	16,241	16,241	16,241	16,241	16,241	16,241	16,241	0.0%	0.0%
DENMARK	0	0	0	0	0	0	0	0	0	0	0	0	0.0%	0.0%
EAST GERMANY	(222,431)	(222,431)	(222,431)	(222,431)	(222,431)	(222,431)	(222,431)	(222,431)	(222,431)	(219,218)	222,431	221,788	-0.1%	-0.2%
EIRE	2,750	2,750	2,750	2,750	2,750	2,750	2,753	2,754	2,758	2,759	2,750	2,755	0.0%	0.0%
FINLAND	0	0	0	0	0	0	0	0	0	0	0	0	0.0%	0.0%
FRANCE	(90,115)	(90,115)	(90,115)	(90,115)	(90,115)	(90,115)	(90,115)	(90,115)	(90,115)	(90,115)	90,115	90,115	0.0%	0.0%
GREECE	16,212	16,212	16,212	16,212	16,212	16,212	16,212	16,212	16,212	16,212	16,212	16,212	0.0%	0.0%
ICELAND	0	0	0	0	0	0	0	0	0	0	0	0	0.0%	0.0%
ITALY	(16,212)	(16,212)	16,212	16,212	16,212	16,212	16,212	16,212	16,212	16,212	16,212	16,212	0.0%	0.0%
LIECHTENSTEIN	0	0	0	0	0	0	0	0	0	0	0	0	0.0%	0.0%
LUXEMBOURG	0	0	0	0	0	0	0	0	0	0	0	0	0.0%	0.0%
NETHERLANDS	23,663	23,663	23,663	23,663	30,000	30,000	30,000	30,000	30,000	30,000	24,930	30,000	3.6%	2.7%
NORWAY	0	0	0	0	0	0	0	0	0	0	0	0	0.0%	0.0%
PORTUGAL	37,011	37,011	37,011	37,011	(37,011)	(37,011)	(37,011)	(37,011)	(37,011)	(37,011)	37,011	37,011	0.0%	0.0%
SPAIN	3,108	3,108	3,108	3,108	3,108	(3,108)	(3,108)	(3,108)	(3,108)	3,108	3,108	3,108	0.0%	0.0%
SWEDEN	(152,229)	(152,229)	(152,229)	(152,229)	(152,229)	(152,229)	(152,229)	(152,229)	(152,229)	(152,229)	152,229	152,229	0.0%	0.0%
SWITZERLAND	(41,689)	(45,723)	(49,757)	(53,791)	(57,825)	61,859	63,630	64,217	64,332	77,984	49,757	66,406	5.9%	7.2%
UK	93,004	93,004	93,004	93,004	93,004	(93,004)	(93,004)	(93,004)	(93,004)	(93,004)	93,004	93,004	0.0%	0.0%
WEST GERMANY	74,667	74,667	65,000	66,000	93,000	95,214	96,458	48,487	47,525	(46,563)	74,667	66,851	-2.2%	-5.1%
EU TOTAL	595,414	595,414	585,747	586,747	620,084	622,298	623,555	575,575	574,617	570,443	596,681	593,298	-0.1%	-0.5%
EFTA TOTAL	194,109	198,143	202,177	206,211	210,245	214,279	216,050	216,637	216,752	230,414	202,177	218,826	1.6%	1.9%
EUROPE TOTAL	789,523	793,557	787,924	792,958	830,329	836,577	839,605	792,212	791,369	800,857	798,858	812,124	0.3%	0.2%

Sector 4 SCHOOLS

	1981	1982	1983	1984	1985	1986	1987	1988	1989	1990	1981–85 Average	1986–90 Average	81/85 – 86/90 Year on Year Increase	Decade: Year on Year Increase
AUSTRIA	(309)	(309)	(309)	(309)	(309)	(309)	(309)	(309)	(309)	(305)	309	308	-0.1%	-0.1%
BELGIUM	759	759	759	759	759	(759)	(759)	(759)	(759)	(759)	759	759	0.0%	0.0%
DENMARK	(408)	(408)	(408)	(408)	(408)	(408)	(408)	(408)	(408)	(408)	408	408	0.0%	0.0%
EAST GERMANY	(688)	(688)	(688)	(688)	(688)	(688)	(688)	(688)	(688)	(672)	688	685	-0.1%	-0.3%
EIRE	372	372	372	372	372	(372)	(372)	(372)	(372)	(372)	372	372	0.0%	0.0%
FINLAND	(679)	(716)	(753)	(790)	(851)	(913)	(955)	(938)	975	1,012	758	959	4.8%	4.5%
FRANCE	4,545	4,545	4,545	4,545	4,545	(4,545)	(4,545)	(4,545)	(4,545)	(4,545)	4,545	4,545	0.0%	0.0%
GREECE	800	800	800	800	800	800	800	800	800	800	800	800	0.0%	0.0%
ICELAND	(25)	(25)	(25)	(25)	(25)	(25)	(25)	(25)	(25)	(25)	25	25	0.0%	0.0%
ITALY	4,818	4,818	4,818	4,818	4,818	4,818	4,818	4,818	4,818	(4,818)	4,818	4,818	0.0%	0.0%
LIECHTENSTEIN	(1)	(1)	(1)	(1)	(1)	(1)	(1)	(1)	(1)	(1)	1	1	0.0%	0.0%
LUXEMBOURG	26	26	26	26	26	26	26	26	26	(26)	26	26	0.0%	0.0%
NETHERLANDS	1,226	1,226	1,226	1,226	1,226	1,226	1,226	1,226	(1,226)	(1,226)	1,226	1,226	0.0%	0.0%
NORWAY	(905)	(905)	(905)	(905)	(913)	(925)	(886)	(933)	(957)	(934)	907	927	0.4%	0.4%
PORTUGAL	(1,495)	(1,885)	(2,275)	(2,665)	(3,055)	2,028	3,670	1,940	5,610	3,980	2,275	3,446	8.7%	11.5%
SPAIN	934	934	934	934	934	(934)	(934)	(934)	(934)	(934)	934	934	0.0%	0.0%
SWEDEN	(6,370)	(6,095)	(5,819)	(5,544)	(4,904)	(4,632)	(4,495)	(4,495)	(4,166)	(3,893)	5,746	4,337	-5.5%	-5.3%
SWITZERLAND	(257)	(257)	(257)	(257)	(257)	(257)	(257)	(257)	(257)	(255)	257	257	0.0%	-0.1%
UK	4,545	4,545	4,545	4,545	4,545	(4,545)	(4,545)	(4,545)	(4,545)	(4,545)	4,545	4,545	0.0%	0.0%
WEST GERMANY	4,525	4,525	4,525	4,525	4,525	(4,525)	(4,525)	(4,525)	(4,525)	(4,525)	4,525	4,525	0.0%	0.0%
EU TOTAL	25,141	25,531	25,921	26,311	26,701	25,874	27,316	25,586	29,256	27,610	25,921	27,088	0.9%	1.0%
EFTA TOTAL	8,546	8,308	8,069	7,831	7,260	7,062	6,928	6,958	6,692	6,425	8,003	6,813	-3.2%	-3.1%
EUROPE TOTAL	33,687	33,839	33,990	34,142	33,961	32,936	34,244	32,544	35,948	34,035	33,924	33,901	-0.0%	0.1%

Figures in parentheses are grossed.

Collections: Manuscripts

	1981	1982	1983	1984	1985	1986	1987	1988	1989	1990	1981–85 Average	1986–90 Average	81/85 – 86/90 Year on Year Increase	Decade: Year on Year Increase
Sector 5														
SPECIAL														
AUSTRIA	(108,933)	(108,933)	(108,933)	(108,933)	(108,933)	(108,933)	(108,933)	(108,933)	(108,933)	(109,680)	108,933	109,082	0.0%	0.1%
BELGIUM	(48,464)	(48,464)	(48,464)	(48,464)	(48,464)	(48,464)	(48,464)	(48,464)	(48,464)	(48,464)	48,464	48,464	0.0%	0.0%
DENMARK	(24,860)	(24,860)	(24,860)	(24,860)	(24,860)	(24,439)	(24,019)	23,599	17,119	12,333	24,860	20,302	-4.0%	-7.5%
EAST GERMANY	(238,351)	(238,351)	(238,351)	(238,351)	(238,351)	(238,351)	(238,351)	(238,351)	(238,351)	(234,554)	238,351	237,592	-0.1%	-0.2%
EIRE	(15,355)	(15,355)	(15,355)	(15,355)	(15,355)	(15,355)	(15,355)	(15,355)	(15,355)	(15,355)	15,355	15,355	0.0%	0.0%
FINLAND	(21,021)	(22,322)	(23,993)	(27,358)	(28,591)	(29,475)	(30,370)	-30,103	(34,257)	(33,834)	24,657	31,608	5.1%	5.4%
FRANCE	(261,944)	(261,944)	(261,944)	(261,944)	(261,944)	(261,944)	(261,944)	(261,944)	(261,944)	(261,944)	261,944	261,944	0.0%	0.0%
GREECE	(47,071)	(47,071)	(47,071)	(47,071)	(47,071)	(47,071)	(47,071)	(47,071)	(47,071)	(47,071)	47,071	47,071	0.0%	0.0%
ICELAND	(221)	(221)	(221)	(221)	(221)	(221)	(221)	(221)	221	(221)	221	221	0.0%	0.0%
ITALY	421,748	421,748	417,713	421,506	426,025	(427,094)	(428,163)	(429,232)	(430,301)	(431,370)	421,748	429,232	0.4%	0.3%
LIECHTENSTEIN	0	0	0	0	0	0	0	0	0	0	0	0	0.0%	0.0%
LUXEMBOURG	(1,857)	(1,857)	(1,857)	(1,857)	(1,857)	(1,857)	(1,857)	(1,857)	(1,857)	(1,857)	1,857	1,857	0.0%	0.0%
NETHERLANDS	32,000	22,000	22,000	25,333	25,333	(26,444)	(27,555)	(28,666)	(29,777)	(30,888)	25,333	28,666	2.5%	-0.4%
NORWAY	(41,669)	(42,634)	(43,598)	(44,562)	(45,526)	(49,864)	(50,982)	(48,844)	(45,258)	(50,348)	43,598	49,061	2.4%	2.1%
PORTUGAL	9,315	9,315	9,315	9,315	9,315	9,380	9,716	15,936	27,876	11,338	9,315	14,849	9.8%	2.2%
SPAIN	57,416	82,058	106,700	131,342	155,984	180,627	(261,797)	261,797	(127,922)	127,922	106,700	192,013	12.5%	9.3%
SWEDEN	(37,774)	(37,774)	(37,774)	(37,774)	(37,774)	32,543	43,004	79,120	88,569	83,705	37,774	65,388	11.6%	9.2%
SWITZERLAND	(96,180)	(96,180)	(96,180)	(96,180)	(96,180)	(96,180)	(96,180)	(96,180)	(96,180)	(96,878)	96,180	96,320	0.0%	0.1%
UK	(270,951)	(270,951)	(270,951)	(270,951)	(270,951)	(270,951)	(270,951)	(270,951)	(270,951)	(270,951)	270,951	270,951	0.0%	0.0%
WEST GERMANY	(310,871)	(310,871)	(310,871)	(310,871)	(310,871)	(310,871)	(310,871)	(310,871)	(310,871)	(310,871)	310,871	310,871	0.0%	0.0%
EU TOTAL	1,740,203	1,754,845	1,775,452	1,807,220	1,836,361	1,862,848	1,946,114	1,954,094	1,827,859	1,804,918	1,782,820	1,879,167	1.1%	0.4%
EFTA TOTAL	305,798	308,064	310,699	315,028	317,225	317,216	329,700	363,401	373,418	374,666	311,363	351,680	2.5%	2.3%
EUROPE TOTAL	2,046,001	2,062,909	2,086,151	2,122,248	2,153,606	2,180,064	2,275,814	2,317,495	2,201,277	2,179,584	2,094,183	2,230,847	1.3%	0.7%
Sector 6														
PUBLIC														
AUSTRIA	(16,316)	(17,037)	(17,758)	(18,479)	(19,200)	(19,244)	(20,706)	(20,104)	(20,731)	(22,804)	17,758	20,718	3.1%	3.8%
BELGIUM	(22,795)	(22,795)	(22,795)	(22,795)	(22,795)	(22,795)	(22,795)	(22,795)	(22,795)	(22,795)	22,795	22,795	0.0%	0.0%
DENMARK	(11,833)	(11,833)	(11,833)	(11,833)	(11,833)	(11,833)	(11,833)	(11,833)	(11,833)	(11,833)	11,833	11,833	0.0%	0.0%
EAST GERMANY	(185,006)	(185,006)	(185,006)	(185,006)	(185,006)	(185,006)	(185,006)	(185,006)	(185,006)	(185,006)	185,006	185,006	0.0%	0.0%
EIRE	(8,106)	(8,106)	(8,106)	(8,106)	(8,106)	(8,106)	(8,106)	(8,106)	(8,106)	(8,106)	8,106	8,106	0.0%	0.0%
FINLAND	(71,551)	(74,578)	(77,604)	(80,630)	(84,173)	(87,526)	(91,180)	(94,199)	(96,500)	(98,788)	77,707	93,639	3.8%	3.6%
FRANCE	(126,482)	(126,482)	(126,482)	(126,482)	(126,482)	(126,482)	(126,482)	(126,482)	(126,482)	(126,482)	126,482	126,482	0.0%	0.0%
GREECE	(12,829)	(12,829)	(12,829)	(12,829)	(12,829)	(12,829)	(12,829)	(12,829)	(12,829)	(12,829)	12,829	12,829	0.0%	0.0%
ICELAND	(2,373)	(2,373)	(2,373)	(2,373)	(2,373)	2,373	2,416	6,207	4,447	4,447	2,373	3,978	10.9%	7.2%
ITALY	(587,740)	(587,740)	(587,740)	(587,740)	(587,740)	(587,740)	(587,740)	(587,740)	(587,740)	(587,740)	587,740	587,740	0.0%	0.0%
LIECHTENSTEIN	(49)	(51)	(53)	(55)	(57)	(58)	(60)	(64)	(64)	(66)	53	62	3.2%	3.4%
LUXEMBOURG	(846)	(846)	(846)	(846)	(846)	(846)	(846)	(846)	(846)	(846)	846	846	0.0%	0.0%
NETHERLANDS	(33,213)	(33,213)	(33,213)	(33,213)	(33,213)	(33,213)	(33,213)	(33,213)	(33,213)	(33,213)	33,213	33,213	0.0%	0.0%
NORWAY	(44,442)	(45,356)	(46,250)	(47,144)	(48,038)	(48,932)	(50,863)	(51,100)	(51,634)	(52,506)	46,250	51,007	2.0%	1.9%
PORTUGAL	156,902	156,902	156,902	156,902	156,902	156,902	156,902	158,071	164,386	123,734	156,902	151,999	-0.6%	-2.6%
SPAIN	19,352	30,365	(24,859)	(24,859)	(24,859)	34,430	(37,585)	40,740	(37,509)	34,277	24,859	36,908	8.2%	6.6%
SWEDEN	(115,145)	(117,033)	(118,922)	(120,811)	(122,699)	(124,588)	(127,201)	(129,530)	(131,411)	(132,143)	118,922	128,975	1.6%	1.5%
SWITZERLAND	402,834	410,910	351,765	367,061	388,621	(380,685)	(377,132)	(373,579)	(370,026)	(366,473)	384,238	373,579	-0.6%	-1.0%
UK	65,092	68,061	71,208	86,495	75,225	101,303	97,103	69,634	58,985	66,910	73,216	78,787	1.5%	0.3%
WEST GERMANY	242,003	253,946	261,462	270,640	294,505	(304,628)	312,188	322,742	321,159	(331,054)	264,511	318,354	3.8%	3.5%
EU TOTAL	1,472,199	1,498,124	1,503,281	1,527,746	1,540,341	1,586,113	1,592,628	1,580,037	1,570,889	1,544,825	1,508,338	1,574,898	0.9%	0.5%
EFTA TOTAL	652,730	667,338	614,725	636,553	665,161	663,406	669,560	674,781	674,813	677,229	647,301	671,958	0.8%	0.4%
EUROPE TOTAL	2,124,929	2,165,462	2,118,006	2,164,299	2,205,502	2,249,519	2,262,188	2,254,818	2,245,702	2,222,054	2,155,640	2,246,856	0.8%	0.5%

Figures in parentheses are grossed.

Collections: Manuscripts

	1981	1982	1983	1984	1985	1986	1987	1988	1989	1990	1981-85 Average	1986-90 Average	81/85 - 86/90 Year on Year Increase	Decade: Year on Year Increase
ALL SECTORS														
AUSTRIA	243,921	247,837	251,042	254,032	257,951	260,296	262,689	261,692	270,214	276,056	250,957	266,189	1.2%	1.4%
BELGIUM	135,567	135,582	135,596	135,609	135,627	135,642	135,657	135,672	135,687	135,702	135,596	135,672	0.0%	0.0%
DENMARK	202,633	202,633	202,633	202,633	202,633	202,595	202,557	194,891	208,715	207,147	202,633	203,181	0.1%	0.2%
EAST GERMANY	802,257	802,929	803,600	804,271	804,943	805,614	806,286	806,957	807,629	801,274	803,600	805,552	0.0%	-0.0%
EIRE	90,685	90,685	90,685	90,685	90,685	90,685	90,688	90,689	90,693	90,694	90,685	90,690	0.0%	0.0%
FINLAND	97,521	101,300	106,289	113,622	118,544	122,829	127,698	130,500	137,083	138,094	107,455	131,241	4.1%	3.9%
FRANCE	744,932	744,932	744,932	744,932	744,932	745,332	745,732	746,132	746,532	746,932	744,932	746,132	0.0%	0.0%
GREECE	92,229	92,229	92,229	92,229	92,229	92,229	92,229	92,229	92,229	92,229	92,229	92,229	0.0%	0.0%
ICELAND	16,819	16,901	16,983	17,065	17,146	17,228	17,356	21,226	19,818	19,629	16,983	19,051	2.3%	1.7%
ITALY	1,900,975	1,900,975	1,895,870	1,901,198	1,905,857	1,907,077	1,908,297	1,909,517	1,910,737	1,911,957	1,900,975	1,909,517	0.1%	0.1%
LIECHTENSTEIN	2,857	2,859	2,861	2,863	2,865	2,868	2,868	2,870	2,872	2,873	2,861	2,870	0.1%	0.1%
LUXEMBOURG	4,757	4,857	4,957	5,057	5,157	5,207	5,237	5,277	5,297	5,307	4,957	5,265	1.2%	1.2%
NETHERLANDS	128,102	118,102	118,102	121,435	127,772	130,912	132,430	133,950	135,479	137,006	122,703	133,955	1.8%	0.7%
NORWAY	107,124	109,226	111,327	113,428	115,537	121,024	124,287	122,666	119,879	126,066	111,328	122,784	2.0%	1.8%
PORTUGAL	278,479	279,279	283,121	283,838	284,651	286,194	292,635	310,190	325,939	282,502	281,882	299,492	1.2%	0.2%
SPAIN	141,641	179,091	202,025	230,296	258,643	284,061	372,223	379,217	267,460	285,601	202,339	317,712	9.4%	8.1%
SWEDEN	926,221	878,540	830,859	783,179	735,133	682,225	697,700	701,246	750,976	647,302	830,786	695,890	-3.5%	-3.9%
SWITZERLAND	925,943	939,277	885,390	905,944	932,762	877,571	920,736	932,347	951,899	901,113	917,863	916,722	-0.0%	-0.3%
UK	709,061	712,030	715,177	730,464	719,194	745,272	743,072	717,603	774,454	849,879	717,185	766,056	1.3%	2.0%
WEST GERMANY	832,733	844,676	836,858	854,036	907,901	931,255	944,576	908,257	907,263	919,068	855,241	922,084	1.5%	1.1%
EU TOTAL	6,064,051	6,108,000	6,125,785	6,196,663	6,280,264	6,362,075	6,471,619	6,430,561	6,408,114	6,465,298	6,154,957	6,427,537	0.9%	0.7%
EFTA TOTAL	2,320,406	2,295,940	2,204,751	2,190,133	2,179,838	2,083,985	2,153,334	2,172,547	2,252,741	2,111,133	2,238,234	2,154,748	-0.8%	-1.0%
EUROPE TOTAL	8,384,457	8,403,940	8,330,536	8,386,816	8,460,202	8,446,060	8,624,953	8,603,128	8,660,855	8,576,431	8,393,190	8,582,285	0.4%	0.3%

Collections: Manuscripts per 1000 Population

	1981	1982	1983	1984	1985	1986	1987	1988	1989	1990	1981-85 Average	1986-90 Average	81/85 - 86/90 Year on Year Increase	Decade: Year on Year Increase
European Union														
Sector 1	5.26	5.26	5.27	5.27	5.27	5.22	5.23	5.20	5.49	5.69	5.27	5.36	0.4%	0.9%
Sector 2	1.34	1.35	1.34	1.38	1.39	1.43	1.47	1.51	1.62	1.74	1.36	1.56	2.7%	3.0%
Sector 3	1.76	1.76	1.73	1.74	1.83	1.83	1.83	1.68	1.70	1.68	1.76	1.74	-0.2%	-0.5%
Sector 4	0.07	0.08	0.08	0.08	0.08	0.08	0.08	0.07	0.09	0.08	0.08	0.08	0.8%	1.0%
Sector 5	5.15	5.19	5.25	5.35	5.42	5.47	5.71	5.71	5.41	5.33	5.27	5.53	0.9%	0.4%
Sector 6	4.36	4.43	4.45	4.52	4.55	4.66	4.67	4.62	4.65	4.56	4.46	4.63	0.8%	0.5%
All Sectors	17.94	18.07	18.12	18.33	18.54	18.67	19.00	18.80	18.96	19.08	18.20	18.90	0.8%	0.7%
EFTA														
Sector 1	9.56	9.66	9.76	9.87	9.97	10.07	10.32	13.49	13.62	11.55	9.76	11.81	3.9%	2.1%
Sector 2	26.51	25.01	23.51	22.01	20.52	17.37	18.66	14.85	16.91	13.87	23.51	16.33	-7.0%	-6.9%
Sector 3	6.04	6.17	6.29	6.42	6.54	6.67	6.72	6.74	6.74	7.12	6.29	6.80	1.6%	1.8%
Sector 4	0.27	0.26	0.25	0.24	0.23	0.22	0.22	0.22	0.21	0.20	0.25	0.21	-3.2%	-3.2%
Sector 5	9.52	9.59	9.67	9.80	9.87	9.87	10.26	11.31	11.62	11.58	9.69	10.93	2.4%	2.2%
Sector 6	20.31	20.77	19.13	19.81	20.70	20.64	20.83	21.00	21.00	20.93	20.14	20.88	0.7%	0.3%
All Sectors	72.20	71.44	68.61	68.15	67.83	64.85	67.01	67.60	70.10	65.26	69.65	66.96	-0.8%	-1.1%
Europe Total														
Sector 1	5.63	5.64	5.66	5.67	5.68	5.64	5.67	5.91	6.20	6.20	5.66	5.92	0.9%	1.1%
Sector 2	3.53	3.40	3.27	3.17	3.05	2.81	2.95	2.66	2.95	2.80	3.28	2.83	-2.9%	-2.5%
Sector 3	2.13	2.14	2.13	2.14	2.24	2.24	2.25	2.12	2.14	2.16	2.16	2.18	0.2%	0.1%
Sector 4	0.09	0.09	0.09	0.09	0.09	0.09	0.09	0.09	0.10	0.09	0.09	0.09	-0.1%	0.1%
Sector 5	5.53	5.57	5.64	5.73	5.81	5.85	6.10	6.19	5.95	5.87	5.66	5.99	1.2%	0.7%
Sector 6	5.74	5.85	5.72	5.85	5.95	6.03	6.07	6.03	6.07	5.99	5.82	6.04	0.7%	0.5%
All Sectors	22.65	22.70	22.51	22.66	22.81	22.65	23.14	22.99	23.40	23.11	22.67	23.06	0.3%	0.2%

- 146 -

Collections: Microforms

	1981	1982	1983	1984	1985	1986	1987	1988	1989	1990	1981–85 Average	1986–90 Average	81/85 – 86/90 Year on Year Increase	Decade: Year on Year Increase
Sector 1														
NATIONAL														
AUSTRIA	(21,205)	(22,368)	(23,531)	(24,694)	(25,857)	27,020	27,959	28,858	29,890	31,674	23,531	29,080	4.3%	4.6%
BELGIUM	(240,997)	(240,997)	(240,997)	(240,997)	(240,997)	(240,997)	(240,997)	(240,997)	(240,997)	(240,997)	240,997	240,997	0.0%	0.0%
DENMARK	67,654	74,438	82,919	93,071	107,938	222,826	337,313	452,000	176,674	168,595	85,204	271,442	26.1%	10.7%
EAST GERMANY	(625,949)	(625,949)	(625,949)	(625,949)	(625,949)	(625,949)	(625,949)	(625,949)	(625,949)	(625,949)	625,949	625,949	0.0%	0.0%
EIRE	(85,699)	(85,699)	(85,699)	(85,699)	(85,699)	(85,699)	(85,699)	(85,699)	(85,699)	(85,699)	85,699	85,699	0.0%	0.0%
FINLAND	89,000	98,000	102,500	118,900	133,200	220,000	248,000	276,500	290,830	317,306	108,320	270,527	20.1%	15.2%
FRANCE	(1,337,207)	(1,337,207)	(1,337,207)	(1,337,207)	(1,337,207)	(1,337,207)	(1,337,207)	(1,337,207)	(1,337,207)	(1,337,207)	1,337,207	1,337,207	0.0%	0.0%
GREECE	(4,000)	(4,000)	(4,000)	(4,000)	(4,000)	(4,000)	(4,000)	(4,000)	(4,000)	(4,000)	4,000	4,000	0.0%	0.0%
ICELAND	(34,225)	(34,913)	(35,602)	(36,290)	(36,978)	(37,577)	(38,237)	(38,919)	(39,559)	(40,420)	35,602	38,942	1.6%	1.9%
ITALY	(1,389,186)	(1,389,186)	(1,389,186)	(1,389,186)	(1,389,186)	(1,389,186)	(1,389,186)	(1,389,186)	(1,389,186)	(1,389,186)	1,389,186	1,389,186	0.0%	0.0%
LIECHTENSTEIN	(450)	(450)	(450)	(450)	(450)	(450)	(450)	(450)	(450)	450	450	450	0.0%	0.0%
LUXEMBOURG	1,000	1,100	1,200	1,300	1,400	1,600	1,800	2,000	2,200	2,400	1,200	2,000	10.8%	10.2%
NETHERLANDS	66,000	76,000	124,000	118,000	96,000	100,000	102,500	103,150	104,299	106,310	96,000	103,252	1.5%	5.4%
NORWAY	(84,913)	(79,359)	(73,805)	(68,251)	(62,697)	57,143	48,422	59,571	72,986	34,928	73,805	54,610	-5.8%	-9.4%
PORTUGAL	919	1,092	2,253	3,976	4,980	4,772	5,817	7,052	7,916	8,883	2,644	6,888	21.1%	28.7%
SPAIN	4,624	5,475	8,300	6,133	6,133	8,423	8,902	13,978	17,418	23,818	6,133	14,108	18.1%	20.0%
SWEDEN	(114,660)	(121,858)	(129,056)	(136,254)	(143,452)	150,650	317,233	162,990	171,274	179,443	129,056	196,318	8.8%	5.1%
SWITZERLAND	(9,409)	(9,656)	(9,903)	(10,150)	(10,397)	10,844	11,040	11,277	11,385	6,947	9,903	10,259	0.7%	-3.3%
UK	2,200,000	2,300,000	2,400,000	2,700,000	2,600,000	3,296,000	3,596,000	3,896,000	3,801,500	3,707,000	2,440,000	3,659,300	8.4%	6.0%
WEST GERMANY	1,537,000	1,288,000	1,452,000	1,625,000	1,783,000	2,004,525	2,193,087	2,452,980	2,713,930	2,976,309	1,537,000	2,468,162	9.9%	7.6%
EU TOTAL	7,560,235	7,429,143	7,753,710	8,230,518	8,282,469	9,318,984	9,928,437	10,610,198	10,506,975	10,676,353	7,851,219	10,208,189	5.4%	3.9%
EFTA TOTAL	353,862	366,604	374,847	394,989	413,031	503,484	691,341	578,565	616,374	611,168	380,667	600,186	9.5%	6.3%
EUROPE TOTAL	7,914,097	7,795,747	8,128,557	8,625,507	8,695,520	9,822,468	10,619,778	11,188,763	11,123,349	11,287,521	8,231,886	10,808,376	5.6%	4.0%
Sector 2														
HIGHER EDUCATION														
AUSTRIA	(857,622)	(896,417)	(916,440)	(930,785)	(969,665)	(984,872)	(965,980)	(928,813)	(1,079,022)	(1,105,134)	914,186	1,012,764	2.1%	2.9%
BELGIUM	(566,649)	(566,649)	(566,649)	(566,649)	(566,649)	(566,649)	(566,649)	(566,649)	(566,649)	(566,649)	566,649	566,649	0.0%	0.0%
DENMARK	(270,198)	(270,198)	(270,198)	(270,198)	(270,198)	(328,374)	(382,551)	438,728	431,816	935,401	270,198	502,974	13.2%	14.8%
EAST GERMANY	(1,637,126)	(1,654,861)	(1,672,596)	(1,690,331)	(1,708,066)	(1,725,800)	(1,743,535)	(1,761,270)	(1,779,005)	(1,796,740)	1,672,596	1,761,270	1.0%	1.0%
EIRE	202,498	202,498	202,498	202,498	202,498	202,498	202,498	202,498	202,498	202,498	202,498	202,498	0.0%	0.0%
FINLAND	636,459	707,705	754,527	946,563	1,030,735	1,112,051	944,286	900,015	926,874	965,492	815,198	969,744	3.5%	4.7%
FRANCE	180,000	300,500	240,250	240,250	240,250	(407,625)	575,000	750,000	962,000	1,065,000	240,250	751,925	25.6%	21.8%
GREECE	(509,297)	(509,297)	(509,297)	(509,297)	(509,297)	(509,297)	(509,297)	(509,297)	(509,297)	(509,297)	509,297	509,297	0.0%	0.0%
ICELAND	(200)	(200)	(200)	(200)	(200)	200	300	400	500	600	200	400	14.9%	13.0%
ITALY	(139,297)	(139,297)	139,297	139,297	139,297	(139,297)	(139,297)	(139,297)	(139,297)	(139,297)	139,297	139,297	0.0%	0.0%
LIECHTENSTEIN	(2,273)	(2,273)	(2,273)	(2,273)	(2,273)	(2,273)	(2,273)	(2,273)	(2,273)	(2,252)	2,273	2,269	-0.0%	-0.1%
LUXEMBOURG	(21,109)	(21,109)	(21,109)	(21,109)	(21,109)	(21,109)	(21,109)	(21,109)	(21,109)	(21,109)	21,109	21,109	0.0%	0.0%
NETHERLANDS	947,000	1,018,000	1,100,000	1,021,667	1,208,000	1,251,000	1,287,000	1,344,000	1,513,000	(1,682,000)	1,058,933	1,415,400	6.0%	6.6%
NORWAY	(372,396)	(383,079)	(393,762)	(404,445)	(415,128)	425,811	475,744	426,614	458,245	468,543	393,762	450,991	2.8%	2.6%
PORTUGAL	(15,103)	(15,103)	(15,103)	(15,103)	(15,103)	18,069	33,138	59,355	63,557	57,912	15,103	46,406	25.2%	16.1%
SPAIN	45,240	59,795	52,518	52,518	52,518	337,766	(124,332)	167,636	(391,674)	434,978	52,518	291,277	40.9%	28.6%
SWEDEN	(331,991)	(331,991)	(331,991)	(331,991)	(331,991)	300,914	331,398	323,080	372,573	2,344,762	331,991	734,545	17.2%	24.3%
SWITZERLAND	(1,127,372)	(1,246,591)	(1,365,810)	(1,485,029)	(1,604,248)	1,723,467	1,871,682	2,002,683	2,074,972	2,200,344	1,365,810	1,974,630	7.7%	7.7%
UK	(3,182,376)	(3,182,376)	(3,182,376)	(3,182,376)	(3,182,376)	(3,182,376)	(3,182,376)	(3,182,376)	(3,182,376)	(3,182,376)	3,182,376	3,182,376	0.0%	0.0%
WEST GERMANY	6,101,750	4,437,000	4,966,000	5,688,000	9,316,000	10,836,954	14,336,231	15,447,038	16,581,911	(17,891,931)	6,101,750	15,018,813	19.7%	12.7%
EU TOTAL	13,817,643	12,376,683	12,937,891	13,599,293	17,431,361	19,524,814	23,103,013	24,589,253	26,344,189	28,485,188	14,032,574	24,409,291	11.7%	8.4%
EFTA TOTAL	3,328,313	3,568,256	3,765,003	4,101,286	4,354,240	4,549,588	4,591,663	4,583,878	4,914,459	7,087,127	3,823,420	5,145,343	6.1%	8.8%
EUROPE TOTAL	17,145,956	15,944,939	16,702,894	17,700,579	21,785,601	24,074,402	27,694,676	29,173,131	31,258,648	35,572,315	17,855,994	29,554,634	10.6%	8.4%

Figures in parentheses are grossed.

Collections: Microforms

Sector 3 – OTHER NON-MAJOR SPEC.

	1981	1982	1983	1984	1985	1986	1987	1988	1989	1990	1981–85 Average	1986–90 Average	81/85 – 86/90 Year on Year Increase	Decade: Year on Year Increase
AUSTRIA	(34,341)	(34,341)	(34,341)	(34,341)	(34,341)	(34,341)	(34,341)	(34,341)	(34,341)	(34,341)	34,341	34,341	0.0%	0.0%
BELGIUM	(24,165)	(24,165)	(24,165)	(24,165)	(24,165)	(24,165)	(24,165)	(24,165)	(24,165)	(24,165)	24,165	24,165	0.0%	0.0%
DENMARK	0	0	0	0	0	0	0	0	0	0	0	0	0.0%	0.0%
EAST GERMANY	(586,108)	(586,108)	(586,108)	(586,108)	(586,108)	(586,108)	(586,108)	(586,108)	(586,108)	(577,641)	586,108	584,415	-0.1%	-0.2%
EIRE	(280)	(280)	(280)	(280)	(280)	280	285	286	288	289	280	286	0.4%	0.4%
FINLAND	0	0	0	0	0	0	0	0	0	0	0	0	0.0%	0.0%
FRANCE	(8,897)	(8,897)	(8,897)	(8,897)	(8,897)	(8,897)	(8,897)	(8,897)	(8,897)	(8,897)	8,897	8,897	0.0%	0.0%
GREECE	(24,123)	(24,123)	(24,123)	(24,123)	(24,123)	(24,123)	(24,123)	(24,123)	(24,123)	(24,123)	24,123	24,123	0.0%	0.0%
ICELAND	0	0	0	0	0	0	0	0	0	0	0	0	0.0%	0.0%
ITALY	(139,297)	(139,297)	(139,297)	(139,297)	(139,297)	(139,297)	(139,297)	(139,297)	(139,297)	(139,297)	139,297	139,297	0.0%	0.0%
LIECHTENSTEIN	0	0	0	0	0	0	0	0	0	0	0	0	0.0%	0.0%
LUXEMBOURG	0	0	0	0	0	0	0	0	0	0	0	0	0.0%	0.0%
NETHERLANDS	(35,209)	(35,209)	(35,209)	(35,209)	(35,209)	(35,209)	(35,209)	(35,209)	(35,209)	(35,209)	35,209	35,209	0.0%	0.0%
NORWAY	0	0	0	0	0	0	0	0	0	0	0	0	0.0%	0.0%
PORTUGAL	(35,880)	(35,880)	(35,880)	(35,880)	(35,880)	(35,880)	(35,880)	(35,880)	(35,880)	(35,880)	35,880	35,880	0.0%	0.0%
SPAIN	(93,558)	(93,558)	(93,558)	(93,558)	(93,558)	(109,796)	(126,032)	(142,268)	(158,504)	(174,740)	93,558	142,268	8.7%	7.2%
SWEDEN	(401,126)	(401,126)	(401,126)	(401,126)	(401,126)	(401,126)	(401,126)	(401,126)	(401,126)	(401,126)	401,126	401,126	0.0%	0.0%
SWITZERLAND	(23,084)	(28,094)	(33,104)	(38,114)	(43,124)	48,134	50,690	69,921	64,402	68,174	33,104	60,264	12.7%	12.8%
UK	(138,384)	(138,384)	(138,384)	(138,384)	(138,384)	(138,384)	(138,384)	(138,384)	(138,384)	(138,384)	138,384	138,384	0.0%	0.0%
WEST GERMANY	156,500	105,000	144,000	186,000	191,000	290,088	375,098	504,460	549,896	(549,896)	156,500	453,888	23.7%	15.0%
EU TOTAL	1,242,401	1,190,901	1,229,901	1,271,901	1,276,901	1,392,227	1,493,478	1,639,077	1,700,751	1,708,521	1,242,401	1,586,811	5.0%	3.6%
EFTA TOTAL	458,551	463,561	468,571	473,581	478,591	483,601	486,157	505,388	499,869	503,641	468,571	495,731	1.1%	1.0%
EUROPE TOTAL	1,700,952	1,654,462	1,698,472	1,745,482	1,755,492	1,875,828	1,979,635	2,144,465	2,200,620	2,212,162	1,710,972	2,082,542	4.0%	3.0%

Sector 4 SCHOOLS

	1981	1982	1983	1984	1985	1986	1987	1988	1989	1990	1981–85 Average	1986–90 Average	81/85 – 86/90 Year on Year Increase	Decade: Year on Year Increase
AUSTRIA	(2,235)	(2,235)	(2,235)	(2,235)	(2,235)	(2,235)	(2,235)	(2,235)	(2,235)	(2,208)	2,235	2,230	-0.0%	-0.1%
BELGIUM	(8,456)	(8,456)	(8,456)	(8,456)	(8,456)	(8,456)	(8,456)	(8,456)	(8,456)	(8,456)	8,456	8,456	0.0%	0.0%
DENMARK	(17,665)	(18,311)	(19,547)	(19,075)	(19,643)	(20,138)	(20,632)	(21,127)	(21,621)	(22,116)	18,848	21,127	2.3%	2.5%
EAST GERMANY	(4,976)	(4,976)	(4,976)	(4,976)	(4,976)	(4,976)	(4,976)	(4,976)	(4,976)	(4,861)	4,976	4,953	-0.1%	-0.3%
EIRE	(4,152)	(4,152)	(4,152)	(4,152)	(4,152)	(4,152)	(4,152)	(4,152)	(4,152)	(4,152)	4,152	4,152	0.0%	0.0%
FINLAND	(4,915)	(5,183)	(5,450)	(5,717)	(6,161)	(6,605)	(6,910)	(6,787)	(7,055)	(7,322)	5,485	6,936	4.8%	4.5%
FRANCE	(50,659)	(50,659)	(50,659)	(50,659)	(50,659)	(50,659)	(50,659)	(50,659)	(50,659)	(50,659)	50,659	50,659	0.0%	0.0%
GREECE	(8,920)	(8,920)	(8,920)	(8,920)	(8,920)	(8,920)	(8,920)	(8,920)	(8,920)	(8,920)	8,920	8,920	0.0%	0.0%
ICELAND	(181)	(181)	(181)	(181)	(181)	(181)	(181)	(181)	(181)	(181)	181	181	0.0%	0.0%
ITALY	(15,398)	(15,396)	(15,396)	(15,396)	(15,396)	(15,396)	(15,398)	(15,396)	(15,398)	(15,396)	15,398	15,398	0.0%	0.0%
LIECHTENSTEIN	(9)	(9)	(9)	(9)	(9)	(9)	(9)	(9)	(9)	(9)	9	9	0.0%	0.0%
LUXEMBOURG	(292)	(292)	(292)	(292)	(292)	(292)	(292)	(292)	(292)	(292)	292	292	0.0%	0.0%
NETHERLANDS	(13,671)	(13,671)	(13,671)	(13,671)	(13,671)	(13,671)	(13,671)	(13,671)	(13,671)	(13,671)	13,671	13,671	0.0%	0.4%
NORWAY	(6,550)	(6,550)	(6,550)	(6,550)	(6,608)	(6,696)	(6,409)	(6,752)	(6,923)	(6,760)	6,562	6,708	5.8%	3.7%
PORTUGAL	(1,963)	(1,589)	(1,825)	(2,614)	(2,732)	3,462	2,862	2,679	2,496	2,732	2,144	2,846	0.0%	0.0%
SPAIN	(2,236)	(2,236)	(2,236)	(2,236)	(2,236)	(2,236)	(2,236)	(2,236)	(2,236)	(2,236)	2,236	2,236	0.0%	0.0%
SWEDEN	(46,096)	(44,104)	(42,112)	(40,121)	(35,488)	(33,516)	(32,531)	(32,531)	(30,165)	(28,173)	41,584	31,383	-5.5%	-5.3%
SWITZERLAND	(1,862)	(1,862)	(1,862)	(1,862)	(1,862)	(1,862)	(1,862)	(1,862)	(1,862)	(1,847)	1,862	1,859	-0.0%	-0.1%
UK	(50,665)	(50,665)	(50,665)	(50,665)	(50,665)	(50,665)	(50,665)	(50,665)	(50,665)	(50,665)	50,665	50,665	0.0%	0.0%
WEST GERMANY	(14,947)	(14,947)	(14,947)	(14,947)	(14,947)	(14,947)	(14,947)	(14,947)	(14,947)	(14,947)	14,947	14,947	0.0%	0.0%
EU TOTAL	194,000	194,272	195,744	196,061	196,747	197,972	197,866	198,178	198,489	199,105	195,365	198,322	0.3%	0.3%
EFTA TOTAL	61,847	60,124	58,399	56,675	52,544	51,104	50,137	50,357	48,430	46,500	57,918	49,306	-3.2%	-3.1%
EUROPE TOTAL	255,847	254,396	254,143	252,736	249,291	249,076	248,003	248,535	246,919	245,605	253,282	247,628	-0.5%	-0.5%

Figures in parentheses are grossed.

- 148 -

Collections: Microforms

Sector 5 SPECIAL

	1981	1982	1983	1984	1985	1986	1987	1988	1989	1990	1981-85 Average	1986-90 Average	81/85 - 86/90 Year on Year Increase	Decade: Year on Year Increase
AUSTRIA	(5,253,677)	(5,253,677)	(5,253,677)	(5,253,677)	(5,253,677)	(5,253,677)	(5,253,677)	(5,253,677)	(5,253,677)	(5,289,707)	(5,253,677)	5,260,883	0.0%	0.1%
BELGIUM	(2,425,794)	(2,425,794)	(2,425,794)	(2,425,794)	(2,425,794)	(2,425,794)	(2,425,794)	(2,425,794)	(2,425,794)	(2,425,794)	2,425,794	2,425,794	0.0%	0.0%
DENMARK	(1,244,356)	(1,244,356)	(1,244,356)	(1,244,356)	(1,244,356)	(1,609,943)	(1,975,529)	2,341,115	2,499,560	3,399,968	1,244,356	2,365,227	13.7%	11.8%
EAST GERMANY	(11,495,304)	(11,495,304)	(11,495,304)	(11,495,304)	(11,495,304)	(11,495,304)	(11,495,304)	(11,495,304)	(11,495,304)	(11,312,188)	11,495,304	11,458,681	-0.1%	-0.2%
EIRE	(768,557)	(768,557)	(768,557)	(768,557)	(768,557)	(768,557)	(768,557)	(768,557)	(768,557)	(768,557)	768,557	768,557	0.0%	0.0%
FINLAND	56,223	108,300	173,355	195,771	233,769	263,259	188,638	286,702	2,682,143	2,864,781	153,484	1,257,165	52.3%	54.8%
FRANCE	(13,111,327)	(13,111,327)	(13,111,327)	(13,111,327)	(13,111,327)	(13,111,327)	(13,111,327)	(13,111,327)	(13,111,327)	(13,111,327)	13,111,327	13,111,327	0.0%	0.0%
GREECE	(13,962,165)	(13,962,165)	(13,962,165)	(13,962,165)	(13,962,165)	(13,962,165)	(13,962,165)	(13,962,165)	(13,962,165)	(13,962,165)	13,962,165	13,962,165	0.0%	0.0%
ICELAND	(40,686)	(44,581)	(49,449)	(55,939)	(65,675)	(75,410)	(85,145)	(94,881)	(114,352)	(133,824)	51,266	100,722	14.5%	14.1%
ITALY	(13,962,165)	(13,962,165)	(13,962,165)	(13,962,165)	(13,962,165)	(13,962,165)	(13,962,165)	(13,962,165)	(13,962,165)	(13,962,165)	13,962,165	13,962,165	0.0%	0.0%
LIECHTENSTEIN	0	0	0	0	0	0	0	0	0	0	0	0	0.0%	0.0%
LUXEMBOURG	(92,939)	(92,939)	(92,939)	(92,939)	(92,939)	(92,939)	(92,939)	(92,939)	(92,939)	(92,939)	92,939	92,939	0.0%	0.0%
NETHERLANDS	8,980,000	10,095,000	11,248,000	10,107,667	7,689,000	8,352,000	8,623,000	8,761,000	8,873,000	(8,985,000)	9,623,933	8,718,800	-2.0%	0.0%
NORWAY	(2,594,140)	(2,662,242)	(2,730,344)	(2,798,446)	(2,866,548)	2,820,024	3,030,416	2,795,727	3,092,432	3,703,868	2,730,344	3,088,493	2.5%	4.0%
PORTUGAL	(62,505)	(74,652)	(86,799)	(98,946)	(111,093)	123,240	(135,367)	(147,534)	159,681	(171,828)	86,799	147,534	11.2%	11.9%
SPAIN	(1,665,122)	(1,665,122)	(1,665,122)	(1,665,122)	(1,665,122)	1,685,122	(2,173,608)	2,173,608	(3,250,982)	3,250,982	1,665,122	2,502,860	8.5%	7.7%
SWEDEN	(3,142,316)	(3,203,270)	(3,264,224)	(3,325,178)	(3,386,132)	2,059,132	2,120,086	4,542,140	5,066,985	(5,307,569)	3,264,224	3,819,182	3.2%	6.0%
SWITZERLAND	(4,638,614)	(4,638,614)	(4,638,614)	(4,638,614)	(4,638,614)	(4,638,614)	(4,638,614)	4,638,614	(4,638,614)	(4,672,289)	4,638,614	4,645,349	0.0%	0.1%
UK	(13,562,190)	(13,562,190)	(13,562,190)	(13,562,190)	(13,562,190)	(13,562,190)	(13,562,190)	(13,562,190)	(13,562,190)	(13,562,190)	13,562,190	13,562,190	0.0%	0.0%
WEST GERMANY	15,378,667	15,378,667	16,369,000	11,748,000	18,019,000	15,475,276	13,995,111	14,490,035	21,662,334	(22,380,519)	15,378,667	17,596,855	2.7%	4.2%
EU TOTAL	96,711,091	97,838,238	99,993,718	94,244,532	98,109,012	96,606,022	96,284,078	97,293,733	105,825,998	107,365,642	97,379,318	100,675,094	0.7%	1.2%
EFTA TOTAL	15,725,656	15,910,684	16,109,663	16,267,625	16,444,415	15,110,116	15,316,876	17,611,741	20,848,203	21,972,038	16,091,609	18,171,795	2.5%	3.8%
EUROPE TOTAL	112,436,747	113,748,922	116,103,381	110,512,157	114,553,427	111,716,138	111,600,952	114,905,474	126,674,201	129,337,680	113,470,927	118,846,889	0.9%	1.6%

Sector 6 PUBLIC

	1981	1982	1983	1984	1985	1986	1987	1988	1989	1990	1981-85 Average	1986-90 Average	81/85 - 86/90 Year on Year Increase	Decade: Year on Year Increase
AUSTRIA	(85,320)	(89,090)	(92,860)	(96,630)	(100,400)	(100,633)	(108,288)	(105,131)	(108,410)	(119,251)	92,860	108,343	3.1%	3.8%
BELGIUM	(174,007)	(174,007)	(174,007)	(174,007)	(174,007)	(174,007)	(174,007)	(174,007)	(174,007)	(174,007)	174,007	174,007	0.0%	0.0%
DENMARK	(39,641)	(39,641)	(39,641)	(39,641)	(39,641)	(39,641)	31,657	37,355	42,670	46,882	39,641	39,641	0.0%	1.9%
EAST GERMANY	(6,740,252)	(6,740,252)	(6,740,252)	(6,740,252)	(6,740,252)	(6,740,252)	(6,740,252)	(6,740,252)	(6,740,252)	(6,740,252)	6,740,252	6,740,252	0.0%	0.0%
EIRE	5,756	6,517	7,315	5,970	7,151	7,519	8,088	7,750	9,726	8,229	6,542	8,229	4.7%	6.0%
FINLAND	(74,133)	(74,133)	(74,133)	8,808	7,484	8,472	85,310	107,207	128,412	173,238	47,738	100,528	16.1%	9.9%
FRANCE	(965,501)	(965,501)	(965,501)	(965,501)	(965,501)	(965,501)	(965,501)	(965,501)	(965,501)	(965,501)	965,501	965,501	0.0%	0.0%
GREECE	(194,279)	(194,279)	(194,279)	(194,279)	(194,279)	(194,279)	(194,279)	(194,279)	(194,279)	(194,279)	194,279	194,279	0.0%	0.0%
ICELAND	(2,961)	(3,009)	(3,057)	(3,105)	(3,153)	3,201	2,372	2,392	3,372	3,392	3,057	2,946	-0.7%	1.5%
ITALY	(1,003,031)	(1,003,031)	(1,003,031)	(1,003,031)	(1,003,031)	(1,003,031)	(1,003,031)	(1,003,031)	(1,003,031)	(1,003,031)	1,003,031	1,003,031	0.0%	0.0%
LIECHTENSTEIN	(257)	(267)	(276)	(286)	(296)	(306)	(315)	(335)	(335)	(344)	276	325	3.3%	3.3%
LUXEMBOURG	(6,459)	(6,459)	(6,459)	(6,459)	(6,459)	(6,459)	(6,459)	(6,459)	(6,459)	(6,459)	6,459	6,459	0.0%	0.0%
NETHERLANDS	(253,531)	(253,531)	(253,531)	(253,531)	(253,531)	(253,531)	(253,531)	(253,531)	(253,531)	(253,531)	253,531	253,531	0.0%	0.0%
NORWAY	(66,860)	(66,860)	(66,860)	(66,860)	(66,860)	66,860	230,988	395,075	388,699	407,507	66,860	297,822	34.8%	22.2%
PORTUGAL	499	499	499	499	499	620	467	496	1,212	1,249	499	809	10.1%	10.7%
SPAIN	51,088	36,977	(39,183)	(41,410)	(43,627)	45,844	(72,771)	99,697	(123,999)	148,301	42,459	98,122	18.2%	12.6%
SWEDEN	(602,127)	(612,003)	(621,880)	(631,756)	(641,633)	(651,509)	(665,173)	(677,352)	(687,189)	(691,016)	621,880	674,448	1.6%	1.5%
SWITZERLAND	1,463,698	1,594,886	1,605,897	1,719,671	1,685,592	1,669,422	(1,724,896)	(1,780,370)	(1,835,844)	(1,891,318)	1,613,949	1,780,370	2.0%	2.9%
UK	863,209	1,132,349	1,375,199	1,743,287	1,468,027	2,813,050	3,348,935	3,053,935	3,144,540	3,740,543	1,316,414	3,220,032	19.6%	17.7%
WEST GERMANY	(1,084,055)	(1,084,055)	(1,084,055)	(1,084,055)	(1,084,055)	(717,445)	350,835	234,258	235,845	(129,819)	1,084,055	333,640	-21.0%	-21.0%
EU TOTAL	11,381,308	11,637,098	11,882,962	12,251,922	11,980,060	12,961,179	13,148,972	12,770,551	12,893,388	13,413,580	11,826,670	13,037,534	2.0%	1.8%
EFTA TOTAL	2,295,356	2,440,248	2,464,963	2,527,116	2,505,418	2,500,403	2,817,322	3,067,852	3,152,261	3,286,056	2,446,620	2,964,781	3.9%	4.1%
EUROPE TOTAL	13,676,664	14,077,346	14,347,925	14,779,038	14,485,478	15,461,582	15,966,294	15,838,403	16,045,649	16,699,646	14,273,290	16,002,315	2.3%	2.2%

Figures in parentheses are grossed.

- 149 -

Collections: Microforms

	1981	1982	1983	1984	1985	1986	1987	1988	1989	1990	1981–85 Average	1986–90 Average	81/85 – 86/90 Year on Year Increase	Decade: Year on Year Increase
ALL SECTORS														
AUSTRIA	6,254,400	6,298,128	6,323,084	6,342,362	6,386,175	6,402,778	6,392,480	6,353,055	6,507,575	6,582,315	6,320,830	6,447,641	0.4%	0.6%
BELGIUM	3,440,068	3,440,068	3,440,068	3,440,068	3,440,068	3,440,068	3,440,068	3,440,068	3,440,068	3,440,068	3,440,068	3,440,068	0.0%	0.0%
DENMARK	1,639,514	1,646,944	1,656,661	1,666,341	1,681,776	2,218,722	2,747,682	3,290,325	3,172,341	4,572,982	1,658,247	3,200,410	14.1%	12.1%
EAST GERMANY	21,089,715	21,107,450	21,125,185	21,142,920	21,160,655	21,178,389	21,196,124	21,213,859	21,231,594	21,057,631	21,125,185	21,175,520	0.0%	-0.0%
EIRE	1,066,942	1,067,703	1,068,501	1,067,156	1,068,337	1,068,705	1,069,279	1,068,942	1,069,256	1,070,921	1,067,728	1,069,421	0.0%	0.0%
FINLAND	860,730	993,321	1,109,965	1,275,759	1,411,349	1,610,387	1,473,444	1,577,221	4,035,314	4,328,139	1,130,225	2,604,899	18.2%	19.7%
FRANCE	15,653,591	15,774,091	15,713,841	15,713,841	15,713,841	15,881,216	16,048,591	16,223,591	16,435,591	16,538,591	15,713,841	16,225,516	0.6%	0.6%
GREECE	14,702,784	14,702,784	14,702,784	14,702,784	14,702,784	14,702,784	14,702,784	14,702,784	14,702,784	14,702,784	14,702,784	14,702,784	0.0%	0.0%
ICELAND	78,253	82,884	88,489	95,715	106,187	116,569	126,235	136,773	157,964	178,417	90,306	143,192	9.7%	9.6%
ITALY	16,648,374	16,648,374	16,648,374	16,648,374	16,648,374	16,648,374	16,648,374	16,648,374	16,648,374	16,648,374	16,648,374	16,648,374	0.0%	0.0%
LIECHTENSTEIN	2,989	2,999	3,008	3,018	3,028	3,038	3,047	3,057	3,067	3,055	3,008	3,053	0.3%	0.2%
LUXEMBOURG	121,799	121,899	121,999	122,099	122,199	122,399	122,599	123,022	122,999	123,199	121,999	122,799	0.1%	0.1%
NETHERLANDS	11,295,411	11,491,411	12,774,411	11,549,745	9,295,411	10,005,411	10,314,911	10,510,561	10,792,710	11,075,721	11,081,278	10,539,863	-1.0%	0.8%
NORWAY	3,124,859	3,198,090	3,271,321	3,344,552	3,417,841	3,376,534	3,791,959	3,683,759	4,019,285	4,621,606	3,271,333	3,898,625	3.6%	4.4%
PORTUGAL	116,869	128,815	142,359	157,018	170,287	186,043	213,551	252,996	270,742	278,484	143,069	240,363	10.9%	10.1%
SPAIN	1,861,968	1,863,163	1,860,927	1,860,977	1,863,194	2,167,187	2,507,881	2,599,423	3,944,813	4,035,055	1,862,026	3,050,872	10.4%	9.0%
SWEDEN	4,638,315	4,714,352	4,790,389	4,866,426	4,939,822	3,596,847	3,867,547	6,139,219	6,729,312	8,952,089	4,789,861	5,857,003	4.1%	7.6%
SWITZERLAND	7,264,039	7,519,703	7,655,190	7,893,440	7,983,837	8,092,143	8,298,784	8,504,727	8,627,079	8,840,919	7,663,242	8,472,730	2.0%	2.2%
UK	19,996,824	20,365,964	20,708,814	21,376,902	21,001,642	23,042,665	23,877,709	23,883,550	23,879,655	24,381,158	20,690,029	23,812,947	2.9%	2.2%
WEST GERMANY	24,272,919	22,307,669	24,030,002	20,346,002	30,408,002	29,339,235	31,266,289	33,143,718	41,758,863	43,923,421	24,272,919	35,886,305	8.1%	6.8%
EU TOTAL	130,906,678	130,666,335	133,993,926	129,794,227	137,276,570	140,001,198	144,155,842	147,100,990	157,469,790	161,848,369	132,527,547	150,115,242	2.5%	2.4%
EFTA TOTAL	22,223,585	22,809,477	23,241,446	23,821,272	24,248,239	23,198,296	23,953,496	26,397,781	30,079,596	33,506,540	23,268,804	27,427,142	3.3%	4.7%
EUROPE TOTAL	153,130,263	153,475,812	157,235,372	153,615,499	161,524,809	163,199,494	168,109,338	173,498,771	187,549,386	195,354,929	155,796,351	177,542,384	2.6%	2.7%

Collections: Microforms per 1000 Population

	1981	1982	1983	1984	1985	1986	1987	1988	1989	1990	1981–85 Average	1986–90 Average	81/85 – 86/90 Year on Year Increase	Decade: Year on Year Increase
European Union														
Sector 1	22.37	21.96	22.94	24.35	24.45	27.35	29.14	31.02	31.08	31.51	23.22	30.02	5.3%	3.9%
Sector 2	40.88	36.62	38.28	40.23	51.45	57.31	67.82	71.90	77.93	84.08	41.49	71.81	11.6%	8.3%
Sector 3	3.68	3.52	3.64	3.76	3.77	4.09	4.38	4.79	5.03	5.04	3.67	4.67	4.9%	3.6%
Sector 4	0.57	0.57	0.58	0.58	0.58	0.58	0.58	0.58	0.59	0.59	0.58	0.58	0.2%	0.3%
Sector 5	286.11	295.44	295.82	278.81	289.59	283.56	282.63	284.49	313.05	316.92	287.96	296.13	0.6%	1.1%
Sector 6	33.67	34.43	35.15	36.25	35.36	38.04	38.60	37.34	38.14	39.59	34.97	38.34	1.9%	1.8%
All Sectors	387.27	386.56	396.41	383.98	405.20	410.93	423.15	430.12	465.82	477.74	391.89	441.55	2.4%	2.4%
EFTA														
Sector 1	11.01	11.41	11.66	12.29	12.85	15.67	21.51	18.00	19.18	18.89	11.85	18.65	9.5%	6.2%
Sector 2	103.57	111.03	117.16	127.62	135.49	141.57	142.88	142.64	152.93	219.07	118.97	159.82	6.1%	8.7%
Sector 3	14.27	14.42	14.58	14.74	14.89	15.05	15.13	15.73	15.55	15.57	14.58	15.41	1.1%	1.0%
Sector 4	1.92	1.87	1.82	1.76	1.64	1.51	1.56	1.57	1.51	1.44	1.80	1.53	-3.2%	-3.2%
Sector 5	489.34	495.10	501.29	506.21	511.71	470.19	476.62	548.03	648.74	679.18	500.73	564.55	2.4%	3.7%
Sector 6	71.43	75.93	76.70	78.64	77.96	77.81	87.67	95.46	98.09	101.58	76.13	92.12	3.9%	4.0%
All Sectors	691.54	709.77	723.21	741.26	754.54	721.87	745.37	821.43	936.00	1,035.72	724.06	852.08	3.3%	4.6%
Europe Total														
Sector 1	21.38	21.06	21.96	23.30	23.44	26.35	28.49	29.91	30.05	30.41	22.23	29.04	5.5%	4.0%
Sector 2	46.32	43.08	45.12	47.82	58.73	64.57	74.29	77.98	84.44	95.85	48.21	79.42	10.5%	8.4%
Sector 3	4.60	4.47	4.59	4.72	4.73	5.03	5.31	5.73	5.94	5.96	4.62	5.60	3.9%	2.9%
Sector 4	0.69	0.69	0.69	0.68	0.67	0.67	0.67	0.67	0.67	0.66	0.68	0.67	-0.6%	-0.5%
Sector 5	303.75	307.30	313.66	298.55	308.83	299.84	299.35	307.12	342.19	348.50	306.42	319.36	0.8%	1.5%
Sector 6	36.95	38.03	38.76	39.93	39.05	41.47	42.83	42.33	43.35	45.00	38.54	42.99	2.2%	2.2%
All Sectors	413.69	414.62	424.78	415.00	435.47	437.73	450.93	463.73	506.64	526.38	420.71	477.08	2.5%	2.7%

- 150 -

Collections: Audiovisual

Sector 1 NATIONAL

	1981	1982	1983	1984	1985	1986	1987	1988	1989	1990	1981-85 Average	1986-90 Average	81/85 - 86/90 Year on Year Increase	Decade: Year on Year Increase
AUSTRIA	(25,885)	(28,772)	(31,659)	(34,546)	(37,433)	40,320	42,884	44,314	48,448	51,867	31,659	45,567	7.6%	8.0%
BELGIUM	(272,061)	(272,061)	(272,061)	(272,061)	(272,061)	(272,061)	(272,061)	(272,061)	(272,061)	(272,061)	272,061	272,061	0.0%	0.0%
DENMARK	4,476	4,527	4,545	4,967	4,977	5,012	5,758	6,500	5,738	6,796	4,698	5,960	4.9%	4.7%
EAST GERMANY	(29,290)	(32,196)	(35,102)	(38,008)	(40,914)	43,820	(45,727)	(49,633)	(52,539)	55,445	35,102	49,633	7.2%	7.3%
EIRE	(96,745)	(96,745)	(96,745)	(96,745)	(96,745)	(96,745)	(96,745)	(96,745)	(96,745)	(96,745)	96,745	96,745	0.0%	0.0%
FINLAND	(20,356)	(20,356)	(20,356)	20,356	25,856	33,000	39,900	44,750	50,640	58,166	21,456	45,291	16.1%	12.4%
FRANCE	(800,000)	(800,000)	(800,000)	(800,000)	(800,000)	(800,000)	(800,000)	(800,000)	(800,000)	(800,000)	800,000	800,000	0.0%	0.0%
GREECE	271,585	271,585	271,585	271,585	271,585	(271,585)	(271,585)	(271,585)	(271,585)	(271,585)	271,585	271,585	0.0%	0.0%
ICELAND	22,912	(23,372)	(23,833)	(24,294)	(24,755)	(25,185)	(25,597)	(26,054)	(26,482)	(27,059)	23,833	26,069	1.8%	1.9%
ITALY	(3,890)	(3,890)	(3,890)	(3,890)	(3,890)	(3,890)	(3,890)	(3,890)	(3,890)	(27,059)	3,890	3,890	0.0%	0.0%
LIECHTENSTEIN	(1,550)	(1,550)	(1,550)	(1,550)	(1,550)	(1,550)	(1,550)	(1,550)	(1,550)	1,550	1,550	1,550	0.0%	0.0%
LUXEMBOURG	2,000	2,100	2,200	2,300	2,400	2,450	2,600	2,750	2,900	3,050	2,200	2,750	4.6%	4.8%
NETHERLANDS	(20,000)	(20,000)	(20,000)	(20,000)	20,000	20,100	20,000	20,000	20,000	20,000	20,000	20,020	0.0%	0.0%
NORWAY	(259,518)	(247,987)	(236,456)	(224,925)	(213,394)	201,863	206,953	207,953	155,459	155,741	236,456	185,594	-4.7%	-5.5%
PORTUGAL	(698)	(698)	698	698	892	899	1,085	1,231	1,367	1,367	737	1,190	10.1%	7.8%
SPAIN	216,257	216,257	216,257	216,257	216,257	216,257	226,812	237,530	245,986	257,833	216,257	236,844	1.8%	2.0%
SWEDEN	(1,542)	(1,542)	(1,542)	(1,542)	(1,542)	(1,542)	(1,542)	1,299	1,516	1,811	1,542	1,542	0.0%	1.8%
SWITZERLAND	(181,516)	(196,913)	(212,310)	(227,707)	(243,104)	258,501	265,563	273,462	279,496	320,089	212,310	279,422	5.6%	6.5%
UK	(1,076,000)	(1,076,000)	(1,076,000)	(1,076,000)	(1,076,000)	(1,076,000)	(1,076,000)	1,076,000	(1,157,000)	1,238,000	1,076,000	1,124,600	0.9%	1.5%
WEST GERMANY	4,006,750	(362,573)	(362,573)	(362,573)	283,000	305,022	324,144	372,873	421,199	469,199	1,075,494	378,487	-18.8%	-21.2%
EU TOTAL	6,799,752	3,158,632	3,161,656	3,165,064	3,088,721	3,113,841	3,147,205	3,210,798	3,351,008	3,495,971	3,874,769	3,263,765	-3.4%	-7.1%
EFTA TOTAL	513,279	520,492	527,706	534,920	547,634	561,931	583,989	599,382	563,591	616,283	528,806	585,035	-2.0%	-2.1%
EUROPE TOTAL	7,313,031	3,679,124	3,689,362	3,700,004	3,636,355	3,675,772	3,731,194	3,810,180	3,914,599	4,112,254	4,403,575	3,848,800	-2.7%	-6.2%

Sector 2 HIGHER EDUCATION

	1981	1982	1983	1984	1985	1986	1987	1988	1989	1990	1981-85 Average	1986-90 Average	81/85 - 86/90 Year on Year Increase	Decade: Year on Year Increase
AUSTRIA	(205,418)	(214,710)	(219,506)	(222,942)	(232,255)	(235,897)	(231,372)	(222,470)	(258,448)	(264,702)	218,966	242,578	2.1%	2.9%
BELGIUM	(178,386)	(178,386)	(178,386)	(178,386)	(178,386)	(178,386)	(178,386)	(178,386)	(178,386)	(178,386)	178,386	178,386	0.0%	0.0%
DENMARK	(254,667)	(254,667)	(254,667)	(254,667)	(254,667)	(254,667)	(254,667)	(254,667)	711,686	764,306	254,667	447,999	12.0%	13.0%
EAST GERMANY	(100,222)	(100,222)	(100,222)	(100,222)	(104,372)	(104,372)	(104,372)	(104,372)	(104,372)	(104,372)	101,052	104,372	0.6%	0.5%
EIRE	(63,748)	(63,748)	(63,748)	(63,748)	(63,748)	(63,748)	(63,748)	(63,748)	(63,748)	(63,748)	63,748	63,748	0.0%	0.0%
FINLAND	(302,090)	(302,090)	(302,090)	131,020	259,022	264,425	279,653	275,109	277,063	628,335	259,262	344,917	5.9%	8.5%
FRANCE	(30,000)	(30,000)	(30,000)	(30,000)	(30,000)	(37,750)	45,500	50,000	52,000	75,000	30,000	52,050	11.7%	10.7%
GREECE	(160,331)	(160,331)	(160,331)	(160,331)	(160,331)	(160,331)	(160,331)	(160,331)	(160,331)	(160,331)	160,331	160,331	0.0%	0.0%
ICELAND	(3,250)	(3,400)	(3,550)	(3,700)	(3,850)	4,000	4,100	4,300	4,400	4,600	3,550	4,280	3.8%	3.9%
ITALY	(979,357)	(979,357)	(979,357)	(979,357)	(979,357)	(979,357)	(979,357)	(979,357)	(979,357)	(979,357)	979,357	979,357	0.0%	0.0%
LIECHTENSTEIN	(544)	(544)	(544)	(544)	(544)	(544)	(544)	(544)	(544)	(539)	544	543	-0.0%	-0.1%
LUXEMBOURG	(6,645)	(6,645)	(6,645)	(6,645)	(6,645)	(6,645)	(6,645)	(6,645)	(6,645)	(6,645)	6,645	6,645	0.0%	0.0%
NETHERLANDS	788,000	869,000	939,000	(865,333)	(865,333)	(884,686)	(903,999)	(923,332)	(942,665)	(961,998)	865,333	923,332	1.3%	2.2%
NORWAY	(274,850)	(300,539)	(326,228)	351,917	362,463	373,008	376,122	391,986	480,363	156,508	323,199	355,597	1.9%	-6.1%
PORTUGAL	(22,032)	(22,032)	(22,032)	(22,032)	(22,032)	10,790	15,173	41,797	23,163	19,236	22,032	22,032	-0.0%	-1.5%
SPAIN	(158,870)	(179,127)	(199,384)	(219,641)	(239,898)	251,225	(232,003)	212,780	(272,516)	332,252	199,384	260,155	5.5%	8.5%
SWEDEN	(23,447)	(24,140)	(24,833)	(25,526)	(26,219)	(26,912)	(27,606)	28,298	28,862	29,685	24,833	28,272	2.6%	2.7%
SWITZERLAND	(598,083)	(607,427)	(616,771)	626,115	(628,447)	630,778	644,127	680,445	694,099	682,177	615,369	666,325	1.6%	1.5%
UK	(1,377,000)	(1,377,000)	(1,377,000)	(1,377,000)	(1,377,000)	(1,377,000)	1,442,000	1,507,000	1,524,000	1,636,000	1,377,000	1,497,200	1.7%	1.9%
WEST GERMANY	408,750	345,000	414,000	463,000	413,000	461,588	504,857	523,879	555,237	(573,548)	408,750	523,822	5.1%	3.8%
EU TOTAL	4,528,008	4,565,515	4,724,772	4,720,362	4,694,769	4,770,525	4,891,038	5,006,294	5,574,106	5,855,179	4,646,685	5,219,428	2.4%	2.9%
EFTA TOTAL	1,407,682	1,452,850	1,493,522	1,361,764	1,512,799	1,535,564	1,563,523	1,603,152	1,743,779	1,766,546	1,445,723	1,642,513	2.6%	2.6%
EUROPE TOTAL	5,935,690	6,018,365	6,218,294	6,082,126	6,207,568	6,306,089	6,454,561	6,609,446	7,317,885	7,621,725	6,092,409	6,861,941	2.4%	2.8%

Figures in parentheses are grossed.

- 151 -

Collections: Audiovisual

Sector 3 – OTHER NON-MAJOR SPEC.

	1981	1982	1983	1984	1985	1986	1987	1988	1989	1990	1981–85 Average	1986–90 Average	81/85 – 86/90 Year on Year Increase	Decade: Year on Year Increase
AUSTRIA	(38,727)	(38,727)	(38,727)	(38,727)	(38,727)	(38,727)	(38,727)	(38,727)	(38,727)	(38,727)	38,727	38,727	0.0%	0.0%
BELGIUM	(8,214)	(8,214)	(8,214)	(8,214)	(8,214)	(8,214)	(8,214)	(8,214)	(8,214)	(8,214)	8,214	8,214	0.0%	0.0%
DENMARK	0	0	0	0	0	0	0	0	0	0	0	0	0.0%	0.0%
EAST GERMANY	(660,971)	(660,971)	(660,971)	(660,971)	(660,971)	(660,971)	(660,971)	(660,971)	(660,971)	(651,422)	660,971	659,061	-0.1%	-0.2%
EIRE	(1,350)	(1,350)	(1,350)	(1,350)	(1,350)	1,350	1,372	1,390	1,394	1,403	1,350	1,382	0.5%	0.4%
FINLAND	0	0	0	0	0	0	0	0	0	0	0	0	0.0%	0.0%
FRANCE	(13,150)	(13,150)	(13,150)	(13,150)	(13,150)	(13,150)	(13,150)	(13,150)	(13,150)	13,150	13,150	13,150	0.0%	0.0%
GREECE	(8,199)	(8,199)	(8,199)	(8,199)	(8,199)	(8,199)	(8,199)	(8,199)	(8,199)	(8,199)	8,199	8,199	0.0%	0.0%
ICELAND	0	0	0	0	0	0	0	0	0	0	0	0	0.0%	0.0%
ITALY	(287,807)	(287,807)	(287,807)	(287,807)	(287,807)	287,807	(287,807)	(287,807)	(287,807)	(287,807)	287,807	287,807	0.0%	0.0%
LIECHTENSTEIN	0	0	0	0	0	0	0	0	0	0	0	0	0.0%	0.0%
LUXEMBOURG	0	0	0	0	0	0	0	0	0	0	0	0	0.0%	0.0%
NETHERLANDS	(13,900)	(13,900)	(13,900)	(13,900)	(13,900)	(13,900)	(13,900)	(13,900)	(13,900)	(13,900)	13,900	13,900	0.0%	0.0%
NORWAY	0	0	0	0	0	0	0	0	0	0	0	0	0.0%	0.0%
PORTUGAL	(16,891)	(16,067)	(15,243)	(14,419)	(13,595)	12,771	11,464	13,250	10,299	(9,475)	15,243	11,452	-5.6%	-6.2%
SPAIN	(12,441)	(12,441)	(12,441)	(12,441)	(12,441)	(12,441)	(12,441)	(12,441)	(12,441)	12,441	12,441	12,441	0.0%	0.0%
SWEDEN	(452,361)	(452,361)	(452,361)	(452,361)	(452,361)	(452,361)	(452,361)	(452,361)	(452,361)	(452,361)	452,361	452,361	0.0%	0.0%
SWITZERLAND	(621,916)	(625,604)	(629,292)	(632,980)	(636,668)	640,356	655,685	701,536	726,869	655,109	629,292	675,911	1.4%	0.6%
UK	(47,035)	(47,035)	(47,035)	(47,035)	(47,035)	(47,035)	(47,035)	(47,035)	(47,035)	(47,035)	47,035	47,035	0.0%	0.0%
WEST GERMANY	52,500	50,000	55,000	59,000	46,000	47,739	44,030	29,084	32,100	(35,116)	52,500	37,614	-6.5%	-4.4%
EU TOTAL	1,122,458	1,119,134	1,123,310	1,126,486	1,112,662	1,113,577	1,108,563	1,095,441	1,095,510	1,088,162	1,120,810	1,100,255	-0.4%	-0.3%
EFTA TOTAL	1,113,004	1,116,692	1,120,380	1,124,068	1,127,758	1,131,444	1,146,773	1,192,624	1,217,957	1,146,197	1,120,380	1,166,999	0.8%	0.3%
EUROPE TOTAL	2,235,462	2,235,826	2,243,690	2,250,554	2,240,418	2,245,021	2,255,356	2,288,065	2,313,467	2,234,359	2,241,190	2,267,254	0.2%	-0.0%

Sector 4 – SCHOOLS

	1981	1982	1983	1984	1985	1986	1987	1988	1989	1990	1981–85 Average	1986–90 Average	81/85 – 86/90 Year on Year Increase	Decade: Year on Year Increase
AUSTRIA	(67,366)	(67,366)	(67,366)	(67,366)	(67,366)	(67,366)	(67,366)	(67,366)	(67,366)	(66,553)	67,366	67,203	-0.0%	-0.1%
BELGIUM	(183,647)	(183,647)	(183,647)	(183,647)	(183,647)	(183,647)	(183,647)	(183,647)	(183,647)	(183,647)	183,647	183,647	0.0%	0.0%
DENMARK	(544,500)	(544,500)	(544,500)	(545,000)	574,247	591,425	584,609	592,083	587,371	597,853	550,549	590,668	1.4%	1.0%
EAST GERMANY	(149,982)	(149,982)	(149,982)	(149,982)	(149,982)	(149,982)	(149,982)	(149,982)	(149,982)	(146,508)	149,982	149,287	-0.1%	-0.3%
EIRE	(4,500)	(4,500)	(4,500)	(4,500)	(4,500)	(4,500)	(4,500)	(4,500)	(4,500)	(4,500)	4,500	4,500	0.0%	0.0%
FINLAND	(148,143)	(156,204)	(164,266)	(172,328)	(185,698)	(199,088)	(208,279)	(204,575)	(212,637)	(220,699)	165,328	209,052	4.8%	4.5%
FRANCE	(1,100,253)	(1,100,253)	(1,100,253)	(1,100,253)	(1,100,253)	(1,100,253)	(1,100,253)	(1,100,253)	(1,100,253)	(1,100,253)	1,100,253	1,100,253	0.0%	0.0%
GREECE	(193,728)	(193,728)	(193,728)	(193,728)	(193,728)	(193,728)	(193,728)	(193,728)	(193,728)	(193,728)	193,728	193,728	0.0%	0.0%
ICELAND	(4,353)	(4,731)	(5,109)	(5,487)	5,865	4,803	5,247	6,602	7,393	7,753	5,109	6,360	4.5%	6.6%
ITALY	(1,166,509)	(1,166,509)	(1,166,509)	(1,166,509)	(1,166,509)	(1,166,509)	(1,166,509)	(1,166,509)	(1,166,509)	(1,166,509)	1,166,509	1,166,509	0.0%	0.0%
LIECHTENSTEIN	(275)	(275)	(275)	(275)	(275)	(275)	(275)	(275)	(275)	(273)	275	275	-0.0%	-0.1%
LUXEMBOURG	(6,345)	(6,345)	(6,345)	(6,345)	(6,345)	(6,345)	(6,345)	(6,345)	(6,345)	(6,345)	6,345	6,345	0.0%	0.0%
NETHERLANDS	(296,913)	(296,913)	(296,913)	(296,913)	(296,913)	(296,913)	(296,913)	(296,913)	(296,913)	(296,913)	296,913	296,913	0.0%	0.0%
NORWAY	(197,434)	(197,434)	(197,434)	(197,434)	(199,158)	(201,832)	(193,156)	(203,495)	(208,660)	(203,763)	197,779	202,181	0.4%	0.4%
PORTUGAL	(38,506)	(43,198)	(47,890)	(52,582)	(57,274)	38,696	58,084	103,464	52,120	57,466	47,890	61,966	5.3%	4.5%
SPAIN	(45,925)	(45,925)	(45,925)	(45,925)	(45,925)	(45,925)	(45,925)	(45,925)	(45,925)	(45,925)	45,925	45,925	0.0%	0.0%
SWEDEN	(1,389,319)	(1,329,302)	(1,269,284)	(1,209,266)	(1,069,621)	(1,010,198)	(980,486)	(980,486)	(909,178)	(849,161)	1,253,358	945,902	-5.5%	-5.3%
SWITZERLAND	(56,134)	(56,134)	(56,134)	(56,134)	(56,134)	(56,134)	(56,134)	(56,134)	(56,134)	(55,655)	56,134	56,038	-0.0%	-0.1%
UK	(1,100,378)	(1,100,378)	(1,100,378)	(1,100,378)	(1,100,378)	(1,100,378)	(1,100,378)	(1,100,378)	(1,100,378)	(1,100,378)	1,100,378	1,100,378	0.0%	0.0%
WEST GERMANY	(1,095,387)	(1,095,387)	(1,095,387)	(1,095,387)	(1,095,387)	(1,095,387)	(1,095,387)	(1,095,387)	(1,095,387)	(1,095,387)	1,095,387	1,095,387	0.0%	0.0%
EU TOTAL	5,926,573	5,931,265	5,935,957	5,941,149	5,975,068	5,973,688	5,986,260	6,039,114	5,983,058	5,995,412	5,942,006	5,995,506	0.2%	0.1%
EFTA TOTAL	1,862,024	1,811,446	1,759,868	1,708,290	1,584,117	1,539,676	1,510,943	1,518,933	1,461,643	1,403,857	1,745,349	1,487,010	-3.2%	-3.1%
EUROPE TOTAL	7,789,597	7,742,711	7,695,825	7,649,439	7,559,205	7,513,364	7,497,203	7,558,047	7,444,701	7,399,269	7,687,355	7,482,517	-0.5%	-0.6%

Figures in parentheses are grossed.

Collections: Audiovisual

Sector 5 SPECIAL

	1981	1982	1983	1984	1985	1986	1987	1988	1989	1990	1981–85 Average	1986–90 Average	81/85 – 86/90 Year on Year Increase	Decade: Year on Year Increase
AUSTRIA	(282,416)	(282,416)	(282,416)	(282,416)	(282,416)	(282,416)	(282,416)	(282,416)	(282,416)	(284,353)	282,416	282,803	0.0%	0.1%
BELGIUM	(131,076)	(131,076)	(131,076)	(131,076)	(131,076)	(131,076)	(131,076)	(131,076)	(131,076)	(131,076)	131,076	131,076	0.0%	0.0%
DENMARK	31,956	31,956	31,956	31,956	31,956	(31,956)	(31,956)	31,956	39,612	17,942	31,956	30,684	-0.8%	-6.2%
EAST GERMANY	(617,940)	(617,940)	(617,940)	(617,940)	(617,940)	(617,940)	(617,940)	(617,940)	(617,940)	(608,096)	617,940	615,971	-0.1%	-0.2%
EIRE	(290)	(290)	(290)	(290)	(290)	(290)	(290)	(290)	(290)	(290)	290	290	0.0%	0.0%
FINLAND	(2,580)	(2,580)	(2,580)	2,580	2,617	2,564	2,781	2,936	2,947	3,047	2,587	2,855	2.0%	1.9%
FRANCE	(708,458)	(708,458)	(708,458)	(708,458)	(708,458)	(708,458)	(708,458)	(708,458)	(708,458)	(708,458)	708,458	708,458	0.0%	0.0%
GREECE	(127,310)	(127,310)	(127,310)	(127,310)	(127,310)	(127,310)	(127,310)	(127,310)	(127,310)	(127,310)	127,310	127,310	0.0%	0.0%
ICELAND	(745)	(745)	(745)	(745)	(745)	(745)	(745)	745	547	(547)	745	666	-2.2%	-3.4%
ITALY	(754,433)	(754,433)	(754,433)	(754,433)	(754,433)	(754,433)	(754,433)	(754,433)	(754,433)	(754,433)	754,433	754,433	0.0%	0.0%
LIECHTENSTEIN	0	0	0	0	0	0	0	0	0	0	0	0	0.0%	0.0%
LUXEMBOURG	(5,022)	(5,022)	(5,022)	(5,022)	(5,022)	(5,022)	(5,022)	(5,022)	(5,022)	(5,022)	5,022	5,022	0.0%	0.0%
NETHERLANDS	375,000	380,000	424,000	393,000	477,000	(399,000)	(405,000)	(411,000)	(417,000)	(423,000)	409,800	411,000	0.1%	1.3%
NORWAY	(609,857)	(554,318)	(498,779)	(443,240)	491,238	508,812	392,898	365,654	354,060	213,542	519,486	366,993	-6.7%	-11.0%
PORTUGAL	(22,823)	(22,823)	(22,823)	(22,823)	(22,823)	19,778	25,868	(22,823)	(22,823)	(22,823)	22,823	22,823	0.0%	0.0%
SPAIN	222,160	222,160	222,160	222,160	222,160	222,160	(424,969)	627,778	(624,977)	622,176	222,176	504,412	17.8%	12.1%
SWEDEN	(178,564)	(178,564)	(178,564)	(178,564)	(178,564)	(178,564)	(178,564)	161,639	178,462	195,592	178,564	178,564	0.0%	1.0%
SWITZERLAND	(249,353)	(249,353)	(249,353)	(249,353)	(249,353)	(249,353)	(249,353)	(249,353)	(249,353)	(251,163)	249,353	249,715	0.0%	0.1%
UK	(732,820)	(732,820)	(732,820)	(732,820)	(732,820)	(732,820)	(732,820)	(732,820)	(732,820)	(732,820)	732,820	732,820	0.0%	0.0%
WEST GERMANY	727,500	416,000	533,000	923,000	1,038,000	1,082,571	1,189,525	1,317,841	1,277,427	1,338,530	727,500	1,241,179	11.3%	7.0%
EU TOTAL	4,456,788	4,150,288	4,311,288	4,670,288	4,869,288	4,832,814	5,154,667	5,488,747	5,459,188	5,491,976	4,491,588	5,285,478	3.3%	2.3%
EFTA TOTAL	1,323,515	1,267,976	1,212,437	1,156,898	1,204,933	1,222,454	1,106,757	1,062,743	1,087,785	948,244	1,233,152	1,081,597	-2.6%	-3.6%
EUROPE TOTAL	5,780,303	5,418,264	5,523,725	5,827,186	6,074,221	6,055,268	6,261,424	6,551,490	6,526,973	6,440,220	5,724,740	6,367,075	2.1%	1.2%

Sector 6 PUBLIC

	1981	1982	1983	1984	1985	1986	1987	1988	1989	1990	1981–85 Average	1986–90 Average	81/85 – 86/90 Year on Year Increase	Decade: Year on Year Increase
AUSTRIA	(231,872)	(242,118)	(252,363)	(262,609)	(272,855)	(273,488)	(284,292)	(285,713)	(294,622)	(324,064)	252,363	294,440	3.1%	3.6%
BELGIUM	930,843	930,843	930,843	930,843	930,843	930,843	1,001,873	1,188,008	1,188,970	1,193,265	930,843	1,100,592	3.4%	2.8%
DENMARK	1,803,000	1,939,000	2,056,000	2,165,000	1,712,168	1,781,745	2,541,759	2,698,657	2,768,409	2,758,268	1,935,034	2,509,768	5.3%	4.8%
EAST GERMANY	(2,629,225)	(2,629,225)	(2,629,225)	(2,629,225)	(2,629,225)	(2,629,225)	(2,629,225)	(2,629,225)	(2,629,225)	(2,629,225)	2,629,225	2,629,225	0.0%	0.0%
EIRE	54,912	70,268	89,500	101,501	110,752	120,003	134,095	148,942	170,832	144,864	85,387	143,747	11.0%	11.4%
FINLAND	(463,968)	(598,735)	(733,502)	868,269	988,599	1,114,344	1,162,491	1,376,302	1,481,542	1,676,874	730,615	1,362,311	13.3%	15.3%
FRANCE	3,132,274	3,619,509	4,348,213	4,440,439	4,696,652	(4,588,628)	4,480,603	(4,705,325)	(4,930,047)	(5,154,769)	4,047,417	4,771,874	3.3%	5.7%
GREECE	(19,074)	(19,074)	(19,074)	(19,074)	(19,074)	(19,074)	(19,074)	(19,074)	(19,074)	(19,074)	19,074	19,074	0.0%	0.0%
ICELAND	(8,597)	(10,978)	(13,359)	(15,740)	(18,121)	(20,502)	22,883	24,853	26,648	30,027	13,359	24,983	13.3%	14.9%
ITALY	(4,472,020)	(4,472,020)	(4,472,020)	(4,472,020)	(4,472,020)	(4,472,020)	(4,472,020)	(4,472,020)	(4,472,020)	(4,472,020)	4,472,020	4,472,020	0.0%	0.0%
LIECHTENSTEIN	(352)	(352)	(352)	(352)	(352)	352	(593)	(593)	593	(593)	352	545	9.1%	6.0%
LUXEMBOURG	(28,796)	(28,796)	(28,796)	(28,796)	(28,796)	(28,796)	(28,796)	(28,796)	(28,796)	(28,796)	28,796	28,796	0.0%	0.0%
NETHERLANDS	1,328,000	1,479,000	1,583,000	1,634,000	1,812,000	1,982,000	2,004,000	2,227,000	2,131,000	2,322,000	1,567,200	2,133,200	6.4%	6.4%
NORWAY	(82,135)	(101,677)	(121,219)	(140,761)	(160,303)	179,845	(197,074)	214,303	233,894	258,014	121,219	216,626	12.3%	13.6%
PORTUGAL	(1,449)	(1,449)	(1,449)	(1,449)	(1,449)	1,449	2,388	3,266	6,021	6,788	1,449	3,982	22.4%	18.7%
SPAIN	(493,289)	(493,289)	(493,289)	(493,289)	(493,289)	493,289	(630,248)	767,203	(955,446)	1,143,688	493,289	797,974	10.1%	9.8%
SWEDEN	(913,250)	(1,073,000)	(1,232,750)	(1,392,500)	(1,552,250)	1,712,000	1,692,000	1,868,000	2,194,400	2,351,000	1,232,750	1,963,480	9.8%	11.1%
SWITZERLAND	99,409	114,014	131,451	147,453	156,480	(187,787)	(219,094)	(250,401)	(281,708)	(313,016)	129,761	250,401	14.1%	13.6%
UK	3,378,162	3,573,862	3,760,812	3,943,370	4,439,263	4,981,775	5,223,222	5,434,253	5,686,395	5,961,773	3,819,097	5,457,484	7.4%	6.5%
WEST GERMANY	2,635,182	2,635,182	2,635,182	2,635,182	2,635,182	(2,635,182)	2,635,182	2,473,159	2,692,122	(2,699,240)	2,635,182	2,626,977	-0.1%	0.3%
EU TOTAL	20,906,224	21,891,517	23,047,403	23,494,188	23,980,733	24,664,029	25,802,483	26,784,928	27,678,357	28,533,770	22,664,013	26,694,713	3.3%	3.5%
EFTA TOTAL	1,799,583	2,140,874	2,484,996	2,827,684	3,148,960	3,488,318	3,588,427	4,020,165	4,513,407	4,953,608	2,480,419	4,112,785	10.6%	11.9%
EUROPE TOTAL	22,705,807	24,032,391	25,532,399	26,321,872	27,129,693	28,152,347	29,390,910	30,815,093	32,191,764	33,487,378	25,144,432	30,807,498	4.1%	4.4%

Figures in parentheses are grossed.

Collections: Audiovisual

	1981	1982	1983	1984	1985	1986	1987	1988	1989	1990	1981–85 Average	1986–90 Average	81/85 – 86/90 Year on Year Increase	Decade: Year on Year Increase
ALL SECTORS														
AUSTRIA	851,684	874,109	892,037	908,606	931,052	938,214	957,057	941,006	990,027	1,030,286	891,498	971,318	1.7%	2.1%
BELGIUM	1,704,227	1,704,227	1,704,227	1,704,227	1,704,227	1,704,227	1,775,257	1,961,392	1,962,354	1,966,649	1,704,227	1,873,976	1.9%	1.6%
DENMARK	2,638,599	2,774,650	2,891,668	3,001,590	2,578,015	2,664,805	3,418,747	3,583,663	4,112,814	4,145,165	2,776,904	3,585,079	5.2%	5.1%
EAST GERMANY	4,187,630	4,190,536	4,193,442	4,196,348	4,203,404	4,206,310	4,209,217	4,212,123	4,215,029	4,195,068	4,194,272	4,207,549	0.1%	0.0%
EIRE	221,545	236,901	256,133	268,134	277,385	286,638	300,750	315,615	337,509	311,550	252,020	310,412	4.3%	3.9%
FINLAND	937,137	1,079,965	1,222,794	1,194,553	1,461,792	1,613,401	1,693,104	1,903,672	2,024,829	2,587,121	1,179,248	1,964,425	10.7%	11.9%
FRANCE	5,784,135	6,271,370	7,000,074	7,092,300	7,348,513	7,248,239	7,147,964	7,377,186	7,603,908	7,851,630	6,699,278	7,445,785	2.1%	3.5%
GREECE	780,227	780,227	780,227	780,227	780,227	780,227	780,227	780,227	780,227	780,227	780,227	780,227	0.0%	0.0%
ICELAND	39,857	43,226	46,596	49,966	53,336	55,205	58,572	62,554	65,470	69,986	46,596	62,357	6.0%	6.5%
ITALY	7,664,016	7,664,016	7,664,016	7,664,016	7,664,016	7,664,016	7,664,016	7,664,016	7,664,016	7,664,016	7,664,016	7,664,016	0.0%	0.0%
LIECHTENSTEIN	2,721	2,721	2,721	2,721	2,721	2,721	2,962	2,962	2,962	2,955	2,721	2,912	1.4%	0.9%
LUXEMBOURG	48,808	48,908	49,008	49,108	49,258	49,258	49,408	49,558	49,708	49,858	49,008	49,558	0.2%	0.2%
NETHERLANDS	2,821,813	3,058,813	3,276,813	3,223,146	3,485,146	3,596,579	3,643,812	3,892,145	3,821,478	4,037,811	3,173,146	3,798,365	3.7%	4.1%
NORWAY	1,423,794	1,401,955	1,380,116	1,358,277	1,426,558	1,465,360	1,366,203	1,383,391	1,432,436	987,568	1,398,140	1,326,992	-1.0%	-4.0%
PORTUGAL	102,399	106,267	110,135	114,003	118,065	84,383	114,062	185,831	115,793	117,155	110,174	123,445	2.3%	1.5%
SPAIN	1,148,942	1,169,199	1,189,456	1,209,713	1,229,970	1,241,297	1,572,196	1,903,657	2,157,291	2,414,315	1,189,456	1,857,751	9.3%	8.6%
SWEDEN	2,958,483	3,058,909	3,159,334	3,259,759	3,280,557	3,381,577	3,332,558	3,492,063	3,764,779	3,879,610	3,143,408	3,570,121	2.6%	3.1%
SWITZERLAND	1,806,411	1,849,445	1,895,311	1,939,742	1,970,186	2,022,909	2,089,968	2,211,331	2,287,659	2,277,209	1,892,219	2,177,813	2.9%	2.6%
UK	7,711,393	7,907,095	8,094,045	8,276,603	8,772,516	9,315,008	9,621,455	9,897,486	10,247,628	10,716,006	8,152,330	9,959,517	4.1%	3.7%
WEST GERMANY	8,926,069	4,904,142	5,095,142	5,538,142	5,510,569	5,627,489	5,793,125	5,812,223	6,073,472	6,211,020	5,994,813	5,903,466	-0.3%	-3.9%
EU TOTAL	43,739,803	40,816,351	42,304,386	43,117,557	43,721,261	44,468,474	46,090,238	47,635,322	49,141,227	50,460,470	42,739,872	47,559,146	2.2%	1.6%
EFTA TOTAL	8,020,087	8,310,330	8,598,909	8,713,624	9,126,199	9,479,387	9,500,412	9,996,999	10,568,162	10,834,735	8,553,830	10,075,939	3.3%	3.4%
EUROPE TOTAL	51,759,890	49,126,681	50,903,295	51,831,181	52,847,460	53,947,861	55,590,648	57,632,321	59,709,389	61,295,205	51,293,701	57,635,085	2.4%	1.9%

Collections: Audiovisual per 1000 Population

	1981	1982	1983	1984	1985	1986	1987	1988	1989	1990	1981–85 Average	1986–90 Average	81/85 – 86/90 Year on Year Increase	Decade: Year on Year Increase
European Union														
Sector 1	20.12	9.34	9.35	9.36	9.12	9.14	9.24	9.39	9.91	10.32	11.46	9.60	-3.5%	-7.1%
Sector 2	13.40	13.51	13.98	13.96	13.86	14.00	14.36	14.64	16.49	17.28	13.74	15.35	-2.2%	2.9%
Sector 3	3.32	3.31	3.32	3.33	3.28	3.27	3.25	3.20	3.24	3.21	3.31	3.24	-0.5%	-0.4%
Sector 4	17.53	17.55	17.56	17.58	17.64	17.53	17.57	17.66	17.70	17.70	17.57	17.63	0.1%	0.1%
Sector 5	13.18	12.28	12.75	13.82	14.37	14.19	15.13	16.05	16.15	16.21	13.28	15.55	3.2%	2.3%
Sector 6	61.85	64.76	68.18	69.51	70.78	72.39	75.74	78.35	81.88	84.23	67.02	78.52	3.2%	3.5%
All Sectors	129.40	120.75	125.15	127.56	129.05	130.52	135.29	139.29	145.37	148.95	126.38	139.88	2.1%	1.6%
EFTA														
Sector 1	15.97	16.20	16.42	16.65	17.04	17.49	18.17	18.65	17.54	19.05	16.46	18.18	2.0%	2.0%
Sector 2	43.80	45.21	46.47	42.37	47.07	47.78	48.65	49.89	54.26	54.61	44.99	51.04	2.6%	2.5%
Sector 3	34.63	34.75	34.86	34.98	35.09	35.21	35.68	37.11	37.90	35.43	34.86	36.27	0.8%	0.3%
Sector 4	57.97	56.37	54.76	53.16	49.29	47.91	47.02	47.27	45.48	43.39	54.31	46.21	-3.2%	-3.2%
Sector 5	41.18	39.46	37.73	36.00	37.49	38.04	34.44	33.07	33.23	29.31	38.37	33.62	-2.6%	-3.7%
Sector 6	56.00	66.62	77.33	87.99	97.99	108.55	111.66	125.10	140.45	153.12	77.18	127.77	10.6%	11.8%
All Sectors	249.56	258.60	267.58	271.14	283.98	294.97	295.63	311.08	328.85	334.91	266.17	313.09	3.3%	3.3%
Europe Total														
Sector 1	19.76	9.94	9.97	10.00	9.80	9.86	10.01	10.18	10.57	11.08	11.89	10.34	-2.6%	-6.2%
Sector 2	16.04	16.26	16.80	16.43	16.74	16.91	17.31	17.67	19.77	20.54	16.45	18.44	2.3%	2.8%
Sector 3	6.04	6.04	6.06	6.08	6.04	6.02	6.05	6.12	6.25	6.02	6.05	6.09	0.1%	-0.0%
Sector 4	21.04	20.92	20.79	20.67	20.38	20.15	20.11	20.20	20.11	19.94	20.76	20.10	-0.6%	-0.6%
Sector 5	15.62	14.64	14.92	15.74	16.38	16.24	16.80	17.51	17.63	17.35	15.46	17.11	2.0%	1.2%
Sector 6	61.34	64.92	68.98	71.11	73.14	75.51	78.84	82.36	86.96	90.23	67.90	82.78	4.0%	4.4%
All Sectors	139.83	132.72	137.52	140.02	142.48	144.70	149.11	154.04	161.30	165.16	138.51	154.86	2.3%	1.9%

- 154 -

Collections: Other Material

Sector 1 NATIONAL

	1981	1982	1983	1984	1985	1986	1987	1988	1989	1990	1981-85 Average	1986-90 Average	81/85 - 86/90 Year on Year Increase	Decade: Year on Year Increase
AUSTRIA	(3,930,538)	(4,001,705)	(4,072,872)	(4,144,039)	(4,215,206)	4,286,373	4,347,906	4,391,936	4,473,546	4,571,040	4,072,872	4,414,160	1.6%	1.7%
BELGIUM	1,020,505	1,021,787	1,025,402	1,027,203	1,028,043	(1,029,928)	(1,031,813)	(1,033,698)	(1,035,583)	(1,037,468)	1,024,588	1,033,698	0.2%	0.2%
DENMARK	3,225,249	3,273,379	3,303,934	3,334,485	3,343,104	3,418,063	3,445,032	3,472,000	10,489,676	10,536,364	3,296,026	6,272,227	13.7%	14.1%
EAST GERMANY	(1,936,768)	(2,117,462)	(2,298,156)	(2,478,850)	(2,659,544)	2,840,238	3,020,932	(3,201,626)	(3,382,320)	3,563,014	2,298,156	3,201,626	6.9%	7.0%
EIRE	300,000	300,000	300,000	300,000	300,000	300,000	(300,000)	(300,000)	300,000	300,000	300,000	300,000	0.0%	0.0%
FINLAND	(30,163)	(32,749)	(35,330)	37,911	39,347	41,100	49,000	50,600	51,980	53,396	35,101	49,215	7.0%	6.5%
FRANCE	3,396,066	3,396,066	3,396,066	3,396,066	3,396,066	(3,396,066)	(3,396,066)	(3,396,066)	(3,396,066)	(3,396,066)	3,396,066	3,396,066	0.0%	0.0%
GREECE	200,000	200,000	200,000	200,000	200,000	200,000	(200,000)	(200,000)	(200,000)	(200,000)	200,000	200,000	0.0%	0.0%
ICELAND	(302,985)	(309,079)	(315,173)	(321,267)	(327,361)	(332,658)	(338,502)	(344,539)	(350,207)	(357,831)	315,173	344,747	1.8%	1.9%
ITALY	143,864	143,864	143,042	143,976	144,574	(144,752)	(144,930)	(145,108)	(145,286)	(145,464)	143,864	145,108	0.2%	0.1%
LIECHTENSTEIN	(900)	(900)	(900)	(900)	(900)	(900)	(900)	(900)	(900)	900	900	900	0.0%	0.0%
LUXEMBOURG	1,100	1,100	1,100	1,100	1,100	1,100	1,180	1,270	1,360	1,500	1,100	1,282	3.1%	3.5%
NETHERLANDS	5,000	6,000	7,000	8,000	6,500	7,100	7,300	8,100	8,375	8,789	6,500	7,933	4.1%	6.5%
NORWAY	(1,929,363)	(1,915,391)	(1,901,420)	(1,784,387)	(1,926,689)	(2,068,992)	(1,908,578)	(2,097,452)	(1,750,752)	(1,714,529)	1,891,450	1,908,061	0.2%	-1.3%
PORTUGAL	8,547	8,797	12,077	53,090	53,157	76,929	78,551	80,065	81,577	83,828	27,134	80,190	24.2%	28.9%
SPAIN	733,876	733,876	733,876	733,876	733,876	733,876	891,690	902,620	1,409,910	1,257,947	733,876	1,039,209	7.2%	6.2%
SWEDEN	(1,546,349)	(1,541,199)	(1,536,049)	(1,530,899)	(1,525,749)	(1,520,599)	(1,515,449)	1,510,299	1,511,260	1,500,000	1,536,049	1,511,521	-0.3%	-0.3%
SWITZERLAND	(1,074,101)	(1,074,101)	(1,074,101)	(1,074,101)	(1,074,101)	(1,087,881)	(1,060,322)	(1,153,172)	(2,154,556)	(2,199,420)	1,074,101	1,531,070	7.3%	8.3%
UK	46,277,000	46,277,000	46,277,000	46,277,000	46,277,000	46,277,000	(49,449,000)	52,621,000	(54,315,500)	56,010,000	46,277,000	51,734,500	2.3%	2.1%
WEST GERMANY	(7,531,918)	(7,345,189)	(7,158,459)	(6,971,730)	(6,785,000)	6,848,727	8,903,064	9,119,875	9,227,533	9,334,656	7,158,459	8,686,371	3.9%	2.4%
EU TOTAL	64,779,893	64,824,520	64,856,112	64,925,356	64,927,964	65,271,779	70,669,558	74,481,428	83,993,186	85,875,096	64,862,769	76,098,209	3.2%	3.2%
EFTA TOTAL	8,814,404	8,875,124	8,935,845	8,893,504	9,109,353	9,338,503	9,220,657	9,548,898	10,293,201	10,397,116	8,925,646	9,759,675	1.8%	1.9%
EUROPE TOTAL	73,594,297	73,699,644	73,791,957	73,818,860	74,037,317	74,610,282	80,090,215	84,030,326	94,286,387	96,272,212	73,788,415	85,857,884	3.1%	3.0%

Sector 2 HIGHER EDUCATION

	1981	1982	1983	1984	1985	1986	1987	1988	1989	1990	1981-85 Average	1986-90 Average	81/85 - 86/90 Year on Year Increase	Decade: Year on Year Increase
AUSTRIA	(1,176,747)	(1,229,979)	(1,257,452)	(1,277,134)	(1,330,482)	(1,351,347)	(1,325,426)	(1,274,428)	(1,480,531)	(1,516,360)	1,254,359	1,389,618	2.1%	2.9%
BELGIUM	168,733	168,733	168,733	168,733	168,733	(168,733)	(168,733)	(168,733)	(168,733)	(168,733)	168,733	168,733	0.0%	0.0%
DENMARK	917,001	917,001	917,001	917,001	917,001	(917,001)	917,001	917,001	996,778	967,657	917,001	943,088	0.6%	0.6%
EAST GERMANY	(3,112,792)	(4,141,601)	(5,170,410)	6,199,219	(7,228,028)	(8,256,837)	9,285,646	(10,314,455)	(11,343,264)	(12,372,073)	5,170,410	10,314,455	14.8%	16.6%
EIRE	315,145	315,145	315,145	315,145	315,145	(315,145)	(315,145)	(315,145)	(315,145)	(315,145)	315,145	315,145	0.0%	0.0%
FINLAND	(104,855)	(104,855)	(104,855)	104,855	113,732	259,032	468,982	472,369	559,172	489,909	106,630	449,893	33.4%	18.7%
FRANCE	3,080,000	3,100,000	(3,090,000)	3,100,000	(3,090,000)	(3,485,000)	3,880,000	3,900,000	3,970,000	4,164,000	3,092,000	3,879,800	4.6%	3.4%
GREECE	792,611	792,611	792,611	792,611	792,611	(792,611)	(792,611)	(792,611)	(792,611)	(792,611)	792,611	792,611	0.0%	0.0%
ICELAND	(501)	(300)	(400)	(400)	(500)	500	600	700	800	1,000	380	720	13.6%	14.3%
ITALY	(3,118)	(501)	(283)	(408)	(813)	(813)	(813)	(813)	(813)	(3,090)	501	813	10.2%	5.5%
LIECHTENSTEIN	(3,118)	(3,118)	(3,118)	(3,118)	(3,118)	(3,118)	(3,118)	(3,118)	(3,118)	(3,090)	3,118	3,112	-0.0%	-0.1%
LUXEMBOURG	32,851	32,851	32,851	32,851	32,851	(32,851)	(32,851)	(32,851)	(32,851)	(32,851)	32,851	32,851	0.0%	0.0%
NETHERLANDS	729,000	336,000	336,000	(467,000)	(467,000)	-(32,851)	(554,334)	(598,000)	(641,668)	(685,335)	467,000	598,001	5.1%	-0.7%
NORWAY	(2,467,770)	(2,640,004)	(2,812,238)	2,984,472	(3,156,705)	(3,328,939)	3,501,173	(3,687,579)	(3,873,984)	4,060,389	2,812,238	3,690,413	5.6%	5.7%
PORTUGAL	43,410	43,410	43,410	43,410	43,410	43,410	43,410	69,313	99,612	168,234	43,410	84,796	14.3%	16.2%
SPAIN	89,205	89,205	89,205	89,205	89,205	89,205	(120,856)	152,506	(132,881)	113,255	89,205	121,740	6.4%	2.7%
SWEDEN	(28,196)	(28,783)	(29,371)	(29,956)	(30,547)	(31,135)	(31,723)	32,311	32,899	77,393	29,371	41,092	6.9%	11.9%
SWITZERLAND	(1,522,258)	(1,522,258)	(1,522,258)	(1,522,258)	(1,603,594)	(1,603,594)	(1,648,887)	(1,708,618)	(1,750,432)	(1,766,675)	1,538,525	1,695,641	2.0%	1.7%
UK	5,000,000	5,000,000	5,000,000	5,000,000	5,000,000	5,000,000	5,000,000	5,000,000	5,000,000	5,000,000	5,000,000	5,000,000	0.0%	0.0%
WEST GERMANY	13,164,000	13,164,000	13,750,000	14,389,000	11,353,000	10,229,181	10,736,938	11,023,168	11,273,091	(11,036,727)	13,164,000	10,859,821	-3.8%	-1.9%
EU TOTAL	27,445,249	28,101,058	29,705,649	31,514,583	29,497,797	29,841,454	31,848,336	33,284,597	34,767,447	35,817,434	29,252,867	33,111,853	2.5%	3.0%
EFTA TOTAL	5,303,243	5,529,297	5,729,692	5,922,196	6,238,678	6,577,665	6,979,909	7,179,123	7,700,936	7,914,816	5,744,621	7,270,490	4.8%	4.5%
EUROPE TOTAL	32,748,492	33,630,355	35,435,341	37,436,779	35,736,475	36,419,119	38,828,245	40,463,720	42,468,383	43,732,250	34,997,488	40,382,343	2.9%	3.3%

Figures in parentheses are grossed.

Collections: Other Material

Sector 3 – OTHER NON-MAJOR SPEC

	1981	1982	1983	1984	1985	1986	1987	1988	1989	1990	1981–85 Average	1986–90 Average	81/85 – 86/90 Year on Year Increase	Decade: Year on Year Increase
AUSTRIA	(62,026)	(62,026)	(62,026)	(62,026)	(62,026)	(62,026)	(62,026)	(62,026)	(62,026)	(62,026)	62,026	62,026	0.0%	0.0%
BELGIUM	55,252	55,252	55,252	55,252	55,252	55,252	55,252	55,252	55,252	55,252	55,252	55,252	0.0%	0.0%
DENMARK	0	0	0	0	0	0	0	0	0	0	0	0	0.0%	0.0%
EAST GERMANY	(1,058,622)	(1,058,622)	(1,058,622)	(1,058,622)	(1,058,622)	(1,058,622)	(1,058,622)	(1,058,622)	(1,058,622)	(1,043,328)	1,058,622	1,055,563	-0.1%	-0.2%
EIRE	2,000	2,000	2,000	2,000	2,000	2,000	2,000	2,000	2,000	2,000	2,000	2,000	0.0%	0.0%
FINLAND	0	0	0	0	0	0	0	0	0	0	0	0	0.0%	0.0%
FRANCE	(16,069)	(16,069)	(16,069)	(16,069)	(16,069)	(16,069)	(16,069)	(16,069)	(16,069)	(16,069)	16,069	16,069	0.0%	0.0%
GREECE	55,155	55,155	55,155	55,155	55,155	55,155	55,155	55,155	55,155	55,155	55,155	55,155	0.0%	0.0%
ICELAND	0	0	0	0	0	0	0	0	0	0	0	0	0.0%	0.0%
ITALY	(95,253)	(95,253)	(95,253)	(95,253)	(95,253)	95,253	(101,480)	(107,706)	113,932	(120,158)	95,253	107,706	2.5%	2.6%
LIECHTENSTEIN	0	0	0	0	0	0	0	0	0	0	0	0	0.0%	0.0%
LUXEMBOURG	0	0	0	0	0	0	0	0	0	0	0	0	0.6%	0.4%
NETHERLANDS	84,300	84,300	84,300	84,300	84,300	87,000	(87,000)	(87,000)	(87,000)	(87,000)	84,300	87,000	0.0%	0.0%
NORWAY	0	0	0	0	0	0	0	0	0	0	0	0	24.0%	4.9%
PORTUGAL	(12,402)	(12,402)	(12,402)	(12,402)	12,402	11,783	52,103	48,217	50,396	19,093	12,402	36,318	0.0%	0.0%
SPAIN	213,911	213,911	213,911	213,911	213,911	(213,911)	(213,911)	(213,911)	(213,911)	(213,911)	213,911	213,911	0.0%	0.0%
SWEDEN	(724,509)	(724,509)	(724,509)	(724,509)	(724,509)	(724,509)	(724,509)	(724,509)	(724,509)	(724,509)	724,509	724,509	1.4%	1.1%
SWITZERLAND	(271,879)	(274,944)	(278,008)	(281,073)	(284,138)	(287,202)	(294,396)	(305,147)	(306,720)	(299,461)	278,008	298,585	0.0%	0.0%
UK	316,401	316,401	316,401	316,401	316,401	(316,401)	(316,401)	(316,401)	(316,401)	(316,401)	316,401	316,401	-6.4%	-4.7%
WEST GERMANY	571,250	280,000	788,000	821,000	396,000	472,557	486,552	354,148	362,666	(371,184)	571,250	409,421		
EU TOTAL	2,480,615	2,189,365	2,697,365	2,730,365	2,305,365	2,384,003	2,444,545	2,314,481	2,331,404	2,299,551	2,480,615	2,354,797	-1.0%	-0.8%
EFTA TOTAL	1,058,414	1,061,479	1,064,543	1,067,608	1,070,673	1,073,737	1,080,931	1,091,682	1,093,255	1,085,996	1,064,543	1,085,120	0.4%	0.3%
EUROPE TOTAL	3,539,029	3,250,844	3,761,908	3,797,973	3,376,038	3,457,740	3,525,476	3,406,163	3,424,659	3,385,547	3,545,158	3,439,917	-0.6%	-0.5%

Sector 4 SCHOOLS

	1981	1982	1983	1984	1985	1986	1987	1988	1989	1990	1981–85 Average	1986–90 Average	81/85 – 86/90 Year on Year Increase	Decade: Year on Year Increase
AUSTRIA	(969)	(969)	(969)	(969)	(969)	(969)	(969)	(969)	(969)	(958)	969	967	-0.0%	-0.1%
BELGIUM	2,026	2,026	2,026	2,026	2,026	(2,026)	(2,026)	(2,026)	(2,026)	(2,026)	2,026	2,026	0.0%	0.0%
DENMARK	(1,090)	(1,090)	(1,090)	(1,090)	(1,090)	(1,090)	(1,090)	(1,090)	(1,090)	(1,090)	1,090	1,090	0.0%	0.0%
EAST GERMANY	(2,158)	(2,158)	(2,158)	(2,158)	(2,158)	(2,158)	(2,158)	(2,158)	(2,158)	(2,108)	2,158	2,148	-0.1%	-0.3%
EIRE	(2,784)	(2,784)	(2,784)	(2,784)	(2,784)	2,784	(2,784)	(2,784)	(2,784)	(2,784)	2,784	2,784	0.0%	0.0%
FINLAND	(2,132)	(2,248)	(2,364)	(2,480)	(2,672)	(2,865)	(2,997)	(2,944)	(3,060)	(3,176)	2,379	3,008	4.8%	4.5%
FRANCE	12,140	12,140	12,140	12,140	12,140	(12,140)	(12,140)	(12,140)	(12,140)	(12,140)	12,140	12,140	0.0%	0.0%
GREECE	2,138	2,138	2,138	2,138	2,138	(2,138)	(2,138)	(2,138)	(2,138)	(2,138)	2,138	2,138	0.0%	0.0%
ICELAND	(79)	(79)	(79)	(79)	(79)	(79)	(79)	(79)	(79)	(79)	79	79	0.0%	0.0%
ITALY	12,871	12,871	12,871	12,871	12,871	(12,871)	(12,871)	(12,871)	(12,871)	(12,871)	12,871	12,871	0.0%	0.0%
LIECHTENSTEIN	(4)	(4)	(4)	(4)	(4)	(4)	(4)	(4)	(4)	(4)	4	4	0.0%	0.0%
LUXEMBOURG	70	70	70	70	70	70	70	70	70	70	70	70	0.0%	0.0%
NETHERLANDS	3,276	3,276	3,276	3,276	3,276	(3,276)	(3,276)	(3,276)	(3,276)	(3,276)	3,276	3,276	0.0%	0.0%
NORWAY	(2,841)	(2,841)	(2,841)	(2,841)	(2,866)	(2,905)	(2,780)	(2,929)	(3,003)	(2,932)	2,846	2,910	0.4%	0.4%
PORTUGAL	(12,701)	(12,701)	(12,701)	(12,701)	(12,701)	10,547	5,517	7,437	8,775	31,228	12,701	12,701	-0.0%	10.5%
SPAIN	9,504	9,504	9,504	9,504	9,504	9,504	9,504	9,504	9,504	9,504	9,504	9,504	0.0%	0.0%
SWEDEN	(19,994)	(19,131)	(18,267)	(17,403)	(15,393)	(14,538)	(14,111)	(14,111)	(13,084)	(12,221)	18,038	13,613	-5.5%	-5.3%
SWITZERLAND	(808)	(808)	(808)	(808)	(808)	(808)	(808)	(808)	(808)	(801)	808	807	0.0%	-0.1%
UK	12,142	12,142	12,142	12,142	12,142	(12,142)	(12,142)	(12,142)	(12,142)	(12,142)	12,142	12,142	0.0%	0.0%
WEST GERMANY	12,087	12,087	12,087	12,087	12,087	(12,087)	(12,087)	(12,087)	(12,087)	(12,087)	12,087	12,087	0.0%	0.0%
EU TOTAL	84,987	84,987	84,987	84,987	84,987	82,833	77,803	79,723	81,061	103,464	84,987	84,977	-0.0%	2.2%
EFTA TOTAL	26,827	26,080	25,332	24,584	22,791	22,168	21,748	21,844	21,007	20,171	25,123	21,388	-3.2%	-3.1%
EUROPE TOTAL	111,814	111,067	110,319	109,571	107,778	105,001	99,551	101,567	102,068	123,635	110,110	106,364	-0.7%	1.1%

Figures in parentheses are grossed

- 156 -

Collections: Other Material

Sector 5 SPECIAL

	1981	1982	1983	1984	1985	1986	1987	1988	1989	1990	1981-85 Average	1986-90 Average	81/85 – 86/90 Year on Year Increase	Decade: Year on Year Increase
AUSTRIA	(3,151,200)	(3,151,200)	(3,151,200)	(3,151,200)	(3,151,200)	(3,151,200)	(3,151,200)	(3,151,200)	(3,151,200)	(3,172,811)	3,151,200	3,155,522	0.0%	0.1%
BELGIUM	101,676	101,676	101,676	101,676	101,676	101,676	101,676	101,676	101,676	101,676	101,676	101,676	0.0%	0.0%
DENMARK	16,696,411	16,696,411	16,696,411	16,696,411	16,696,411	16,696,411	16,696,411	16,696,411	16,696,411	18,862,259	16,696,411	17,036,137	0.4%	1.4%
EAST GERMANY	(6,894,981)	(6,894,981)	(6,894,981)	(6,894,981)	(6,894,981)	(6,894,981)	(6,894,981)	(6,894,981)	(6,894,981)	(6,785,147)	6,894,981	6,873,014	-0.1%	-0.2%
EIRE	630	630	630	630	630	630	630	630	630	630	630	630	0.0%	0.0%
FINLAND	(112,100)	(112,100)	(112,100)	112,100	112,100	112,100	117,078	119,266	19,570,117	20,384,893	112,100	8,060,691	135.2%	78.3%
FRANCE	549,556	549,556	549,556	549,556	549,556	549,556	549,558	549,556	549,556	549,556	549,556	549,556	0.0%	0.0%
GREECE	98,755	98,755	98,755	98,755	98,755	98,755	98,755	98,755	98,755	98,755	98,755	98,755	0.0%	0.0%
ICELAND	(2,115)	(2,115)	(2,115)	(2,115)	(2,115)	(2,115)	(2,115)	(2,115)	2,578	2,578	2,115	2,300	1.7%	2.2%
ITALY	141,831	141,881	114,680	137,811	173,152	180,970	(188,768)	(196,606)	(204,424)	(212,242)	141,881	196,606	6.7%	4.6%
LIECHTENSTEIN	0	0	0	0	0	0	0	0	0	0	0	0	0.0%	0.0%
LUXEMBOURG	3,896	3,896	3,896	3,896	3,896	3,896	(3,896)	(3,896)	(3,896)	(3,896)	3,896	3,896	0.0%	0.0%
NETHERLANDS	539,000	619,000	738,000	832,000	966,600	1,073,500	1,180,400	1,287,300	1,394,200	1,501,100	738,920	1,287,300	11.7%	12.1%
NORWAY	(121,074)	(121,074)	(121,074)	(121,074)	121,074	121,074	121,074	121,074	121,074	121,074	121,074	121,074	0.0%	0.0%
PORTUGAL	(46,566)	(46,566)	(46,566)	(46,566)	(46,566)	46,566	157,353	346,137	152,742	300,761	46,566	200,712	33.9%	23.0%
SPAIN	853,872	853,872	853,872	853,872	853,872	853,872	1,083,953	1,314,033	1,711,378	2,108,723	853,872	1,414,392	10.6%	10.6%
SWEDEN	(1,301,555)	(1,313,352)	(1,263,114)	(1,328,201)	(1,348,740)	(1,112,400)	(1,523,461)	1,410,360	403,379	2,756,645	1,310,992	1,441,249	1.9%	8.7%
SWITZERLAND	(2,782,280)	(2,782,280)	(2,782,280)	(2,782,280)	(2,782,280)	(2,782,280)	(2,782,280)	(2,782,280)	(2,782,280)	(2,802,479)	2,782,280	2,786,320	0.0%	0.1%
UK	568,454	568,454	568,454	568,454	568,454	568,454	568,454	(568,454)	(568,454)	(568,454)	568,454	568,454	0.0%	0.0%
WEST GERMANY	652,205	652,205	652,205	652,205	652,205	652,205	7,878,411	32,470,253	53,388,093	59,247,636	652,205	35,052,405	121.9%	65.0%
EU TOTAL	27,147,883	27,227,883	27,319,682	27,436,813	27,606,754	49,346,898	35,403,264	60,528,688	81,297,979	90,340,835	27,347,803	63,383,533	18.3%	14.3%
EFTA TOTAL	7,470,324	7,482,121	7,431,883	7,496,970	7,517,509	7,281,169	7,697,208	7,586,295	26,030,628	29,240,480	7,479,761	15,567,156	15.8%	16.4%
EUROPE TOTAL	34,618,207	34,710,004	34,751,565	34,933,783	35,124,263	56,628,067	43,100,472	68,114,983	107,328,607	119,581,315	34,827,564	78,950,689	17.8%	14.8%

Sector 6 PUBLIC

	1981	1982	1983	1984	1985	1986	1987	1988	1989	1990	1981-85 Average	1986-90 Average	81/85 – 86/90 Year on Year Increase	Decade: Year on Year Increase
AUSTRIA	(168,704)	(176,159)	(183,613)	(191,068)	(198,522)	(198,963)	(214,119)	(207,878)	(214,360)	(235,795)	183,613	214,227	3.1%	3.8%
BELGIUM	116,421	138,740	172,444	195,474	211,035	234,689	258,343	(281,997)	(305,651)	(329,305)	166,823	281,997	11.1%	12.2%
DENMARK	565,864	565,864	565,864	565,864	565,864	607,422	38,610	39,183	42,065	45,076	565,864	154,471	-22.9%	-24.5%
EAST GERMANY	(1,912,958)	(1,912,958)	(1,912,958)	(1,912,958)	(1,912,958)	(1,912,958)	(1,912,958)	(1,912,958)	(1,912,958)	(1,912,958)	1,912,958	1,912,958	0.0%	0.0%
EIRE	1,632	2,311	3,105	2,373	3,779	4,376	4,455	2,757	2,791	2,332	2,640	3,342	4.8%	4.0%
FINLAND	(739,837)	(771,130)	(802,422)	(833,714)	(870,349)	(905,014)	(942,796)	(974,017)	(997,810)	(1,021,468)	803,490	968,221	3.8%	3.6%
FRANCE	1,080,400	1,336,600	1,592,724	1,848,900	1,955,582	(2,174,378)	(2,393,174)	(2,611,970)	(2,830,766)	(3,049,562)	1,562,841	2,611,970	10.8%	12.2%
GREECE	6,235	6,235	6,235	6,235	6,235	15,140	(15,140)	(15,140)	(15,140)	(15,140)	6,235	15,140	19.4%	10.4%
ICELAND	(2,729)	(2,865)	(3,001)	(3,137)	(3,273)	(3,409)	3,240	3,623	3,870	3,647	3,001	3,518	3.2%	3.3%
ITALY	(2,210,209)	(2,210,209)	(2,210,209)	(2,210,209)	(2,210,209)	(2,210,209)	(2,210,209)	(2,210,209)	(2,210,209)	(2,210,209)	2,210,209	2,210,209	0.0%	0.0%
LIECHTENSTEIN	(508)	(527)	(547)	(566)	(585)	(604)	(623)	(643)	(662)	(681)	547	643	3.3%	3.3%
LUXEMBOURG	9,528	9,528	9,528	9,528	9,528	9,528	9,528	9,528	9,528	9,528	9,528	9,528	0.0%	0.0%
NETHERLANDS	879,000	979,000	985,000	1,128,000	1,208,500	1,211,720	1,214,940	1,218,160	1,289,000	1,289,000	1,035,900	1,244,564	3.7%	4.3%
NORWAY	(121,898)	(121,898)	(121,898)	(121,898)	(121,898)	121,898	(121,898)	(121,898)	(121,898)	(121,898)	121,898	121,898	0.0%	0.0%
PORTUGAL	11,603	11,603	11,603	11,603	11,603	11,603	34,467	32,440	38,731	13,835	11,603	26,215	17.7%	2.0%
SPAIN	78,163	78,163	78,163	78,163	78,163	78,163	(110,518)	142,872	123,107	123,107	78,163	117,530	8.5%	5.2%
SWEDEN	(1,190,591)	(1,210,120)	(1,229,649)	(1,249,178)	(1,268,707)	(1,288,236)	(1,315,253)	(1,339,335)	(1,358,785)	(1,366,352)	1,229,649	1,333,592	1.6%	1.5%
SWITZERLAND	1,156,200	1,222,591	1,260,760	1,260,215	1,319,005	(1,284,455)	(1,325,156)	(1,365,857)	(1,406,558)	(1,447,259)	1,243,754	1,365,857	1.9%	2.5%
UK	850,739	900,995	914,651	1,024,911	1,082,984	10,493,576	11,208,984	12,092,646	12,229,898	7,718,648	954,856	10,748,750	62.3%	27.8%
WEST GERMANY	1,599,187	1,599,187	1,599,187	1,599,187	1,599,187	1,599,187	1,599,187	1,599,187	1,599,187	1,599,187	1,599,187	1,599,187	0.0%	0.0%
EU TOTAL	9,321,939	9,751,393	10,061,671	10,593,405	10,855,627	20,562,249	21,010,513	22,169,047	22,618,914	18,317,887	10,116,807	20,935,862	15.7%	7.8%
EFTA TOTAL	3,380,467	3,505,290	3,601,890	3,659,776	3,782,339	3,802,599	3,923,085	4,013,251	4,103,743	4,197,100	3,585,952	4,007,956	2.3%	2.4%
EUROPE TOTAL	12,702,406	13,256,683	13,663,561	14,253,181	14,637,966	24,365,548	24,933,598	26,182,298	26,722,657	22,514,987	13,702,759	24,943,817	12.7%	6.6%

Figures in parentheses are grossed.

Collections: Other Material

	1981	1982	1983	1984	1985	1986	1987	1988	1989	1990	1981-85 Average	1986-90 Average	81/85 - 86/90 Year on Year Increase	Decade: Year on Year Increase
ALL SECTORS														
AUSTRIA	8,490,184	8,622,038	8,728,132	8,826,436	8,958,405	9,050,898	9,101,646	9,088,437	9,382,632	9,558,990	8,725,039	9,236,521	1.1%	1.3%
BELGIUM	1,464,613	1,488,214	1,525,533	1,550,364	1,566,765	1,592,304	1,617,843	1,643,382	1,668,921	1,694,460	1,519,098	1,643,382	1.6%	1.6%
DENMARK	21,405,615	21,453,745	21,484,300	21,514,831	21,523,470	21,639,987	21,098,144	21,125,685	27,758,803	30,412,446	21,476,392	24,407,013	2.6%	4.0%
EAST GERMANY	14,918,279	16,127,782	17,337,285	18,546,788	19,756,291	20,965,794	22,175,297	23,384,800	24,594,303	25,678,628	17,337,285	23,359,764	6.1%	6.2%
EIRE	622,191	622,870	623,316	622,932	624,338	624,935	625,014	623,316	623,350	622,891	623,199	623,901	0.0%	0.0%
FINLAND	989,092	1,023,062	1,057,071	1,091,060	1,138,200	1,320,111	1,580,853	1,819,196	21,182,139	21,952,842	1,059,701	9,531,028	55.2%	41.1%
FRANCE	8,134,231	8,410,431	8,656,555	8,922,731	9,019,413	9,633,209	10,247,005	10,485,801	10,774,597	11,187,393	8,628,672	10,465,601	3.9%	3.6%
GREECE	1,154,894	1,154,894	1,154,894	1,154,894	1,154,894	1,163,799	1,163,799	1,163,799	1,163,799	1,163,799	1,154,894	1,163,799	0.2%	0.1%
ICELAND	308,208	314,438	320,768	328,998	333,328	338,761	344,536	351,056	357,334	365,135	320,748	351,364	1.8%	1.9%
ITALY	2,604,579	2,604,579	2,576,338	2,600,528	2,636,872	2,644,868	2,659,091	2,673,313	2,687,535	2,701,757	2,604,579	2,673,313	0.5%	0.4%
LIECHTENSTEIN	4,530	4,549	4,569	4,588	4,607	4,626	4,645	4,665	4,684	4,675	4,569	4,659	0.4%	0.4%
LUXEMBOURG	47,445	47,445	47,445	47,445	47,445	47,445	47,525	47,615	47,705	47,845	47,445	47,627	0.1%	0.1%
NETHERLANDS	2,239,576	2,027,576	2,153,576	2,522,576	2,736,176	2,893,263	3,047,250	3,201,837	3,423,519	3,574,500	2,335,896	3,228,074	6.7%	5.3%
NORWAY	4,642,946	4,801,208	4,959,471	5,014,672	5,329,232	5,643,808	5,655,503	6,030,932	5,870,711	6,020,822	4,949,506	5,844,355	3.4%	2.9%
PORTUGAL	135,229	135,479	138,759	179,772	179,839	200,838	371,401	583,609	431,833	616,979	153,816	440,932	23.4%	18.4%
SPAIN	1,978,531	1,978,531	1,978,531	1,978,531	1,978,531	1,978,531	2,430,431	2,735,446	3,610,573	3,826,447	1,978,531	2,916,286	8.1%	7.6%
SWEDEN	4,811,193	4,837,094	4,800,959	4,880,149	4,913,645	4,691,417	5,124,506	5,030,925	4,043,916	6,437,120	4,848,608	5,065,577	0.9%	3.3%
SWITZERLAND	6,807,526	6,876,962	6,918,215	6,920,735	7,063,926	7,046,220	7,111,849	7,315,882	8,401,354	8,516,095	6,917,477	7,678,280	2.1%	2.5%
UK	53,024,736	53,074,992	53,088,648	53,198,908	53,256,981	62,667,573	66,554,981	70,610,643	72,442,395	69,625,645	53,128,853	68,380,247	5.2%	3.1%
WEST GERMANY	23,530,647	23,052,668	23,959,938	24,445,209	20,797,479	41,437,370	29,616,237	54,578,718	75,862,657	81,601,477	23,157,188	56,619,292	19.6%	14.8%
EU TOTAL	131,260,566	132,179,206	134,725,466	137,285,509	135,278,494	167,489,916	161,654,017	192,857,964	225,089,990	232,754,267	134,145,848	195,969,231	7.6%	6.6%
EFTA TOTAL	26,053,679	26,479,391	26,789,185	27,064,638	27,741,343	28,095,841	28,923,538	29,441,093	49,242,770	52,855,679	26,825,647	37,711,784	7.0%	8.2%
EUROPE TOTAL	157,314,245	158,658,597	161,514,651	164,350,147	163,019,837	195,585,757	190,577,555	222,299,057	274,332,760	285,609,946	160,971,495	233,681,015	7.7%	6.9%

Collections: Other Material per 1000 Population

	1981	1982	1983	1984	1985	1986	1987	1988	1989	1990	1981-85 Average	1986-90 Average	81/85 - 86/90 Year on Year Increase	Decade: Year on Year Increase
European Union														
Sector 1	191.64	191.78	191.87	192.07	191.65	191.59	208.03	217.78	248.47	253.48	191.80	223.87	3.1%	3.2%
Sector 2	81.19	83.13	87.88	93.23	87.07	87.59	93.49	97.32	102.85	105.72	86.50	97.39	2.4%	3.0%
Sector 3	7.34	6.48	7.98	8.08	6.80	7.00	7.18	6.77	6.90	6.79	7.34	6.93	-1.1%	-0.9%
Sector 4	0.25	0.25	0.25	0.25	0.25	0.24	0.23	0.23	0.24	0.31	0.25	0.25	-0.1%	2.2%
Sector 5	80.31	80.55	80.82	81.17	81.49	144.84	103.92	176.99	240.49	266.67	80.87	186.58	18.2%	14.3%
Sector 6	27.58	28.85	29.77	31.34	32.04	60.38	61.67	64.82	66.91	54.07	29.92	61.57	15.5%	7.8%
All Sectors	388.32	391.04	398.57	406.15	399.30	491.62	474.51	563.92	665.85	687.04	396.68	576.59	7.8%	6.5%
EFTA														
Sector 1	274.28	276.17	278.06	276.74	283.46	290.59	286.92	297.14	320.30	321.39	277.74	303.27	1.8%	1.8%
Sector 2	165.02	172.06	178.29	184.28	194.13	204.68	217.20	223.40	239.63	244.66	178.76	225.91	4.8%	4.5%
Sector 3	32.94	33.03	33.13	33.22	33.32	33.41	33.64	33.97	34.02	33.72	33.13	33.72	0.4%	0.2%
Sector 4	0.83	0.81	0.79	0.76	0.71	0.69	0.68	0.68	0.65	0.62	0.78	0.66	-3.2%	-3.2%
Sector 5	232.46	232.82	231.26	233.29	233.93	226.57	239.52	236.07	810.00	903.86	232.75	483.20	15.7%	16.3%
Sector 6	105.19	109.08	112.08	113.88	117.70	118.33	122.08	124.88	127.70	129.74	111.59	124.54	2.2%	2.4%
All Sectors	810.72	823.97	833.61	842.18	863.24	874.27	900.02	916.13	1,532.31	1,633.83	834.74	1,171.31	7.0%	8.1%
Europe Total														
Sector 1	198.82	199.10	199.35	199.43	199.60	200.12	214.83	224.60	254.70	259.40	199.26	230.73	3.0%	3.0%
Sector 2	88.47	90.85	95.73	101.14	96.34	97.68	104.15	108.15	114.72	117.84	94.51	108.51	2.8%	3.2%
Sector 3	9.56	8.78	10.16	10.26	9.10	9.27	9.46	9.10	9.25	9.12	9.57	9.24	-0.7%	-0.5%
Sector 4	0.30	0.30	0.30	0.30	0.29	0.28	0.27	0.27	0.28	0.33	0.30	0.29	-0.8%	1.1%
Sector 5	93.52	93.77	93.88	94.38	94.69	151.89	115.61	182.06	289.93	322.21	94.05	212.34	17.7%	14.7%
Sector 6	34.32	35.81	36.91	38.51	39.46	65.35	68.88	69.98	72.19	60.67	37.00	67.01	12.6%	6.5%
All Sectors	424.99	428.62	436.34	444.00	439.50	524.60	511.19	594.17	741.07	769.57	434.69	628.12	7.6%	6.8%

- 158 -

Library Users

Sector 1 NATIONAL

	1981	1982	1983	1984	1985	1986	1987	1988	1989	1990	1981–85 Average	1986–90 Average	81/85 – 86/90 Year on Year Increase	Decade: Year on Year Increase
AUSTRIA	(453,925)	(459,471)	(465,017)	(470,563)	(476,109)	506,042	487,245	497,205	389,557	528,227	465,017	481,655	0.7%	1.7%
BELGIUM	113,636	112,451	97,466	109,222	89,948	(104,544)	(104,544)	(104,544)	(104,544)	(104,544)	104,544	104,544	0.0%	-0.9%
DENMARK	(105,443)	(105,443)	(105,443)	(105,443)	(105,443)	(105,443)	(105,443)	(105,443)	(105,443)	(105,443)	105,443	105,443	0.0%	0.0%
EAST GERMANY	(505,811)	(505,811)	(505,811)	(505,811)	(505,811)	505,811	(505,811)	(505,811)	(505,811)	(505,811)	505,811	505,811	0.0%	0.0%
EIRE	(33,000)	(33,000)	(33,000)	(33,000)	(33,000)	(33,000)	(33,000)	(33,000)	33,000	28,300	33,000	32,060	-0.6%	-1.7%
FINLAND	80,735	82,883	84,140	86,314	88,266	90,366	92,530	94,617	96,670	98,914	84,468	94,619	2.3%	2.3%
FRANCE	(37,140)	(37,140)	(37,140)	(37,140)	(37,140)	37,140	38,595	40,963	41,859	42,463	37,140	40,204	1.6%	1.5%
GREECE	202,779	202,779	202,779	202,779	202,779	202,779	202,779	202,779	202,779	(202,779)	202,779	202,779	0.0%	0.0%
ICELAND	(11,689)	(11,689)	(11,689)	(11,689)	(11,689)	12,285	12,124	12,411	10,564	10,283	11,689	11,533	-0.5%	-1.4%
ITALY	646,052	646,052	579,617	656,492	702,048	(646,052)	(646,052)	(646,052)	(646,052)	(646,052)	646,052	646,052	0.0%	0.0%
LIECHTENSTEIN	12,000	12,000	12,000	12,000	12,000	10,100	10,800	12,100	13,050	13,950	12,000	12,000	-0.0%	1.7%
LUXEMBOURG	13,000	13,000	14,000	15,000	16,000	18,000	19,550	20,800	22,700	24,650	14,000	21,140	8.6%	8.3%
NETHERLANDS	(50,000)	(50,000)	(50,000)	(50,000)	(50,000)	50,000	61,763	73,788	84,978	96,770	50,000	73,456	8.0%	7.6%
NORWAY	(77,527)	(77,527)	(77,527)	(77,527)	(77,527)	(77,527)	(77,527)	78,595	81,382	72,605	77,527	77,527	0.0%	-0.7%
PORTUGAL	34,009	60,142	36,638	36,906	43,156	70,568	67,780	68,604	65,099	43,433	42,170	63,097	8.4%	2.6%
SPAIN	(44,806)	(47,073)	(105,092)	(109,496)	(113,900)	118,304	122,709	38,402	55,364	55,909	84,074	78,138	-1.5%	2.5%
SWEDEN	(3,100)	(3,100)	(3,100)	(3,100)	(3,100)	3,100	3,400	(3,400)	(3,400)	3,400	3,100	3,340	1.5%	1.0%
SWITZERLAND	(12,888)	(12,888)	(12,888)	(12,888)	(12,888)	12,888	9,359	9,644	7,094	7,603	12,888	9,318	-6.3%	-5.7%
UK	3,198,696	2,881,395	2,863,822	2,982,697	3,099,433	(3,005,209)	(3,005,209)	(3,005,209)	(3,005,209)	(3,005,209)	3,005,209	3,005,209	0.0%	-0.7%
WEST GERMANY	75,784	71,024	72,930	72,385	86,798	(81,222)	(75,645)	(70,068)	64,491	(64,491)	75,784	71,183	-1.2%	-1.6%
EU TOTAL	5,059,158	4,765,310	4,703,738	4,916,371	5,085,454	4,978,073	4,988,680	4,915,443	4,937,329	4,925,854	4,906,006	4,949,116	0.2%	-0.3%
EFTA TOTAL	651,864	659,558	666,361	674,081	682,357	712,308	692,985	707,972	601,717	734,982	666,844	689,993	0.7%	1.3%
EUROPE TOTAL	5,711,022	5,424,868	5,370,099	5,590,452	5,767,811	5,690,381	5,681,665	5,623,415	5,539,046	5,660,836	5,572,851	5,639,109	0.2%	-0.1%

Sector 2 HIGHER EDUCATION

	1981	1982	1983	1984	1985	1986	1987	1988	1989	1990	1981–85 Average	1986–90 Average	81/85 – 86/90 Year on Year Increase	Decade: Year on Year Increase
AUSTRIA	1,320,854	1,506,707	1,962,750	2,062,772	2,341,758	2,266,209	2,459,655	2,811,210	2,604,384	3,066,340	1,838,968	2,641,560	7.5%	9.5%
BELGIUM	(73,246)	(73,246)	(73,246)	(73,246)	(73,246)	(76,561)	(79,874)	(83,187)	86,500	87,400	73,246	82,704	2.5%	2.0%
DENMARK	(55,522)	(56,445)	(58,242)	(59,603)	(61,866)	(61,866)	(65,246)	(68,627)	(64,406)	(69,364)	58,336	65,902	2.5%	2.5%
EAST GERMANY	(222,897)	(222,897)	(222,897)	222,897	(225,005)	(227,113)	(229,221)	(229,221)	(229,221)	(229,221)	223,319	228,799	0.5%	0.3%
EIRE	(51,049)	(51,049)	(51,049)	(51,049)	(51,049)	(51,049)	(51,049)	(51,049)	(51,049)	(51,049)	51,049	51,049	0.0%	0.0%
FINLAND	(123,342)	(123,342)	(123,342)	(123,342)	(123,342)	117,759	113,812	121,065	129,414	134,662	123,342	123,342	0.0%	1.0%
FRANCE	485,000	485,000	462,000	463,000	560,000	595,000	615,000	642,000	723,000	794,000	491,000	673,800	6.5%	5.6%
GREECE	(128,391)	(128,391)	(128,391)	(128,391)	(128,391)	(128,391)	(128,391)	(128,391)	(128,391)	(128,391)	128,391	128,391	0.0%	0.0%
ICELAND	(1,752)	(1,850)	(1,948)	(2,045)	(2,143)	(2,241)	(2,348)	2,437	(2,535)	(2,632)	1,948	2,439	4.6%	4.6%
ITALY	(1,394,895)	(1,394,895)	1,142,317	1,365,906	1,676,462	(1,394,895)	(1,394,895)	(1,394,895)	(1,394,895)	(1,394,895)	1,394,895	1,394,895	0.0%	0.0%
LIECHTENSTEIN	(265)	(265)	(265)	(265)	(265)	(265)	(265)	(265)	(265)	(265)	265	264	-0.0%	-0.1%
LUXEMBOURG	(5,321)	(5,321)	(5,321)	(5,321)	(5,321)	(5,321)	(5,321)	(5,321)	(5,321)	(5,321)	5,321	5,321	0.0%	0.0%
NETHERLANDS	(223,599)	(223,599)	(223,599)	(223,599)	(223,599)	(223,599)	(223,599)	(223,599)	(223,599)	(223,599)	223,599	223,599	0.0%	0.0%
NORWAY	(54,340)	(54,340)	(54,340)	54,340	(57,247)	(60,153)	63,059	(71,804)	(80,548)	89,292	54,921	72,971	5.8%	5.7%
PORTUGAL	145,936	145,936	145,936	145,936	(145,836)	158,008	170,080	142,916	157,691	154,883	145,936	156,716	1.4%	0.7%
SPAIN	319,740	379,802	573,816	767,861	961,905	1,155,961	(987,985)	819,989	(866,174)	912,359	600,625	948,498	9.6%	12.4%
SWEDEN	(108,814)	(108,814)	(108,814)	(108,814)	(108,814)	106,409	111,219	(108,814)	(108,814)	(108,814)	108,814	108,814	0.0%	0.0%
SWITZERLAND	(139,380)	(139,380)	(139,380)	139,380	(156,007)	172,633	209,423	215,358	176,701	189,980	142,705	192,819	6.2%	3.5%
UK	(1,088,000)	(1,088,000)	(1,088,000)	(1,088,000)	(1,088,000)	1,088,000	1,118,000	1,152,000	1,221,000	1,331,000	1,088,000	1,182,000	1.7%	2.3%
WEST GERMANY	1,105,907	1,011,240	1,010,065	1,058,591	1,343,731	1,212,025	1,232,837	1,278,921	1,289,164	1,312,071	1,105,907	1,265,004	2.7%	1.9%
EU TOTAL	5,299,503	5,265,821	5,184,879	5,653,400	6,544,511	6,377,809	6,301,498	6,220,116	6,440,411	6,693,553	5,589,623	6,406,677	2.8%	2.6%
EFTA TOTAL	1,748,747	1,934,698	2,390,839	2,490,958	2,789,576	2,725,669	2,959,781	3,330,953	3,102,661	3,591,982	2,270,964	3,142,209	6.7%	8.3%
EUROPE TOTAL	7,048,250	7,200,519	7,575,718	8,144,358	9,334,087	9,103,478	9,261,279	9,551,069	9,543,072	10,285,535	7,860,566	9,548,887	4.0%	4.3%

Figures in parentheses are grossed

Library Users

Sector 3 – OTHER NON-MAJOR SPEC

	1981	1982	1983	1984	1985	1986	1987	1988	1989	1990	1981-85 Average	1986-90 Average	81/85 – 86/90 Year on Year Increase	Decade: Year on Year Increase
AUSTRIA	(68,556)	(68,556)	(68,556)	(68,556)	(68,556)	(68,556)	(68,556)	(68,556)	68,556	(68,556)	68,556	68,556	0.0%	0.0%
BELGIUM	(55,262)	(55,262)	(55,262)	(55,262)	(55,262)	(55,262)	(55,262)	(55,262)	(55,262)	(55,262)	55,262	55,262	0.0%	0.0%
DENMARK	0	0	0	0	0	0	0	0	0	0	0	0	0.0%	0.0%
EAST GERMANY	(137,839)	(137,839)	(137,839)	(137,839)	(137,839)	(137,839)	(137,839)	(137,839)	(137,839)	(135,848)	137,839	137,441	-0.1%	-0.2%
EIRE	(13,316)	(13,316)	(13,316)	(13,316)	(13,316)	13,316	12,633	11,565	10,801	10,323	13,316	11,728	-2.5%	-2.8%
FINLAND	0	0	0	0	0	0	0	0	0	0	0	0	0.0%	0.0%
FRANCE	(3,998,752)	(3,998,752)	(3,998,752)	(3,998,752)	(3,998,752)	3,998,752	4,296,697	4,109,155	3,328,059	3,938,463	3,998,752	3,934,225	-0.3%	-0.2%
GREECE	(55,166)	(55,166)	(55,166)	(55,166)	(55,166)	(55,166)	(55,166)	(55,166)	(55,166)	(55,166)	55,166	55,166	0.0%	0.0%
ICELAND	0	0	0	0	0	0	0	0	0	0	0	0	0.0%	0.0%
ITALY	(43,263)	(43,263)	(43,263)	(43,263)	(43,263)	43,263	(44,063)	(44,863)	45,663	(45,663)	43,263	44,703	0.7%	0.6%
LIECHTENSTEIN	0	0	0	0	0	0	0	0	0	0	0	0	0.0%	0.0%
LUXEMBOURG	0	0	0	0	0	0	0	0	0	0	0	0	0.0%	0.0%
NETHERLANDS	(80,518)	(80,518)	(80,518)	(80,518)	(80,518)	(80,518)	(80,518)	(80,518)	(80,518)	(80,518)	80,518	80,518	0.0%	0.0%
NORWAY	0	0	0	0	0	0	0	0	0	0	0	0	0.0%	0.0%
PORTUGAL	6,185	6,185	6,185	6,185	6,185	3,836	2,906	3,989	5,808	5,711	6,185	4,450	-6.4%	-0.9%
SPAIN	(213,951)	(213,951)	(213,951)	(213,951)	(213,951)	(213,951)	(213,951)	(213,951)	(213,951)	(213,951)	213,951	213,951	0.0%	0.0%
SWEDEN	(94,335)	(94,335)	(94,335)	(94,335)	(94,335)	(94,335)	(94,335)	(94,335)	(94,335)	(94,335)	94,335	94,335	0.0%	0.0%
SWITZERLAND	(191,228)	(191,228)	(191,228)	(191,228)	(191,228)	191,228	213,702	235,903	(245,669)	255,435	191,228	228,387	3.6%	3.3%
UK	(316,460)	(316,460)	(316,460)	(316,460)	(316,460)	(316,460)	(316,460)	(316,460)	(316,460)	(316,460)	316,460	316,460	0.0%	0.0%
WEST GERMANY	147,882	133,327	132,917	166,926	158,358	144,573	148,506	174,547	179,310	(179,310)	147,882	164,849	2.2%	2.2%
EU TOTAL	5,068,594	5,054,039	5,053,629	5,087,638	5,079,070	5,062,938	5,362,001	5,203,315	4,428,837	5,036,675	5,068,594	5,018,753	-0.2%	-0.1%
EFTA TOTAL	354,119	354,119	354,119	354,119	354,119	354,119	376,593	398,794	408,560	418,326	354,119	391,278	2.0%	1.9%
EUROPE TOTAL	5,422,713	5,408,158	5,407,748	5,441,757	5,433,189	5,417,055	5,738,594	5,602,109	4,837,397	5,455,001	5,422,713	5,410,031	-0.0%	0.1%

Sector 4 SCHOOLS

	1981	1982	1983	1984	1985	1986	1987	1988	1989	1990	1981-85 Average	1986-90 Average	81/85 – 86/90 Year on Year Increase	Decade: Year on Year Increase
AUSTRIA	(2,273)	(2,273)	(2,273)	(2,273)	(2,273)	(2,273)	(2,273)	(2,273)	(2,273)	(2,245)	2,273	2,267	-0.0%	-0.1%
BELGIUM	(663,604)	(663,604)	(663,604)	(663,604)	(663,604)	(663,604)	(663,604)	(663,604)	(663,604)	(663,604)	663,604	663,604	0.0%	0.0%
DENMARK	(357,000)	(357,000)	(357,000)	(357,000)	(357,000)	(357,000)	(357,000)	(357,000)	(357,000)	(357,000)	357,000	357,000	0.0%	0.0%
EAST GERMANY	(5,060)	(5,060)	(5,060)	(5,060)	(5,060)	(5,060)	(5,060)	(5,060)	(5,060)	(4,943)	5,060	5,037	-0.1%	-0.3%
EIRE	652,093	539,428	671,973	662,086	567,011	618,518	(611,803)	626,278	617,139	608,150	618,518	616,378	-0.1%	-0.8%
FINLAND	(666,500)	(666,500)	(666,500)	(666,500)	(666,500)	(668,500)	666,500	(676,777)	(687,053)	697,329	666,500	678,832	0.4%	0.5%
FRANCE	(3,975,733)	(3,975,733)	(3,975,733)	(3,975,733)	(3,975,733)	(3,975,733)	(3,975,733)	(3,975,733)	(3,975,733)	(3,975,733)	3,975,733	3,975,733	0.0%	0.0%
GREECE	(700,033)	(700,033)	(700,033)	(700,033)	(700,033)	(700,033)	(700,033)	(700,033)	(700,033)	(700,033)	700,033	700,033	0.0%	0.0%
ICELAND	(184)	(184)	(184)	(184)	(184)	(184)	(184)	(184)	(184)	(184)	184	184	0.0%	0.0%
ITALY	4,215,151	(4,215,151)	(4,215,151)	(4,215,151)	(4,215,151)	(4,215,151)	(4,215,151)	(4,215,151)	(4,215,151)	(4,215,151)	4,215,151	4,215,151	0.0%	0.0%
LIECHTENSTEIN	(9)	(9)	(9)	(9)	(9)	(9)	(9)	(9)	(9)	(9)	9	9	0.0%	0.0%
LUXEMBOURG	(22,927)	(22,927)	(22,927)	(22,927)	(22,927)	(22,927)	(22,927)	(22,927)	(22,927)	(22,927)	22,927	22,927	0.0%	0.0%
NETHERLANDS	(1,072,887)	(1,072,887)	(1,072,887)	(1,072,887)	(1,072,887)	(1,072,887)	(1,072,887)	(1,072,887)	(1,072,887)	(1,072,887)	1,072,887	1,072,887	0.0%	0.0%
NORWAY	(6,661)	(6,661)	(6,661)	(6,661)	6,719	(6,809)	(6,517)	(6,865)	(7,040)	(6,874)	6,673	6,821	0.4%	0.4%
PORTUGAL	(819,164)	(819,164)	(819,164)	(819,164)	819,164	887,921	910,483	992,051	(992,051)	(992,051)	819,164	914,911	2.2%	2.2%
SPAIN	(211,768)	(211,768)	(211,768)	(211,768)	(211,768)	(211,768)	(211,768)	(211,768)	(211,768)	(211,768)	211,768	211,768	0.0%	0.0%
SWEDEN	(1,377,000)	(1,377,000)	(1,377,000)	1,377,000	(1,377,000)	(1,377,000)	(1,377,000)	(1,377,000)	(1,377,000)	(1,377,000)	1,377,000	1,377,000	0.0%	0.0%
SWITZERLAND	(1,894)	(1,894)	(1,894)	(1,894)	(1,894)	(1,894)	(1,894)	(1,894)	(1,894)	(1,878)	1,894	1,891	-0.0%	-0.1%
UK	(663,604)	(663,604)	(663,604)	(663,604)	(663,604)	(663,604)	(663,604)	(663,604)	(663,604)	(663,604)	663,604	663,604	0.0%	0.0%
WEST GERMANY	(3,958,151)	(3,958,151)	(3,958,151)	(3,958,151)	(3,958,151)	(3,958,151)	(3,958,151)	(3,958,151)	(3,958,151)	(3,958,151)	3,958,151	3,958,151	0.0%	0.0%
EU TOTAL	17,317,175	17,204,510	17,337,055	17,327,168	17,232,093	17,152,357	17,368,204	17,464,247	17,455,108	17,446,002	17,283,600	17,377,184	0.1%	0.1%
EFTA TOTAL	2,054,521	2,054,521	2,054,521	2,054,521	2,054,579	2,054,669	2,054,377	2,065,002	2,075,453	2,085,519	2,054,533	2,067,004	0.1%	0.2%
EUROPE TOTAL	19,371,696	19,259,031	19,391,576	19,381,689	19,286,672	19,207,026	19,422,581	19,529,249	19,530,561	19,531,521	19,338,133	19,444,188	0.1%	0.1%

Figures in parentheses are grossed.

Library Users

Sector 5 SPECIAL

	1981	1982	1983	1984	1985	1986	1987	1988	1989	1990	1981-85 Average	1986-90 Average	81/85 – 86/90 Year on Year Increase	Decade: Year on Year Increase
AUSTRIA	(194,533)	(194,533)	(194,533)	(194,533)	(194,533)	(194,533)	(194,533)	(194,533)	(194,533)	(195,867)	194,533	194,800	0.0%	0.1%
BELGIUM	(61,271)	(61,271)	(61,271)	(61,271)	(61,271)	(61,271)	(61,271)	(61,271)	(61,271)	(61,271)	61,271	61,271	0.0%	0.0%
DENMARK	(31,430)	(31,430)	(31,430)	(31,430)	(31,430)	(31,430)	(31,430)	(31,430)	(31,430)	(31,430)	31,430	31,430	0.0%	0.0%
EAST GERMANY	(425,648)	(425,648)	(425,648)	(425,648)	(425,648)	(425,648)	(425,648)	(425,648)	(425,648)	(418,868)	425,648	424,292	-0.1%	-0.2%
EIRE	(3,149)	(3,149)	(3,149)	(3,149)	(3,149)	(3,149)	(3,149)	(3,149)	(3,149)	(3,149)	3,149	3,149	0.0%	0.0%
FINLAND	(37,539)	(39,863)	(42,847)	(48,857)	(51,058)	(52,637)	(54,235)	(53,758)	(61,176)	(60,421)	44,033	56,445	5.1%	5.4%
FRANCE	(331,168)	(331,168)	(331,168)	(331,168)	(331,168)	(331,168)	(331,168)	(331,168)	(331,168)	(331,168)	331,168	331,168	0.0%	0.0%
GREECE	(59,511)	(59,511)	(59,511)	(59,511)	(59,511)	(59,511)	(59,511)	(59,511)	(59,511)	(59,511)	59,511	59,511	0.0%	0.0%
ICELAND	(1,507)	(1,651)	(1,831)	(2,071)	(2,432)	(2,792)	(3,153)	(3,513)	(4,234)	(4,955)	1,898	3,729	14.5%	14.1%
ITALY	505,640	505,640	532,972	479,508	504,441	(505,640)	(505,640)	(505,640)	(505,640)	(505,640)	505,640	505,640	-0.0%	0.0%
LIECHTENSTEIN	0	0	0	0	0	0	0	0	0	0	0	0	0.0%	0.0%
LUXEMBOURG	(2,051)	(2,051)	(2,051)	(2,051)	(2,051)	(2,051)	(2,051)	(2,051)	(2,051)	(2,051)	2,051	2,051	0.0%	0.0%
NETHERLANDS	(90,152)	(90,152)	(90,152)	(90,152)	(90,152)	(90,152)	(90,152)	(90,152)	(90,152)	(90,152)	90,152	90,152	0.0%	0.0%
NORWAY	(64,476)	(64,476)	(64,476)	(64,476)	(64,476)	(64,476)	(64,476)	(64,476)	(64,476)	(64,476)	64,476	64,476	0.0%	0.0%
PORTUGAL	(44,273)	(44,273)	(44,273)	(44,273)	(44,273)	44,273	65,889	178,784	121,659	(121,659)	44,273	106,453	19.2%	11.9%
SPAIN	215,621	215,621	276,442	337,264	398,085	458,906	(489,831)	520,755	(469,359)	417,962	288,607	471,363	10.3%	7.6%
SWEDEN	(34,448)	(34,448)	(34,448)	(34,448)	(34,448)	34,448	34,695	34,695	(34,695)	(34,695)	34,448	34,646	0.1%	0.1%
SWITZERLAND	(171,759)	(171,759)	(171,759)	(171,759)	(171,759)	(171,759)	(171,759)	(171,759)	(171,759)	(173,006)	171,759	172,008	0.0%	0.1%
UK	(342,556)	(342,556)	(342,556)	(342,556)	(342,556)	(342,556)	(342,556)	(342,556)	(342,556)	(342,556)	342,556	342,556	0.0%	0.0%
WEST GERMANY	288,981	275,131	244,243	353,666	356,565	359,464	327,118	391,001	310,947	310,947	303,717	339,895	2.3%	0.8%
EU TOTAL	2,401,451	2,387,601	2,444,866	2,561,647	2,650,300	2,715,219	2,735,414	2,943,116	2,754,541	2,696,364	2,489,173	2,768,931	2.2%	1.3%
EFTA TOTAL	504,262	506,730	509,894	516,144	518,706	520,845	522,851	522,734	530,873	533,420	511,147	526,105	0.6%	0.6%
EUROPE TOTAL	2,905,713	2,894,331	2,954,760	3,077,791	3,169,006	3,235,864	3,258,265	3,465,850	3,285,414	3,229,784	3,000,320	3,295,035	1.9%	1.2%

Sector 6 PUBLIC

	1981	1982	1983	1984	1985	1986	1987	1988	1989	1990	1981-85 Average	1986-90 Average	81/85 – 86/90 Year on Year Increase	Decade: Year on Year Increase
AUSTRIA	(813,102)	(813,102)	(813,102)	813,102	(794,993)	(798,615)	802,237	815,508	782,860	869,292	809,480	813,702	0.1%	0.7%
BELGIUM	1,429,818	1,559,313	1,628,537	1,686,527	1,743,269	1,743,269	(1,743,269)	(1,743,269)	(1,743,269)	(1,743,269)	1,609,093	1,743,269	1.6%	2.2%
DENMARK	2,561,000	2,559,500	2,557,000	2,555,500	2,555,500	(2,557,700)	(2,557,700)	(2,557,700)	(2,557,700)	(2,557,700)	2,557,700	2,557,700	0.0%	-0.0%
EAST GERMANY	(4,621,032)	(4,621,032)	(4,621,032)	(4,621,032)	(4,621,032)	(4,621,032)	(4,621,032)	(4,621,032)	(4,621,032)	(4,621,032)	4,621,032	4,621,032	0.0%	0.0%
EIRE	677,653	703,307	657,752	654,579	647,437	668,043	697,807	689,420	683,133	742,414	668,146	696,163	0.8%	1.0%
FINLAND	(1,978,560)	(1,978,560)	(1,978,560)	1,978,560	2,072,135	2,074,417	2,149,494	2,178,355	2,176,190	2,198,665	1,997,275	2,155,424	1.5%	1.2%
FRANCE	2,991,200	3,201,800	3,532,200	3,577,000	3,783,393	(3,943,295)	4,103,197	(4,263,098)	4,423,000	4,605,240	3,417,119	4,267,566	4.5%	4.9%
GREECE	(1,170,049)	(1,170,049)	(1,170,049)	(1,170,049)	(1,170,049)	1,399,719	(1,399,719)	(1,399,719)	(1,399,719)	(1,399,719)	1,170,049	1,399,719	3.6%	2.0%
ICELAND	92,948	92,402	80,364	83,892	76,997	81,215	75,157	74,140	83,094	94,578	85,321	81,637	-0.9%	0.2%
ITALY	(6,756,359)	(6,756,359)	(6,756,359)	(6,756,359)	(6,756,359)	(6,756,359)	(6,756,359)	(6,756,359)	(6,756,359)	(6,756,359)	6,756,359	6,756,359	0.0%	0.0%
LIECHTENSTEIN	(64)	(66)	(69)	(71)	(74)	(76)	(79)	(81)	(83)	(86)	69	81	3.3%	3.3%
LUXEMBOURG	(43,505)	(43,505)	(43,505)	(43,505)	(43,505)	(43,505)	(43,505)	(43,505)	(43,505)	(43,505)	43,505	43,505	0.0%	0.0%
NETHERLANDS	4,117,000	4,270,000	4,160,000	4,047,000	4,162,000	4,182,000	4,220,000	4,246,000	4,261,000	4,346,000	4,151,200	4,251,000	0.5%	0.6%
NORWAY	(57,950)	(59,115)	(60,280)	(61,445)	(62,810)	(63,776)	(66,292)	(66,601)	(67,297)	(68,436)	60,280	66,480	2.0%	1.9%
PORTUGAL	(189,374)	(189,374)	(189,374)	(189,374)	(189,374)	(189,374)	283,274	238,624	329,997	381,006	189,374	280,455	8.2%	8.1%
SPAIN	1,341,674	1,546,112	1,863,929	2,181,727	2,499,535	2,817,342	(3,135,150)	3,452,957	(3,770,765)	4,088,572	1,886,595	3,452,957	12.9%	13.2%
SWEDEN	(150,074)	(152,535)	(154,997)	(157,459)	(159,920)	(162,382)	(165,787)	(168,823)	(171,275)	(172,228)	154,997	168,099	1.6%	1.5%
SWITZERLAND	303,397	310,433	320,449	333,126	351,444	351,444	(351,444)	(351,444)	(351,444)	(351,444)	323,770	351,444	1.7%	1.6%
UK	33,076,783	33,076,783	33,076,783	33,076,783	33,076,783	33,076,783	33,014,661	33,090,160	33,196,109	33,292,696	33,076,783	33,134,082	0.0%	0.1%
WEST GERMANY	6,058,796	6,340,133	6,174,357	6,217,684	6,585,721	6,627,100	6,827,100	6,723,291	6,566,950	6,566,950	6,275,338	6,622,278	1.1%	0.9%
EU TOTAL	65,034,243	66,037,267	66,428,877	66,777,119	67,833,957	68,625,521	69,182,773	69,825,134	70,352,538	71,144,462	66,422,293	69,826,086	1.0%	1.0%
EFTA TOTAL	3,396,095	3,406,213	3,407,821	3,427,655	3,518,173	3,531,925	3,610,490	3,654,362	3,632,243	3,754,729	3,431,191	3,636,868	1.2%	1.1%
EUROPE TOTAL	68,430,338	69,443,480	69,836,698	70,204,774	71,352,130	72,157,446	72,793,263	73,480,086	73,984,781	74,899,191	69,853,484	73,462,953	1.0%	1.0%

Figures in parentheses are grossed.

Library Users

ALL SECTORS	1981	1982	1983	1984	1985	1986	1987	1988	1989	1990	1981-85 Average	1986-90 Average	81/85 – 86/90 Year on Year Increase	Decade: Year on Year Increase
AUSTRIA	2,853,243	3,044,642	3,506,231	3,611,799	3,878,222	3,836,228	4,014,499	4,389,285	4,042,163	4,730,527	3,378,827	4,202,540	4.5%	5.8%
BELGIUM	2,396,837	2,525,147	2,577,386	2,649,132	2,686,598	2,704,511	2,707,824	2,711,137	2,714,450	2,715,350	2,567,020	2,710,655	1.1%	1.4%
DENMARK	3,110,395	3,109,818	3,109,115	3,108,976	3,111,239	3,113,439	3,116,819	3,120,200	3,115,979	3,120,937	3,109,909	3,117,475	0.0%	0.0%
EAST GERMANY	5,918,287	5,918,287	5,918,287	5,918,287	5,920,395	5,922,503	5,924,611	5,924,611	5,924,611	5,915,723	5,918,709	5,922,412	0.0%	-0.0%
EIRE	1,430,260	1,343,249	1,430,239	1,417,179	1,314,962	1,387,075	1,409,441	1,414,461	1,398,271	1,443,385	1,387,178	1,410,527	0.3%	0.1%
FINLAND	2,886,676	2,891,148	2,895,389	2,903,573	3,001,301	3,001,075	3,076,571	3,124,572	3,150,503	3,189,991	2,915,617	3,108,663	1.3%	1.1%
FRANCE	11,818,993	12,029,593	12,336,993	12,382,793	12,686,186	12,881,088	13,360,390	13,362,117	12,822,819	13,687,067	12,250,912	13,222,696	1.5%	1.6%
GREECE	2,315,929	2,315,929	2,315,929	2,315,929	2,315,929	2,545,599	2,545,599	2,545,599	2,545,599	2,545,599	2,315,929	2,545,599	1.9%	1.1%
ICELAND	108,080	107,776	96,016	99,881	94,223	98,717	92,966	92,685	100,611	112,632	101,195	99,522	-0.3%	0.5%
ITALY	13,561,360	13,561,360	13,269,679	13,516,679	13,897,724	13,561,360	13,562,160	13,562,960	13,563,760	13,563,760	13,561,360	13,562,800	0.0%	0.0%
LIECHTENSTEIN	12,338	12,340	12,343	12,345	12,348	10,450	11,153	12,455	13,407	14,307	12,343	12,354	0.0%	1.7%
LUXEMBOURG	85,804	86,804	87,804	88,804	89,804	91,804	93,354	94,604	96,504	98,454	87,804	94,944	1.6%	1.5%
NETHERLANDS	5,634,156	5,787,156	5,677,156	5,564,156	5,679,156	5,699,156	5,748,919	5,786,924	5,813,134	5,909,926	5,668,356	5,791,612	0.4%	0.5%
NORWAY	260,954	262,119	263,284	264,449	268,579	272,741	277,871	288,341	300,743	301,683	263,877	288,276	1.8%	1.6%
PORTUGAL	1,238,941	1,265,074	1,241,570	1,241,838	1,248,088	1,153,961	1,480,412	1,624,968	1,672,305	1,698,743	1,247,102	1,526,082	4.1%	3.6%
SPAIN	2,347,562	2,614,327	3,244,998	3,822,067	4,399,144	4,976,252	5,161,394	5,257,822	5,587,381	5,900,521	3,285,620	5,376,674	10.4%	10.8%
SWEDEN	1,767,771	1,770,232	1,772,694	1,775,156	1,777,617	1,777,674	1,786,436	1,787,067	1,789,519	1,790,472	1,772,694	1,786,234	0.2%	0.1%
SWITZERLAND	820,546	827,582	837,558	850,275	885,220	901,846	957,581	986,002	954,561	979,346	844,244	955,867	2.5%	2.0%
UK	38,686,099	38,368,798	38,351,225	38,470,100	38,586,836	38,492,612	38,460,490	38,569,989	38,744,938	38,951,525	38,492,612	38,643,911	0.1%	0.1%
WEST GERMANY	11,635,501	11,789,006	11,592,663	11,827,403	12,489,324	12,382,535	12,367,357	12,595,979	12,369,013	12,391,920	11,866,779	12,421,361	0.9%	0.7%
EU TOTAL	100,180,124	100,714,548	101,153,044	102,323,343	104,425,385	104,911,916	105,938,770	106,571,371	106,368,765	107,942,910	101,759,289	106,346,746	0.9%	0.8%
EFTA TOTAL	8,709,608	8,915,839	9,383,555	9,517,478	9,917,510	9,899,335	10,217,077	10,680,407	10,351,507	11,118,958	9,288,798	10,453,457	2.4%	2.8%
EUROPE TOTAL	108,889,732	109,630,387	110,536,599	111,840,821	114,342,895	114,811,251	116,155,847	117,251,778	116,720,272	119,061,868	111,048,087	116,800,203	1.0%	1.0%

Library Users per 1000 Population

European Union	1981	1982	1983	1984	1985	1986	1987	1988	1989	1990	1981-85 Average	1986-90 Average	81/85 – 86/90 Year on Year Increase	Decade: Year on Year Increase
Sector 1	14.97	14.10	13.92	14.54	15.01	14.61	14.64	14.37	14.61	14.54	14.51	14.55	0.1%	-0.3%
Sector 2	15.68	15.58	15.34	16.73	19.32	18.72	18.50	18.19	19.05	19.76	16.53	18.84	2.7%	2.6%
Sector 3	14.99	14.95	14.95	15.05	14.99	14.86	15.74	15.21	13.10	14.87	14.99	14.76	-0.3%	-0.1%
Sector 4	51.23	50.90	51.29	51.26	50.86	50.35	50.98	51.07	51.64	51.50	51.11	51.10	-0.0%	1.3%
Sector 5	7.10	7.06	7.23	7.58	7.82	7.97	8.03	8.61	8.15	7.96	7.36	8.14	2.0%	1.0%
Sector 6	192.40	195.36	196.52	197.55	200.23	201.43	203.08	204.17	208.11	210.00	196.41	205.36	0.9%	1.0%
All Sectors	296.37	297.95	299.25	302.71	308.23	307.94	310.97	311.61	314.66	318.62	300.90	312.76	0.8%	0.8%

EFTA	1981	1982	1983	1984	1985	1986	1987	1988	1989	1990	1981-85 Average	1986-90 Average	81/85 – 86/90 Year on Year Increase	Decade: Year on Year Increase
Sector 1	20.28	20.52	20.74	20.98	21.23	22.17	21.56	22.03	18.72	22.72	20.75	21.44	0.7%	1.3%
Sector 2	54.42	60.20	74.40	77.51	86.80	84.82	92.10	103.65	96.55	111.03	70.67	97.63	6.7%	8.2%
Sector 3	11.02	11.02	11.02	11.02	11.02	11.02	11.72	12.41	12.71	12.93	11.02	12.16	2.0%	1.8%
Sector 4	63.93	63.93	63.93	63.93	63.93	63.94	63.93	64.26	64.58	64.23	63.93	64.23	0.1%	0.1%
Sector 5	15.69	15.77	15.87	16.06	16.14	16.20	16.27	16.27	16.52	16.49	15.91	16.35	0.6%	0.6%
Sector 6	105.68	105.99	106.04	106.66	109.48	109.90	112.35	113.73	113.03	116.06	106.77	113.01	1.1%	1.0%
All Sectors	271.02	277.44	291.99	296.16	308.61	308.04	317.93	332.35	322.11	343.70	289.04	324.83	2.4%	2.7%

Europe Total	1981	1982	1983	1984	1985	1986	1987	1988	1989	1990	1981-85 Average	1986-90 Average	81/85 – 86/90 Year on Year Increase	Decade: Year on Year Increase
Sector 1	15.43	14.66	14.51	15.10	15.55	15.26	15.24	15.03	14.96	15.25	15.05	15.15	0.1%	-0.1%
Sector 2	19.04	19.45	20.47	22.00	25.16	24.42	24.84	25.53	25.78	27.71	21.23	25.66	3.9%	4.3%
Sector 3	14.65	14.61	14.61	14.70	14.65	14.53	15.39	14.97	13.07	14.70	14.64	14.53	-0.2%	0.0%
Sector 4	52.33	52.03	52.39	52.36	52.00	51.52	52.10	52.20	52.76	52.63	52.22	52.24	0.0%	0.1%
Sector 5	7.85	7.82	7.98	8.31	8.54	8.68	8.74	9.26	8.88	8.70	8.10	8.85	1.8%	1.2%
Sector 6	184.87	187.61	188.67	189.66	192.36	193.54	195.26	196.40	199.86	201.81	188.63	197.37	0.9%	1.0%
All Sectors	294.17	296.17	298.62	302.14	308.27	307.95	311.57	313.40	315.30	320.81	299.87	313.80	0.9%	1.0%

- 162 -

Library Consultations

Sector 1 - NATIONAL

	1981	1982	1983	1984	1985	1986	1987	1988	1989	1990	1981-85 Average	1986-90 Average	81/85 - 86/90 Year on Year Increase	Decade: Year on Year Increase
AUSTRIA	(317,040)	(321,195)	(325,350)	(329,505)	(333,661)	(338,771)	(341,067)	(344,944)	(349,795)	(354,437)	325,350	345,803	1.2%	1.2%
BELGIUM	305,719	364,120	310,396	342,021	358,422	(336,136)	(336,136)	(336,136)	(336,136)	(336,136)	336,136	336,136	0.0%	1.1%
DENMARK	251,600	262,628	282,375	(279,800)	(277,100)	(280,195)	(283,289)	286,383	327,356	386,873	270,701	312,819	2.9%	4.9%
EAST GERMANY	(1,546,483)	(1,546,483)	(1,546,483)	(1,546,483)	(1,546,483)	(1,546,483)	(1,546,483)	(1,546,483)	(1,546,483)	(1,546,483)	1,546,483	1,546,483	0.0%	0.0%
EIRE	(119,770)	(119,770)	(119,770)	(119,770)	(119,770)	(119,770)	(119,770)	(119,770)	(119,770)	(119,770)	119,770	119,770	0.0%	0.0%
FINLAND	(458,837)	(458,837)	(458,837)	(458,837)	(458,837)	(458,837)	(458,837)	458,837	417,368	(417,368)	458,837	442,249	-0.7%	-1.0%
FRANCE	1,819,534	1,676,918	1,748,226	1,748,226	1,748,226	(1,576,151)	(1,404,076)	1,232,000	1,362,000	1,256,000	1,748,226	1,366,045	-4.8%	-4.0%
GREECE	(22,286)	22,286	38,500	37,000	34,987	34,987	(34,987)	(34,987)	(34,987)	(34,987)	31,012	34,987	2.4%	5.1%
ICELAND	(37,443)	(37,443)	(37,443)	(37,443)	(37,443)	(37,443)	37,443	35,301	(35,301)	(35,301)	37,443	36,158	-0.7%	-0.7%
ITALY	(55,682)	(55,682)	(55,682)	(55,682)	(55,682)	(55,682)	(55,682)	(55,682)	(55,682)	(55,682)	55,682	55,682	0.0%	0.0%
LIECHTENSTEIN	(45,380)	(45,380)	(45,380)	(45,380)	(45,380)	29,500	35,500	51,800	53,600	56,500	45,380	45,380	0.0%	2.5%
LUXEMBOURG	60,000	70,000	80,000	90,000	100,000	110,000	116,000	125,000	132,000	135,000	80,000	123,600	9.1%	9.4%
NETHERLANDS	125,000	60,000	118,000	132,000	144,000	154,000	168,000	169,000	169,200	(169,200)	115,800	165,480	7.4%	3.4%
NORWAY	(105,000)	(105,000)	(105,000)	105,000	91,462	77,923	95,000	(95,000)	(95,000)	(95,000)	102,292	91,585	-2.2%	-1.1%
PORTUGAL	221,751	234,773	173,154	177,435	206,831	354,428	349,684	249,919	354,412	340,161	202,789	329,721	10.2%	4.9%
SPAIN	(1,303,975)	(1,303,975)	(1,303,975)	(1,303,975)	(1,303,975)	(1,303,975)	(1,303,975)	(1,303,975)	(1,303,975)	(1,303,975)	1,303,975	1,303,975	0.0%	0.0%
SWEDEN	(114,000)	(114,000)	(114,000)	114,000	(122,561)	131,121	130,252	123,275	118,452	121,511	115,712	124,922	1.5%	0.7%
SWITZERLAND	(100,846)	(100,846)	(100,846)	(100,846)	(100,846)	101,458	104,487	102,833	95,878	99,578	100,846	100,846	0.0%	-0.1%
UK	(4,285,000)	(4,285,000)	(4,285,000)	(4,285,000)	(4,285,000)	4,285,000	(4,345,500)	4,406,000	(4,430,500)	4,455,000	4,285,000	4,384,400	0.5%	0.4%
WEST GERMANY	1,796,000	1,628,000	1,710,000	1,864,000	1,982,000	1,989,880	1,997,761	2,005,642	2,013,523	2,013,523	1,796,000	2,004,066	2.2%	1.3%
EU TOTAL	11,912,800	11,629,635	11,771,561	11,981,392	12,162,476	12,146,687	12,059,343	11,870,977	12,186,024	12,152,790	11,891,573	12,083,164	0.3%	0.2%
EFTA TOTAL	1,178,546	1,182,701	1,186,856	1,191,011	1,190,190	1,175,051	1,202,586	1,211,990	1,165,394	1,179,695	1,185,861	1,186,943	0.0%	0.0%
EUROPE TOTAL	13,091,346	12,812,336	12,958,417	13,172,403	13,352,666	13,321,738	13,261,929	13,082,967	13,351,418	13,332,485	13,077,434	13,270,107	0.3%	0.2%

Sector 2 - HIGHER EDUCATION

	1981	1982	1983	1984	1985	1986	1987	1988	1989	1990	1981-85 Average	1986-90 Average	81/85 - 86/90 Year on Year Increase	Decade: Year on Year Increase
AUSTRIA	793,198	777,685	917,982	974,305	1,145,580	1,161,036	1,267,284	1,387,408	1,408,753	1,350,909	921,750	1,315,078	7.4%	6.1%
BELGIUM	(632,632)	(632,632)	(632,632)	(632,632)	(632,632)	632,632	682,872	660,562	676,766	704,766	632,632	671,520	1.2%	1.2%
DENMARK	1,927,000	2,053,000	2,361,000	2,366,200	2,370,400	(2,079,331)	(1,788,262)	1,497,193	1,559,967	1,760,029	2,215,520	1,736,960	-4.8%	-1.0%
EAST GERMANY	(5,493,958)	(5,493,958)	(5,493,958)	5,493,958	(5,711,749)	(5,929,541)	6,147,333	(6,147,333)	(6,147,333)	(6,147,333)	5,537,516	6,103,775	2.0%	1.3%
EIRE	932,000	885,000	989,000	1,088,000	1,077,000	1,072,000	1,116,000	1,205,000	1,157,000	1,164,000	994,200	1,142,800	2.8%	2.5%
FINLAND	1,904,755	2,050,224	2,204,907	2,210,049	2,359,903	2,325,164	2,458,510	2,618,202	2,587,034	2,612,449	2,145,968	2,520,272	3.3%	3.6%
FRANCE	3,460,000	3,600,000	7,129,000	7,343,000	7,679,000	8,391,000	8,652,000	9,279,000	9,711,000	9,275,800	5,842,200	9,275,800	9.7%	12.9%
GREECE	(1,766,360)	(1,766,360)	(1,766,360)	(1,766,360)	(1,766,360)	(1,766,360)	(1,766,360)	(1,766,360)	(1,766,360)	(1,766,360)	1,766,360	1,766,360	0.0%	0.0%
ICELAND	(30,600)	(30,600)	(30,600)	(30,600)	(30,600)	27,500	28,800	28,900	31,500	36,300	30,600	30,600	0.0%	1.8%
ITALY	(60,546)	(60,546)	46,871	55,848	78,919	(81,260)	83,641	(78,977)	(88,170)	(97,363)	60,546	85,886	7.2%	5.4%
LIECHTENSTEIN	(9,437)	(9,437)	(9,437)	(9,437)	(9,437)	(9,437)	(9,437)	(9,437)	(9,437)	(9,352)	9,437	9,420	-0.0%	-0.1%
LUXEMBOURG	(73,210)	(73,210)	(73,210)	(73,210)	(73,210)	(73,210)	(73,210)	(73,210)	(73,210)	(73,210)	73,210	73,210	0.0%	0.0%
NETHERLANDS	3,883,000	3,891,000	3,929,000	3,901,000	4,151,000	4,151,000	4,210,000	4,187,000	4,132,000	(4,132,000)	3,939,800	4,162,400	1.1%	0.7%
NORWAY	(815,393)	(815,393)	(815,393)	815,393	(1,005,197)	1,195,000	(1,199,500)	1,204,000	1,348,000	1,523,000	853,354	1,293,900	8.7%	7.2%
PORTUGAL	(305,940)	(305,940)	(305,940)	(305,940)	(305,940)	305,940	513,934	404,424	499,260	535,942	305,940	451,900	8.1%	6.4%
SPAIN	(7,396,170)	(7,396,170)	(7,396,170)	(7,396,170)	(7,396,170)	(7,396,170)	(7,396,170)	7,396,170	(7,491,176)	7,586,181	7,396,170	7,453,173	0.2%	0.3%
SWEDEN	(1,896,469)	(1,896,469)	(1,896,469)	1,168,153	2,001,000	1,954,498	1,915,296	1,993,432	2,067,023	2,175,878	1,771,712	2,021,225	2.7%	1.5%
SWITZERLAND	(1,260,276)	(1,260,276)	(1,896,469)	1,260,276	(1,315,215)	1,370,153	1,785,154	1,420,009	1,861,309	1,749,039	1,271,264	1,637,133	5.2%	3.7%
UK	(30,152,000)	(30,152,000)	(30,152,000)	(30,152,000)	(30,152,000)	30,152,000	30,996,000	31,926,000	33,842,000	34,897,000	30,152,000	32,362,600	1.4%	1.6%
WEST GERMANY	29,601,750	26,572,000	29,338,000	31,704,000	30,793,000	(32,643,823)	(34,494,647)	(36,345,471)	38,196,295	(38,196,295)	29,601,750	35,975,306	4.0%	2.9%
EU TOTAL	85,684,566	82,881,816	89,613,141	92,278,318	94,674,287	(97,920,429)	100,966,700	105,340,557	107,406,479	88,517,844	101,261,690	2.7%	2.5%
EFTA TOTAL	6,710,128	6,840,084	7,135,064	6,468,213	7,866,932	8,042,788	8,663,981	8,661,388	9,313,056	9,456,927	7,004,064	8,827,628	4.7%	3.9%
EUROPE TOTAL	92,394,694	89,721,900	96,748,205	98,746,531	99,998,312	102,717,075	106,584,410	109,628,088	114,653,613	116,863,406	95,521,928	110,089,318	2.9%	2.6%

Figures in parentheses are grossed.

Library Consultations

Sector 3 – OTHER NON-MAJOR SPEC.

	1981	1982	1983	1984	1985	1986	1987	1988	1989	1990	1981–85 Average	1986–90 Average	81/85 – 86/90 Year on Year Increase	Decade: Year on Year Increase
AUSTRIA	(479,047)	(479,047)	(479,047)	(479,047)	(479,047)	(479,047)	(479,047)	(479,047)	(479,047)	(479,047)	479,047	479,047	0.0%	0.0%
BELGIUM	(332,961)	(332,961)	(332,961)	(332,961)	(332,961)	(332,961)	(332,961)	(332,961)	(332,961)	(332,961)	332,961	332,961	0.0%	0.0%
DENMARK	0	0	0	0	0	0	0	0	0	0	0	0	0.0%	0.0%
EAST GERMANY	(8,176,064)	(8,176,064)	(8,176,064)	(8,176,064)	(8,176,064)	(8,176,064)	(8,176,064)	(8,176,064)	(8,176,064)	(8,057,945)	8,176,064	8,152,440	-0.1%	-0.2%
EIRE	(108,982)	(108,982)	(108,982)	(108,982)	(108,982)	108,982	102,978	98,002	100,668	91,955	108,982	100,517	-1.6%	-1.9%
FINLAND	0	0	0	0	0	0	0	0	0	0	0	0	0.0%	0.0%
FRANCE	(1,847,483)	(1,847,483)	(1,847,483)	(1,847,483)	(1,847,483)	(1,847,483)	(1,847,483)	(1,847,483)	(1,847,483)	(1,847,483)	1,847,483	1,847,483	0.0%	0.0%
GREECE	(332,379)	(332,379)	(332,379)	(332,379)	(332,379)	(332,379)	(332,379)	(332,379)	(332,379)	(332,379)	332,379	332,379	0.0%	0.0%
ICELAND	0	0	0	0	0	0	0	0	0	0	0	0	0.0%	0.0%
ITALY	84,525	84,525	72,126	75,969	105,481	177,351	(169,766)	(162,182)	154,598	(154,598)	84,525	163,699	14.1%	6.9%
LIECHTENSTEIN	0	0	0	0	0	0	0	0	0	0	0	0	0.0%	0.0%
LUXEMBOURG	0	0	0	0	0	0	0	0	0	0	0	0	0.0%	0.0%
NETHERLANDS	(203,600)	(203,600)	(203,600)	(203,600)	(256,000)	256,000	(221,067)	(221,067)	(221,067)	(221,067)	214,080	228,054	1.3%	0.9%
NORWAY	0	0	0	0	0	0	0	0	0	0	0	0	0.0%	0.0%
PORTUGAL	(9,022)	(9,022)	(9,022)	(9,022)	(9,022)	9,022	6,017	7,932	9,969	11,116	9,022	8,811	-0.5%	2.3%
SPAIN	(1,289,080)	(1,289,080)	(1,289,080)	(1,289,080)	(1,289,080)	(1,289,080)	(1,289,080)	(1,289,080)	(1,289,080)	(1,289,080)	1,289,080	1,289,080	0.0%	0.0%
SWEDEN	(1,637,876)	(1,637,876)	(1,637,876)	(1,637,876)	(1,637,876)	(1,637,876)	1,906,408	1,798,511	1,208,708	(1,637,876)	1,637,876	1,637,876	-0.0%	0.0%
SWITZERLAND	(6,256,041)	(6,256,041)	(6,256,041)	(6,256,041)	(6,256,041)	6,243,738	6,923,413	3,315,676	7,766,320	7,031,061	6,256,041	6,256,041	0.0%	1.3%
UK	(1,906,712)	(1,906,712)	(1,906,712)	(1,906,712)	(1,906,712)	(1,906,712)	(1,906,712)	(1,906,712)	(1,906,712)	(1,906,712)	1,906,712	1,906,712	0.0%	0.0%
WEST GERMANY	3,134,500	2,849,000	2,801,000	3,325,000	3,563,000	3,979,182	3,916,147	3,514,413	3,717,073	(3,717,073)	3,134,500	3,768,778	3.8%	1.9%
EU TOTAL	17,425,308	17,139,808	17,079,409	17,607,252	17,927,164	18,415,216	18,300,654	17,888,275	18,088,054	17,962,369	17,435,788	18,130,914	0.8%	0.3%
EFTA TOTAL	8,372,964	8,372,964	8,372,964	8,372,964	8,372,964	8,360,659	9,308,868	5,593,234	9,454,075	9,147,984	8,372,964	8,372,964	0.0%	1.0%
EUROPE TOTAL	25,798,272	25,512,772	25,452,373	25,980,216	26,300,128	26,775,875	27,609,522	23,481,509	27,542,129	27,110,353	25,808,752	26,503,878	0.5%	0.6%

Sector 4 SCHOOLS

	1981	1982	1983	1984	1985	1986	1987	1988	1989	1990	1981–85 Average	1986–90 Average	81/85 – 86/90 Year on Year Increase	Decade: Year on Year Increase
AUSTRIA	(7,388,954)	(7,388,954)	(7,388,954)	(7,388,954)	(7,388,954)	(7,388,954)	(7,388,954)	(7,388,954)	(7,388,954)	(7,299,856)	7,388,954	7,371,134	-0.0%	-0.1%
BELGIUM	(26,571,344)	(26,571,344)	(26,571,344)	(26,571,344)	(26,571,344)	(26,571,344)	(26,571,344)	(26,571,344)	(26,571,344)	(26,571,344)	26,571,344	26,571,344	0.0%	0.0%
DENMARK	(37,450,000)	(38,280,000)	(38,490,000)	(39,200,000)	41,374,839	40,917,827	40,714,057	39,356,179	39,409,207	36,590,181	38,958,968	39,397,490	0.2%	-0.3%
EAST GERMANY	(16,450,685)	(16,450,685)	(16,450,685)	(16,450,685)	(16,450,685)	(16,450,685)	(16,450,685)	(16,450,685)	(16,450,685)	(16,069,573)	16,450,685	16,374,463	-0.1%	-0.3%
EIRE	(3,410,630)	(3,410,630)	(3,410,630)	(3,410,630)	(3,410,630)	3,410,630	(3,410,630)	(3,410,630)	(3,410,630)	(3,410,630)	3,410,630	3,410,630	0.0%	0.0%
FINLAND	(16,248,910)	(17,133,159)	18,017,408	18,901,657	20,368,164	21,834,672	22,844,833	22,438,658	23,322,907	24,207,156	18,133,860	22,929,665	4.5%	4.5%
FRANCE	(159,192,111)	(159,192,111)	(159,192,111)	(159,192,111)	(159,192,111)	(159,192,111)	(159,192,111)	(159,192,111)	(159,192,111)	(159,192,111)	159,192,111	159,192,111	0.0%	0.0%
GREECE	(28,029,967)	(28,029,967)	(28,029,967)	(28,029,967)	(28,029,967)	(28,029,967)	(28,029,967)	(28,029,967)	(28,029,967)	(28,029,967)	28,029,967	28,029,967	0.0%	0.0%
ICELAND	(134,288)	(134,288)	(134,288)	(134,288)	97,607	113,012	112,035	140,432	156,140	186,502	126,952	141,624	2.2%	3.7%
ITALY	(168,778,622)	(168,778,622)	(168,778,622)	(168,778,622)	(168,778,622)	(168,778,622)	(168,778,622)	(168,778,622)	(168,778,622)	(168,778,622)	168,778,622	168,778,622	0.0%	-0.1%
LIECHTENSTEIN	(30,164)	(30,164)	(30,164)	(30,164)	(30,164)	(30,164)	(30,164)	(30,164)	(29,927)	(29,927)	30,164	30,117	0.0%	0.0%
LUXEMBOURG	(918,023)	(918,023)	(918,023)	(918,023)	(918,023)	(918,023)	(918,023)	(918,023)	(918,023)	(918,023)	918,023	918,023	0.0%	0.0%
NETHERLANDS	(42,959,398)	(42,959,398)	(42,959,398)	(42,959,398)	(42,959,398)	(42,959,398)	(42,959,398)	(42,959,398)	(42,959,398)	(42,959,398)	42,959,398	42,959,398	0.0%	0.0%
NORWAY	(4,792,826)	(4,792,826)	(4,792,826)	5,362,441	5,283,000	4,894,016	4,373,143	4,354,105	4,534,661	4,748,415	5,004,784	4,580,668	-1.8%	-0.1%
PORTUGAL	(352,327)	(352,327)	(352,327)	(352,327)	(352,327)	222,800	395,751	407,034	383,722	(352,327)	352,327	352,327	0.0%	0.0%
SPAIN	(271,233)	(271,233)	(271,233)	(271,233)	(271,233)	(271,233)	(271,233)	(271,233)	(271,233)	(271,233)	271,233	271,233	0.0%	0.0%
SWEDEN	24,800,000	24,800,000	24,800,000	24,800,000	22,000,000	23,000,000	19,000,000	20,000,000	16,000,000	(16,000,000)	24,240,000	18,800,000	-5.0%	-4.8%
SWITZERLAND	(6,157,032)	(6,157,032)	(6,157,032)	(6,157,032)	(6,157,032)	(6,157,032)	(6,157,032)	(6,157,032)	(6,157,032)	(6,104,502)	6,157,032	6,146,526	-0.0%	-0.1%
UK	(159,210,241)	(159,210,241)	(159,210,241)	(159,210,241)	(159,210,241)	(159,210,241)	(159,210,241)	(159,210,241)	(159,210,241)	(159,210,241)	159,210,241	159,210,241	0.0%	0.0%
WEST GERMANY	(158,488,080)	(158,488,080)	(158,488,080)	(158,488,080)	(158,488,080)	(158,488,080)	(158,488,080)	(158,488,080)	(158,488,080)	(158,488,080)	158,488,080	158,488,080	0.0%	0.0%
EU TOTAL	802,082,661	802,912,661	803,122,661	803,832,661	806,007,500	805,420,961	805,390,142	804,043,547	804,073,263	800,841,730	803,591,629	803,953,929	0.0%	-0.0%
EFTA TOTAL	59,552,174	60,436,423	61,320,672	62,774,536	61,324,921	63,417,850	59,906,261	60,509,345	57,589,858	58,576,358	61,081,745	59,999,934	-0.4%	-0.2%
EUROPE TOTAL	861,634,835	863,349,084	864,443,333	866,607,197	867,332,421	868,838,811	865,296,403	864,552,892	861,663,121	859,418,088	864,673,374	863,953,863	-0.0%	-0.0%

Figures in parentheses are grossed.

Library Consultations

Sector 5 SPECIAL

	1981	1982	1983	1984	1985	1986	1987	1988	1989	1990	1981-85 Average	1986-90 Average	81/85 - 86/90 Year on Year Increase	Decade: Year on Year Increase
AUSTRIA	(1,077,411)	(1,077,411)	(1,077,411)	(1,077,411)	(1,077,411)	(1,077,411)	(1,077,411)	(1,077,411)	(1,077,411)	(1,084,800)	1,077,411	1,078,889	0.0%	0.1%
BELGIUM	(464,531)	(464,531)	(464,531)	(464,531)	(464,531)	(464,531)	(464,531)	(464,531)	(464,531)	(464,531)	464,531	464,531	0.0%	0.0%
DENMARK	375,000	362,000	362,300	340,000	290,900	(499,092)	(707,264)	915,476	856,194	832,379	346,040	762,085	17.1%	9.3%
EAST GERMANY	(2,357,429)	(2,357,429)	(2,357,429)	(2,357,429)	(2,357,429)	(2,357,429)	(2,357,429)	(2,357,429)	(2,357,429)	(2,319,876)	2,357,429	2,349,918	-0.1%	-0.2%
EIRE	(14,438)	(14,438)	(14,438)	(14,438)	(14,438)	(14,438)	(14,438)	(14,438)	(14,438)	(14,438)	14,438	14,438	0.0%	0.0%
FINLAND	197,600	217,350	218,800	238,970	252,649	251,500	269,775	263,568	283,568	264,793	225,074	266,641	3.4%	3.3%
FRANCE	(2,510,771)	(2,510,771)	(2,510,771)	(2,510,771)	(2,510,771)	(2,510,771)	(2,510,771)	(2,510,771)	(2,510,771)	(2,510,771)	2,510,771	2,510,771	0.0%	0.0%
GREECE	(451,186)	(451,186)	(451,186)	(451,186)	(451,186)	(451,186)	(451,186)	(451,186)	(451,186)	(451,186)	451,186	451,186	0.0%	0.0%
ICELAND	(34,634)	(34,634)	(34,634)	(34,634)	(34,634)	(34,634)	(34,634)	30,777	38,491	(34,634)	34,634	34,634	0.0%	0.0%
ITALY	(65,290)	(65,290)	(68,232)	64,825	62,812	(65,290)	(65,290)	(65,290)	(65,290)	(65,290)	65,290	65,290	0.0%	0.0%
LIECHTENSTEIN	0	0	0	0	0	0	0	0	0	0	0	0	0.0%	0.0%
LUXEMBOURG	(17,797)	(17,797)	(17,797)	(17,797)	(17,797)	(17,797)	(17,797)	(17,797)	(17,797)	(17,797)	17,797	17,797	0.0%	0.0%
NETHERLANDS	2,279,000	2,242,000	2,374,000	2,298,333	2,687,000	2,825,000	2,916,000	2,782,000	2,593,000	(2,593,000)	2,376,067	2,741,800	2.9%	1.4%
NORWAY	(477,600)	(477,600)	(477,600)	(477,600)	(477,600)	548,000	523,000	455,000	433,000	429,000	477,600	477,600	0.0%	-1.2%
PORTUGAL	(161,853)	(161,853)	(161,853)	(161,853)	161,853	211,696	192,987	176,227	232,987	111,415	161,853	185,062	2.7%	-4.1%
SPAIN	(3,074,059)	(3,074,059)	(3,074,059)	(3,074,059)	(3,074,059)	1,898,090	(2,598,233)	3,298,375	(3,624,658)	3,950,941	3,074,059	3,074,059	0.0%	2.8%
SWEDEN	(413,624)	(413,624)	(413,624)	(413,624)	196,181	319,422	294,545	609,668	609,000	452,927	370,135	457,112	4.3%	1.0%
SWITZERLAND	(951,276)	(951,276)	(951,276)	(951,276)	(951,276)	(951,276)	(951,276)	(951,276)	(951,276)	(958,182)	951,276	952,657	0.0%	0.1%
UK	(2,597,109)	(2,597,109)	(2,597,109)	(2,597,109)	(2,597,109)	(2,597,109)	(2,597,109)	(2,597,109)	(2,597,109)	(2,597,109)	2,597,109	2,597,109	0.0%	0.0%
WEST GERMANY	3,654,000	3,314,000	3,650,000	3,911,000	3,741,000	4,689,762	4,446,059	4,670,977	4,894,068	(4,894,068)	3,654,000	4,718,987	5.2%	3.3%
EU TOTAL	18,022,463	17,632,463	18,103,705	18,263,331	18,430,885	18,602,191	19,339,114	20,321,606	20,679,458	20,822,801	18,090,569	19,953,034	2.0%	1.6%
EFTA TOTAL	3,152,145	3,171,895	3,173,345	3,193,515	2,989,751	3,182,243	3,150,641	3,387,700	3,392,746	3,224,336	3,136,130	3,267,533	0.8%	0.3%
EUROPE TOTAL	21,174,608	20,804,358	21,277,050	21,456,846	21,420,636	21,784,434	22,489,755	23,709,306	24,072,204	24,047,137	21,226,700	23,220,567	1.8%	1.4%

Sector 6 PUBLIC

	1981	1982	1983	1984	1985	1986	1987	1988	1989	1990	1981-85 Average	1986-90 Average	81/85 - 86/90 Year on Year Increase	Decade: Year on Year Increase
AUSTRIA	(13,385,564)	(13,385,564)	(13,385,564)	13,385,564	(13,392,273)	(13,396,982)	13,405,691	12,988,018	12,479,044	13,899,522	13,386,906	13,234,251	-0.2%	0.4%
BELGIUM	38,362,629	43,267,536	46,569,587	48,344,501	(48,344,501)	(48,344,501)	(48,344,501)	(48,344,501)	(48,344,501)	(48,344,501)	44,977,751	48,344,501	1.5%	2.6%
DENMARK	85,100,000	93,500,000	94,500,000	87,344,000	94,600,000	92,346,651	93,580,956	91,842,145	87,395,123	87,760,342	91,008,800	90,585,043	-0.1%	0.3%
EAST GERMANY	(185,965,818)	(185,965,818)	(185,965,818)	(185,965,818)	(185,965,818)	(185,965,818)	(185,965,818)	(185,965,818)	(185,965,818)	(185,965,818)	185,965,818	185,965,818	0.0%	0.0%
EIRE	14,785,329	14,822,053	15,092,959	14,426,293	14,627,968	14,119,482	13,649,803	12,912,432	12,417,896	12,431,817	14,750,960	13,106,286	-2.3%	-1.9%
FINLAND	78,638,513	78,638,513	78,638,513	78,638,513	80,002,975	83,248,696	86,653,350	86,240,024	85,669,070	85,719,168	78,911,405	85,506,062	1.6%	1.0%
FRANCE	60,659,000	69,508,000	77,699,000	77,894,000	82,388,483	(85,271,983)	88,155,482	(91,038,982)	97,217,000	96,805,981	73,629,697	91,697,886	4.5%	5.3%
GREECE	(957,719)	(957,719)	(957,719)	(957,719)	(957,719)	957,719	(957,719)	(957,719)	(957,719)	(957,719)	957,719	957,719	0.0%	0.0%
ICELAND	2,317,487	2,284,252	2,253,803	2,224,924	2,053,300	1,976,209	1,778,190	1,624,927	1,647,580	1,701,662	2,226,753	1,745,714	-4.8%	-3.4%
ITALY	(356,515,548)	(356,515,548)	(356,515,548)	(356,515,548)	(356,515,548)	(356,515,548)	(356,515,548)	(356,515,548)	(356,515,548)	(356,515,548)	356,515,548	356,515,548	0.0%	0.0%
LIECHTENSTEIN	(54,623)	(56,666)	(58,748)	(60,811)	(62,873)	(64,936)	(66,995)	(69,057)	(71,120)	(73,182)	58,748	69,058	3.5%	3.3%
LUXEMBOURG	2,295,646	2,295,646	2,295,646	2,295,646	2,295,646	(2,295,646)	(2,295,646)	(2,295,646)	(2,295,646)	(2,295,646)	2,295,646	2,295,646	0.0%	0.0%
NETHERLANDS	170,352,000	177,983,000	179,735,000	172,795,000	172,636,000	168,604,000	179,882,000	185,443,000	184,946,000	185,724,000	174,700,200	180,919,800	0.7%	1.0%
NORWAY	(17,919,000)	(17,919,000)	(17,919,000)	(17,919,000)	(17,919,000)	17,919,000	17,794,194	17,801,321	19,130,000	19,680,492	17,919,000	18,465,001	0.6%	1.0%
PORTUGAL	(742,998)	(742,998)	(742,998)	(742,998)	(742,998)	742,998	810,538	804,848	955,407	885,934	742,998	839,945	2.5%	2.0%
SPAIN	(16,773,684)	(16,773,684)	(16,773,684)	(16,773,684)	(16,773,684)	14,357,850	(16,121,376)	17,884,902	17,981,601	18,078,300	16,773,684	16,884,806	0.1%	0.8%
SWEDEN	(72,904,080)	(72,904,080)	(72,904,080)	(72,904,080)	(72,904,080)	73,752,600	73,885,700	72,759,600	72,132,500	71,990,000	72,904,080	72,904,080	0.0%	-0.1%
SWITZERLAND	7,363,818	7,082,911	3,916,581	3,950,765	6,716,458	(5,806,107)	(5,806,107)	(5,806,107)	(5,806,107)	(5,806,107)	5,806,107	5,806,107	0.0%	-2.6%
UK	659,000,000	656,000,000	652,000,000	646,000,000	645,000,000	643,437,508	632,821,968	608,349,313	594,013,927	588,458,103	651,600,000	613,476,164	-1.2%	-1.3%
WEST GERMANY	189,722,105	193,021,842	196,253,123	199,489,748	204,640,300	212,983,189	217,887,662	221,055,372	219,679,102	(219,679,102)	196,625,424	218,256,885	2.1%	1.6%
EU TOTAL	1,781,252,476	1,811,374,044	1,825,121,082	1,809,564,955	1,825,508,665	1,825,962,893	1,837,009,017	1,823,430,226	1,809,005,288	1,803,922,811	1,810,564,244	1,819,866,047	0.1%	0.1%
EFTA TOTAL	192,583,085	192,271,006	189,076,289	189,083,657	193,050,959	196,166,530	199,390,227	197,289,054	196,935,421	198,870,133	191,212,999	197,730,273	0.7%	0.4%
EUROPE TOTAL	1,973,835,561	2,003,645,050	2,014,197,371	1,998,648,612	2,018,559,624	2,022,129,423	2,036,399,244	2,020,719,280	2,005,940,709	2,002,792,944	2,001,777,244	2,017,596,320	0.2%	0.2%

Figures in parentheses are grossed.

Library Consultations

	1981	1982	1983	1984	1985	1986	1987	1988	1989	1990	1981-85 Average	1986-90 Average	81/85 - 86/90 Year on Year Increase	Decade: Year on Year Increase
ALL SECTORS														
AUSTRIA	23,441,214	23,429,856	23,574,308	23,634,786	23,816,926	23,844,201	23,959,454	23,665,782	23,183,004	24,468,571	23,579,418	23,824,202	0.2%	0.5%
BELGIUM	66,669,816	71,633,124	74,881,451	76,687,990	76,704,391	76,682,105	76,732,345	76,710,035	76,726,239	76,754,239	73,315,354	76,720,993	0.9%	1.6%
DENMARK	125,103,600	134,457,628	135,995,675	129,530,000	138,913,239	136,123,096	137,073,848	133,897,376	129,547,867	127,329,804	132,800,028	132,794,398	-0.0%	0.2%
EAST GERMANY	220,010,437	220,010,437	220,010,437	220,010,437	220,228,228	220,446,020	220,663,812	220,663,812	220,663,812	220,127,028	220,053,995	220,512,897	0.2%	0.0%
EIRE	19,371,149	19,361,073	19,735,779	19,168,113	19,358,788	18,845,302	18,413,619	17,760,272	17,220,402	17,232,610	19,398,980	17,894,441	-1.6%	-1.3%
FINLAND	97,448,615	98,498,083	99,538,465	100,448,026	103,442,528	108,118,869	112,685,405	112,019,289	112,279,947	113,220,934	99,875,143	111,664,889	2.3%	1.7%
FRANCE	229,488,899	238,335,283	250,126,591	250,535,591	255,366,074	258,789,498	261,761,923	265,100,347	271,840,365	271,958,346	244,770,488	265,890,096	1.7%	1.9%
GREECE	31,559,897	31,559,897	31,576,011	31,574,611	31,572,598	31,572,598	31,572,598	31,572,598	31,572,598	31,572,598	31,568,623	31,572,598	0.0%	0.0%
ICELAND	2,554,452	2,521,217	2,490,768	2,461,889	2,253,584	2,188,798	1,991,102	1,860,337	1,909,012	1,994,399	2,456,382	1,988,730	-4.1%	-2.7%
ITALY	525,560,213	525,560,213	525,537,081	525,546,494	525,537,064	525,673,773	525,662,549	525,656,301	525,657,910	525,667,103	525,560,213	525,664,727	0.0%	0.1%
LIECHTENSTEIN	139,604	141,667	143,729	145,792	147,854	142,096	134,037	160,458	164,321	168,961	143,729	153,975	1.4%	2.1%
LUXEMBOURG	3,364,676	3,374,676	3,384,676	3,394,676	3,404,676	3,414,676	3,420,676	3,429,676	3,436,676	3,439,676	3,384,676	3,428,276	0.3%	0.2%
NETHERLANDS	219,801,998	227,338,998	229,318,998	222,289,331	222,777,398	218,949,398	230,354,465	235,761,465	235,020,665	235,798,665	224,305,345	231,176,932	0.6%	0.8%
NORWAY	24,109,819	24,109,819	24,109,819	24,109,434	24,776,259	24,633,939	23,984,837	23,909,426	25,540,661	26,475,907	24,357,030	24,908,954	0.4%	1.0%
PORTUGAL	1,793,891	1,806,913	1,745,294	1,749,575	1,778,971	1,846,884	2,268,911	2,050,384	2,435,757	2,236,895	1,774,929	2,167,766	4.1%	2.5%
SPAIN	30,108,201	30,108,201	30,108,201	30,108,201	30,108,201	26,516,398	28,980,067	31,443,735	31,961,723	32,479,710	30,108,201	30,276,326	0.1%	0.8%
SWEDEN	101,766,049	101,766,049	101,766,049	101,037,733	98,861,693	100,795,517	97,132,201	97,284,486	92,135,683	92,378,192	101,039,516	95,945,216	-1.0%	-1.1%
SWITZERLAND	22,089,289	21,808,382	18,642,052	18,676,236	21,496,868	20,629,760	21,727,469	17,752,933	22,637,922	21,748,469	20,542,565	20,899,311	0.3%	-0.2%
UK	857,151,062	854,151,062	850,151,062	844,151,062	843,151,062	841,588,570	831,877,530	808,395,375	796,300,489	791,524,165	849,751,062	813,937,226	-0.9%	-0.9%
WEST GERMANY	386,396,435	385,872,922	392,240,203	398,781,828	403,207,380	414,773,916	421,230,356	426,079,955	426,988,141	426,988,141	393,299,754	423,212,102	1.5%	1.1%
EU TOTAL	2,716,380,274	2,743,570,427	2,764,811,559	2,753,527,909	2,772,168,070	2,775,222,234	2,790,018,698	2,778,521,331	2,769,372,644	2,763,108,980	2,750,091,648	2,775,248,777	0.2%	0.2%
EFTA TOTAL	271,549,042	272,275,073	270,265,190	271,083,896	274,795,717	280,345,121	281,622,564	276,652,711	277,850,550	280,455,433	271,993,784	279,385,276	0.5%	0.4%
EUROPE TOTAL	2,987,929,316	3,015,845,500	3,035,076,749	3,024,611,805	3,046,963,787	3,055,567,355	3,071,641,262	3,055,174,042	3,047,223,194	3,043,564,413	3,022,085,431	3,054,634,053	0.2%	0.2%

Library Consultations per 1000 Population

	1981	1982	1983	1984	1985	1986	1987	1988	1989	1990	1981-85 Average	1986-90 Average	81/85 - 86/90 Year on Year Increase	Decade: Year on Year Increase
European Union														
Sector 1	35.24	34.41	34.82	35.45	35.90	35.65	35.40	34.71	36.05	35.87	35.16	35.54	0.2%	0.2%
Sector 2	253.49	245.20	265.11	273.00	271.95	277.89	287.43	295.23	311.61	317.04	261.75	297.84	2.6%	2.5%
Sector 3	51.55	50.71	50.53	52.09	52.92	54.05	53.72	52.31	53.51	53.02	51.56	53.32	0.7%	0.3%
Sector 4	2,372.88	2,375.33	2,375.96	2,378.06	2,379.10	2,364.07	2,364.12	2,351.02	2,378.58	2,363.90	2,376.27	2,364.34	-0.1%	-0.0%
Sector 5	53.32	52.16	53.56	54.03	54.40	54.60	56.77	59.42	61.17	61.46	53.49	58.69	1.9%	1.6%
Sector 6	5,269.65	5,358.76	5,399.43	5,353.41	5,388.08	5,359.56	5,392.30	5,331.71	5,351.33	5,324.77	5,353.93	5,351.93	-0.0%	0.1%
All Sectors	8,036.13	8,116.57	8,179.41	8,146.03	8,182.65	8,145.83	8,189.73	8,124.39	8,192.25	8,156.07	8,132.16	8,161.65	0.1%	0.2%
EFTA														
Sector 1	36.67	36.80	36.93	37.06	37.04	36.56	37.42	37.71	36.26	36.47	36.90	36.89	-0.0%	-0.1%
Sector 2	208.80	212.85	222.02	201.27	244.80	250.27	269.60	269.52	289.80	292.32	217.95	274.30	4.7%	3.8%
Sector 3	260.54	260.54	260.54	260.54	260.54	260.16	289.67	174.05	294.19	282.77	260.54	260.17	-0.0%	0.9%
Sector 4	1,853.11	1,880.62	1,908.14	1,953.38	1,908.27	1,973.40	1,864.12	1,882.89	1,792.04	1,810.66	1,900.70	1,864.62	-0.4%	-0.3%
Sector 5	98.09	98.70	98.75	99.37	93.03	99.02	98.04	105.42	105.57	99.67	97.59	101.54	0.8%	0.2%
Sector 6	5,992.68	5,982.97	5,883.56	5,883.78	6,007.24	6,104.18	6,204.50	6,139.11	6,128.11	6,147.29	5,950.04	6,144.64	0.6%	0.3%
All Sectors	8,449.89	8,472.48	8,409.94	8,435.42	8,550.92	8,723.60	8,763.35	8,608.70	8,645.98	8,669.19	8,463.73	8,682.16	0.5%	0.3%
Europe Total														
Sector 1	35.37	34.61	35.01	35.59	36.00	35.73	35.57	34.97	36.07	35.92	35.31	35.65	0.2%	0.2%
Sector 2	249.61	242.39	261.37	266.77	269.59	275.51	285.90	293.02	309.72	314.89	257.95	295.81	2.8%	2.6%
Sector 3	69.70	68.92	68.76	70.19	70.90	71.82	74.06	62.76	74.40	73.05	69.69	71.22	0.4%	0.5%
Sector 4	2,327.75	2,332.38	2,335.34	2,341.19	2,338.31	2,330.40	2,321.02	2,310.81	2,327.66	2,315.68	2,335.00	2,321.11	-0.1%	-0.1%
Sector 5	57.20	56.20	57.48	57.97	57.75	58.43	60.33	63.37	65.03	64.79	57.32	62.39	1.7%	1.4%
Sector 6	5,332.42	5,412.96	5,441.46	5,399.46	5,442.00	5,423.75	5,462.31	5,401.06	5,418.76	5,396.47	5,405.66	5,420.47	0.1%	0.1%
All Sectors	8,072.05	8,147.47	8,199.42	8,171.15	8,214.56	8,195.63	8,239.18	8,165.99	8,231.64	8,200.60	8,160.93	8,206.65	0.2%	0.2%

- 166 -

ALL SECTORS Estimated Average Expenditure and Income per annum (1986-1990) at constant 1990 prices in ECUs.

	Staff Expenditure	Premises and Operating Costs	New Buildings and Refurbishment	Acquisition of Stock	Cost of Borrowing	Miscellaneous Expenditure	TOTAL EXPENDITURE	Government and Municipal Funds	Fees and Charges	Other Income	TOTAL INCOME
Austria	100,331,299	11,930,060	857,955	35,249,745	3,074,564	15,936,721	167,380,344	154,704,048	5,350,161	7,326,135	167,380,344
Belgium	148,753,282	22,688,329	1,027,163	54,003,595	6,644,158	27,607,553	260,724,080	223,215,725	19,000,273	18,508,083	260,724,081
Denmark	258,037,569	58,514,383	308,171	79,452,151	3,469,345	16,229,258	416,010,877	399,893,396	5,293,456	10,824,024	416,010,876
East Germany	445,740,137	48,490,526	1,202,440	161,292,372	12,133,576	57,289,266	726,148,317	671,154,577	23,210,674	31,783,067	726,148,318
Eire	31,458,790	12,728,046	343,433	9,318,384	4,629,637	13,360,046	71,838,336	62,596,620	2,450,507	6,791,208	71,838,335
Finland	154,618,774	30,561,979	503,057	73,602,147	3,734,514	18,197,580	281,218,051	274,841,095	2,691,459	3,685,496	281,218,050
France	503,060,790	64,686,773	4,583,196	156,887,728	15,868,243	79,656,000	824,742,730	760,644,498	21,822,305	42,275,927	824,742,730
Greece	93,441,593	11,105,899	435,094	33,340,945	2,784,636	13,823,872	154,932,039	143,198,497	4,952,262	6,781,280	154,932,039
Iceland	3,942,304	611,979	14,905	1,692,112	119,846	676,786	7,057,932	6,467,563	473,667	116,702	7,057,932
Italy	349,484,381	40,876,979	1,773,485	120,865,360	10,225,658	51,247,162	574,473,025	527,421,882	18,795,263	28,255,881	574,473,026
Liechtenstein	430,104	72,917	881	219,958	12,336	83,647	819,843	738,612	10,031	71,200	819,843
Luxembourg	4,898,236	524,916	18,833	1,886,015	126,976	708,948	8,163,924	7,168,239	307,034	688,651	8,163,924
Netherlands	315,416,203	92,951,079	785,913	118,570,549	9,732,333	53,362,348	590,818,425	514,779,070	38,461,242	37,578,114	590,818,426
Norway	108,172,364	13,116,657	513,870	31,491,586	3,288,803	16,326,728	172,910,008	165,776,597	3,010,708	4,122,704	172,910,009
Portugal	20,959,612	2,600,881	41,184	7,411,335	448,887	2,254,411	33,716,310	28,637,413	659,798	4,419,100	33,716,311
Spain	172,548,950	21,132,458	44,172	70,943,577	1,451,828	11,120,009	277,240,994	256,244,569	8,861,757	12,134,688	277,241,014
Sweden	364,655,757	69,675,447	2,384,937	123,777,660	17,074,412	84,583,749	662,151,962	602,315,864	22,789,531	37,046,567	662,151,962
Switzerland	146,402,362	13,343,236	130,251	45,820,545	3,331,716	14,881,507	223,909,617	211,732,364	1,482,516	10,694,737	223,909,617
UK	934,862,684	157,344,716	10,710,834	378,793,626	70,186,286	194,218,095	1,746,116,241	1,615,020,103	35,655,287	95,440,851	1,746,116,241
West Germany	554,350,206	57,494,851	4,246,608	230,761,747	14,397,283	90,572,997	951,823,692	879,738,770	30,424,183	41,660,739	951,823,692
EU TOTAL	3,833,012,433	591,139,836	25,520,526	1,423,527,384	152,098,846	611,449,965	6,636,748,990	6,089,713,359	209,894,041	337,141,613	6,636,749,013
EFTA TOTAL	878,552,964	139,312,275	4,405,856	311,853,753	30,636,191	150,686,718	1,515,447,757	1,416,576,143	35,808,073	63,063,541	1,515,447,757
STUDY TOTAL	4,711,565,397	730,452,111	29,926,382	1,735,381,137	182,735,037	762,136,683	8,152,196,747	7,506,289,502	245,702,114	400,205,154	8,152,196,770

ALL SECTORS Estimated Average Expenditure and Income per annum (1981-1985) at constant 1990 prices in ECUs.

	Staff Expenditure	Premises and Operating Costs	New Buildings and Refurbishment	Acquisition of Stock	Cost of Borrowing	Miscellaneous Expenditure	TOTAL EXPENDITURE	Government and Municipal Funds	Fees and Charges	Other Income	TOTAL INCOME
Austria	92,173,209	10,884,037	670,782	32,548,559	2,753,784	13,997,907	153,028,278	141,438,914	4,891,410	6,697,954	153,028,278
Belgium	128,779,924	19,198,072	859,598	46,670,300	5,556,075	23,404,285	224,468,254	192,490,253	16,090,125	15,887,875	224,468,253
Denmark	241,919,383	42,052,071	274,933	82,596,630	2,872,872	13,522,900	383,238,789	369,426,449	4,580,877	9,231,463	383,238,789
East Germany	440,636,762	47,883,970	1,178,677	159,471,434	11,981,491	56,534,266	717,686,600	663,333,696	22,940,202	31,412,703	717,686,601
Eire	29,675,373	12,136,408	345,512	10,244,406	4,964,955	12,754,117	70,120,771	61,333,377	2,082,556	6,704,838	70,120,771
Finland	124,336,033	25,065,279	336,111	60,720,553	2,495,077	12,158,091	225,111,144	220,329,094	2,018,313	2,763,736	225,111,143
France	459,038,756	59,136,832	3,283,101	141,191,783	13,710,940	67,235,595	743,597,007	687,676,247	18,993,862	36,926,898	743,597,007
Greece	93,441,585	11,105,898	435,094	33,340,942	2,784,636	13,823,871	154,932,026	143,198,485	4,952,262	6,781,280	154,932,027
Iceland	3,144,052	494,550	11,723	1,346,162	94,877	537,426	5,628,790	5,148,088	395,443	85,259	5,628,790
Italy	337,346,979	39,444,818	1,714,665	116,588,473	9,866,938	49,458,729	554,420,602	508,943,987	18,147,481	27,239,134	554,330,602
Liechtenstein	420,017	71,718	834	216,358	12,035	82,155	803,117	709,392	9,496	84,230	803,118
Luxembourg	4,810,452	497,497	18,833	1,822,395	123,769	649,335	7,922,281	7,007,465	291,671	623,146	7,922,282
Netherlands	303,630,427	66,305,928	709,196	106,616,234	19,604,107	55,009,354	551,875,246	489,390,895	28,065,708	34,418,644	551,875,247
Norway	99,815,433	12,065,264	472,681	28,645,916	3,025,182	15,018,024	159,042,500	152,403,346	2,802,129	3,837,025	159,042,500
Portugal	16,796,700	1,615,865	29,070	5,924,835	342,588	1,631,124	26,340,182	21,413,736	385,074	4,541,373	26,340,183
Spain	126,127,570	18,083,501	44,172	50,516,776	1,060,294	7,865,978	203,698,291	188,271,510	6,511,031	8,915,750	203,698,291
Sweden	375,862,844	68,149,517	2,397,488	128,474,999	16,850,823	84,013,223	675,748,894	616,334,459	22,867,105	36,547,330	675,748,894
Switzerland	130,706,921	11,843,884	130,148	41,032,794	2,957,853	13,273,258	199,944,858	188,912,168	1,481,342	9,551,348	199,944,858
UK	873,959,616	140,734,534	10,394,951	336,107,976	60,160,001	169,688,599	1,591,045,677	1,470,788,066	31,388,755	88,868,855	1,591,045,676
West Germany	470,405,829	48,732,200	3,679,925	195,307,678	12,202,903	76,396,704	806,725,239	745,629,128	25,786,242	35,309,868	806,725,238
EU TOTAL	3,526,569,356	506,927,594	22,967,727	1,286,399,862	145,231,569	547,974,857	6,036,070,965	5,548,903,294	180,215,846	306,861,827	6,035,980,967
EFTA TOTAL	826,458,509	128,574,249	4,019,767	292,985,341	28,189,631	139,080,084	1,419,307,581	1,325,275,461	34,465,238	59,566,882	1,419,307,581
STUDY TOTAL	4,353,027,865	635,501,843	26,987,494	1,579,385,203	173,421,200	687,054,941	7,455,378,546	6,874,178,755	214,681,084	366,428,709	7,455,288,548

National Libraries Estimated Average Expenditure and Income per annum (1986-1990) at constant 1990 prices in ECUs.

	Staff Expenditure	Premises and Operating Costs	New Buildings and Refurbishment	Acquisition of Stock	Cost of Borrowing	Miscellaneous Expenditure	TOTAL EXPENDITURE	Government and Municipal Funds	Fees and Charges	Other Income	TOTAL INCOME
Austria	3914350	470528	409005	847161	201260	1672671	7,514,975	6945839	240210	328926	7,514,975
Belgium	11,495,428	1,366,277	53,527	4,101,690	342,573	1,700,649	19,060,144	17,616,652	609,240	834,251	19,060,143
Denmark	8,452,011	1,556,318	0	1,219,906	388,064	1,668,882	13,285,181	9,329,367	66,768	3,889,048	13,285,183
East Germany	35,692,317	4,242,172	166,195	12,735,395	1,063,660	5,280,368	59,180,107	54,698,192	1,891,638	2,590,277	59,180,107
Eire	2,769,856	329,208	38,570	208,202	82,544	409,776	3,838,156	295,609	20,272	3,522,275	3,838,156
Finland	3,252,398	290,430	0	1,051,416	72,418	311,437	4,978,099	4,601,090	159,120	217,888	4,978,098
France	38,138,097	4,532,862	177,584	13,608,075	1,136,546	5,642,200	63,235,364	46,938,356	0	16,297,008	63,235,364
Greece	7,720,262	917,583	35,948	2,754,671	230,070	1,142,146	12,800,680	11,831,240	409,162	560,278	12,800,680
Iceland	403,163	89,902	0	55,192	19,648	163,290	731,195	577,024	138,501	15,669	731,194
Italy	11,199,300	670,472	198,317	274,718	144,486	1,200,821	13,688,114	9,107,165	870,280	3,710,669	13,688,114
Liechtenstein	240,824	50,421	0	152,421	6,695	55,644	506,005	448,540	0	57,464	506,004
Luxembourg	853,541	44,188	0	442,826	6,441	110,570	1,457,566	969,778	92,671	395,117	1,457,566
Netherlands	5,931,185	3,541,264	0	1,520,384	0	0	10,992,833	10,992,832	0	0	10,992,832
Norway	5,689,149	218,764	8,570	551,387	54,852	272,303	6,795,025	6,280,414	217,197	297,414	6,795,025
Portugal	1,959,480	955,476	0	70,002	37,151	308,758	3,330,867	2,952,422	105,355	273,090	3,330,867
Spain	9,290,465	4,454,769	0	1,125,584	0	0	14,870,818	13,744,600	475,332	650,887	14,870,819
Sweden	6,280,142	3,071,620	0	731,637	382,456	2,667,310	13,133,165	3,796,127	633,857	8,703,182	13,133,166
Switzerland	3,733,906	359,798	0	513,647	89,715	385,821	5,082,887	5,036,215	0	46,672	5,082,887
UK	61,116,606	18,238,516	10,318,772	15,392,205	2,665,103	22,149,652	129,880,854	98,006,613	0	31,874,240	129,880,853
West Germany	46,227,431	5,033,365	1,599,436	18,518,116	1,255,058	5,397,414	78,030,820	72,121,273	2,494,184	3,415,361	78,030,818
EU TOTAL	240,845,979	45,882,470	12,588,349	71,971,774	7,351,696	45,011,236	423,651,504	348,604,099	7,034,902	68,012,501	423,651,502
EFTA TOTAL	23,513,932	4,551,463	417,575	3,902,861	827,044	5,528,476	38,741,351	27,685,249	1,388,885	9,667,215	38,741,349
STUDY TOTAL	264,359,911	50,433,933	13,005,924	75,874,635	8,178,740	50,539,712	462,392,855	376,289,348	8,423,787	77,679,716	462,392,851

National Libraries Estimated Average Expenditure and Income per annum (1981-1985) at constant 1990 prices in ECUs

	Staff Expenditure	Premises and Operating Costs	New Buildings and Refurbishment	Acquisition of Stock	Cost of Borrowing	Miscellaneous Expenditure	TOTAL EXPENDITURE	Government and Municipal Funds	Fees and Charges	Other Income	TOTAL INCOME
Austria	3,047,538	291,102	255,783	747,580	97,767	812,538	5,252,308	4,854,532	167,885	229,890	5,252,307
Belgium	8,756,599	1,040,756	40,774	3,124,447	260,954	1,295,463	14,518,993	13,419,417	464,087	635,488	14,518,992
Denmark	6,992,425	1,324,775	0	1,023,390	330,330	1,420,592	11,091,512	7,788,888	55,742	3,246,882	11,091,512
East Germany	33,694,314	4,004,701	156,892	12,022,486	1,004,118	4,984,781	55,867,292	51,636,268	1,785,747	2,445,277	55,867,292
Eire	2,970,652	353,073	40,649	152,631	88,528	439,482	4,045,015	261,403	24,430	3,759,182	4,045,015
Finland	3,091,645	156,516	0	624,273	39,027	167,836	4,079,297	3,770,357	130,391	178,548	4,079,296
France	38,138,097	4,532,862	177,584	13,608,075	1,136,546	5,642,200	63,235,364	46,927,037	0	16,308,327	63,235,364
Greece	7,720,262	917,583	35,948	2,754,671	230,070	1,142,146	12,800,680	11,831,240	409,162	560,278	12,800,680
Iceland	356,329	82,202	0	45,689	16,011	133,065	633,296	497,214	122,359	13,724	633,297
Italy	11,022,705	659,900	195,190	270,386	142,208	1,181,886	13,472,275	8,963,561	856,557	3,652,158	13,472,276
Liechtenstein	240,824	50,421	0	152,420	6,695	55,644	506,004	434,778	0	71,226	506,004
Luxembourg	765,757	16,769	0	379,206	3,234	50,957	1,215,923	809,004	77,308	329,612	1,215,924
Netherlands	4,772,200	2,849,282	0	1,223,293	0	0	8,844,775	8,844,774	0	0	8,844,774
Norway	5,639,622	216,860	8,496	546,587	54,374	269,932	6,735,871	6,225,743	215,305	294,823	6,735,871
Portugal	1,441,072	280,465	23	321,152	8,581	71,312	2,122,605	2,089,080	0	33,525	2,122,605
Spain	13,485,270	6,466,174	0	1,633,805	0	0	21,585,249	19,950,523	689,953	944,773	21,585,249
Sweden	5,569,408	2,270,579	0	648,836	339,173	2,818,867	11,646,863	3,578,949	538,117	7,529,798	11,646,864
Switzerland	2,619,470	252,411	0	360,342	62,938	270,668	3,565,829	3,533,084	0	32,745	3,565,829
UK	59,245,676	17,680,190	10,002,889	14,921,012	2,583,517	21,471,597	125,904,881	95,003,741	0	30,901,140	125,904,881
West Germany	39,394,786	4,289,408	1,363,031	15,781,046	1,069,554	4,599,650	66,497,475	61,461,389	2,125,531	2,910,554	66,497,474
EU TOTAL	228,399,815	44,415,938	12,012,980	67,215,600	6,857,640	42,300,066	401,202,039	328,986,325	6,488,517	65,727,196	401,202,038
EFTA TOTAL	20,564,836	3,320,091	264,279	3,125,727	615,985	4,528,550	32,419,468	22,894,657	1,174,057	8,350,754	32,419,468
STUDY TOTAL	248,964,651	47,736,029	12,277,259	70,341,327	7,473,625	46,828,616	433,621,507	351,880,982	7,662,574	74,077,950	433,621,506

HIGHER EDUCATION LIBRARIES : Estimated Average Expenditure and Income per annum (1986-1990) at constant 1990 prices in ECUs

	Staff Expenditure	Premises and Operating Costs	New Buildings and Refurbishment	Acquisition of Stock	Cost of Borrowing	Miscellaneous Expenditure	TOTAL EXPENDITURE	Government and Municipal Funds	Fees and Charges	Other Income	TOTAL INCOME
Austria	40,971,765	4,869,655	190,778	14,619,158	1,220,992	6,061,417	67,933,765	62,788,904	2,171,442	2,973,419	67,933,765
Belgium	18,491,833	2,197,827	86,104	6,598,081	551,072	2,735,706	30,660,623	28,338,587	980,039	1,341,997	30,660,623
Denmark	22,555,131	2,501,034	0	8,775,299	623,627	2,681,927	37,137,018	34,529,771	1,194,150	1,413,097	37,137,018
East Germany	71,252,876	8,468,683	331,777	25,423,777	2,123,394	10,541,244	118,141,751	109,194,465	3,776,294	5,170,992	118,141,751
Eire	8,331,000	657,600	0	4,124,800	164,200	705,000	13,982,600	12,923,912	446,773	611,915	13,982,600
Finland	16,933,844	1,041,249	0	14,460,031	259,633	1,116,560	33,811,317	31,250,668	1,080,748	1,479,901	33,811,317
France	62,715,219	7,553,943	3,388,003	18,660,831	1,579,986	13,131,253	107,029,235	91,604,977	5,843,989	9,580,269	107,029,235
Greece	20,018,196	2,379,241	93,211	7,142,703	596,559	2,961,518	33,191,428	30,677,726	1,060,934	1,452,768	33,191,428
Iceland	338,078	141,618	0	350,050	4,804	39,926	874,476	863,279	11,197	0	874,476
Italy	3,687,356	438,257	17,169	1,202,647	109,886	545,512	6,000,827	5,546,364	191,811	262,652	6,000,827
Liechtenstein	91,775	10,908	427	32,746	2,735	13,578	152,169	140,645	4,863	6,660	152,168
Luxembourg	829,690	98,612	3,863	296,042	24,725	122,746	1,375,678	1,271,493	43,972	60,213	1,375,678
Netherlands	79,121,383	9,403,886	368,415	22,064,622	2,357,882	2,699,969	116,016,157	107,229,850	3,708,351	5,077,956	116,016,157
Norway	26,214,924	3,115,747	122,065	9,353,761	781,226	3,878,271	43,465,994	40,174,176	1,389,323	1,902,495	43,465,994
Portugal	1,965,753	79,289	0	1,834,010	19,770	85,024	3,983,846	3,555,726	46,033	382,087	3,983,846
Spain	31,760,581	2,498,836	0	25,972,339	0	0	60,231,756	55,670,196	1,925,254	2,636,307	60,231,757
Sweden	34,493,645	4,377,141	0	12,380,117	1,091,430	4,693,727	57,036,060	50,736,465	3,896,929	2,402,666	57,036,060
Switzerland	38,368,013	3,876,652	0	14,380,515	966,634	4,157,040	61,748,854	59,188,025	0	2,630,829	61,818,854
UK	150,491,445	12,335,846	0	97,349,275	3,075,915	13,228,065	276,480,546	259,891,897	4,147,048	12,441,601	276,480,546
West Germany	138,679,106	6,569,796	0	121,587,536	1,638,164	7,044,972	275,519,574	254,653,517	8,806,734	12,059,323	275,519,574
EU TOTAL	609,899,569	55,182,850	4,288,542	341,031,962	12,865,180	56,482,936	1,079,751,039	995,088,481	32,171,382	52,491,177	1,079,751,040
EFTA TOTAL	157,412,044	17,432,970	313,270	65,576,378	4,327,454	19,960,519	265,022,635	245,142,162	8,554,502	11,395,970	265,092,634
STUDY TOTAL	767,311,613	72,615,820	4,601,812	406,608,340	17,192,634	76,443,455	1,344,773,674	1,240,230,643	40,725,884	63,887,147	1,344,843,674

HIGHER EDUCATION LIBRARIES : Estimated Average Expenditure and Income per annum (1981-1985) at constant 1990 prices in ECUs

	Staff Expenditure	Premises and Operating Costs	New Buildings and Refurbishment	Acquisition of Stock	Cost of Borrowing	Miscellaneous Expenditure	TOTAL EXPENDITURE	Government and Municipal Funds	Fees and Charges	Other Income	TOTAL INCOME
Austria	36,983,749	4,395,663	172,208	13,196,192	1,102,146	5,471,425	61,321,383	56,677,301	1,960,083	2,683,999	61,321,383
Belgium	18,491,833	2,197,827	86,104	6,598,081	551,072	2,735,706	30,660,623	28,338,587	980,039	1,341,997	30,660,623
Denmark	21,672,343	2,187,440	0	8,669,300	545,433	2,345,652	35,420,168	32,933,455	1,138,944	1,347,769	35,420,168
East Germany	67,665,530	8,042,313	315,073	24,143,774	2,016,488	10,010,528	112,193,706	103,696,887	3,586,170	4,910,650	112,193,707
Eire	7,351,800	531,000	0	3,855,800	132,400	570,000	12,441,000	11,498,442	397,897	544,661	12,441,000
Finland	11,506,029	652,223	0	10,323,018	162,630	699,396	23,343,296	21,575,427	746,147	1,021,722	23,343,296
France	56,143,803	7,512,932	2,087,909	12,289,887	796,321	6,618,223	85,449,075	77,207,725	3,911,727	4,329,624	85,449,076
Greece	20,018,196	2,379,241	93,211	7,142,703	596,559	2,961,518	33,191,428	30,677,726	1,060,934	1,452,768	33,191,428
Iceland	270,018	113,109	0	279,580	3,837	31,889	698,433	689,478	8,955	0	698,433
Italy	3,844,361	456,917	17,901	1,253,855	114,565	568,740	6,256,339	5,782,525	199,978	273,836	6,256,339
Liechtenstein	91,939	10,927	428	32,805	2,740	13,602	152,441	140,897	4,872	6,672	152,441
Luxembourg	829,690	98,612	3,863	296,042	24,725	122,746	1,375,678	1,271,493	43,972	60,213	1,375,678
Netherlands	65,497,649	7,784,652	304,979	19,598,185	1,951,883	2,274,469	97,411,817	90,034,482	3,113,681	4,263,656	97,411,819
Norway	23,382,512	2,779,103	108,877	8,343,127	696,818	3,459,239	38,769,676	35,833,536	1,239,234	1,696,906	38,769,676
Portugal	880,755	28,595	0	1,241,444	7,130	30,663	2,188,587	1,988,723	23,956	175,910	2,188,589
Spain	23,302,195	1,833,353	0	19,055,460	0	0	44,191,008	40,844,270	1,412,526	1,934,214	44,191,010
Sweden	28,786,588	3,430,414	0	10,460,811	855,366	3,678,527	47,211,706	41,997,204	3,225,691	1,988,811	47,211,706
Switzerland	34,049,706	3,207,374	0	12,656,304	799,751	3,439,354	54,152,489	51,868,171	0	2,284,318	54,152,489
UK	139,072,374	11,399,820	0	89,962,555	2,842,519	12,224,339	255,501,607	240,171,681	3,832,376	11,497,550	255,501,607
West Germany	115,696,096	5,480,997	0	101,437,077	1,366,674	5,877,423	229,858,267	212,450,299	7,347,212	10,060,755	229,858,266
EU TOTAL	540,466,625	49,933,699	2,909,040	295,544,163	10,945,769	46,340,007	946,139,303	876,896,295	27,049,412	42,193,603	946,139,310
EFTA TOTAL	135,070,541	14,588,813	281,513	55,291,837	3,623,288	16,793,432	225,649,424	208,782,014	7,184,982	9,682,428	225,649,424
STUDY TOTAL	675,537,166	64,522,512	3,190,553	350,836,000	14,569,057	63,133,439	1,171,788,727	1,085,678,309	34,234,394	51,876,031	1,171,788,734

OTHER MAJOR NON-SPECIALISED LIBRARIES Estimated Average Expenditure and Income per annum (1986-1990) at constant 1990 prices in ECUS

	Staff Expenditure	Premises and Operating Costs	New Buildings and Refurbishment	Acquisition of Stock	Cost of Borrowing	Miscellaneous Expenditure	TOTAL EXPENDITURE	Government and Municipal Funds	Fees and Charges	Other Income	TOTAL INCOME
Austria	384,105	45,652	1,789	137,053	11,447	56,825	636,871	588,639	20,357	27,875	636,871
Belgium	4,327,982	514,398	20,153	1,544,270	128,977	640,287	7,176,067	6,632,598	229,377	314,092	7,176,067
Denmark	0	0	0	0	0	0	0	0	0	0	0
East Germany	81,142,551	9,644,110	377,827	28,952,518	2,418,115	12,004,336	134,539,457	124,350,315	4,300,432	5,888,710	134,539,457
Eire	245,703	8,379	0	42,072	2,089	8,985	307,228	301,628	509	5,091	307,228
Finland	0	0	0	0	0	0	0	0	0	0	0
France	2,403,628	285,680	11,192	857,640	71,630	355,596	3,985,366	3,683,541	127,388	174,437	3,985,366
Greece	4,320,410	513,498	20,117	1,541,568	128,752	639,167	7,163,512	6,620,994	228,975	313,543	7,163,512
Iceland	0	0	0	0	0	0	0	0	0	0	0
Italy	22,380,221	2,659,977	104,210	7,985,499	666,949	3,310,960	37,107,816	34,297,511	1,186,118	1,624,186	37,107,815
Liechtenstein	0	0	0	0	0	0	0	0	0	0	0
Luxembourg	0	0	0	0	0	0	0	0	0	0	0
Netherlands	2,861,481	903,602	35,400	846,353	226,564	1,124,742	5,998,142	5,543,882	191,725	262,535	5,998,142
Norway	0	0	0	0	0	0	0	0	0	0	0
Portugal	988,654	117,566	0	64,097	29,315	126,069	1,325,701	850,053	0	475,647	1,325,700
Spain	2,292,678	296,375	0	647,793	31,831	264,544	3,533,221	3,265,638	112,936	154,647	3,533,221
Sweden	40,920,422	4,572,383	179,132	14,889,900	1,146,456	5,691,393	67,399,686	62,295,273	2,154,370	2,950,043	67,399,686
Switzerland	20,172,782	2,156,257	0	4,496,390	537,657	2,312,213	29,675,299	27,893,199	0	1,782,101	29,675,300
UK	24,784,313	2,945,713	115,404	8,843,304	738,593	3,666,624	41,093,951	37,981,763	1,313,531	1,798,657	41,093,951
West Germany	25,210,023	1,862,660	922,249	8,285,306	464,450	1,997,381	38,742,069	35,807,997	1,238,355	1,695,717	38,742,069
EU TOTAL	170,957,644	19,751,958	1,606,552	59,610,420	4,907,265	24,138,691	280,972,530	259,335,920	8,929,346	12,707,262	280,972,528
EFTA TOTAL	61,477,309	6,774,292	180,921	19,523,343	1,695,560	8,060,431	97,711,856	90,777,111	2,174,727	4,760,019	97,711,857
STUDY TOTAL	232,434,953	26,526,250	1,787,473	79,133,763	6,602,825	32,199,122	378,684,386	350,113,031	11,104,073	17,467,281	378,684,385

OTHER MAJOR NON-SPECIALISED LIBRARIES Estimated Average Expenditure and Income per annum (1981-1985) at constant 1990 prices in ECUs

	Staff Expenditure	Premises and Operating Costs	New Buildings and Refurbishment	Acquisition of Stock	Cost of Borrowing	Miscellaneous Expenditure	TOTAL EXPENDITURE	Government and Municipal Funds	Fees and Charges	Other Income	TOTAL INCOME
Austria	384,105	45,652	1,789	137,053	11,447	56,825	636,871	588,639	20,357	27,875	636,871
Belgium	4,327,982	514,398	20,153	1,544,270	128,977	640,287	7,176,067	6,632,598	229,377	314,092	7,176,067
Denmark	0	0	0	0	0	0	0	0	0	0	0
East Germany	81,377,682	9,672,056	378,922	29,036,415	2,425,122	12,039,122	134,929,319	124,710,651	4,312,894	5,905,774	134,929,319
Eire	241,455	8,234	0	41,345	2,053	8,830	301,917	296,389	450	5,078	301,917
Finland	0	0	0	0	0	0	0	0	0	0	0
France	2,403,628	285,681	11,192	857,640	71,630	355,596	3,985,367	3,683,542	127,388	174,437	3,985,367
Greece	4,320,410	513,498	20,117	1,541,568	128,752	639,167	7,163,512	6,620,994	228,975	313,543	7,163,512
Iceland	0	0	0	0	0	0	0	0	0	0	0
Italy	12,799,645	1,521,288	59,600	4,567,048	381,440	1,893,596	21,222,617	19,615,354	678,362	928,901	21,222,617
Liechtenstein	0	0	0	0	0	0	0	0	0	0	0
Luxembourg	0	0	0	0	0	0	0	0	0	0	0
Netherlands	4,577,100	1,445,362	56,625	1,353,790	362,403	1,799,088	9,594,368	8,867,752	306,676	419,939	9,594,367
Norway	0	0	0	0	0	0	0	0	0	0	0
Portugal	1,087,307	129,297	0	70,493	32,240	138,649	1,457,986	1,116,805	10,673	330,507	1,457,985
Spain	2,292,678	296,375	0	647,793	31,831	264,544	3,533,221	3,265,638	112,936	154,647	3,533,221
Sweden	40,920,422	4,572,383	179,132	14,889,900	1,146,456	5,691,393	67,399,686	62,295,273	2,154,370	2,950,043	67,399,686
Switzerland	18,782,597	2,007,660	0	4,186,526	500,606	2,152,869	27,630,258	25,970,026	0	1,660,233	27,630,259
UK	24,784,313	2,945,713	115,404	8,843,304	738,593	3,666,624	41,093,951	37,981,763	1,313,531	1,798,657	41,093,951
West Germany	23,465,023	1,733,729	858,413	7,711,810	432,301	1,859,126	36,060,402	33,329,423	1,152,638	1,578,341	36,060,402
EU TOTAL	161,677,223	19,065,631	1,520,426	56,215,476	4,735,342	23,304,629	266,518,727	246,120,909	8,473,900	11,923,916	266,518,725
EFTA TOTAL	60,087,124	6,625,695	180,921	19,213,479	1,658,509	7,901,087	95,666,815	88,853,938	2,174,727	4,638,151	95,666,816
STUDY TOTAL	221,764,347	25,691,326	1,701,347	75,428,955	6,393,851	31,205,716	362,185,542	334,974,847	10,648,627	16,562,067	362,185,541

SCHOOL LIBRARIES : Estimated Average Expenditure and Income per annum (1986-1990) at constant 1990 prices in ECUs.

	Staff Expenditure	Premises and Operating Costs	New Buildings and Refurbishment	Acquisition of Stock	Cost of Borrowing	Miscellaneous Expenditure	TOTAL EXPENDITURE	Government and Municipal Funds	Fees and Charges	Other Income	TOTAL INCOME
Austria	6,984,808	830,172	32,523	2,492,253	208,153	1,033,342	11,581,251	10,704,163	370,184	506,904	11,581,251
Belgium	26,489,024	3,148,324	123,342	9,451,563	789,395	3,918,821	43,920,469	40,594,219	1,403,878	1,922,372	43,920,469
Denmark	66,183,116	7,866,123	308,171	23,614,833	1,972,311	9,791,217	109,735,771	101,425,098	3,507,605	4,803,067	109,735,770
East Germany	15,516,267	1,844,169	72,249	5,536,367	462,398	2,295,497	25,726,947	23,778,556	822,338	1,126,052	25,726,946
Eire	1,528,455	7,696,974	301,544	528,454	1,929,900	9,580,673	21,566,000	19,121,331	1,031,797	1,412,872	21,566,000
Finland	21,727,908	2,582,447	101,172	7,752,747	647,509	3,214,455	36,026,238	33,297,846	1,151,546	1,576,846	36,026,238
France	158,698,916	18,861,988	738,955	56,625,446	4,729,358	23,478,127	263,132,790	243,204,827	8,410,802	11,517,161	263,132,790
Greece	27,943,126	3,321,150	130,112	9,970,402	832,728	4,133,943	46,331,461	42,822,618	1,480,943	2,027,900	46,331,461
Iceland	104,169	12,381	485	37,169	3,104	15,411	172,719	159,638	5,521	7,560	172,719
Italy	48,236,827	5,733,136	224,607	17,211,408	1,437,497	7,136,220	79,979,695	73,922,555	2,556,478	3,500,662	79,979,695
Liechtenstein	28,538	3,392	133	10,183	851	4,222	47,319	43,735	1,513	2,071	47,319
Luxembourg	915,178	108,773	4,261	326,545	27,273	135,393	1,517,423	1,402,503	48,503	66,417	1,517,423
Netherlands	42,826,304	5,090,074	199,414	15,280,877	1,276,259	6,335,780	71,008,708	65,630,971	2,269,729	3,108,008	71,008,708
Norway	24,057,479	2,859,326	112,020	3,537,412	716,933	3,559,095	34,842,265	32,203,538	1,113,702	1,525,025	34,842,265
Portugal	8,844,832	1,051,243	41,184	3,155,930	263,583	1,308,516	14,665,288	13,554,635	468,762	641,891	14,665,288
Spain	6,396,091	1,127,505	44,172	2,358,863	282,705	1,403,442	11,612,778	10,733,302	371,192	508,284	11,612,778
Sweden	98,312,912	11,684,875	457,778	35,079,083	2,929,805	14,544,542	163,008,995	150,663,756	5,210,435	7,134,804	163,008,995
Switzerland	5,824,383	692,251	27,121	2,078,201	173,571	861,667	9,657,194	8,925,821	308,683	422,689	9,657,193
UK	142,506,606	11,528,623	0	61,005,649	0	0	215,040,878	198,755,083	6,873,587	9,412,208	215,040,878
West Germany	46,825,286	5,565,369	218,034	16,707,755	1,395,432	6,927,394	77,639,270	71,759,378	2,481,669	3,398,223	77,639,270
EU TOTAL	592,910,028	72,943,451	2,406,045	221,774,092	15,398,839	76,445,023	981,877,478	906,705,076	31,727,283	43,445,117	981,877,476
EFTA TOTAL	157,040,197	18,664,844	731,232	50,987,048	4,679,926	23,232,734	255,335,981	235,998,497	8,161,584	11,175,899	255,335,980
STUDY TOTAL	749,950,225	91,608,295	3,137,277	272,761,140	20,078,765	99,677,757	1,237,213,459	1,142,703,573	39,888,867	54,621,016	1,237,213,456

SCHOOL LIBRARIES : Estimated Average Expenditure and Income per annum (1981-1985) at constant 1990 prices in ECUs.

	Staff Expenditure	Premises and Operating Costs	New Buildings and Refurbishment	Acquisition of Stock	Cost of Borrowing	Miscellaneous Expenditure	TOTAL EXPENDITURE	Government and Municipal Funds	Fees and Charges	Other Income	TOTAL INCOME
Austria	7,001,694	832,179	32,602	2,498,840	208,656	1,035,840	11,609,811	10,730,040	371,079	508,130	11,609,249
Belgium	26,489,024	3,148,324	123,342	9,451,563	789,395	3,918,821	43,920,469	40,594,219	1,403,878	1,922,372	43,920,469
Denmark	59,044,966	7,017,726	274,933	21,067,866	1,759,588	8,735,190	97,900,269	90,485,941	3,129,293	4,285,035	97,900,269
East Germany	15,588,495	1,852,754	72,585	5,562,139	464,550	2,306,182	25,846,705	23,889,245	826,166	1,131,294	25,846,705
Eire	1,528,455	7,696,974	301,544	528,454	1,929,900	9,580,672	21,565,999	19,121,330	1,031,798	1,412,872	21,566,000
Finland	17,183,453	2,042,321	80,012	6,131,237	512,081	2,542,143	28,491,247	26,333,505	910,697	1,247,044	28,491,246
France	158,698,916	18,861,988	738,955	56,625,446	4,729,358	23,478,127	263,132,790	243,204,827	8,410,802	11,517,161	263,132,790
Greece	27,943,126	3,321,150	130,112	9,970,402	832,728	4,133,943	46,331,461	42,822,618	1,480,943	2,027,900	46,331,461
Iceland	57,164	6,794	266	20,397	1,703	8,457	94,781	87,603	3,029	4,149	94,781
Italy	48,236,827	5,733,136	224,607	17,211,408	1,437,497	7,136,220	79,979,695	73,922,555	2,556,478	3,500,662	79,979,695
Liechtenstein	28,583	3,397	133	10,199	852	4,229	47,393	43,804	1,515	2,074	47,393
Luxembourg	915,178	108,773	4,261	326,545	27,273	135,393	1,517,423	1,402,503	48,503	66,417	1,517,423
Netherlands	42,826,304	5,090,074	199,414	15,280,877	1,276,259	6,335,780	71,008,708	65,630,971	2,269,729	3,108,008	71,008,708
Norway	23,533,649	2,797,066	109,581	3,460,388	701,322	3,481,559	34,083,565	31,502,236	1,089,452	1,491,819	34,083,507
Portugal	6,238,121	741,425	29,047	2,225,827	185,901	922,876	10,343,197	9,559,871	330,611	452,715	10,343,197
Spain	6,396,091	1,127,505	44,172	2,358,863	282,705	1,403,442	11,612,778	10,733,302	371,192	508,284	11,612,778
Sweden	130,268,623	15,482,936	606,574	46,481,217	3,882,112	19,272,112	215,993,574	199,635,629	6,904,039	9,453,906	215,993,574
Switzerland	5,834,338	693,434	27,167	2,081,753	173,868	863,140	9,673,700	8,941,078	309,211	423,411	9,673,700
UK	142,506,606	11,528,623	0	61,005,649	0	0	215,040,878	198,755,084	6,873,587	9,412,207	215,040,878
West Germany	46,825,286	5,565,369	218,034	16,707,755	1,395,432	6,927,394	77,639,270	71,759,378	2,481,669	3,398,223	77,639,270
EU TOTAL	583,237,395	71,793,821	2,361,006	218,322,794	15,110,586	75,014,040	965,839,642	891,881,844	31,214,649	42,743,150	965,839,643
EFTA TOTAL	183,907,504	21,858,127	856,335	60,684,031	5,480,594	27,207,480	299,994,071	277,273,895	9,589,022	13,130,533	299,993,450
STUDY TOTAL	767,144,899	93,651,948	3,217,341	279,006,825	20,591,180	102,221,520	1,265,833,713	1,169,155,739	40,803,671	55,873,683	1,265,833,093

SPECIAL LIBRARIES : Estimated Average Expenditure and Income per annum (1986-1990) at constant 1990 prices in ECS.

	Staff Expenditure	Premises and Operating Costs	New Buildings and Refurbishment	Acquisition of Stock	Cost of Borrowing	Miscellaneous Expenditure	TOTAL EXPENDITURE	Government and Municipal Funds	Fees and Charges	Other Income	TOTAL INCOME
Austria	25,083,215	2,981,238	116,796	8,949,956	747,500	3,710,844	41,589,549	38,439,828	1,329,372	1,820,349	41,589,549
Belgium	10,627,328	1,263,100	49,484	3,791,943	316,703	1,572,221	17,620,779	16,286,295	563,233	771,251	17,620,779
Denmark	8,626,789	1,946,450	0	3,276,826	485,343	2,087,232	16,422,640	15,178,894	524,934	718,812	16,422,640
East Germany	54,633,521	6,493,408	254,392	19,493,816	1,628,123	8,082,555	90,585,815	83,725,436	2,895,494	3,964,886	90,585,816
Eire	369,439	55,857	3,319	167,689	14,005	69,527	679,836	628,349	21,731	29,756	679,836
Finland	5,633,500	733,386	0	2,050,757	182,868	786,429	9,386,940	8,676,035	300,045	410,861	9,386,941
France	57,440,310	6,827,006	267,461	20,495,308	1,711,768	8,497,795	95,239,648	88,026,818	3,044,249	4,168,581	95,239,648
Greece	10,322,044	1,226,815	48,063	3,683,014	307,605	1,527,057	17,114,598	15,818,450	547,053	749,095	17,114,598
Iceland	480,232	57,077	2,236	171,352	14,311	71,046	796,254	735,951	25,452	34,852	796,255
Italy	16,839,875	2,001,485	78,412	6,008,645	501,842	2,491,313	27,921,572	25,806,975	892,488	1,222,110	27,921,573
Liechtenstein	0	0	0	0	0	0	0	0	0	0	0
Luxembourg	407,164	48,393	1,896	145,280	12,134	60,236	675,103	623,975	21,579	29,549	675,103
Netherlands	39,233,355	4,663,038	182,683	27,415,712	1,169,186	4,119,887	76,783,861	70,968,752	2,454,327	3,360,782	76,783,861
Norway	4,527,999	273,951	10,733	3,865,507	68,689	340,995	9,087,874	8,399,616	290,486	397,771	9,087,873
Portugal	4,024,802	186,355	0	1,846,350	46,467	199,834	6,303,808	4,057,106	31,500	2,215,201	6,303,807
Spain	73,700,389	4,043,795	0	24,735,109	434,303	3,609,492	106,523,088	98,455,724	3,404,914	4,662,450	106,523,088
Sweden	12,254,565	1,350,643	0	5,649,777	336,780	1,448,331	21,040,096	20,080,106	9,080	950,910	21,040,096
Switzerland	22,148,428	2,632,428	103,131	7,902,793	660,041	3,276,668	36,723,489	33,942,290	1,173,833	1,607,364	36,723,487
UK	59,415,530	7,061,769	276,658	21,200,087	1,770,631	8,790,012	98,514,687	91,053,828	3,148,932	4,311,927	98,514,687
West Germany	29,569,363	4,196,166	164,393	12,597,283	1,052,125	5,223,104	52,802,434	48,803,522	1,687,782	2,311,130	52,802,434
EU TOTAL	365,209,909	40,013,637	1,326,761	144,857,062	9,450,235	46,330,265	607,187,869	559,434,124	19,238,216	28,515,530	607,187,870
EFTA TOTAL	70,127,939	8,028,723	232,896	28,590,142	2,010,189	9,634,313	118,624,202	110,273,826	3,128,268	5,222,107	118,624,201
STUDY TOTAL	435,337,848	48,042,360	1,559,657	173,447,204	11,460,424	55,964,578	725,812,071	669,707,950	22,366,484	33,737,637	725,812,071

SPECIAL LIBRARIES : Estimated Average Expenditure and Income per annum (1981-1985) at constant 1990 prices in ECS.

	Staff Expenditure	Premises and Operating Costs	New Buildings and Refurbishment	Acquisition of Stock	Cost of Borrowing	Miscellaneous Expenditure	TOTAL EXPENDITURE	Government and Municipal Funds	Fees and Charges	Other Income	TOTAL INCOME
Austria	25,048,858	2,977,155	116,636	8,937,697	746,476	3,705,761	41,532,583	38,387,176	1,327,551	1,817,856	41,532,583
Belgium	10,627,328	1,263,100	49,484	3,791,943	316,703	1,572,221	17,620,779	16,286,295	563,233	771,251	17,620,779
Denmark	4,221,847	952,569	0	1,603,639	237,521	1,021,466	8,037,042	7,428,368	256,897	351,777	8,037,042
East Germany	54,808,136	6,514,162	255,205	19,556,120	1,633,327	8,108,388	90,875,338	83,993,032	2,904,748	3,977,558	90,875,338
Eire	369,439	55,857	3,319	167,689	14,005	69,527	679,836	628,349	21,731	29,756	679,836
Finland	4,224,592	570,654	0	1,679,826	142,291	611,927	7,229,290	6,681,790	231,078	316,422	7,229,290
France	57,440,310	6,827,006	267,461	20,495,308	1,711,768	8,497,795	95,239,648	88,026,818	3,044,249	4,168,581	95,239,648
Greece	10,322,044	1,226,815	48,063	3,683,014	307,605	1,527,057	17,114,598	15,818,450	547,053	749,095	17,114,598
Iceland	244,428	29,051	1,138	87,215	7,284	36,161	405,277	374,584	12,954	17,739	405,277
Italy	14,302,639	1,699,925	66,598	5,103,332	426,230	2,115,951	23,714,675	21,918,680	758,018	1,037,977	23,714,675
Liechtenstein	0	0	0	0	0	0	0	0	0	0	0
Luxembourg	407,164	48,393	1,896	145,280	12,134	60,236	675,103	623,975	21,579	29,549	675,103
Netherlands	31,823,032	3,782,292	148,179	22,474,427	948,352	4,230,100	63,406,382	58,604,396	2,026,727	2,775,259	63,406,382
Norway	4,023,786	243,445	9,537	3,435,065	61,040	303,024	8,075,897	7,464,281	258,139	353,477	8,075,897
Portugal	3,283,316	198,163	0	1,559,655	49,412	212,495	5,303,041	2,225,018	13,016	3,065,007	5,303,041
Spain	48,534,164	2,662,974	0	16,288,895	286,003	2,376,971	70,149,007	64,836,378	2,242,250	3,070,379	70,149,007
Sweden	11,360,498	1,252,103	0	5,237,581	312,209	1,342,664	19,505,055	18,615,104	8,418	881,534	19,505,056
Switzerland	22,116,316	2,628,611	102,981	7,891,335	659,084	3,271,917	36,670,244	33,893,079	1,172,131	1,605,034	36,670,244
UK	59,415,530	7,061,769	276,658	21,200,087	1,770,631	8,790,012	98,514,687	91,053,828	3,148,932	4,311,927	98,514,687
West Germany	22,485,138	3,190,849	125,008	9,579,227	800,057	3,971,753	40,152,032	37,111,179	1,283,423	1,757,430	40,152,032
EU TOTAL	318,040,087	35,483,874	1,241,871	125,648,616	8,513,748	42,553,972	531,482,168	488,554,766	16,831,856	26,095,546	531,482,168
EFTA TOTAL	67,018,478	7,701,019	230,292	27,268,719	1,928,384	9,271,454	113,418,346	105,416,014	3,010,271	4,992,062	113,418,347
STUDY TOTAL	385,058,565	43,184,893	1,472,163	152,917,335	10,442,132	51,825,426	644,900,514	593,970,780	19,842,127	31,087,608	644,900,515

PUBLIC LIBRARIES : Estimated Average Expenditure and Income per annum (1986-1990) at constant 1990 prices in ECUs.

	Staff Expenditure	Premises and Operating Costs	New Buildings and Refurbishment	Acquisition of Stock	Cost of Borrowing	Miscellaneous Expenditure	TOTAL EXPENDITURE	Government and Municipal Funds	Fees and Charges	Other Income	TOTAL INCOME
Austria	22,993,056	2,732,815	107,063	8,204,165	685,212	3,401,623	38,123,934	35,236,675	1,218,597	1,668,661	38,123,933
Belgium	77,321,688	14,198,404	694,553	28,516,048	4,515,438	17,039,869	142,286,000	113,747,374	15,214,505	13,324,121	142,286,000
Denmark	152,220,522	44,644,458	0	42,565,288	0	0	239,430,268	239,430,267	0	0	239,430,267
East Germany	187,502,605	17,797,984	0	69,150,500	4,437,886	19,085,265	297,974,240	275,407,613	9,524,477	13,042,150	297,974,240
Eire	18,214,336	3,980,028	0	4,247,167	2,436,899	2,586,084	31,464,514	29,325,792	929,424	1,209,298	31,464,514
Finland	107,071,124	25,914,467	401,884	48,287,196	2,572,085	12,768,699	197,015,455	197,015,455	0	0	197,015,455
France	183,664,620	26,625,293	0	46,640,429	6,638,955	28,551,029	292,120,326	287,185,979	4,395,878	538,470	292,120,327
Greece	23,117,555	2,747,612	107,643	8,248,587	688,922	3,420,041	38,330,360	35,427,469	1,225,195	1,677,696	38,330,360
Iceland	2,616,661	311,000	12,184	1,078,350	77,979	387,112	4,483,286	4,131,670	292,996	58,621	4,483,287
Italy	247,140,802	29,373,652	1,150,770	88,182,443	7,364,998	36,562,336	409,775,001	378,741,312	13,098,088	17,395,601	409,235,001
Liechtenstein	68,967	8,197	321	24,608	2,055	10,203	114,351	105,692	3,655	5,005	114,352
Luxembourg	1,892,663	224,950	8,813	675,322	56,403	280,003	3,138,154	2,900,490	100,309	137,355	3,138,154
Netherlands	145,442,496	69,349,216	0	51,442,601	4,702,442	39,081,970	310,018,725	254,412,782	29,837,109	25,768,832	310,018,723
Norway	47,682,814	6,648,870	260,483	14,183,518	1,667,103	8,276,064	78,718,852	78,718,853	0	0	78,718,853
Portugal	3,176,091	210,953	0	440,947	52,601	226,211	4,106,803	3,667,472	8,148	431,184	4,106,804
Spain	49,108,746	8,711,178	0	16,103,888	702,988	5,842,532	80,469,332	74,375,109	2,572,129	3,522,093	80,469,331
Sweden	172,394,069	44,618,785	1,748,027	55,047,146	11,187,484	55,538,446	340,533,957	314,744,136	10,884,860	14,904,962	340,533,958
Switzerland	56,154,850	3,625,851	0	16,448,999	904,098	3,888,099	81,021,897	76,816,814	0	4,205,083	81,021,897
UK	496,548,185	105,234,249	0	175,003,105	61,936,044	146,383,742	985,105,325	929,330,918	20,172,189	35,602,219	985,105,326
West Germany	267,838,997	34,267,495	1,342,496	53,065,752	8,592,055	63,982,732	429,089,527	396,593,083	13,715,458	18,780,985	429,089,526
EU TOTAL	1,876,182,362	360,098,287	3,411,338	592,486,242	102,810,843	366,443,437	3,301,432,509	3,055,782,335	112,011,506	133,098,665	3,300,892,506
EFTA TOTAL	385,988,485	81,127,170	2,422,899	135,069,817	16,410,804	80,868,623	701,887,798	671,532,620	11,181,511	19,173,671	701,887,802
STUDY TOTAL	2,262,170,847	441,225,457	5,834,237	727,556,059	119,221,647	447,312,060	4,003,320,307	3,727,314,955	123,193,017	152,272,336	4,002,780,308

PUBLIC LIBRARIES : Estimated Average Expenditure and Income per annum (1981-1985) at constant 1990 prices in ECUs.

	Staff Expenditure	Premises and Operating Costs	New Buildings and Refurbishment	Acquisition of Stock	Cost of Borrowing	Miscellaneous Expenditure	TOTAL EXPENDITURE	Government and Municipal Funds	Fees and Charges	Other Income	TOTAL INCOME
Austria	19,707,264	2,342,286	91,764	7,031,760	587,293	2,915,519	32,675,886	30,201,226	1,044,455	1,430,203	32,675,884
Belgium	60,087,158	11,033,667	539,741	22,159,996	3,508,975	13,241,787	110,571,324	87,219,137	12,449,511	10,902,675	110,571,323
Denmark	149,987,803	30,569,560	0	50,232,434	0	0	230,789,797	230,789,797	0	0	230,789,797
East Germany	187,502,605	17,797,984	0	69,150,500	4,437,886	19,085,265	297,974,240	275,407,613	9,524,477	13,042,150	297,974,240
Eire	17,213,572	3,491,270	0	5,498,487	2,798,070	2,085,606	31,087,005	29,527,465	606,251	953,289	31,087,005
Finland	88,330,315	21,643,566	256,099	41,962,199	1,639,048	8,136,789	161,968,016	161,968,015	0	0	161,968,015
France	146,214,002	21,116,364	0	37,315,426	5,265,317	22,643,653	232,554,762	228,626,298	3,499,696	428,768	232,554,762
Greece	23,117,547	2,747,611	107,643	8,248,584	688,922	3,420,040	38,330,347	35,427,457	1,225,195	1,677,696	38,330,348
Iceland	2,216,113	263,394	10,319	913,280	66,042	327,855	3,797,003	3,499,210	248,145	49,648	3,797,003
Italy	247,140,802	29,373,652	1,150,770	88,182,443	7,364,998	36,562,336	409,775,001	378,741,312	13,098,088	17,935,601	409,775,001
Liechtenstein	58,671	6,973	273	20,934	1,748	8,680	97,279	89,913	3,109	4,258	97,280
Luxembourg	1,892,663	224,950	8,813	675,322	56,403	280,003	3,138,154	2,900,490	100,309	137,355	3,138,154
Netherlands	154,134,142	45,354,266	0	46,685,662	15,065,210	40,369,917	301,609,197	257,408,519	20,348,895	23,851,783	301,609,197
Norway	43,235,864	6,028,790	236,190	12,860,748	1,511,628	7,504,230	71,377,450	71,377,449	0	0	71,377,449
Portugal	3,866,127	237,920	0	506,264	59,325	255,129	4,924,765	4,434,239	6,818	483,709	4,924,766
Spain	32,117,171	5,697,119	0	10,531,960	459,755	3,821,022	52,627,027	48,641,399	1,682,175	2,303,453	52,627,027
Sweden	158,957,304	41,141,101	1,611,782	50,756,653	10,315,508	51,209,661	313,992,009	290,212,301	10,036,471	13,743,237	313,992,009
Switzerland	47,304,494	3,054,394	0	13,856,534	761,606	3,275,310	68,252,338	64,706,730	0	3,545,608	68,252,338
UK	448,935,117	90,118,419	0	140,175,369	52,224,741	123,536,027	854,989,673	807,821,970	16,220,329	30,947,373	854,989,672
West Germany	222,539,499	28,471,848	1,115,440	44,090,764	7,138,884	53,161,359	356,517,794	329,517,460	11,395,769	15,604,565	356,517,794
EU TOTAL	1,694,748,208	286,234,630	2,922,407	523,453,211	99,068,486	318,462,144	2,924,889,086	2,716,463,156	90,157,513	118,268,417	2,924,889,086
EFTA TOTAL	359,810,025	74,480,504	2,206,427	127,402,108	14,882,873	73,378,044	652,159,981	622,054,844	11,332,180	18,772,954	652,159,978
STUDY TOTAL	2,054,558,233	360,715,134	5,128,834	650,855,319	113,951,359	391,840,188	3,577,049,067	3,338,518,000	101,489,693	137,041,371	3,577,049,064

APPENDIX 5

ECONOMETRIC DATA

GDP : National currencies

Exchange Rates : National currencies/ECU

GDP : ECU

Consumer Price Indices

Libraries expenditure as a % of GDP

Growth in Salaries compared to Growth in Consumer Prices

Sector population served, Sectors 1-6

Population changes for the EU and EFTA

ECONOMETRIC DATA

Sources

Eurostat
Statistical Office of the European Communities
Monetary and Financial Statistics
Jean Monet Building
L-2920
Luxembourg

OECD
Main Economic Indicators
February 1994
2 rue André-Pascal
75775 Paris
1SSN 0474 5523

OECD
Quarterly National Accounts No 4 1993
2 rue André-Pascal
75775 Paris
ISSN 0304 3738

Statistical Bureau of Iceland
Skuggasund 3
150 Reykjavik

Income Data Services Ltd
193 St John Street
London
EC1V 4LS

LIST OF DATA

Gross Domestic Product (GDP)

Source OECD

These data proved to be the most comprehensive and consistent data available. However, OECD GDP data does not include GDP data for Liechtenstein.

Exchange rates National currencies/ECUs

Source Eurostat and OECD

The table presents the annual exchange ratio to ECUs for the countries participating in the study.

Liechtenstein use the Swiss Franc.

GROSS DOMESTIC PRODUCT

GDP (ECU - Million Currency Units)

Data taken from OECD source and converted to the common currency unit, ECUs, using the annual average exchange rates.

Consumer Price Indices
Source OECD and Statistical Bureau of Iceland

Using 1990 as the base year this table shows the indices of real purchasing power throughout the decade.

The CPI for Switzerland has been replicated for Liechtenstein.

It is worth noting that inflation was particularly high in Iceland.

Using the annual average ECU exchange rates and the Consumer Price Indices Library expenditure and income for each individual country were converted to a common and consistent basis, that of 1990 constant price in ECUs.

Library expenditure and income tables are shown at Appendix 4.

GDP (NATIONAL CURRENCIES - MILLION CURRENCY UNITS)

COUNTRY	1981	1982	1983	1984	1985	1986	1987	1988	1989	1990
AUSTRIA	-	1,133,535	1,201,217	1,276,775	1,348,425	1,422,497	1,481,388	1,561,700	1,663,891	1,789,386
BELGIUM	-	3,888,986	4,122,259	4,429,036	4,738,039	4,985,952	5,205,543	5,542,673	6,015,975	6,429,346
DENMARK	-	464,467	512,540	565,284	615,072	666,496	699,908	732,054	769,801	800,014
EAST GERMANY	-	263,858	276,505	293,271	311,755	321,935	332,810	346,129	-	-
FINLAND	-	245,716	274,647	308,357	334,986	357,566	391,597	441,539	496,935	524,781
FRANCE	-	3,626,021	4,006,498	4,361,913	4,700,143	5,069,296	5,336,652	5,723,206	6,136,070	6,484,109
GREECE	-	2,574,652	3,079,178	3,805,686	4,617,816	5,514,766	6,258,478	7,526,471	8,777,535	-
ICELAND	-	38,132	65,837	87,508	119,091	158,597	208,099	254,639	300,595	341,790
EIRE	-	13,382	14,779	16,407	17,790	18,877	20,263	21,815	24,308	25,693
ITALY	-	545,124,000	633,436,000	725,760,000	810,580,000	899,903,000	983,803,000	1,091,837,000	1,192,725,000	1,306,833,000
LIECHTENSTEIN	-	-	-	-	-	-	-	-	-	-
LUXEMBOURG	-	158,786	174,683	193,666	205,255	223,304	227,846	248,387	279,033	291,505
NETHERLANDS	-	368,860	381,020	400,250	418,180	428,610	430,170	449,820	475,300	508,310
NORWAY	-	362,269	402,269	452,512	500,199	513,718	561,480	583,277	621,383	661,670
PORTUGAL	-	1,850,407	2,301,713	2,815,728	3,523,945	4,420,400	5,174,732	6,002,751	7,130,260	8,507,434
SPAIN	-	19,567,000	22,235,000	25,111,000	28,201,000	32,324,000	36,144,000	40,164,000	45,025,000	-
SWEDEN	-	633,682	709,852	794,298	865,788	945,583	1,019,547	1,110,471	1,226,313	1,350,138
SWITZERLAND	-	195,980	203,865	213,230	227,950	243,350	254,350	268,410	290,360	312,355
UK	-	278,087	303,377	324,081	354,911	381,731	419,983	466,477	510,020	549,181
WEST GERMAN	-	1,588,090	1,668,540	1,750,890	1,823,180	1,925,290	1,990,480	2,095,980	2,220,880	2,404,540

EXCHANGE RATES (CURRENCY/ECU)

COUNTRY	1981	1982	1983	1984	1985	1986	1987	1988	1989	1990
AUSTRIA	17.715	16.699	15.969	15.735	15.643	14.964	14.545	14.586	14.569	14.440
BELGIUM	41.295	44.712	45.438	45.442	44.914	43.798	43.039	43.428	43.381	42.425
DENMARK	7.926	8.157	8.132	8.146	8.019	7.936	7.884	7.952	8.049	7.856
EAST GERMANY	2.514	2.376	2.271	2.238	2.226	2.128	2.072	2.074	2.070	2.052
FINLAND	4.793	4.708	4.948	4.724	4.694	4.980	5.065	4.844	4.723	4.855
FRANCE	6.039	6.431	6.771	6.872	6.795	6.800	6.928	7.038	7.024	6.914
GREECE	61.624	65.342	78.088	88.340	105.739	137.425	156.220	167.575	178.840	201.412
ICELAND	74.658	74.658	74.658	74.658	74.658	74.658	74.658	74.658	74.658	74.658
EIRE	0.691	0.690	0.715	0.726	0.715	0.734	0.775	0.776	0.777	0.768
ITALY	1,263.180	1,323.780	1,349.820	1,381.380	1,447.990	1,461.870	1,494.710	1,537.330	1,510.470	1,521.940
LIECHTENSTEIN	2.187	1.986	1.868	1.848	1.856	1.761	1.718	1.728	1.800	1.762
LUXEMBOURG	41.295	44.712	45.438	45.442	44.914	43.798	43.039	43.428	43.381	42.425
NETHERLANDS	2.775	2.614	2.537	2.523	2.511	2.401	2.334	2.335	2.335	2.312
NORWAY	6.386	6.313	6.491	6.409	6.511	7.278	7.766	7.701	7.604	7.948
PORTUGAL	68.495	78.007	98.689	115.680	130.251	147.088	162.581	170.059	173.413	181.108
SPAIN	102.676	107.558	127.503	126.569	129.165	137.456	142.191	137.601	130.406	129.316
SWEDEN	5.635	6.145	6.821	6.511	6.521	6.996	7.313	7.242	7.099	7.520
SWITZERLAND	2.187	1.986	1.868	1.848	1.856	1.761	1.718	1.728	1.800	1.762
UK	0.553	0.580	0.587	0.591	0.589	0.672	0.705	0.664	0.573	0.714
WEST GERMAN	2.514	2.376	2.271	2.238	2.226	2.128	2.072	2.074	2.070	2.052

GDP (ECU - MILLION CURRENCY UNITS)

COUNTRY	1981	1982	1983	1984	1985	1986	1987	1988	1989	1990
AUSTRIA	-	67,880	75,222	81,143	86,201	95,059	101,846	107,068	114,204	123,918
BELGIUM	-	86,980	90,723	97,466	105,492	113,840	120,949	127,628	138,679	151,545
DENMARK	-	56,942	63,028	69,390	76,704	83,988	88,774	92,065	95,636	101,829
EAST GERMANY	-	111,052	121,780	131,035	140,032	151,272	160,654	166,857		
FINLAND	-	52,188	55,505	65,274	71,361	71,804	77,312	91,159	105,216	108,094
FRANCE	-	563,820	591,734	634,769	691,704	745,511	770,249	813,137	873,602	937,803
GREECE	-	39,403	39,432	43,080	43,672	40,129	40,062	44,914	49,080	
ICELAND	-	511	882	1,172	1,595	2,124	2,787	3,411	4,026	4,578
EIRE	-	19,405	20,674	22,601	24,875	25,735	26,131	28,124	31,292	33,464
ITALY	-	411,794	469,274	525,388	559,797	615,583	658,190	710,216	789,638	858,663
LIECHTENSTEIN	-									
LUXEMBOURG	-	3,551	3,844	4,262	4,570	5,099	5,294	5,719	6,432	6,871
NETHERLANDS	-	141,115	150,173	158,619	166,539	178,521	184,284	192,660	203,532	219,844
NORWAY	-	57,385	61,972	70,606	76,823	70,590	72,296	75,745	81,720	83,246
PORTUGAL	-	23,721	23,323	24,341	27,055	30,053	31,829	35,298	41,117	46,974
SPAIN	-	181,920	174,388	198,398	218,333	235,159	254,193	291,887	345,268	
SWEDEN	-	103,116	104,066	121,996	132,762	135,167	139,422	153,340	172,735	179,535
SWITZERLAND	-	98,664	109,163	115,414	122,836	138,200	148,052	155,310	161,302	177,263
UK	-	479,085	516,814	548,708	602,589	568,440	595,823	702,067	889,618	769,316
WEST GERMAN	-	668,391	734,871	782,307	818,921	904,661	960,846	1,010,403	1,072,811	1,171,740
EU TOTAL	-	2,787,179	3,000,060	3,240,363	3,480,282	3,697,990	3,897,278	4,220,976	4,536,707	4,298,049
EFTA TOTAL	-	379,743	406,810	455,604	491,580	512,945	541,715	586,032	639,204	676,633

CONSUMER PRICE INDICES (1990 = 100)

COUNTRY	1981	1982	1983	1984	1985	1986	1987	1988	1989	1990
AUSTRIA	75.651	79.784	82.390	87.062	89.847	91.375	92.633	94.429	96.855	100.000
BELGIUM	70.894	71.234	75.404	80.255	85.106	88.426	91.319	91.574	94.553	100.000
DENMARK	62.409	66.774	71.625	75.990	80.841	84.640	88.682	91.835	95.150	100.000
EAST GERMANY	67.011	74.677	80.706	83.807	86.133	90.009	92.679	93.712	96.555	100.000
FINLAND	58.445	64.022	69.285	74.234	78.555	81.461	84.368	88.452	94.266	100.000
FRANCE	70.429	74.103	76.990	81.715	87.489	89.589	90.814	91.864	95.276	100.000
GREECE	71.453	81.549	82.071	85.901	87.032	81.027	82.942	87.815	93.560	100.000
ICELAND	8.364	12.632	23.278	30.069	39.803	48.271	57.327	71.921	87.083	100.000
EIRE	62.855	74.291	79.323	85.087	91.491	92.498	90.119	92.040	95.517	100.000
ITALY	56.550	62.859	70.687	76.597	79.872	83.626	85.623	87.540	94.649	100.000
LIECHTENSTEIN	76.325	80.654	83.039	85.424	88.339	88.958	90.283	92.049	94.876	100.000
LUXEMBOURG	71.577	72.357	77.296	82.322	86.655	89.168	90.641	91.161	94.281	100.000
NETHERLANDS	69.788	78.269	82.862	85.954	88.339	92.580	94.788	95.583	96.643	100.000
NORWAY	54.505	60.635	65.805	69.867	73.855	79.173	86.041	91.802	96.012	100.000
PORTUGAL	65.334	70.799	69.821	76.509	81.566	80.587	79.690	83.442	92.251	100.000
SPAIN	59.238	64.809	61.290	68.695	73.314	74.780	76.173	82.478	92.962	100.000
SWEDEN	53.960	58.623	63.805	68.912	74.019	77.128	80.385	85.048	90.526	100.000
SWITZERLAND	76.325	80.654	83.039	85.424	88.339	88.958	90.283	92.049	94.876	100.000
UK	76.636	82.000	82.000	85.364	90.909	82.727	81.818	91.091	96.909	100.000
WEST GERMAN	67.011	74.677	80.706	83.807	86.133	90.009	92.679	93.712	96.555	100.000

Libraries Expenditure as a percentage of GDP

This table shows the data employed to generate Figure 1. The GDP has been repriced to 1990 constant prices in order that a meaningful comparison might be made with the Library expenditure which is shown at 1990 constant prices in ECUs.

LIBRARIES EXPENDITURE AS A % OF GDP

COUNTRY	1981	1982	1983	1984	1985	1986	1987	1988	1989	1990
AUSTRIA	-	0.18%	0.17%	0.17%	0.17%	0.16%	0.15%	0.14%	0.15%	0.14%
BELGIUM	-	0.18%	0.19%	0.19%	0.19%	0.19%	0.19%	0.19%	0.18%	0.18%
DENMARK	-	0.45%	0.45%	0.42%	0.40%	0.42%	0.41%	0.43%	0.41%	0.41%
EAST GERMANY	-	0.48%	0.48%	0.46%	0.44%	0.43%	0.42%	0.41%	-	-
FINLAND	-	0.26%	0.28%	0.26%	0.28%	0.29%	0.29%	0.27%	0.27%	0.28%
FRANCE	-	0.10%	0.10%	0.10%	0.10%	0.09%	0.09%	0.09%	0.09%	0.09%
GREECE	-	0.32%	0.32%	0.31%	0.31%	0.31%	0.32%	0.30%	0.30%	-
ICELAND	-	0.14%	0.14%	0.14%	0.15%	0.14%	0.14%	0.16%	0.16%	0.16%
EIRE	-	0.22%	0.22%	0.22%	0.22%	0.22%	0.20%	0.18%	0.17%	0.17%
ITALY	-	0.08%	0.08%	0.08%	0.08%	0.08%	0.07%	0.07%	0.07%	0.07%
LIECHTENSTEIN	-	-	-	-	-	-	-	-	-	-
LUXEMBOURG	-	0.16%	0.16%	0.15%	0.15%	0.14%	0.14%	0.13%	0.12%	0.12%
NETHERLANDS	-	0.31%	0.31%	0.29%	0.30%	0.30%	0.30%	0.29%	0.28%	0.28%
NORWAY	-	0.17%	0.17%	0.16%	0.16%	0.21%	0.20%	0.21%	0.20%	0.20%
PORTUGAL	-	0.08%	0.08%	0.08%	0.08%	0.08%	0.08%	0.08%	0.09%	0.07%
SPAIN	-	0.07%	0.07%	0.08%	0.08%	0.07%	0.08%	0.09%	0.08%	-
SWEDEN	-	0.39%	0.42%	0.38%	0.37%	0.38%	0.38%	0.38%	0.35%	0.36%
SWITZERLAND	-	0.16%	0.16%	0.15%	0.15%	0.14%	0.13%	0.13%	0.14%	0.13%
UK	-	0.27%	0.25%	0.25%	0.24%	0.24%	0.23%	0.22%	0.21%	0.23%
WEST GERMAN	-	0.09%	0.09%	0.09%	0.09%	0.09%	0.09%	0.09%	0.09%	0.08%
EU TOTAL	-	0.15%	0.15%	0.15%	0.15%	0.15%	0.15%	0.14%	0.15%	0.16%
EFTA TOTAL	-	0.25%	0.25%	0.24%	0.24%	0.24%	0.23%	0.23%	0.23%	0.23%

GDP AT 1990 PRICES (ECU - MILLION CURRENCY UNITS)

COUNTRY	1981	1982	1983	1984	1985	1986	1987	1988	1989	1990
AUSTRIA	-	85,080	91,300	93,201	95,942	104,033	109,946	113,384	117,912	123,918
BELGIUM	-	122,104	120,315	121,445	123,953	128,741	132,446	139,371	146,668	151,545
DENMARK	-	85,275	87,998	91,314	94,883	99,229	100,104	100,250	100,511	101,829
EAST GERMANY	-	148,710	150,893	156,353	162,577	168,064	173,345	178,053	-	-
FINLAND	-	81,515	80,110	87,929	90,843	88,145	91,637	103,060	111,616	108,094
FRANCE	-	760,857	768,581	776,811	790,618	832,148	848,164	885,157	916,922	937,803
GREECE	-	48,318	48,046	50,151	50,179	49,526	48,301	51,146	52,459	-
ICELAND	-	4,043	3,788	3,898	4,008	4,401	4,862	4,742	4,623	4,578
EIRE	-	26,121	26,063	26,562	27,189	27,822	28,996	30,556	32,760	33,464
ITALY	-	655,102	663,877	685,908	700,865	736,113	768,707	811,306	834,285	858,663
LIECHTENSTEIN	-	-	-	-	-	-	-	-	-	-
LUXEMBOURG	-	4,908	4,974	5,177	5,274	5,718	5,841	6,274	6,822	6,871
NETHERLANDS	-	180,296	181,233	184,539	188,522	192,830	194,417	201,563	210,602	219,844
NORWAY	-	94,640	94,175	101,057	104,019	89,159	84,024	82,509	85,114	83,246
PORTUGAL	-	33,505	33,404	31,814	33,169	37,292	39,941	42,302	44,571	46,974
SPAIN	-	280,701	284,528	288,809	297,806	314,467	333,705	353,897	371,408	-
SWEDEN	-	175,895	163,102	177,031	179,362	175,250	173,443	180,297	190,814	179,535
SWITZERLAND	-	122,330	131,460	135,107	139,051	155,355	163,987	168,725	170,013	177,263
UK	-	584,250	630,261	642,789	662,848	687,125	728,228	770,732	917,993	769,316
WEST GERMAN	-	895,042	910,550	933,462	950,767	1,005,082	1,036,750	1,078,197	1,111,092	1,171,740
EU TOTAL	-	3,825,189	3,910,724	3,995,134	4,088,650	4,284,157	4,438,944	4,648,803	4,746,092	4,298,049
EFTA TOTAL	-	563,504	563,936	598,224	613,224	616,343	627,899	652,717	680,094	676,633

LIBRARIES EXPENDITURE - ALL SECTORS (ECU - MILLION CURRENCY UNITS)

COUNTRY	1981	1982	1983	1984	1985	1986	1987	1988	1989	1990
AUSTRIA	146	150	153	156	160	162	163	161	172	179
BELGIUM	209	221	226	231	235	244	252	262	270	275
DENMARK	372	381	395	385	383	414	408	427	413	418
EAST GERMANY	715	716	718	719	720	721	724	727	730	729
FINLAND	204	216	224	230	252	253	263	282	302	306
FRANCE	710	733	744	755	775	788	791	822	847	876
GREECE	155	155	155	155	155	155	155	155	155	155
ICELAND	6	6	5	6	6	6	7	7	8	7
EIRE	57	57	58	58	59	60	59	56	56	58
ITALY	551	553	551	555	561	571	573	575	576	578
LIECHTENSTEIN	1	1	1	1	1	1	1	1	1	1
LUXEMBOURG	8	8	8	8	8	8	8	8	8	8
NETHERLANDS	523	552	568	544	573	572	590	590	594	607
NORWAY	154	157	159	161	164	184	169	173	172	167
PORTUGAL	25	27	27	26	28	29	32	34	39	35
SPAIN	165	190	204	221	238	232	259	326	291	280
SWEDEN	685	682	679	673	659	661	656	681	672	641
SWITZERLAND	189	195	205	198	214	210	216	227	230	237
UK	1,595	1,553	1,605	1,608	1,594	1,647	1,663	1,724	1,960	1,736
WEST GERMAN	776	772	798	824	863	907	931	953	976	992
EU TOTAL	5,861	5,918	6,057	6,088	6,193	6,349	6,446	6,659	6,913	6,747
EFTA TOTAL	1,385	1,406	1,426	1,424	1,455	1,477	1,474	1,532	1,557	1,538

Growth in Salaries compared to the growth in Consumer Prices (Figure 2)

In order that the Gross Domestic Product is consistent with the data relating to salaries and retail prices. The Gross Domestic Product plotted in this figure differs slightly to that quoted in the main body of the report. The GDP compared in this figure excludes Liechtenstein and the former German Democratic Republic and is derived from the OECD "Growth of Nominal GDP".

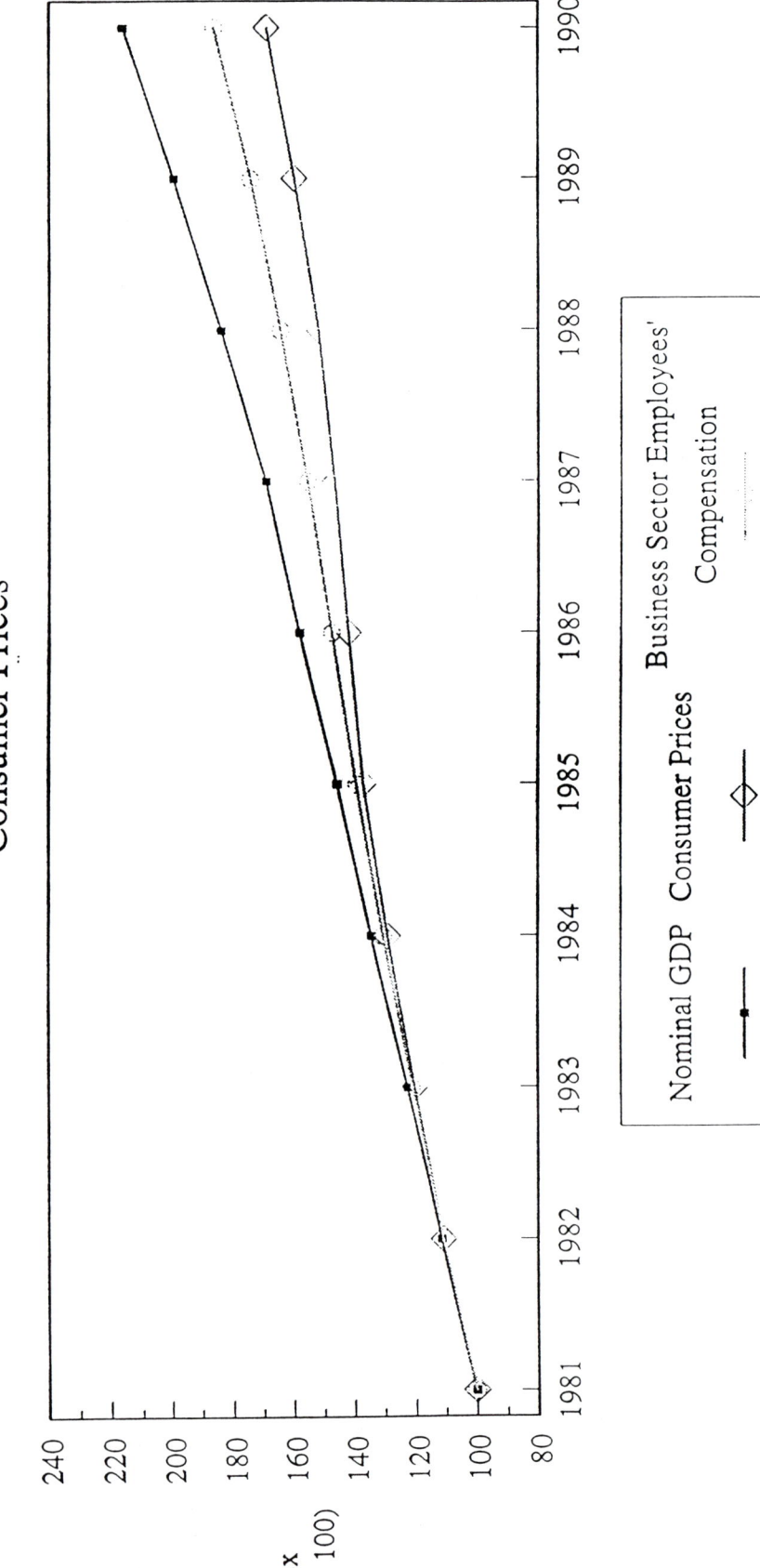

Population Served

Source Eurostat and OECD

In order to create estimated (grossed) data for "Activity" data, the average number per head of population were calculated for those countries which had returned "activity" data. These averages were then multiplied by the national or relevant sector populations for those sectors where data were not available.

The following population bands were applied to the six library sectors:

Sector	Age Range
National	Total Population
Institutes of Higher Education	20-24 Population Age Band
Other Major Non-Specialised	Total Population
School	5-19 Population Age Band
Special	15-64 Population Age Band
Public (or Popular)	Total Population

The tables showing population changes by sector over the decade and the two quinquennia show a slight increase in the total population and decreases within the School and Higher Education Sector Age Band Population. Thus, while the 20-24 Age Band Population has decreased, the number of students entering Higher Education has increased during the decade.

Sector Population Served

Sector 1
NATIONAL

	1981	1982	1983	1984	1985	1986	1987	1988	1989	1990	1981-85 Average	1986-90 Average	81/85 - 86/90 Year on Year Increase	Decade: Year on Year Increase
AUSTRIA	7,602,300	7,602,300	7,602,300	7,602,300	7,602,300	7,602,300	7,602,300	7,602,300	7,602,300	7,660,500	7,602,300	7,613,940	0.0%	0.1%
BELGIUM	9,853,300	9,853,300	9,853,300	9,853,300	9,857,700	9,858,900	9,884,700	9,927,600	9,853,300	9,853,300	9,854,180	9,871,560	0.0%	0.0%
DENMARK	5,112,000	5,112,000	5,112,000	5,112,000	5,077,100	5,116,300	5,124,800	5,129,800	5,129,700	5,135,200	5,105,020	5,127,160	0.1%	0.1%
EAST GERMANY	16,674,900	16,674,900	16,674,900	16,674,900	16,674,900	16,674,900	16,674,900	16,674,900	16,674,900	16,434,000	16,674,900	16,626,720	-0.1%	-0.2%
EIRE	3,523,000	3,523,000	3,523,000	3,523,000	3,537,300	3,540,500	3,539,300	3,521,800	3,523,000	3,523,000	3,525,660	3,529,520	0.0%	0.0%
FINLAND	4,954,600	4,954,600	4,954,600	4,954,600	4,954,600	4,954,600	4,954,600	4,954,600	4,954,600	4,974,500	4,954,600	4,958,580	0.0%	0.0%
FRANCE	54,830,900	54,830,900	54,830,900	54,830,900	55,062,400	55,278,400	55,510,000	56,017,000	54,830,900	54,830,900	54,877,200	55,293,440	0.2%	0.0%
GREECE	9,872,100	9,872,100	9,872,100	9,872,100	9,869,500	9,949,100	9,988,900	10,019,000	9,872,100	9,872,100	9,871,580	9,940,240	0.1%	0.0%
ICELAND	251,919	251,919	251,919	251,919	251,919	251,919	251,919	251,919	251,919	253,785	251,919	252,292	0.0%	0.1%
ITALY	56,929,100	56,929,100	56,929,100	56,929,100	57,080,600	58,202,100	57,290,500	57,504,700	56,929,100	56,929,100	56,959,400	57,371,100	0.1%	0.0%
LIECHTENSTEIN	28,181	28,181	28,181	28,181	28,181	28,181	28,181	28,181	28,181	28,452	28,181	28,235	0.0%	0.1%
LUXEMBOURG	365,600	365,600	365,600	365,600	366,200	365,600	371,700	374,900	374,900	378,300	365,720	373,080	0.4%	0.4%
NETHERLANDS	14,430,600	14,430,600	14,430,600	14,430,600	14,453,800	14,529,400	14,615,100	14,805,200	14,430,600	14,430,600	14,435,640	14,562,180	0.2%	0.0%
NORWAY	4,220,500	4,220,500	4,220,500	4,220,500	4,220,500	4,220,500	4,220,500	4,220,500	4,220,500	4,233,200	4,220,500	4,223,040	0.0%	0.0%
PORTUGAL	10,049,700	10,049,700	10,049,700	10,049,700	10,128,900	10,185,000	10,229,900	10,304,800	10,049,700	10,049,700	10,065,540	10,163,820	0.2%	0.0%
SPAIN	38,260,500	38,260,500	38,260,500	38,260,500	38,423,100	38,588,300	38,750,100	38,851,900	38,260,500	38,260,500	38,293,020	38,541,860	0.1%	0.0%
SWEDEN	8,458,800	8,458,800	8,458,800	8,458,800	8,458,800	8,458,800	8,458,800	8,458,800	8,458,800	8,526,800	8,458,800	8,472,400	0.0%	0.1%
SWITZERLAND	6,620,100	6,620,100	6,620,100	6,620,100	6,620,100	6,620,100	6,620,100	6,620,100	6,620,100	6,673,600	6,620,100	6,630,800	0.0%	0.1%
UK	56,403,900	56,403,900	56,403,900	56,403,900	56,539,300	56,690,600	56,997,700	57,150,500	56,403,900	56,403,900	56,430,980	56,729,320	0.1%	0.0%
WEST GERMANY	61,715,300	61,715,300	61,715,300	61,715,300	61,715,300	61,715,300	61,715,300	61,715,300	61,715,300	62,678,900	61,715,300	61,908,020	0.1%	0.2%
EU TOTAL	338,020,900	338,020,900	338,020,900	338,020,900	338,786,100	340,692,400	340,872,800	341,997,400	338,047,900	338,779,500	338,173,940	340,038,020	0.1%	0.0%
EFTA TOTAL	32,136,400	32,136,400	32,136,400	32,136,400	32,136,400	32,136,400	32,136,400	32,136,400	32,136,400	32,350,837	32,136,400	32,179,287	0.0%	0.1%
EUROPE TOTAL	370,157,300	370,157,300	370,157,300	370,157,300	370,922,500	372,828,800	372,809,300	374,133,800	370,184,300	371,130,337	370,310,340	372,217,307	0.1%	0.0%

Sector 2
HIGHER EDUCATION

	1981	1982	1983	1984	1985	1986	1987	1988	1989	1990	1981-85 Average	1986-90 Average	81/85 - 86/90 Year on Year Increase	Decade: Year on Year Increase
AUSTRIA	648,700	648,700	648,700	648,700	648,700	648,700	648,700	648,700	648,700	645,400	648,700	648,040	-0.0%	-0.1%
BELGIUM	792,000	792,000	792,000	792,000	789,500	793,200	782,500	761,400	792,000	792,000	791,500	784,220	-0.2%	0.0%
DENMARK	381,800	381,800	381,800	381,800	391,900	403,400	417,400	413,500	413,500	402,100	383,820	409,980	1.3%	0.6%
EAST GERMANY	1,315,300	1,315,300	1,315,300	1,315,300	1,315,300	1,315,300	1,315,300	1,315,300	1,315,300	1,230,100	1,315,300	1,298,260	-0.3%	-0.7%
EIRE	284,000	284,000	284,000	284,000	285,700	286,300	275,300	269,100	284,000	284,000	284,340	279,740	-0.3%	0.0%
FINLAND	363,800	363,800	363,800	363,800	363,800	363,800	363,800	363,800	363,800	353,400	363,800	361,720	-0.1%	-0.3%
FRANCE	4,266,900	4,266,900	4,266,900	4,266,900	4,288,600	4,303,900	4,298,500	4,248,100	4,266,900	4,266,900	4,271,240	4,276,940	0.0%	0.0%
GREECE	721,100	721,100	721,100	721,100	724,900	724,100	761,500	770,600	721,100	721,100	721,860	739,680	0.5%	0.0%
ICELAND	22,028	22,028	22,028	22,028	22,028	22,028	22,028	22,028	22,028	21,341	22,028	21,891	-0.1%	-0.4%
ITALY	4,448,500	4,448,500	4,448,500	4,448,500	4,613,200	4,738,200	4,824,900	4,854,600	4,448,500	4,448,500	4,481,440	4,662,920	0.8%	0.0%
LIECHTENSTEIN	2,571	2,571	2,571	2,571	2,571	2,571	2,571	2,571	2,571	2,548	2,571	2,566	-0.0%	-0.1%
LUXEMBOURG	29,500	29,500	29,500	29,500	29,600	29,500	29,300	28,600	28,600	28,100	29,520	28,820	-0.5%	-0.5%
NETHERLANDS	1,256,800	1,256,800	1,256,800	1,256,800	1,267,900	1,276,100	1,273,400	1,262,800	1,256,800	1,256,800	1,259,020	1,265,180	0.1%	0.0%
NORWAY	338,000	338,000	338,000	338,000	338,000	338,000	338,000	338,000	338,000	338,500	338,000	338,100	0.0%	0.0%
PORTUGAL	829,700	829,700	829,700	829,700	849,800	859,700	865,600	862,100	829,700	829,700	833,720	849,360	0.4%	0.0%
SPAIN	3,129,500	3,129,500	3,129,500	3,129,500	3,189,100	3,244,700	3,286,900	3,309,700	3,129,500	3,129,500	3,141,420	3,220,060	0.5%	0.0%
SWEDEN	622,600	622,600	622,600	622,600	622,600	622,600	622,600	622,600	622,600	612,500	622,600	620,580	-0.1%	-0.2%
SWITZERLAND	522,700	522,700	522,700	522,700	522,700	522,700	522,700	522,700	522,700	513,500	522,700	520,860	-0.1%	-0.2%
UK	4,567,100	4,567,100	4,567,100	4,567,100	4,692,900	4,765,700	4,756,300	4,689,000	4,567,100	4,567,100	4,592,260	4,669,040	0.3%	0.0%
WEST GERMANY	5,315,800	5,315,800	5,315,800	5,315,800	5,315,800	5,315,800	5,315,800	5,315,800	5,315,800	5,294,500	5,315,800	5,311,540	-0.0%	-0.0%
EU TOTAL	27,338,000	27,338,000	27,338,000	27,338,000	27,754,200	28,055,900	28,203,000	28,100,600	27,368,800	27,250,400	27,421,240	27,795,740	0.3%	-0.0%
EFTA TOTAL	2,520,399	2,520,399	2,520,399	2,520,399	2,520,399	2,520,399	2,520,399	2,520,399	2,520,399	2,487,189	2,520,399	2,513,757	-0.1%	-0.1%
EUROPE TOTAL	29,858,399	29,858,399	29,858,399	29,858,399	30,274,599	30,576,299	30,723,399	30,620,999	29,889,199	29,737,589	29,941,639	30,309,497	0.2%	-0.0%

Sector Population Served

Sector 3 - OTHER NON-MAJOR SPEC.

	1981	1982	1983	1984	1985	1986	1987	1988	1989	1990	1981-85 Average	1986-90 Average	81/85 - 86/90 Year on Year Increase	Decade: Year on Year Increase
AUSTRIA	7,602,300	7,602,300	7,602,300	7,602,300	7,602,300	7,602,300	7,602,300	7,602,300	7,602,300	7,660,500	7,602,300	7,613,940	0.0%	0.1%
BELGIUM	9,853,300	9,853,300	9,853,300	9,853,300	9,857,700	9,858,900	9,884,700	9,927,600	9,853,300	9,853,300	9,854,180	9,871,560	0.0%	0.0%
DENMARK	0	0	0	0	0	0	0	0	0	0	0	0	0.0%	0.0%
EAST GERMANY	16,674,900	16,674,900	16,674,900	16,674,900	16,674,900	16,674,900	16,674,900	16,674,900	16,674,900	16,434,000	16,674,900	16,626,720	-0.1%	-0.2%
EIRE	3,523,000	3,523,000	3,523,000	3,523,000	3,537,300	3,540,500	3,539,200	3,521,800	3,523,000	3,523,000	3,525,860	3,529,520	0.0%	0.0%
FINLAND	4,954,600	4,954,600	4,954,600	4,954,600	4,954,600	4,954,600	4,954,600	4,954,600	4,954,600	4,974,500	4,954,600	4,958,560	0.0%	0.0%
FRANCE	54,830,900	54,830,900	54,830,900	54,830,900	55,062,400	55,278,400	55,510,000	56,017,000	54,830,900	54,830,900	54,877,200	55,293,440	0.2%	0.0%
GREECE	9,872,100	9,872,100	9,872,100	9,872,100	9,869,500	9,949,100	9,988,500	10,019,000	9,872,100	9,872,100	9,871,580	9,940,240	0.1%	0.0%
ICELAND	251,919	251,919	251,919	251,919	251,919	- 251,919	251,919	251,919	251,919	253,785	251,919	252,292	0.0%	0.1%
ITALY	56,929,100	56,929,100	56,929,100	56,929,100	57,080,600	58,202,100	57,290,500	57,504,700	56,929,100	56,929,100	56,959,400	57,371,100	0.1%	0.0%
LIECHTENSTEIN	28,181	28,181	28,181	28,181	28,181	28,181	28,181	28,181	28,181	28,452	28,181	28,235	0.0%	0.1%
LUXEMBOURG	365,600	365,600	365,600	365,600	366,200	365,600	371,700	374,900	374,900	378,300	365,720	373,080	0.4%	0.4%
NETHERLANDS	14,430,600	14,430,600	14,430,600	14,430,600	14,453,800	14,529,400	14,615,100	14,805,200	14,430,600	14,430,600	14,435,240	14,562,180	0.2%	0.0%
NORWAY	4,220,500	4,220,500	4,220,500	4,220,500	4,220,500	4,220,500	4,220,500	4,220,500	4,220,500	4,233,200	4,220,500	4,223,040	0.0%	0.0%
PORTUGAL	10,049,700	10,049,700	10,049,700	10,049,700	10,128,900	10,185,000	10,229,900	10,304,800	10,049,700	10,049,700	10,065,540	10,163,820	0.2%	0.0%
SPAIN	38,260,500	38,260,500	38,260,500	38,260,500	38,423,100	38,586,300	38,750,100	38,851,900	38,260,500	38,260,500	38,293,020	38,541,860	0.1%	0.0%
SWEDEN	8,458,800	8,458,800	8,458,800	8,458,800	8,458,800	8,458,800	8,458,800	8,458,800	8,458,800	8,526,800	8,458,800	8,472,400	0.0%	0.1%
SWITZERLAND	6,620,100	6,620,100	6,620,100	6,620,100	6,620,100	6,620,100	6,620,100	6,620,100	6,620,100	6,673,600	6,620,100	6,630,800	0.0%	0.1%
UK	56,403,900	56,403,900	56,403,900	56,403,900	56,539,300	56,690,600	56,997,700	57,150,500	56,403,900	56,403,900	56,430,980	56,729,320	0.1%	0.0%
WEST GERMANY	61,715,300	61,715,300	61,715,300	61,715,300	61,715,300	61,715,300	61,715,300	61,715,300	61,715,300	62,678,900	61,715,300	61,908,020	0.1%	0.2%
EU TOTAL	332,908,900	332,908,900	332,908,900	332,908,900	333,709,000	335,576,100	335,548,100	336,867,600	332,918,200	333,644,300	333,068,920	334,910,660	0.1%	0.0%
EFTA TOTAL	32,136,400	32,136,400	32,136,400	32,136,400	32,136,400	32,136,400	32,136,400	32,136,400	32,136,400	32,350,837	32,136,400	32,179,287	0.0%	0.1%
EUROPE TOTAL	365,045,300	365,045,300	365,045,300	365,045,300	365,845,400	367,712,500	367,684,500	369,004,000	365,054,600	365,995,137	365,205,320	367,090,147	0.1%	0.0%

Sector 4 SCHOOLS

	1981	1982	1983	1984	1985	1986	1987	1988	1989	1990	1981-85 Average	1986-90 Average	81/85 - 86/90 Year on Year Increase	Decade: Year on Year Increase
AUSTRIA	1,434,700	1,434,700	1,434,700	1,434,700	1,434,700	1,434,700	1,434,700	1,434,700	1,434,700	1,417,400	1,434,700	1,431,240	0.0%	-0.1%
BELGIUM	2,041,900	2,041,900	2,041,900	2,041,900	2,000,500	1,967,600	1,939,900	1,903,100	2,041,900	2,041,900	2,033,620	1,978,880	-0.5%	0.0%
DENMARK	1,104,700	1,104,700	1,104,700	1,104,700	1,082,700	1,057,200	1,028,000	977,700	977,700	960,100	1,100,300	999,740	-1.9%	-1.5%
EAST GERMANY	3,194,200	3,194,200	3,194,200	3,194,200	3,194,200	3,194,200	3,194,200	3,194,200	3,194,200	3,120,200	3,194,200	3,179,400	-0.1%	-0.3%
EIRE	1,033,000	1,033,000	1,033,000	1,033,000	1,034,500	1,032,400	1,030,600	1,022,600	1,033,000	1,033,000	1,033,300	1,030,320	-0.1%	0.0%
FINLAND	953,100	953,100	953,100	953,100	953,100	953,100	953,100	953,100	953,100	954,200	953,100	953,320	0.0%	0.0%
FRANCE	12,342,000	12,342,000	12,342,000	12,342,000	12,213,500	12,137,000	12,067,300	11,918,200	12,342,000	12,342,000	12,316,300	12,161,300	-0.3%	0.0%
GREECE	2,197,200	2,197,200	2,197,200	2,197,200	2,191,300	2,184,000	2,141,400	2,121,000	2,197,200	2,197,200	2,195,860	2,168,080	-0.3%	0.0%
ICELAND	63,648	63,648	63,648	63,648	63,648	63,648	63,648	63,648	63,648	63,389	63,648	63,596	0.0%	0.0%
ITALY	13,145,100	13,145,100	13,145,100	13,145,100	12,861,800	12,553,100	12,215,000	11,583,200	13,145,100	13,145,100	13,088,440	12,528,300	-0.9%	0.0%
LIECHTENSTEIN	5,857	5,857	5,857	5,857	5,857	5,857	5,857	5,857	5,857	5,811	5,857	5,848	0.0%	-0.1%
LUXEMBOURG	70,200	70,200	70,200	70,200	68,600	70,200	65,200	65,200	65,200	65,100	69,880	66,300	-1.0%	-0.8%
NETHERLANDS	3,291,500	3,291,500	3,291,500	3,291,500	3,210,500	3,146,000	3,087,600	2,961,900	3,291,500	3,291,500	3,275,300	3,155,700	-0.7%	0.0%
NORWAY	861,900	861,900	861,900	861,900	861,900	861,900	861,900	861,900	861,900	844,600	861,900	858,440	-0.1%	-0.2%
PORTUGAL	2,562,400	2,562,400	2,562,400	2,562,400	2,550,600	2,523,600	2,493,800	2,444,200	2,562,400	2,562,400	2,560,040	2,517,280	-0.3%	0.0%
SPAIN	9,839,000	9,839,000	9,839,000	9,839,000	9,760,700	9,656,700	9,513,400	9,160,300	9,839,000	9,839,000	9,823,340	9,601,680	-0.5%	0.0%
SWEDEN	1,552,200	1,552,200	1,552,200	1,552,200	1,552,200	1,552,200	1,552,200	1,552,200	1,552,200	1,548,600	1,552,200	1,551,480	0.0%	-0.1%
SWITZERLAND	1,195,500	1,195,500	1,195,500	1,195,500	1,195,500	1,195,500	1,195,500	1,195,500	1,195,500	1,185,300	1,195,500	1,193,460	0.0%	0.0%
UK	12,178,600	12,178,600	12,178,600	12,178,600	11,934,600	11,731,100	11,351,200	11,179,300	12,178,600	12,178,600	12,129,800	11,723,760	-0.7%	-0.1%
WEST GERMANY	9,854,000	9,854,000	9,854,000	9,854,000	9,854,000	9,854,000	9,854,000	9,854,000	9,854,000	9,760,800	9,854,000	9,835,360	0.0%	0.0%
EU TOTAL	72,853,600	72,853,600	72,853,600	72,853,600	71,957,500	71,107,100	69,980,200	68,384,900	72,721,600	72,536,700	72,674,380	70,946,100	-0.5%	-0.0%
EFTA TOTAL	6,066,905	6,066,905	6,066,905	6,066,905	6,066,905	6,066,905	6,066,905	6,066,905	6,066,905	6,019,300	6,066,905	6,057,364	-0.0%	-0.1%
EUROPE TOTAL	78,920,505	78,920,505	78,920,505	78,920,505	78,024,405	77,174,005	76,047,105	74,451,805	78,788,505	78,556,000	78,741,285	77,003,484	-0.4%	-0.1%

Sector Population Served

Sector 5 SPECIAL

	1981	1982	1983	1984	1985	1986	1987	1988	1989	1990	1981–85 Average	1986–90 Average	81/85 – 86/90 Year on Year Increase	Decade: Year on Year Increase
AUSTRIA	5,132,700	5,132,700	5,132,700	5,132,700	5,132,700	5,132,700	5,132,700	5,132,700	5,132,700	5,167,900	5,132,700	5,139,740	0.0%	0.1%
BELGIUM	6,609,200	6,609,200	6,609,200	6,609,200	6,636,200	6,648,500	6,652,100	6,676,600	6,609,200	6,609,200	6,614,600	6,639,120	0.1%	0.0%
DENMARK	3,381,100	3,381,100	3,381,100	3,381,100	3,394,300	3,404,400	3,421,000	3,444,500	3,444,500	3,454,500	3,383,740	3,433,780	0.3%	0.2%
EAST GERMANY	11,230,600	11,230,600	11,230,600	11,230,600	11,230,600	11,230,600	11,230,600	11,230,600	11,230,600	11,051,700	11,230,600	11,194,820	-0.1%	-0.2%
EIRE	2,101,800	2,101,800	2,101,800	2,101,800	2,119,000	2,129,400	2,147,100	2,144,200	2,101,800	2,101,800	2,105,240	2,124,860	0.2%	0.0%
FINLAND	3,343,600	3,343,600	3,343,600	3,343,600	3,343,600	3,343,600	3,343,600	3,343,600	3,343,600	3,350,500	3,343,600	3,344,980	0.0%	0.0%
FRANCE	35,900,800	35,900,800	35,900,800	35,900,800	36,261,500	36,394,000	36,566,100	36,950,500	35,900,800	35,900,800	35,972,940	36,342,440	0.2%	0.0%
GREECE	6,442,700	6,442,700	6,442,700	6,442,700	6,502,700	6,560,700	6,637,400	6,668,600	6,442,700	6,442,700	6,454,700	6,550,420	0.3%	0.0%
ICELAND	162,309	162,309	162,309	162,309	162,309	162,309	162,309	162,309	162,309	163,501	162,309	162,547	0.0%	0.1%
ITALY	38,159,100	38,159,100	38,159,100	38,159,100	38,632,200	38,854,400	39,085,000	39,467,800	38,159,100	38,159,100	38,253,720	38,745,080	0.3%	0.0%
LIECHTENSTEIN	19,906	19,906	19,906	19,906	19,906	19,906	19,906	19,906	19,906	20,088	19,906	19,942	0.0%	0.1%
LUXEMBOURG	253,000	253,000	253,000	253,000	254,400	253,000	259,200	260,700	260,700	262,300	253,280	259,180	0.5%	0.4%
NETHERLANDS	9,756,100	9,756,100	9,756,100	9,756,100	9,873,800	9,972,000	10,065,800	10,218,600	9,756,100	9,756,100	9,779,640	9,953,680	0.4%	0.0%
NORWAY	2,733,800	2,733,800	2,733,800	2,733,800	2,733,800	2,733,800	2,733,800	2,733,800	2,733,800	2,741,300	2,733,800	2,735,300	0.0%	0.0%
PORTUGAL	6,433,800	6,433,800	6,433,800	6,433,800	6,517,900	6,582,200	6,642,700	6,762,400	6,433,800	6,433,800	6,450,620	6,570,980	0.4%	0.0%
SPAIN	24,607,300	24,607,300	24,607,300	24,607,300	24,870,800	25,114,500	25,344,900	25,758,000	24,607,300	24,607,300	24,660,000	25,086,400	0.3%	0.0%
SWEDEN	5,446,400	5,446,400	5,446,400	5,446,400	5,446,400	5,446,400	5,446,400	5,446,400	5,446,400	5,487,400	5,446,400	5,454,600	0.0%	0.1%
SWITZERLAND	4,531,800	4,531,800	4,531,800	4,531,800	4,531,800	4,531,800	4,531,800	4,531,800	4,531,800	4,564,700	4,531,800	4,538,380	0.0%	0.1%
UK	36,922,300	36,922,300	36,922,300	36,922,300	37,121,500	37,222,800	37,394,800	37,439,500	36,922,300	36,922,300	36,962,220	37,180,340	0.1%	0.0%
WEST GERMANY	43,076,700	43,076,700	43,076,700	43,076,700	43,076,700	43,076,700	43,076,700	43,076,700	43,076,700	43,628,400	43,076,700	43,187,040	0.1%	0.1%
EU TOTAL	224,874,500	224,874,500	224,874,500	224,874,500	226,492,000	227,443,200	228,523,200	230,098,700	224,945,600	225,330,000	225,198,000	227,268,140	0.2%	0.0%
EFTA TOTAL	21,370,515	21,370,515	21,370,515	21,370,515	21,370,515	21,370,515	21,370,515	21,370,515	21,370,515	21,495,389	21,370,515	21,395,490	0.0%	0.1%
EUROPE TOTAL	246,245,015	246,245,015	246,245,015	246,245,015	247,862,515	248,813,715	249,893,715	251,469,215	246,316,115	246,825,389	246,568,515	248,663,630	0.2%	0.0%

Sector 6 PUBLIC

	1981	1982	1983	1984	1985	1986	1987	1988	1989	1990	1981–85 Average	1986–90 Average	81/85 – 86/90 Year on Year Increase	Decade: Year on Year Increase
AUSTRIA	7,602,300	7,602,300	7,602,300	7,602,300	7,602,300	7,602,300	7,602,300	7,602,300	7,602,300	7,660,500	7,602,300	7,613,940	0.0%	0.1%
BELGIUM	9,853,300	9,853,300	9,853,300	9,853,300	9,857,700	9,858,900	9,864,700	9,927,400	9,853,300	9,853,300	9,854,180	9,871,560	0.0%	0.0%
DENMARK	5,112,000	5,112,000	5,112,000	5,112,000	5,077,100	5,116,300	5,124,800	5,129,800	5,129,700	5,135,200	5,105,020	5,127,160	0.1%	0.1%
EAST GERMANY	16,674,900	16,674,900	16,674,900	16,674,900	16,674,900	16,674,900	16,674,900	16,674,900	16,674,900	16,434,000	16,674,900	16,626,720	-0.1%	-0.2%
EIRE	3,523,000	3,523,000	3,523,000	3,523,000	3,537,800	3,540,900	3,539,300	3,521,800	3,523,000	3,523,000	3,525,860	3,529,520	0.0%	0.0%
FINLAND	4,954,600	4,954,600	4,954,600	4,954,600	4,954,600	4,954,600	4,954,600	4,954,600	4,954,600	4,974,500	4,954,600	4,958,580	0.0%	0.0%
FRANCE	54,830,900	54,830,900	54,830,900	54,830,900	55,062,400	55,278,400	55,510,000	56,017,000	54,830,900	54,830,900	54,877,200	55,293,440	0.2%	0.0%
GREECE	9,872,100	9,872,100	9,872,100	9,872,100	9,869,500	9,949,100	9,988,900	10,019,000	9,872,100	9,872,100	9,871,580	9,940,240	0.1%	0.0%
ICELAND	251,919	251,919	251,919	251,919	251,919	251,919	251,919	251,919	251,919	253,785	251,919	252,292	0.0%	0.1%
ITALY	56,929,100	56,929,100	56,929,100	56,929,100	57,080,600	58,202,100	57,290,500	57,504,700	56,929,100	56,929,100	56,959,400	57,371,100	0.1%	0.1%
LIECHTENSTEIN	28,181	28,181	28,181	28,181	28,181	28,181	28,181	28,181	28,181	28,452	28,181	28,235	0.0%	0.0%
LUXEMBOURG	365,600	365,600	365,600	365,600	366,200	365,600	371,700	374,900	374,900	378,300	365,720	373,080	0.4%	0.4%
NETHERLANDS	14,430,600	14,430,600	14,430,600	14,430,600	14,453,800	14,529,400	14,615,100	14,805,200	14,430,600	14,430,600	14,435,240	14,562,180	0.2%	0.0%
NORWAY	4,220,500	4,220,500	4,220,500	4,220,500	4,220,500	4,220,500	4,220,500	4,220,500	4,220,500	4,233,200	4,220,500	4,223,040	0.0%	0.0%
PORTUGAL	10,049,700	10,049,700	10,049,700	10,049,700	10,128,900	10,185,000	10,229,900	10,304,800	10,049,700	10,049,700	10,065,540	10,163,820	0.2%	0.0%
SPAIN	38,260,500	38,260,500	38,260,500	38,260,500	38,423,100	38,586,300	38,750,100	38,851,900	38,260,500	38,293,020	38,293,020	38,541,860	0.1%	0.0%
SWEDEN	8,458,800	8,458,800	8,458,800	8,458,800	8,458,800	8,458,800	8,458,800	8,458,800	8,458,800	8,526,800	8,458,800	8,472,400	0.0%	0.1%
SWITZERLAND	6,620,100	6,620,100	6,620,100	6,620,100	6,620,100	6,620,100	6,620,100	6,620,100	6,620,100	6,673,600	6,620,100	6,630,800	0.0%	0.1%
UK	56,403,900	56,403,900	56,403,900	56,403,900	56,539,300	56,690,600	56,997,700	57,150,500	56,403,900	56,403,900	56,430,980	56,729,320	0.1%	0.0%
WEST GERMANY	61,715,300	61,715,300	61,715,300	61,715,300	61,715,300	61,715,300	61,715,300	61,715,300	61,715,300	62,678,900	61,715,300	61,908,020	0.1%	0.2%
EU TOTAL	338,020,900	338,020,900	338,020,900	338,020,900	338,786,100	340,692,400	340,672,900	341,997,400	338,047,900	338,779,500	338,173,940	340,038,020	0.1%	0.0%
EFTA TOTAL	32,136,400	32,136,400	32,136,400	32,136,400	32,136,400	32,136,400	32,136,400	32,136,400	32,136,400	32,350,837	32,136,400	32,179,287	0.0%	0.1%
EUROPE TOTAL	370,157,300	370,157,300	370,157,300	370,157,300	370,922,500	372,828,800	372,809,300	374,133,800	370,184,300	371,130,337	370,310,340	372,217,307	0.1%	0.0%

- 196 -

POPULATION CHANGE BY SECTOR 1981-1990

EUROPEAN UNION MEMBER STATES

SECTOR	1981	1990	% Change
National	338,020,900	338,779,500	0.22 %
Higher Education	27,338,000	27,250,400	-0.32 %
Other Major Non-Specialised	284,429,500	285,152,200	0.25 %
School	72,853,600	72,536,700	-0.43 %
Special	224,874,500	225,330,000	0.20%
Public	338,020,900	338,779,500	0.22 %
TOTAL	338,020,900	338,779,500	0.22 %

EUROPEAN FREE TRADE AGREEMENT STATES

SECTOR	1981	1990	% Change
National	32,136,400	32,350,837	0.67 %
Higher Education	2,520,399	2,487,189	-1.32 %
Other Major Non-Specialised	22,681,200	22,860,900	0.79 %
School	6,066,905	6,019,300	-0.78 %
Special	21,350,609	21,475,301	0.58 %
Public	32,136,400	32,350,837	0.67 %
TOTAL	32,136,400	32,350,837	0.67 %

POPULATION CHANGE BY SECTOR - FIVE YEAR AVERAGES; 1981-1985 AND 1986-1990

EUROPEAN UNION MEMBER STATES

SECTOR	1981-1985	1986-1990	% Change
National	338,173,940	340,038,020	0.55 %
Higher Education	27,421,240	27,795,740	1.37 %
Other Major Non-Specialised	284,556,000	286,124,360	0.55 %
School	72,674,380	70,946,100	-2.38 %
Special	225,198,000	227,268,140	0.92 %
Public	338,173,940	340,038,020	0.55 %
TOTAL	338,173,940	340,038,020	0.55 %

EUROPEAN FREE TRADE AGREEMENT STATES

SECTOR	1981-1985	1986-1990	% Change
National	32,136,400	32,179,287	0.13 %
Higher Education	2,520,399	2,513,757	-0.26 %
Other Major Non-Specialised	22,681,200	22,717,140	0.16 %
School	6,066,905	6,057,384	-0.16 %
Special	21,350,609	21,375,547	0.12 %
Public	32,136,400	32,179,287	0.13 %
TOTAL	32,136,400	32,179,287	0.13 %

APPENDIX 6

COUNTRY PROFILES

1. STUDY QUESTIONNAIRES RETURNED

2. NATIONAL PUBLICATIONS EMPLOYED IN THE STUDY

3. INDIVIDUALS AND INSTITUTIONS WHO PROVIDED DATA FOR THE STUDY

4. UNESCO DATA

5. NOTES RELATING TO NATIONAL DATA

AUSTRIA

1. <u>Study Questionnaires returned</u>

   National.

2. <u>National Publications employed in the Study</u>

   "Kulturstatistik 1989" October 1990
   "Kulturstatistik 1990" October 1991

   Österreichisches Statistisches Zentralamt
   Hintere Zollamtsstraße 2b
   Postfach 9000
   A-1033 Wien
   Vienna

3. <u>Individuals and Institutions who provided data for the Study</u>

   National Sector :
   Drs Angelika Ander and Herbert Rieser
   Österreichische Nationalbibliothek
   Josefsplatz 1
   A-1015 Wien
   Vienna

   Dr Alois Gehart
   Director of the Library
   Österreichische Statistisches Zentralamt
   Hintere Zollamtsstraße 2b
   1033 Wien
   Vienna

4. <u>UNESCO Data</u>

   National : 1989
   Higher Education : 1984-1990 partial data only
   Other Major Non-Specialised 1989

BELGIUM

1. Study Questionnaires Returned

    National
    Higher Education
    Public

2. National Publications employed in the Study

3. Individuals and Institutions who provided data for the Study

    Pierre Cockshaw
    Conservateur en Chef
    Bibliothèque Royale Albert 1er
    Boulevard de l'Empereur 4
    B-1000 Bruxelles

    Jean-Pierre Devroye
    Président
    Conférence des Bibliothécaires en Chef des Universités belges
    Bibliothèque de l'Université Libre de Bruxelles
    Avenue Fr. Roosevelt 50
    B-1050 Bruxelles

    Monsieur Labiau
    Ministere de la Communaute française de Belgique
    Service de la Lecture publique
    Boulevard Léopold II, 44
    B-1080 Bruxelles

    De Heer Geert Roelandts
    Ministerie van de Vlaamse Gemeenschap
    Dienst voor Openbaar Bibliothekenwerk
    Markiesstraat 1
    B-1000 Bruxelles

    Jan Roegiers
    Vice President
    Conférence des Bibliothecaires en Chef des Universités Belges
    Centrale Bibliotheek K.U.L.
    Place Ladeuze
    B-3000
    Leuven

Pierre Gordinne
Directeur Général
Médiathèque de la Communauté
Francaise de Belgique
18 Place Flagey
B-1050
Bruxelles

Marc Walckiers
Administrateur délégué
LIBRIME
Chemin des Vieux Amis 17
B-1380 Bruxelles

4. <u>UNESCO Data</u>

National : 1989
Special : 1985

5. <u>Notes relating to National Data</u>

Public Library Sector :

Responsibility for this sector is shared between two government ministries; the Ministère de la Communauté de Belgique (15 Administrative Units) and the Ministerie van de Vlaamse Gemeenschap (24 Administrative Units). Neither ministry were able to provide financial data and the activity data supplied by each were not always compatible. Therefore, some estimations relating to activity data were created in order to complete the "national" perspective of this sector.

Higher Education Sector :

Data relating to the French-speaking and Dutch-speaking universities (9 and 8 Administrative units respectively; however, the data relating to the Dutch-Speaking Universities relates to 7 Administrative units only) are maintained separately. Similar problems were encountered when creating the "national" perspective of this sector as to those met with the Public Library sector.

DENMARK

1. <u>Study questionnaires returned</u>

   National
   Higher Education
   School
   Special
   Public

2. <u>National Publications employed in the study</u>

   Folkebiblioteksstatistik 1986; ISSN 0105-6077; ISBN 87552-1239-4
   Folkebiblioteksstatistik 1987; ISSN 0105-6077; ISBN 87-552-1454-1
   Folkebiblioteksstatistik 1988; ISSN 0105-6077; ISBN 87-552-1588-2

   Biblioteksårbog 1988; ISSN 0905-0825; ISBN 87-552-1697-8
   Biblioteksårbog 1989; ISSN 0905-6386; ISBN 87-552-1788-5
   Biblioteksårbog 1990; ISSN 0905-6378; ISBN 87-552-1877-6
   Biblioteksårbog 1991; ISSN 0905-6378; ISSN 87-552-1965-9

   Compiled and published by
   Statens Bibliotekstjeneste (National Library Authority)
   Nyhavn 31 E
   DK-1051 Copenhagen K
   Denmark

   "Nordisk Forskningsbiblioteksstatistik 1988" (Nordic Research Library Statistics) ISSN 0109-8047
   "Nordisk Forskningsbiblioteksstatistik 1989" ISSN 0109-8047

   Compiled and Published by:
   Nordisk statistisk sekretariat
   Sejrøgade 11
   DK-2100 Copenhagen

3. <u>Individuals and Institutions who provided data for the study</u>

   Olga Porotnikoff
   Senior Librarian
   Statens Bibliotekstjeneste
   Nyhavn 31 E
   DK-1051 Copenhagen K
   Denmark

John Jensen
Library Consultant
Statens Bibliotekstjeneste
Nyhavn 31 E
DK-1051 Copenhagen K
Denmark

4. <u>UNESCO Data</u>

National : 1984;1986-1989
Higher Education 1987 and 1990
School 1984; 1986 and 1990.
Special 1985 and 1990

5. <u>Notes relating to the national data</u>

i. Other Major Non-Specialised and University Libraries :

The previous study recorded 8 administrative units within this library sector. The UNESCO data for this sector recorded 5 administrative units in 1989. John Jensen of Statens Bibliotekstjeneste supplied a nil return for Other Major Non-Specialised Libraries for the years 1986-1990.

The Danish Library Authority regard the 5 university libraries and the National library as Non-Specialised libraries, hence UNESCO's figure of 5 Other Major Non-Specialised relates to the 5 University Libraries. The other 13 (now 12) main libraries of other institutions of Higher Education are regarded as Specialised libraries in the Danish national statistics

For the original study 6 administrative units within the Higher Education Library sector were recorded; while *Biblioteksårbog 1990;* records 18 administrative units, this figure includes the 5 University libraries and the 13 libraries of other institutions of Higher Education.

In order to provide a consistent approach throughout the decade the data previously included in the Other Major Non-Specialised Library sector have been transferred to the Higher Education sector.

ii. All sectors:

As with the majority of Scandinavian states the Danish published statistics do not contain data relating to Registered Borrowers or Library Users, but do record the number of Loans and Library consultations made.

EIRE

1. <u>IPF Questionnaires</u>

    National
    Institutions of Higher Education
    Other Major Non-Specialised
    Special
    Public

2. <u>National Publications employed in the study</u>

    Public Library Statistics 1986-1990 provided by
    An Chomhairle Leabharlanna (The Library Council)
    53 & 54 Upper Mount Street
    Dublin 2

    1980/81-1990/91 University Library Statistics provided by
    The Committee of National and University Librarians (CONUL)
    c/o Main Library
    University College Dublin
    Belfield
    Dublin 4

    Extract of *"Directory of Libraries and Information Services in Ireland"*
    4th Edition
    The Library Association of Ireland and The Library Association
    Northern Ireland Branch 1993.
    53 & 54 Upper Mount Street
    Dublin 2

    An Chomhairle Leabharlanna (The Library Council)
    44th Annual Report Year ended December 31, 1991
    53 & 54 Upper Mount Street
    Dublin 2

3. <u>Individuals and Institutions who provided data for the study</u>

    Dr P Donlan
    Director
    The National Library of Ireland
    Kildare Street
    Dublin 2

    Helen Kavanagh
    Project Officer
    The National Library of Ireland
    Kildare Street   Dublin 2

Sean Phillips
Chairman
The Committee of National and University Librarians (CONUL)
Main Library
University College
Belfield
Dublin 4

Alun Bevan
Research & Information Officer
An Chomhairle Leabharlanna (The Library Council)
53 & 54 Upper Mount Street
Dublin 2

Mary Kelleher
Librarian
Royal Dublin Society
Ballsbridge
Dublin 4

Siobhán O'Rafferty
Librarian
Royal Irish Academy
19 Dawson Street
Dublin 2

Fr Vincent Ryan
Librarian
Glenstall Abbey
Murroe
Co. Limerick

Daisy Downes
Librarian
The Institute of Chartered Accountants in Ireland
Chartered Accountants House
87/89 Pembroke Road
Dublin 4

James C. O'Reilly
Library & Information Services
Electricity Supply Board
Lower Fitzwilliam Street
Dublin 2

Barry Lyons
Librarian
Grand Lodge of Freemasons of Ireland
Freemasons Hall
17, Molesworth Street
Dublin 2

June Carr
Resource Centre
Agency For Personal Services Overseas (APSO)
Resource Centre
30 Fitzwilliam Street
Dublin 2

I. O. Deirg
Librarian
The Linguistics Institute of Ireland
31 Fitzwilliam Place
Dublin 2

4. <u>UNESCO Data</u>

National: 1986
Higher Education; 1984
Special 1985
Public 1986

5. <u>Notes relating to the national data</u>

National Library:

i. The National Library was unable to provide acurate financial returns since their staffing costs are met by the Department of Arts, Culture and the Gaeltach while their premises costs are met by the Department of Finance.

Higher Education Sector:

ii. The period of account for which the data for this sector are collected corresponds to that of the academic year (i.e. 1st October - 30 September).

iii. The published statistics do not include the costs of premises, new buildings or refurbishment since these elements are funded by the respective College's administrative or buildings department. This difficulty was replicated across a number of the states participating in this study.

Other Major Non-Specialised Sector

i) The two librarians of the two libraries belonging to this sector, The Royal Irish Academy and The Royal Dublin Society were contacted directly and requested to complete a questionnaire for their respective libraries. The two returns were collated to establish a national perspective.

Special Library Sector :

ii) There are no centrally collected statistics for this library sector; however, the Library Association of Ireland and The Librray Association Northern Ireland Branch maintain a *"Directory of Libraries and Information Services in Ireland"*. All major Special Libraries listed in this directory were contacted and asked to complete a questionnaire for their respective libraries. From the returns received estimates were created to equate to the number of principal libraries listed in the Directory.

FINLAND

1. **Study Questionnaires Returned**

    National
    Institutions of Higher Education
    Special
    Public

2. **National Publications employed in the study**

    "Tieteellisten Kirjastojen Yhteistilasto 1986"; ISSN 0782-9663
    "Tieteellisten Kirjastojen Yhteistilasto 1987"; ISSN 0782-9663
    "Tieteellisten Kirjastojen Yhteistilasto 1988"; ISSN 0782-9663
    "Tieteellisten Kirjastojen Yhteistilasto 1989"; ISSN 0782-9663
    "Tieteellisten Kirjastojen Yhteistilasto 1990"; ISSN 0782-9663
    "Tieteellisten Kirjastojen Yhteistilasto 1991"; ISSN 0782-9663

    Compiled and Published by :
    Tieteellisen informoinnin neuvosto Rådet för vetenskaplig information
    (Finnish Council for Scientific Information and Research Libraries)
    PL 293PB
    SF-00171 Helsinki

    "Nordisk Forskningsbiblioteksstatistik 1988" (Nordic Research Library Statistics) ISSN 0109-8047
    "Nordisk Forskningsbiblioteksstatistik 1989" ISSN 0109-8047

    Compiled and Published by:
    Nordisk statistisk sekretariat
    Sejrogade 11
    DK-2100 Copenhagen

3. **Individuals and Institutions who provided data for the study**

    Riitta Maajärvi
    Secretary General
    Secretariat for National Planning and Co-ordination
    Helsinki University Library
    Box 26
    00014 Helsinki

    Anneli Äyräs
    Ministry of Education
    POB 293
    00171 Helsinki

4. UNESCO Data

   National 1984: 1986; 1988 and 1990
   Higher Education: 1984;1986; and 1988-1990
   School : 1984; 1986; 1987 and 1990
   Special: 1985; 1986 and 1990
   Public: 1984-1990

5. Notes relating to the national data

i. As with a number of the Scandinavian states data relating to the number of "Registered Borrowers" and "Library Users" were not available, except for the Public Library sector.

ii. The Helsinki University Library is also the National Library of Finland (see paragraph 6. 2). It has not proved possible to allocate the costs and activity data between these two library sectors.

iii There are no reported libraries within the Other Major Non-Specialised Library sector in Finland.

FRANCE

1. <u>Study Questionnaires Returned</u>

    National
    Institutions of Higher Education
    Other Major Non-Specialised

2. <u>National Publications employed in the study</u>

    "Annuaire des bibliothèques universitaires 1988"; ISBN 2-11-002521-2
    "Annuaire des bibliothèques universitaires 1989"; ISBN 2-11-002716-9

    Published by:
    La Documentation francaise
    29-31, quai Voltaire
    75344 Paris

    "Bibliothèques Municipales Donnees 1990"
    Ministère de la Culture et de la francophonie
    Direction du Livre et de la Lecture
    27, avenue de l'Opéra
    75001 Paris

3. <u>Individuals and Institutions who provided data for the study</u>

    Jean-Sébastien Dupuit
    Directeur du Livre et de la Lecture
    Ministère de la Culture et de la francophonie
    27 avenue de l'Opéra
    75001 Paris

    Daniel Renoult
    Sous-Directeur des Bibliothèques
    Ministère de l'enseignement supérieur et de la recherche
    Direction de la Programmation et du développement universitaire
    61-65 rue Dutot
    75015 Paris

    Mme Alix Chevallier
    Directeur scientifique
    Bibliothèque nationale
    58 rue de Richelieu
    75002 Paris

4. <u>UNESCO Data</u>

   Higher Education: 1984; 1987 and 1990
   Other Major Non-Specialised: 1991
   Public: 1987

5. <u>Notes relating to the national data</u>

i. During the intervening period of the two studies a reclassification of the Other Major Non-Specialised Library sector occurred, reducing the number of Administrative units from an estimated 25 units for the previous study to 1 Administrative Unit. In order to ensure a consistent approach throughout the decade the number of administrative units for the first half of the decade were amended to mirror those relating to the second quinquennium.

GERMANY

1. Study Questionnaires Returned
   National
   Institutions of Higher Education
   Other Major Non-Specialised
   Special

2. National Publications employed in the study

   "Deutsche Bibliotheksstatistik Teil A 1987-1991"; Disketten-Versiomen
   "Deutsche Bibliotheksstatistik Teil B 1989-1991"; Disketten-Versiomen
   "Deutsche Bibliotheksstatistik Teil C 1991"; Disketten-Versiomen

   Compiled and Produced by :
   Deuches Bibliotheksinstituts
   Bundesallee 184/185
   Berlin HD 10717

3. Individuals and Institutions who provided data for the study

   Andreas Heise
   Deuches Bibliotheksinstituts
   Bundesallee 184/185
   Berlin HD 10717

4. UNESCO Data

   Germany :

   National: 1989
   Other Major Non-Specialised: 1989

   Former German Democratic Republic

   National: 1986
   Higher Education: 1984 and 1987
   Other Major Non-Specialised: 1986
   Special: 1985
   Public: 1986

   Former Federal Republic of Germany

   National: 1986-1988
   Higher Education: 1985-1987 and 1990
   Other Major Non-Specialised: 1986
   Public: 1986-1988

GREECE

1. ## Study Questionnaires Returned

   None

2. ## National Publications employed in the study

   "Libraries and Information Profile - Greece" 1986
   The British Council
   Libraries Department
   10 Spring Gardens
   London
   SW1A 2BN

3. ## Individuals and Institutions who provided data for the study

   Mark Hoy
   Librarian
   The British Council
   17 Kolonaki Square
   P.O Box 3488
   10210 Athens

   ### Individuals or Institutions who were not able to be of assistance to the study

   Dr P Nicolopoulos
   Director
   National Library
   Odos Venizelou 32
   10679 Athens

   Michael Tzekakis
   Librarian
   University of Crete
   Rethymnon
   Crete

   Mrs Sofia Exarchakou
   Ministry of Education
   Mitropolios 15
   Athens

   Mrs K. Chatzopoulou
   The Greek Library Association
   c/o Institut Français d'Athène
   31 Rue Cinar
   10680 Athens

Penelope Spilioti
Ministry of Industry, Energy & Technology
14-18 Messogion Avenue
11510 Athens

Mrs Drekaki
Pantheon University of Political and Social Sciences
136 Syngrou Avenue
17671 Athens

Alexandra Papazoglou
President
Greek Librray Association
Athens College Library
P.O Box 65005
15410 Psychico
Athens

Katerina Synellis
Librarian
Central Library
University of Patras
26500 Rio Patras

4. UNESCO Data

National : 1984; 1986 & 1989
Public : 1986

5. Notes relating to the national data

Data relating to libraries in Greece are particularly sparse; some of which appear implausible.

Public Libraries :

The UNESCO extract includes 615 Administrative Units and Service Points. The scale of these figures is significantly larger than those recorded during the previous study. The British Council *"Libraries and Information Profile-Greece."(1986)* states that :

> "There is no cohesive public library in Greece. Many municipalities maintain municipal librraies, several opened earlier this century, often based upon the private collection of a local benefactor and expanded over the years by donations from individuals and local organisations. These libraries are seldom anything more than showpieces or local archive

collections; the books are seldom available for loan, new books are rarely added and no qualified librarians are employed to develop them."

In the light of the above comments the same number of administrative units (51) which were recorded for the previous study have been carried forward for the second quinquennium.

ICELAND

1. **Study Questionnaires Returned**

    National
    Institutions of Higher Education
    School
    Special
    Public

2. **National Publications employed in the study**

    "Nordisk Forskningsbiblioteksstatistik 1988" (Nordic Research Library Statistics) ISSN 0109-8047
    "Nordisk Forskningsbiblioteksstatistik 1989" ISSN 0109-8047

    Compiled and Published by:
    Nordisk statistisk sekretariat
    Sejrogade 11
    DK-2100 Copenhagen

3. **Individuals and Institutions who provided data for the study**

    Hildur G. Eythórsdóttir
    President
    Icelandic Library Association
    POB 1497
    121 Reykjavík

    Finnbogi Gudmundsson
    Chief Librarian
    Landsbókasafn Islands
    P.O.Box 1210
    121 Reykjavík

    Einar Sigurdsson
    University Librarian
    Háskólabókasafn
    101 Reykjavík

    Thóra Óskarsdóttir
    State Library Director
    Ministry of Education
    Bókafulltrúi ríkisins
    Menntamáláraduneytid
    Sölvhólsgötu 4
    150 Reykjavík

Thóra Gylfadóttir
Statistical Bureau of Iceland
Skuggasund 3
150 Reyjavík

Thórdís Thorvaldsdóttir
Chief
Reykjavík City Library
Borgarbókasafn Reykjavikur
Thingholtsstraeti 27
101 Reykjavík

4. **UNESCO Data**

   National: 1989 and 1990
   Higher Education: 1985 and 1990
   School: 1987 and 1990
   Public: 1985; 1986 and 1988

5. **Notes relating to the national data**

   National Library :

i. Building work began on a new building to house the amalgamated National and University Libraries in 1978, and is expected to be commissioned during the 1994/95 academic year.

ii. Data relating to Library Users in the National and Public Library sectors were available, but not for the other sectors. This information is not collated by Nordisk statistisk sekretariat, however, some of the Nordic states do collect this information at the local level for some, but not all, of their library sectors

   Other Major Non-Specialised Sector

i. There are no libraries within this classification in Iceland.

ITALY

1. **Study Questionnaires Returned**

   National

2. **National Publications employed in the study**

   "Bollettino AIB Rivista italiana di biblioteconomia e scienze dell'informazione'"
   Volume 32 n.3 ISSN 1121-1490 September 1992
   "Bollettino AIB Rivista italiana di biblioteconomia e scienze dell'informazione"
   Volume 32 n.4 ISSN 1121-1490 December 1992

   Published by :
   Associazione Italiana Biblioteche
   Viale Castro Pretorio 105
   00185 Roma

   "Notiziario" VII 38 July-September 1992
   Compiled and published by :
   Ministerio per i beni culturali e ambientali
   Via del Collegio Romano n.27
   00186 Roma

   "Catalogo delle biblioteche d'Italia" ISBN 88-7107-030-5. (1993)
   Ministerio per i beni culturali e ambientali
   Ufficio centrale per i beni e gli istituti culturali
   Istituto centrale per il catalogo unico delle biblioteche italiane e per le informazioni bibliografiche
   Viale Castro Pretorio 105
   00185 Roma

   "La Documentazione Educativa 5 : Indagine sulle biblioteche scolastiche" 1982
   Ministero della publica istruzione
   Istituto della enciclopedia Italiana
   Fondata da Giovanni Treccani

3. **Individuals and Institutions who provided data for the study**

   Mr Paolo Veneziani
   Il Direttore
   Biblioteca Nazionale Centrale Vittorio Emanuele II
   Viale Castro Pretorio 105
   00185 Roma

Dr Franco Toni
Ufficio Automazione
Biblioteca Nazionale Centrale Vittorio Emanuele II
Viale Castro Pretorio 105
00185 Roma

Dr Luca Bellingeri
Ufficio Automazione
Biblioteca Nazionale Centrale Vittorio Emanuele II
Viale Castro Pretorio 105
00185 Roma

Luisa Marquardt
Istituto Tecnico commerciale Sandro Pertini
Via Argoli n. 45
00143 Roma

Martin Rose
Assistant Director
British Council
Via Quattro Fontane 20
00184 Roma

Guiseppe Vitello
Piazza Cavalleggeri 1
50122 Firenze

<u>People or Institutions who were contacted and were either unable to be of assistance or did not respond to the requests for assistance</u>

Professor Alberto Petrucciani
via A. Carrara 77/6
I-16147 Genova

Dr Paolo Carini
Ministero per i beni culturali e ambientali
via del Collegio Romano n.27
00186 Roma

4. <u>UNESCO Data</u>

National : 1986 and 1989
University Libraries : 1987 and 1990 (Partial Data Only)
Other Major-Non-Specialised : 1986 and 1989
Public : 1984-19898 (Partial Data Only)

5. **Notes relating to the national data**

A representative attended the conference "La diffusione dell'informazione in Italia" 17-18 November 1993 in Milan.

Positive moves have been initiated to collect library statistics in Italy, these include:

- "*Le Biblioteche Communali della Lombardia*" (Milan 1990). This publication covers public libraries in the Region of Lombardy for 1989. However, Lombardy is one of the richest of the 20 regions in Italy, therefore the data for Lombardy is not suitable to use as a basis for estimating data for the other regions in Italy.

- "*Le Regioni in cifre*", published by ISTAT.

- "*Notiziario*", Ministerio per i beni culturalie ambientali.

Unfortunately, for this study these publications do not follow ISO/UNESCO library sector definitions and so other than for the National Library sector, the data contained within these publications were not of assistance to this study.

- "*Notiziario*", details the libraries for which the Ministerio per i beni culturali e ambientali is responsible for and so presents an incomplete picture of the national perspective of Italian libraries.

- The Central Institute for a Union Catalogue (ICCU) are undertaking a survey of some 13,500 libraries. However, this will not facilitate international comparisons since the study framework does not follow the ISO/UNESCO library sector definitions.

LIECHTENSTEIN

1. ## Study Questionnaires Returned

    National

2. ## National Publications employed in the study

    None

3. ## Individuals and Institutions who provided data for the study

    Dr Alois Ospelt
    Librarian
    Liechtensteinische Landesbibliotek
    FL-9490 Vaduz

4. ## UNESCO Data

    National: 1896 and 1989
    School: 1987
    Public: 1986 and 1989

5. ## Notes relating to the national data

i. The National Library also provides the serves associated with the Public and Special Library sectors; however the data provided by the National Library were not dissagregated between these sectors.

ii. There are no principal libraries in Liechtenstein belonging to the classifications of Other Major Non-Specialised or Special Library sectors.

LUXEMBOURG

1. ## Study Questionnaires Returned

   National

2. ## National Publications employed in the study

   "Guide des Bibliothèques Luxembourgeoises": ISBN 2-87980-003-X 1991 Bibliothèque nationale Luxembourg

3. ## Individuals and Institutions who provided data for the study

   Dr Jul Christophory
   Directeur
   Bibliotheque National
   37 boulevard F.D.Roosevelt
   2450 Luxembourg

4. ## UNESCO Data

   National: 1986
   Higher Education: 1984

5. ## Notes relating to the national data

   Public Libraries

   i. There are no centrally collected statistics for the Public Libraries in Luxembourg. All Public Libraries listed in the *"Guide des Bibliothèques Luxembourgeoises"* wre contacted individually for data relating to their activity levels and theri associated costs. Estimates for the national perspective were created based upon the individual returns received.

   Other Major Non-Specialised Library Sector :

   i. There are no libraries recorded in Luxembourg which accord with this classification.

THE NETHERLANDS

1. ## Study Questionnaires Returned

   National
   Institutions of Higher Education
   Other Major Non-Specialised
   Special
   Public

2. ## National Publications employed in the study

   "Wetenschappelijke en speciale bibliotheken 1986"; ISBN 906786145 6; ISSN 0168-4191.
   "Wetenschappelijke en speciale bibliotheken 1988"; ISBN 906786320 3; ISSN 0168-4191.
   "Wetenschappelijke en speciale bibliotheken 1989"; ISBN 906786397 1; ISSN 0168-4191.

   Compiled and published by :
   Central bureau voor de statistiek
   prinses beatrixlaan 428
   Postbus 959
   2270 AZ voorburg

3. ## Individuals and Institutions who provided data for the study

   Pierre Poell
   Nederlands Bibliotheek en Lektuur Centrum
   Hoofkantoor
   Postbus 93054
   2509 AB s'- Gravenhage

   Wilco de Gier
   Nederlands Bibliotheek en Lektuur Centrum
   Hoofkantoor
   Postbus 93054
   2509 AB s'- Gravenhage

4. ## UNESCO Data

   Higher Education: 1987 and 1989
   Other Major Non-Specialised: 1986 and 1989
   Special:1985
   Public: 1984-1989

NORWAY

1. <u>Study Questionnaires Returned</u>

    National
    Higher Education
    School
    Special
    Public

2. <u>National Publications employed in the study</u>

    "Kulturstatistik 1988"(Cultural Statistics): ISBN 82-537-2846-8; ISSN 0800-2959.
    Statistisk Sentralbyrå
    P.O.Box 8131 DEP
    N-0033 Oslo

    "Nordisk Forskningsbiblioteksstatistik 1988" (Nordic Research Library Statistics) ISSN 0109-8047
    "Nordisk Forskningsbiblioteksstatistik 1989" ISSN 0109-8047

    Compiled and Published by:
    Nordisk statistisk sekretariat
    Sejrøgade 11
    DK-2100 Copenhagen

3. <u>Individuals and Institutions who provided data for the study</u>

    Hilde Rødland
    Head Librarian
    Statistisk Sentralbyrå
    P.O.Box 8131 DEP
    N-0033 Oslo

    Asbjørn Langeland
    Director General
    Statens Bibliotektilsyn
    Norwegian Directorate for Public Libraries
    Munkedamsveien 62
    Postboks 8145 DEP
    N-0033 Oslo

Ellen Oyno
Head of Library Administration Department
Statens Bibliotektilsyn
Norwegian Directorate for Public Libraries
Munkedamsveien 62
Postboks 8145 DEP
N-0033 Oslo

Tove Molvig
National Office for Research and Special Libraries
Riksbibliotektjenesten
P.O. Box 2439 Solli
N-0201 Oslo

Libena Vokac
National Office for Research and Special Libraries
Riksbibliotektjenesten
P.O. Box 2439 Solli
N-0201 Oslo

4. <u>UNESCO Data</u>

National: 1984; 1986; 1987; 1989 and 1990
Higher Education: 1984; 1986; 1987 and 1990
School: 1984-1988 and 1990
Special: 1985
Public: 1986-1989

PORTUGAL

1. <u>Study Questionnaires Returned</u>

    National
    Higher Education
    Other Major Non-Specilaised
    School
    Special
    Public

2. <u>National Publications employed in the study</u>

    "Estatísticas da cultura desporto e recreio 1991/1992" ISSN 0870-1628
    Instituto Nacional de Estatística
    Avendia António José de Almeida
    1078 Lisboa

3. <u>Individuals and Institutions who provided data for the study</u>

    Fernanda Maria Guedes de Campos
    Vice-Presidente
    Instituto da Biblioteca Nacional e do Livro
    Campo Grande, 83
    1751 Lisboa

    Rodrigo Magalhães
    Director
    Departmento de Marketing e Difusão
    Instituto Nacional de Estatística
    Avendia António José de Almeida
    1078 Lisboa

4. <u>UNESCO Data</u>

    National: 1987-1990
    Higher Education: 1984; 1987 and 1990
    Other Major Non-Specialised: 1986-1990
    School: 1987 and 1990
    Special: 1985
    Public: 1987-1990

5. Notes relating to the national data

Some 15% of total library income in Portugal is classified as "Other Income". This proportion is higher than in most of the other countries participating in the study since tax incentives are offered to those business which wish to support libraries financially in Portugal.

SPAIN

1. **Study Questionnaires Returned**

    National
    Higher Education
    Other Major Non-Specialised
    School
    Special
    Public

2. **National Publications employed in the study**

    "Estadistica Bibliotecas 1988" ; ISBN 84-260-2114-X
    "Estadistica Bibliotecas 1990"; ISBN 84-260-2328-5
    Instituto Nacional de Estadistica
    Paseo de la Castellana 183
    28046 Madrid

3. **Individuals and Institutions who provided data for the study**

    Carmen Lacambra Montero
    Directora General
    Biblioteca Nacional
    Paseo de Recoletos 20
    28071 Madrid

    Xavier Agenjo Bullón
    Director del Departmento de Acceso a la Información y al Documento
    Ministerio de Cultura
    Biblioteca Nacional
    Paseo de Recoletos 20
    28071 Madrid

    José Quevedo
    Director
    Instituto Nacional de Estadistica
    Paseo de la Castellana 183
    28046 Madrid

    Ramón Abad
    Instituto Cervantes
    122 East 42nd Street
    Suite 807
    New York NY 10168

4. <u>UNESCO Data</u>

   National: 1986-1988
   Higher Education: 1986; 1988 and 1990
   Special: 1987 and 1988
   Public: 1986-1988

SWEDEN

1. ## Study Questionnaires Returned

    National
    Higher Education
    Special
    Public

2. ## National Publications employed in the study

    "Statistiska meddelanden : Folkbiblioteken 1986"; Ku 11 SM 8701 ISSN 0282-3519.
    "Statistiska meddelanden : Folkbiblioteken 1987"; Ku 11 SM 8801 ISSN 0282-3519.
    "Statistiska meddelanden : Folkbiblioteken 1988"; Ku 11 SM 8901 ISSN 0282-3519.
    "Statistiska meddelanden : Folkbiblioteken 1989"; Ku 11 SM 9001 ISSN 0282-3519.
    "Statistiska meddelanden : Folkbiblioteken 1990"; Ku 11 SM 9201 ISSN 0282-3519.
    "Statistiska meddelanden : Forskningsbiblioteken 1987"; Ku 13 SM 8801 ISSN 0282-3519.
    "Statistiska meddelanden : Forskningsbiblioteken 1988"; Ku 13 SM 9001 ISSN 0282-3519.
    "Statistiska meddelanden : Forskningsbiblioteken 1989"; Ku 13 SM 9101 ISSN 0282-3519.
    "Statistiska meddelanden : Forskningsbiblioteken 1990"; Ku 13 SM 9201 ISSN 0282-3519.
    "Statistiska meddelanden :Forskningsbiblioteken 1991"; Ku 13 SM 9301 ISSN 0282-3519.
    Sverges officilla statistik
    Statistika centralbyrån
    S-11581 Stockholm

    "Nordisk Forskningsbiblioteksstatistik 1988" (Nordic Research Library Statistics) ISSN 0109-8047
    "Nordisk Forskningsbiblioteksstatistik 1989" ISSN 0109-8047

    Compiled and Published by:
    Nordisk statistisk sekretariat
    Sejrogade 11
    DK-2100 Copenhagen

3. Individuals and Institutions who provided data for the study

   Birgit Antonsson
   National Librarian
   Kungl Biblioteket (The Royal Library)
   Box 5039
   S-10241 Stockholm

   Rolf-Allan Norrmosse
   Chief Librarian
   Statistiska centralbyråns bibliotek
   S-11581 Stockholm

   Thomas Lidman
   President
   Svenska Bibliotekariesamfundet (Swedish Association of University
   and Research Libraries)
   Box 874
   50115 Borå

   Jakob Harnesk
   BIBSAM
   The Royal Library's Office for National Planning and Co-ordination
   Box 5039
   S-10241
   Stockholm

   Barbro Thomas
   STATENS KULTURRÅD
   Swedish National Council for Cultural Affairs
   Långa Raden 4
   Skeppsholmen
   P.O. Box 7843
   103 98 Stockholm

4. UNESCO Data

   National: 1984; 1986-1988 and 1990
   Higher Education: 1984;1985; 1989 and 1990
   Other Major Non-Specialised: 1987-1989
   School: 1984-1988 (No of volumes and loans only)
   Special: 1985; 1987 and 1989
   Public: 1987-1990

5. Notes relating to the national data

   Most research libraries in Sweden use the year 1st July- 30th June as their accounting period.

SWITZERLAND

1. <u>Study Questionnaires Returned</u>

   National
   Higher Education
   Other Major Non-Specialised
   Public

2. <u>National Publications employed in the study</u>

   "Bibliothèques suisses 1986"; ISBN 3-303-16004-X
   "Bibliothèques suisses 19867; ISBN 3-303-16006-6
   "Bibliothèques suisses 1988"; ISBN 3-303-16008-2
   "Bibliothèques suisses 1989"; ISBN 3-303-16011-2
   "Bibliothèques suisses 1990"; ISBN 3-303-16012-0

   Office fédéral de la statistique
   Schwarzterstrasse 96
   3003 Berne

3. <u>Individuals and Institutions who provided data for the study</u>

   Carla Amez-Droz
   Division Societe et Formation
   Section de la culture, de la politique et des conditions de vie.
   Office fédéral de la statistique
   Schwarzterstrasse 96
   3003 Berne

   E.Wiss
   Der Präsident
   Universitätsbibliothek
   Schönbeinstr, 18-20
   4056 Basel

   Schweizerische Landesbibliothek
   Hallwylstrasse 15
   3003 Berne

4. <u>UNESCO Data</u>

   National: 1986; 1988 and 1989
   Higher Education: 1984; 1987 and 1990
   Other Major Non-Specialised: 1986; 1987 and 1989

5. <u>Notes relating to the national data</u>

Public Libraries : Data for this sector relates to the 46 principal administrative units.

Higher Education Libraries : The central University Libraries of Basle, Zurich, Geneva, Bern, Fribourg and Luasanne have the additional functions of regional libraries. Since the ISO standard states that Higher Education libraries "may also serve as a public library" data have not been disaggregated.

UNITED KINGDOM

1. <u>Study Questionnaires Returned</u>

    National
    Higher Education
    Other Major Non-Specialised
    School
    Special
    Public

2. <u>National Publications employed in the study</u>

    "Public Library Statistics 1986-87 Actuals"; ISSN 0309-6629
    "Public Library Statistics 1987-88 Actuals"; ISSN 0309-6629
    "Public Library Statistics 1988-89 Actuals"; ISSN 0309-6629
    "Public Library Statistics 1989-90 Actuals"; ISSN 0309-6629
    "Public Library Statistics 1990-91 Actuals"; ISSN 0309-6629

    Institute of Public Finance Ltd
    Suffolk House
    College Road
    Croydon CR0 1PF

    "LISU Annual Library Statistics 1992": IBSN 0 948848 49 9; ISSN 0967-487X
    John Sumsion and Deborah R Fossey
    Library and Information Statistics Unit
    Department of Information and Library Studies
    Loughborough University of Technology
    Loughborough
    Leicestershire LE11 3TV

    Standing Conference of National & University Librairans (SCONUL)
    102 Euston Street
    London NW1 2HA

3. <u>Individuals and Institutions who provided data for the study</u>

    John Sumsion
    Director
    Library and Information Statistics Unit
    Loughborough University of Technology
    Loughborough
    Leicestershire LE11 3TV

4. <u>UNESCO Data</u>

    National: 1989-1990
    Public: 1989

APPENDIX 7

LIB1 - ECON

EXECUTIVE SUMMARY

A Study of the Library Economics

of the European Community 1981-85

APPENDIX 7

Chapter 1

EXECUTIVE SUMMARY

A Study of the Library Economics of the EC 1981-85

This summary provides an overview of the main findings of a study which we believe is the first attempt to measure the costs of library services throughout the European Community. For a discussion of these findings, and further explanation of the points set out in this chapter, it is necessary to read the whole report.

1.1 Introduction

The purpose of this study was to attempt an up-to-date measure of the extent of library activities in the European Community (EC). We set out to build on the work of the United Nations Educational and Cultural Organisation (UNESCO), with their support and the use of their survey data to guide us. However, so as to advance the knowledge about libraries in the EC we have found it necessary to build on and collect more up to date figures than have hitherto been made available at a central level. We collected such data in our own survey, undertaken in late 1986 and early 1987. This exercise gave us an insight into the practicability of collecting information from the diverse sources throughout the EC using the accepted definitions describing library services. It is our hope that the publication of this report is seen as being timely by the International Organisation for Standardisation (ISO), which is concerned with the development of robust definitions for the description of those library activities we have described.

1.1.1 Survey Data

The six sector definitions developed by UNESCO, (National; Other Major Non-specialised; Public; Higher Education; School and Specialised Libraries), were seen by us at the outset of the study as a convenient and recognisable framework to use in the collection of internationally consistent data. However, the pattern of library provision throughout the EC is so diverse as to make the strict interpretation of the more detailed UNESCO definitions impossible for certain of the libraries activities we attempted to measure. Therefore, **the results of this study provide an insight into the extent of library activities throughout the EC rather than exact measure of the importance and utility of libraries to the economy of the community. WHERE WE HAVE QUOTED FIGURES THESE MUST BE INTERPRETED WITH SOME CAUTION.** In this respect, we sought information for five years, 1980 to 1985 inclusive, describing the scale of each library sector and the costs associated with each.

1.1.2 Types of Data

There were two types of data we were seeking in the survey: "Activity" or data concerning the physical aspects of the library service, such as the number of books, staff, users, etcetera and "Financial" which were the descriptive measures of the scale of the libraries in the national economies covered in our study. The activity data were in most cases much more amenable than the financial information, which has caused us to undertake more estimates for the latter. Where we have reported expenditures, these are all shown in ECU equivalents and at constant 1985 prices. A major problem which we have identified is the lack of standard financial forms of account which can be operated throughout the European Community (EC). Therefore, the practicability of gaining precise assessments of expenditure on libraries for the EC is limited.

1.2 Financial Statistics

In the early 1980s revenue (current) plus capital expenditure on library activities approximated to 4.7 billion ECUs per annum (at 1985 prices). This was equivalent to 14.8 ECU per head of population.

1.2.1 Revenue Expenditure

Library revenue spending, in real terms, remained relatively constant during the period under review:)13.80 ECU to 13.97 ECU per capital). There were fluctuations in overall government public expenditure programmes and such movements will have served to emphasise the small, but real, drop in the proportion of national resources input into libraries: (from 0.41% to 0.39% of total Government Public Expenditure, after deduction of their defence programmes). A discernible increase in the spending on National libraries was evident, and a decrease in school library spending traced a decline in pupil numbers during this time. Taking all libraries sectors in aggregate, it is apparent that the direct cost of staff in libraries account for just over 50% of the overall revenue budget, whilst support staff overheads account for a further 6%. Stock Acquisitions comprise the second biggest expenditure heading in the analysis of the revenue budgets for libraries. From the figures submitted it seems as though the average per annum revenue expenditure on stock acquisitions in the EC was approximately 874 million ECU. It is interesting to note that whereas the proportion of Public Libraries expenditure on acquisitions was roughly 15%, in institutions of Higher Education it was closer to 31% reflecting the higher cost of technical and current literature which are demanded by academic bodies.

ANNUAL AVERAGE REVENUE SPENDING ON LIBRARIES (1981 : 1985)

LIBRARY SECTOR	REVENUE EXPENDITURE AT 1985 PRICES (MILLIONS ECU)	% OF TOTAL
National	207.7	4.6%
Other Major Non-Special	105.5	2.4%
Public (Popular)	2,509.8	56.4%
Higher Education	523.0	11.8%
School	936.5	21.1%
Special	165.4	3.7%
ALL SECTORS	4,447.9	100.0%

1.2.2 Capital Expenditure

The cost of investment, in terms of capital payments on libraries infrastructure has been even more difficult to establish. We estimate that the average annual capital expenditure over the EC was at least 285 million ECU. Spending on Public Libraries accounted for 87% of this amount, and the investment in School Libraries is excluded from this estimate.

ANNUAL AVERAGE CAPITAL SPENDING ON LIBRARIES (1981 : 1985)

LIBRARY SECTOR	CAPITAL EXPENDITURE AT 1985 PRICES (MILLION ECU)	% OF TOTAL
National	12.6	4.4%
Other Major Non-Special	11.2	3.9%
Public (Popular)	247.0	86.6%
Higher Education	5.4	1.9%
School	-	-
Special	8.9	3.2%
ALL SECTORS	285.1	100.0%

1.2.3 Sources of Income

The form of funding has been particularly difficult to trace and the distribution is influenced by the fact that not all libraries fall within the scope of the Public Sector. Between 87% and 100% of the total Public Libraries budgets were funded from the public purse. The split of this funding between the National Exchequer and Local tax sources was not uniform. However, fees and charges accounted for approximately 5% of Public Libraries' revenue and local administrations appear to directly provide 43% of income toward revenue expenditure.

ANNUAL AVERAGE SOURCES OF REVENUE FUNDING (1981 : 1985)

MILLIONS OF ECU AT 1985 CONSTANT PRICES

LIBRARY SECTOR	NATIONAL GOVERNMENT	LOCAL GOVERNMENT	FEES & CHARGES	OTHER SOURCES
National	135.8	-	23.1	48.9
Other Major Non- Special	-	-	-	105.5
Public (Popular)	1,181.7	1,083.3	120.1	124.6
Higher Education	480.8	2.8	12.1	27.2
School	476.6	459.5	-	0.5
Special	-	-	-	165.4
ALL SECTORS 100% →	2,274.9 51.1%	1,545.6 34.8%	155.3 3.5%	472.1 10.6%

1.3 Activity Statistics

There are at least 75,000 "Static library Service Points" in the EC. About half of these are Public Libraries and more than one third are School Libraries. The estimated number of books held in all sectors of libraries is approximately 1.2 billion (i.e. thousands of millions). EC libraries employ the full-time equivalent (FTE) of about 188,000 staff, with a further 56,000 equivalent staff in support. The average school library is thought to possess 9,200 books, against a mean figure of 76,000 for Libraries serving institutions of Higher Education and 13,100 for branches of Public Libraries.

1.3.1 Availability of Library Services

Overall, there were about 3.8 library books per man, woman and child resident in the EC during the period examined. Whereas, a high number of books per head of population in any particular country demonstrates a greater degree of availability to the population at large, it follows that a low number of loans per registered borrower does not necessarily show a poor level of use of the library facilities. Thus in general, in the North of Europe there is a greater level of provision, allowing for larger choice, but in the South of the EC, there is a lower level of provision, and a higher usage as measured in loans per book held in stock. However, a significant measure of the availability of library services to the population at large is demonstrated in the average population catchment size of Public Library service points, where it is evident that there is a clear difference: The United Kingdom, Denmark, West Germany and Belgium have catchment populations of less than the EC average of 8,500 persons per Public Library service point. In all sectors the volume of bookstock was increasing steadily. During the period 1981 to 1985 it is estimated that the number of books in Public Libraries rose by 8.6% (from 467 million to 509 million), an annual growth rate of 2.1%. On a per capita basis this meant an increase in public library bookstock from 1.47 books per head of population to 1.58.

1.3.2 Library Usage

Approximately 23% of the total population are regular library users or registered borrowers. It is clear that Denmark stands out in that its libraries maintain 62% of the national population as library clients. Since 1983, at least, there does appear to have been an increase in the number of users of EC library facilities (3.0% p.a. National; 5.0% p.m. Other Major; 1.0% p.a. Public; 11.5% p.a. Higher Education) although, with a decline in the school age population this was not the case in school libraries. 95% of all loan transactions are made from Public Libraries.

1.3.3 Development of Library Services

There is likely to be a very small growth in the aggregate population of the EC over the next 25 years. Measured from 1990, by which time the decline in school age population will have halted, the growth of the EC will be only just over 1% during the two decades. However, the flow of population change is likely to show a general decline in some of the more "advanced Library States", whereas those that at present show lesser library resource infrastructures will be those where the population growth will be most. Despite the growth in the national economies of the EC during the early 1980s, there has been no evidence to suggest a corresponding increase in libraries investment. Therefore, the "development gap" between the more advanced library states and the less well developed will widen, unless there is a change in the approach to planning and investing in library resources in the coming years. The challenge of the future development of library services within the EC will be to extend the availability book stocks to those areas where the access to service points is particularly difficult. In this respect, 58% of the population of the EC at present reside in areas where the catchment size of Public Library service points exceeds the EC average of 8,500 persons. However, the responsibility for funding library facilities are often divided between different Central Government Departments or responsible Ministries and local administrations (local municipal organisations and educational establishments). There appears to be ample scope for better co-operation on library policies at Member State level and a positive step towards achieving this will be to enhance the systems for collecting and exchanging data on library services for the mutual benefit of all responsible for the efficient management of libraries within the EC.

1.4 Statistical Review

We have encountered problems when collecting data for this study, and these problems will need to be addressed if the development of libraries in the EC is to be monitored in future:

i. It is not common practice to include financial breakdowns in the same surveys used nationally to collect activity based data about libraries, consequently the figures drawn from different sources are inconsistent. In many instances the interest in maintaining the statistical frameworks describing libraries activities lies with librarians alone and so a wider recognition of their problems in collecting the data and the assistance of other professions in their administrations would considerably strengthen the consistent survey coverage of the libraries services.

ii. There are no commonly held standards defining the major headings under which financial information about libraries should be kept. In the accountancy profession these are known as "Standard Forms of Account". In this respect alone, serious work needs to be undertaken, if reliable international comparisons of financial inputs to libraries are to be made.

iii. Responsibility for libraries often crosses several government Departments/ Ministries, each with their own priorities for identifying the costs of such activities. Indeed, the mixed funding pattern for Public Libraries, which constitute the largest sector of libraries activities appears to suffer from a funding dichotomy between the aspirations of Central and Local forms of administration.

1.4.1 Standardisation

Not all the information which UNESCO seeks to collect is useful for policy formulation at national level in a European context, and the quality of the data are such that they can only be used with extreme caution. This can only be improved by better co-ordination and co-operation at international level between government departments responsible for libraries, agencies responsible for collecting and publishing the statistics and library managers. The EC might consider how to sponsor improved co-ordination and co-operation to benefit not only Member States but UNESCO which would ultimately receive better quality data for the countries concerned. One alternative approach would be for the EC to act as a collecting agent for UNESCO, passing on validated data on its behalf, for the mutual benefit of all concerned. A forum to agree a form for EC libraries statistics would be a useful start, and urgent consideration should be given by the International Organisation for Standardisation (ISO) to the integration of financial and activity based statistics.

1.4.2 Suggested Action

In summary, we see the appropriate course of action as:

i. Promote recognition by Member States of the need to consider the practicability of assembling financial information consistent with their activity statistics and within the same surveys to ensure such consistency;

ii. **Define which of those sectors**, described as libraries activities within the UNESCO definitions, which require most emphasis for policy evaluation: School libraries may be better considered as part of dedicated education programmes and Specialised libraries are so diverse in their scope and services as to remain out of effective information policy influence. With a clearer understanding of the objectives of any policy appraisal for developing EC libraries statistics, it will be easier to specify which areas of libraries activities need their statistical reporting frameworks developing as a priority. This will facilitate a phased, but efficient, development of definitions where not all sectors require the same degree of emphasis;

iii. Initiate a forum for the wider development of European statistics on libraries which would act as the agent for the provision of such information to other organisations interested in library activities;

iv. Compile a central register of statistical sources to supplement those identified during the course of this study, which can be used by a review group representing constituent national Ministerial interests, in developing appropriate EC "Activity" and "Financial" forms of account;

v. Continue to monitor the structure of funding of libraries throughout the EC, as well as taking a note of the volume of such funding. In this respect, we have noted the mixed channels of funding through different National Ministries and local Municipal administrations. We believe that developing a consistent statistical reporting process is the only means of providing those individuals and organisations diversely involved with the information which can allow them to develop their services in an efficient and co-ordinated manner.

The Communities research and development information service
CORDIS

A vital part of your programme's dissemination strategy

CORDIS is the information service set up under the VALUE programme to give quick and easy access to information on European Community research programmes. It is available free-of-charge online via the European Commission host organization (ECHO), and now also on a newly released CD-ROM.

CORDIS offers the European R&D community:

— a comprehensive up-to-date view of EC R&TD activities, through a set of databases and related services,
— quick and easy access to information on EC research programmes and results,
— a continuously evolving Commission service tailored to the needs of the research community and industry,
— full user support, including documentation, training and the CORDIS help desk.

The CORDIS Databases are:

**R&TD-programmes – R&TD-projects – R&TD-partners – R&TD-results
R&TD-publications – R&TD-comdocuments – R&TD-acronyms – R&TD-news**

Make sure your programme gains the maximum benefit from CORDIS

— Inform the CORDIS unit of your programme initiatives,
— contribute information regularly to CORDIS databases such as R&TD-news, R&TD-publications and R&TD-programmes,
— use CORDIS databases, such as R&TD-partners, in the implementation of your programme,
— consult CORDIS for up-to-date information on other programmes relevant to your activities,
— inform your programme participants about CORDIS and the importance of their contribution to the service as well as the benefits which they will derive from it,
— contribute to the evolution of CORDIS by sending your comments on the service to the CORDIS Unit.

For more information about contributing to CORDIS,
contact the DG XIII CORDIS Unit

Brussels	*Luxembourg*
Ms I. Vounakis	M. B. Niessen
Tel. +(32) 2 299 0464	Tel. +(352) 4301 33638
Fax +(32) 2 299 0467	Fax +(352) 4301 34989

To register for online access to CORDIS, contact:

ECHO Customer Service
BP 2373
L-1023 Luxembourg
Tel. +(352) 3498 1240
Fax +(352) 3498 1248

If you are already an ECHO user, please mention your customer number.

European Commission

EUR 15903 — Library economics in Europe — An update — 1981-90

Phillip Ramsdale

Luxembourg: Office for Official Publications of the European Communities

1995 – VI, 244 pp. – num. tab., fig. – 21.0 x 29.7 cm

Information management series

ISBN 92-826-9197-7

Price (excluding VAT) in Luxembourg: ECU 21.50

Overall library expenditure has remained static throughout the decade for the European Union. The 'library industry' employed approximately 237 000 persons in the latter half of the l980s, and consumed ECU 6.6 billion per annum, equivalent to approximately ECU 8 014 million when repriced at 1993 constant prices.

Maintenance of libraries continues to be a central element in the cultural programmes of the Member States of the European Union. However, there has been a marked change in the relative focus of libraries' investment during the decade. Although public libraries remain the principal source of library services, accounting for just under one half of gross library expenditure (49%), the main areas of investment growth have been devoted towards the higher education sector. This reflects an implicit policy to employ the resources of the library services in education programmes, and to some extent illustrates the switch in public sector resources from secondary towards tertiary education.

These are some of the findings of the study on library economics in Europe, which provides statistical information on library economics in the EU and EFTA countries for the years 1981-90.